Directory of MARYLAND BURIAL GROUNDS

Genealogical Council of Maryland

HERITAGE BOOKS
2012

HERITAGE BOOKS
AN IMPRINT OF HERITAGE BOOKS, INC.

Books, CDs, and more—Worldwide

For our listing of thousands of titles see our website
at
www.HeritageBooks.com

Published 2012 by
HERITAGE BOOKS, INC.
Publishing Division
100 Railroad Ave. #104
Westminster, Maryland 21157

Copyright © 1996 Genealogical Council of Maryland

Other Heritage Books by the author:
Inventory of Maryland Bible Records, Volume 1
Directory of Maryland Burial Grounds
Directory of Maryland Church Records
Edna A. Kanely, under the auspices of the
Genealogical Council of Maryland

All rights reserved. No part of this book may be reproduced or transmitted in any form or by any means, electronic or mechanical, including photocopying, recording or by any information storage and retrieval system without written permission from the author, except for the inclusion of brief quotations in a review.

International Standard Book Numbers
Paperbound: 978-1-58549-328-9
Clothbound: 978-0-7884-9331-7

INTRODUCTION

One of the long range objectives of the Genealogical Council of Maryland has been to publish a *DIRECTORY OF MARYLAND'S BURIAL GROUNDS*. This book (Volume 1) begins to achieve that goal. The number of burial grounds appearing in each database made it impossible to limit the Directory to a single volume. Volume I, covers Anne Arundel, Carroll, Montgomery and Prince George's Counties. Subsequent volumes will cover the remaining counties.

Many of Maryland's genealogical societies have already published transcriptions of the grave markers found in their counties and other societies are in the process of transcribing and publishing the cemetery data. It is the intention of the Cemetery Committee to augment these efforts and in no way duplicate these fine publications. The Committee's goal was to publish a Directory of burial grounds which describes the location of the sites and the location of the records, identifying those which have been published.

The Cemetery Committee has always been active. From inception its members had visualized producing a Directory. However, the limited manpower available to the Council prevented all goals being met at the same time. In 1993, the Council began to focus its energy and resources on the Cemetery Committee. By building upon and revising its questionnaires, the Committee developed a format for a comprehensive database. The result was a series of 17 informational headings, each listed with multiple fields under every heading. A computer programmer worked with the Committee in developing a modified database. The Committee understood from the beginning that all of the requested information could not be supplied for every cemetery. Notwithstanding, the Committee members believed it was important to supply all the information available.

In order to beta test the program and, at the same time, begin to develop the first county databases, the Committee distributed material, disks, and instructions to the first ten county societies requested to participate in this project: Anne Arundel, Baltimore County, Carroll, Charles, Calvert, Frederick, Howard, Montgomery, Prince George's, and St. Mary's. As each county's database was completed it was submitted to the editor. After merging the first four databases, the editor advised that the total was big enough for one volume. The data for Frederick County is already been keyed and is in the hands of the editor. It will appear in Volume 2. The other five listed county databases are works in progress.

The computer program is now running smoothly. Since Volume I is published, and Volume 2 is well advanced, the Council's Cemetery Committee will be requesting societies representing the remaining 13 counties and Baltimore City to participate in the project.

The following outline displays the format used for obtaining and inputting the information for the *DIRECTORY OF MARYLAND'S BURIAL GROUNDS*:

MARYLAND CEMETERY DIRECTORY HEADINGS

1. County:_____
    Does cemetery cross county or state boundaries? ___Yes ___No

2. Name of Cemetery:_____

3. Previous or other name:_____
    Previous or other name:_____
    Previous or other name:_____

4. Cemetery's mailing address:
    Name_____
    Street or P.O Box_____
    City/Town_____ State_____ Zip_____

5. Directions to cemetery:_____
    _____
    _____

6. Tax Map #:_____ Grid #:_____ Parcel #:_____

7. A.D.C. map location:
    Edition_____   Page #_____
    Grid coordinates_____   Latitude_____
    Longitude_____

8. Type of cemetery:
   ___Private   ___Active   ___Relocated
   ___Church   ___Inactive   ___Non-extant
   ___Public

9. Permission required to visit: ___Yes ___No

10. Condition/description of cemetery:_____
    _____

11. Year of earliest known death:_____
    Year of most recent death if cemetery inactive, defunct, or non-extant:_____

12. Prominent/famous individual(s) interred:_____
    _____

13. Veterans interred:
    _____Revolutionary War   _____Civil War
    _____WWI   _____WWII
    _____Other Wars

14. Are burial records kept? ___Yes ___No

    Types of records:
    ___Deed and plat records
    ___Interment records
    ___Tombstone records
    ___Maps

    Location of records:_____
    _____
    _____

15. Are the gravemarkers transcribed?: ___Yes ___No
    Dates transcribed:_____

    Location of transcribed records (name and full address):
    _____
    _____
    _____

v

16. Are the transcribed records published?: ____Yes ____No
If yes, please list all bibliographic information for each published cemetery:
Author:_____
Title:_____
Publisher:_____
Publisher's address:_____
Date of publication:_____

17. Additional comments:_____
_____
_____

Submitting organization:

Prepared by: Name:_____
              Address:_____
              _____
              Phone:_____

ACKNOWLEDGEMENTS

First Cemetery Committee Chairperson:	Ann Paxton Brown
Second Cemetery Committee Chairperson:	Eleanor C. Lukanich
Third Cemetery Committee Chairperson:	Larry T. Moore
Maryland Cemetery Directory Headings:	Susan Johnston and Diane Winsor
Computer programmer:	Benny Flonnoya Moore

Data contributors: Anne Arundel County Genealogical Society
Carroll County Genealogical Society
Genealogy Club of Montgomery County Historical Society
Prince George's County Genealogical Society

Data entry by: Tina Simmons, Anne Arundel County Genealogical Society
Mimi Ashcraft, Carroll County Genealogical Society
Ann Brown, Montgomery County Genealogy Society
(Janet Manuel completed, by hand, the information requested in the original outline issued by the Council's Cemetery Committee for a majority of Montgomery County's cemeteries.)
William L. Shook, Prince George's County Genealogical Society

Editorial advisor: F. Edward Wright

DIRECTORY OF MARYLAND'S BURIAL GROUNDS

ANNE ARUNDEL COUNTY

Private Cemeteries

205TH STREET CEMETERY
Location: At #809 205th Street. [A.D.C. map location: 1989 Edition, page 9, grid coordinates B-6.] No longer there. No burial records kept. A single stone with first name Joseph.

ALBERT COREY CEMETERY (SPIT POINT CEMETERY)
Location: Spit Point vicinity. [A.D.C. map location: 1989 Edition, page 10, grid coordinates G-8.] No burial records are maintained. Very old stones, not known who was buried there.

ANDERSON FAMILY CEMETERY
Location: On east side of Crownsville Road south of Fairgrounds near roadside barn, in woods. [A.D.C. map location: 1989 Edition, page 19, grid coordinates D/E-3/4.] The cemetery is in fair condition. Year of earliest death: 1863. Year of latest death: 1905. No burial records are maintained. The gravemarkers were transcribed in 1990; maintained by Anne Arundel Genealogical Society.

ANDOVER/CAMP MEADE CEMETERY
Location: At intersection of Andover Road and Route 170. [A.D.C. map location: 1989 Edition, page 2, grid coordinates E-9.] No burial records are maintained. Possibly same as Smith Family Cemetery.

ANNAPOLIS NECK CEMETERY
Location: Annapolis Neck Road southwest of junction with Forest Drive. It can be seen from Forest Dr. [A.D.C. map location: 1989 Edition, page 25, grid coordinates J-2.] Maintained. Year of earliest death: 1910. Year of latest death: 1975. WWI and Korean War Veterans. Records held by Anne Arundel Genealogical Society. The gravemarkers were transcribed in 1975; published by Anne Arundel Genealogical Society. Title: *Cemetery Inscriptions of Anne Arundel County, Maryland*, Vol. I (1982), p. 33.

ANNAPOLIS HEBREW CEMETERY (KNESETH ISRAEL CONGREGATIONAL CEMETERY)
Location: Junction of Route 178 and Route 450 at Threemile Oak Corner. [A.D.C. map location: 1989 Edition, page p. 20, grid coordinates A-8.] Well-maintained. Hebrew Cemetery.

AVERY FAMILY CEMETERY
Location: East West Shady Side Road near museum. [A.D.C. map location: 1989 Edition, page 30, grid coordinates G-7.] No longer exists. No burial records are maintained.

BALDWIN MARKER
Location: West side of right 178, 4 miles north of junction of Route 32 and Route 178, south of Waterbury Road. [A.D.C. map location: 1989 Edition, page 14, grid coordinates B-10.] Single stone of ---- Baldwin, Revolutionary War Veteran, died 1783. Year of earliest death: 1783. Year of latest death: 1783. Revolutionary War Veteran. No burial records are maintained. The gravemarker was transcribed in 1975; published by Anne Arundel Genealogical Society. Title: *Cemetery Inscriptions of Anne Arundel County, Maryland*, Vol. II (1982), p. 36.

BARCHET CEMETERY
Location: No location given. [A.D.C. map location: 1989 Edition, page 21, grid coordinates J-2.] Year of earliest death: 1905. Year of latest death: 1960. No burial records are maintained. The gravemarkers were transcribed in 1984; published by Anne Arundel Genealogical Society. Records held by Anne Arundel Genealogical Society. Title: *Cemetery Inscriptions of Anne Arundel County, Maryland*, Vol. II (1987), p. 13.

BATTEE CEMETERY (SOUTHERN HIGH SCHOOL CEMETERY)
Location: Off Route 2 on Southern High School property, on right when facing building, surrounded by white picket fence. [A.D.C. map location: 1989 Edition, page 29, grid coordinates A-3.] Maintained. Year of earliest death: 1803. Year of latest death: 1803. No burial records are maintained by Anne Arundel Genealogical Society. Compiled in 1991 by Anne Arundel Genealogical Society, published by NSDAR. Title: *Tombstone Inscriptions of Southern Anne Arundel County*.

BAY FRONG ROAD CEMETERY
Location: On first hard surfaced road north of Route 258 on east side. Wrought iron fence. [A.D.C. map location: 1989 Edition, page 33, grid coordinates D-4.] Dr. Weems is buried here. Possibly same as

Weems-Sellman Cemetery since a Dr. Weems is buried within wrought iron fence there.

BAYSIDE BEACH ROAD CEMETERY
Location: Bayside Beach Road to north, before Shipley Road, at edge of woods beside brick house. [A.D.C. map location: 1989 Edition, page 10, grid coordinates E-7.] It may no longer be there. No burial records are maintained. Supposedly no stones remain. Once had fence surrounding cemetery.

BELVOIR CEMETERY
Location: East off Route 178 in Belvoir Community. [A.D.C. map location: 1989 Edition, page 19, grid coordinates G-2.] Year of earliest death: 1811. Year of latest death: 1860. Francis Scott Key's grandmother is buried here. No burial records are maintained by Anne Arundel Genealogical Society. See *Anne Arundel's Legacy*, p. 72, 145; *Historic Graves of Maryland and the District of Columbia*, p. 12-13. Colonial Dames marker.

BENTON-SHIPLEY CEMETERY
Location: East of Camp Meade Road behind Linthicum Elementary School across from park. [A.D.C. map location: 1989 Edition, page 2, grid coordinates F-8.] Year of earliest death: 1810. Year of latest death: 1966. No burial records are maintained. The gravemarkers were transcribed and published by Anne Arundel Genealogical Society. Title: *Cemetery Inscriptions of Anne Arundel County, Maryland*, Vol. II (1987), p. 95.

BETHEL CEMETERY (FT. MEADE CEMETERY #2)
Location: Located on Rock Avenue across from Building 2250. [A.D.C. map location: 1989 Edition, page 12, grid coordinates E-2.] Year of earliest death: 1934. Year of latest death: 1973. WWI Veterans. Maintained and published by Anne Arundel Genealogical Society. Title: *Cemetery Inscriptions of Anne Arundel County, Maryland*, II (1987), p. 69. No burial records are maintained; it was copied by Ft. Meade BSA Troop 379, grid 5027.

BEVAN FAMILY CEMETERY
Location: Near Bristol, approx. 1½ miles from Route 4 and Fisher Station Road intersection on Talbott Farm. [A.D.C. map location: 1989 Edition, page 32, grid coordinates C-5.] Year of earliest death: 1842. Year of latest death: 1857. No burial records are maintained. The

gravemarkers were transcribed and published by Daughters of the American Revolution. Title: *Tombstone Inscriptions of Southern Anne Arundel County* (1971), p. 60.

BIGGS AND WATERS CEMETERY (FT. MEADE CEMETERY #10)
Location: Off Road 834 in area T33 on southeast side of DZ. [A.D.C. map location: 1989 Edition, page 11, grid coordinates G-4.] Poor condition. Year of earliest death: 1850. Year of latest death: 1895. No burial records are maintained. Published by Anne Arundel Genealogical Society. Title: *Cemetery Inscriptions of Anne Arundel County, Maryland*, Vol. II (1987), p. 76. Copied by Ft. Meade BSA Troop 379, grid 4526.

BIRD-CHANEY-CHEW CEMETERY
Location: At #2 Chew Chapel Road in grove of trees behind barn. [A.D.C. map location: 1989 Edition, page 29, grid coordinates F-4.] In good condition, very legible. Year of earliest death: 1815. Year of latest death: 1873. No burial records are maintained. The gravemarkers were transcribed and maintained in 1991 by Anne Arundel Genealogical Society.

BODKIN POINT CEMETERY (PINEHURST CEMETERY)
Location: By C&P telephone tower in Pinehurst-On-The-Bay between Bodkin Creek and Chesapeake Bay. [A.D.C. map location: 1989 Edition, page 10, grid coordinates J-8.] Year of earliest death: 1822. Year of latest death: 1872. No burial records are maintained. The gravemarkers were transcribed and published by Anne Arundel Genealogical Society. Title: *Cemetery Inscriptions of Anne Arundel County, Maryland*, Vol. II. (1987), p. 18.

BOHMEN CEMETERY
Location: Off Benfield Road beside Severna Park Baptist Church. [A.D.C. map location: 1989 Edition, page 14, grid coordinates F-4.] Year of earliest death: 1921. Year of latest death: 1921. No burial records are maintained. The gravemarkers were transcribed in 1962. Single stone remains, formerly large family cemetery.

BOONE-LINSTID FAMILY CEMETERY
Location: At #17 Boone Train between Linstead and Sullivan Roads. [A.D.C. map location: 1989 Edition, page 15, grid coordinates A-7.] Maintained. Year of earliest death: 1832. Year of latest death: 1900. No burial records are maintained. Records held by Anne Arundel

ANNE ARUNDEL COUNTY CEMETERIES - PRIVATE

Genealogical Society. The gravemarkers were transcribed in 1992 and published by Anne Arundel Genealogical Society. Title: *Cemetery Inscriptions of Anne Arundel County, Maryland*, Vol. II (1987), p. 53. Some family history information also available in Anne Arundel Genealogical Society maintained records.

BOONE-MERRIKEN CEMETERY
Location: At Hidden Point Road southwest of junction. Pleasant Plains Road, in middle of field. [A.D.C. map location: 1989 Edition, page 21, grid coordinates F-5.] No longer exists. Year of earliest death: 1806. Year of latest death: 1896. No burial records are maintained. Published by Anne Arundel Genealogical Society. Title: *Cemetery Inscriptions of Anne Arundel County, Maryland*, Vol. II (1987), p. 79.

BOYER BURIAL GROUND
Location: Off Ridge Chapel Road between Harmans Elementary School and Chesapeake Mobile Homes. [A.D.C. map location: 1989 Edition, page 6, grid coordinates F-5.] Year of earliest death: 1880. Year of latest death: 1895. No burial records are maintained. Records held by Anne Arundel Genealogical Society. The gravemarkers were transcribed in 1983; published by Anne Arundel Genealogical Society. Title: *Cemetery Inscriptions of Anne Arundel County, Maryland*, Vol. II (1987), p. 145.

BREWER FAMILY GRAVESTONE
Location: Between Old Cedar Point and Pocahontas Drive on bluff in woods on right. [A.D.C. map location: 1989 Edition, page 25, grid coordinates D-7.] Good condition. No burial records are maintained by Anne Arundel Genealogical Society. The gravemarker was transcribed in 1992. Published in *Anne Arundel's Legacy*, p. 170.

BREWER CEMETERY
Location: At #510 Bayview Point Drive in Loch Haven Community. [A.D.C. map location: 1989 Edition, page 25, grid coordinates F-7.] Nicholas Brewer is buried here. No burial records are maintained.

BREWER HILL CEMETERY
Location: In 800 block of West Street just west of Taylor Avenue next to The National Cemetery. [A.D.C. map location: 1989 Edition, page 20, grid coordinates H-10.] Maintained. Year of earliest death: 1861. Year of latest death: 1962. WWI and WWII Veterans. No burial records are maintained. Records held by and published by Anne Arundel

Genealogical Society. Title: *Cemetery Inscriptions of Anne Arundel County, Maryland*, Vol. II (1987), p. 148. African-American Cemetery.

BROOKSLY POINT CEMETERY
Location: 1/2 mile east on private dirt road, 1/4 mile north of Cedarcroft. [A.D.C. map location: 1989 Edition, page 13, grid coordinates K-6.] No burial records maintained.

BROWN-CARSON FAMILY CEMETERY
Location: Southwest corner of Cypress Creek Road and Dill Road. [A.D.C. map location: 1989 Edition, page 15, grid coordinates D-6.] Year of earliest death: 1907. Year of latest death: 1910. No burial records are maintained. The gravemarkers were transcribed in 1980 and published by Anne Arundel Genealogical Society. Title: *Cemetery Inscriptions of Anne Arundel County, Maryland*, Vol. II (1987), p. 42.

BROWNS-OXBOURNES (MEEK FAMILY CEMETERY)
Location: Unknown. [A.D.C. map location: 1989 Edition, page 9, grid coordinates G-10.] Year of earliest death: 1874. Year of latest death: 1885. No burial records are maintained by Anne Arundel Genealogical Society. The gravemarkers were transcribed and published by Anne Arundel Genealogical Society. Title: *Cemetery Inscriptions of Anne Arundel County*, Vol. II (1987), p. 20.

BRUNS/BRAEN CEMETERY
Location: Between Brauns Avenue and Braen Lane near Burns Crossing Road. [A.D.C. map location: 1989 Edition, page 13, grid coordinates A/B-1.] Possible cemetery.

BURGESS GRAVES (MT. STEUART CEMETERY)
Location: Unknown. [A.D.C. map location: 1989 Edition, page 24, grid coordinates H-7.] The cemetery no longer exists; reinterred at All Hallows in late 19th century. Col. William Burgess is buried here. No burial records are maintained. The gravemarkers were transcribed in 1967 and published by Daughters of the American Revolution. Title: *Tombstone Inscriptions of Anne Arundel County* (1971), p. 323.

BURLEY CREEK CEMETERY
Location: St. Margaret's Church to head of Burley Creek (2 cemeteries on each side of creek, unpaved roads). [A.D.C. map location: 1989 Edition, page 21?.] No burial records are maintained.

CARPENTERS HILL CEMETERY
Location: On east side of Baltimore-Annapolis Boulevard across from entrance to Round Bay Community. [A.D.C. map location: 1989 Edition, page 15, grid coordinates BC-7/8.] Maintained. No burial records are maintained. African-American Cemetery.

CARR FAMILY CEMETERY
Location: Mt. Zion on Route 422 at Carr's Hill. [A.D.C. map location: 1989 Edition, page 28.] Year of earliest death: 1843. Year of latest death: 1852. No burial records are maintained. The gravemarkers were transcribed in 1968 and published by Daughters of the American Revolution. Title: *Tombstone Inscriptions of Southern Anne Arundel County* (1971), p. 184.

CARROLL FAMILY BURIAL GROUNDS
Location: South of Forest Drive on Route 2 in vicinity of Route 655 (now Annapolis Harbor Shopping Center). [A.D.C. map location: 1989 Edition, page 20, grid coordinates B-10/11.] No longer exists. Year of earliest death: 1696. Year of latest death: 1825. Charles Carroll was buried here. Tombstone records maintained by Carroll House, Annapolis, MD 21401. Reinterred at Carroll Gardens Cemetery.

CEDAR DRIVE CEMETERY
Location: #15 Cedar Drive in Marley, Lot 21. [A.D.C. map location: 1989 Edition, page 8, grid coordinates E-4/5.] No burial records are maintained. 200 yr. old graveyard, possibly same as Scheminart Family Cemetery?

CEDAR GROVE CEMETERY
Location: At corner of Route 256 and Deale Road on Mason Beach Road. [A.D.C. map location: 1989 Edition, page 34, grid coordinates A-7.] No burial records are maintained.

CEDARWOOD COVE CEMETERY (LINSTEAD/LINSTID FAMILY CEMETERY)
Location: Cedarwood Cove at northeast corner of junction of Marco Drive and Capel Drive. [A.D.C. map location: 1989 Edition, page 10, grid coordinates D-11.] No longer exists. Year of earliest death: 1843. Year of latest death: 1901. No burial records are maintained by Anne Arundel Genealogical Society. Gravemarkers transcribed and published by Anne Arundel Genealogical Society. Title: *Cemetery Inscriptions of*

Anne Arundel County, Maryland, Vol. II (1987), p. 23. Vandalized; all statues removed in 1987.

CEMETERY
Location: Shore Road in Cape St. Claire near Little Magothy River. Possibly same as Stinchcomb-Tydings Family Cemetery.

CEMETERY
Location: Broadneck Road just north of Persimmon Point Road near Broadneck Church. [A.D.C. map location: 1989 Edition, page 16?.] No burial records are maintained. Possibly same as Stinchcomb-Tydings Family Cemetery.

CHARTWELL GOLF CEMETERY
Location: North of St. Andrews Road and east of lake on the golf course. [A.D.C. map location: 1989 Edition, page 14, grid coordinates D3.] No burial records are maintained.

CLARK CEMETERY
Location: South of Disney Road and southwest of Old Mill Court/New Disney, high above road. [A.D.C. map location: 1989 Edition, page 6, grid coordinates F-8.] Year of earliest death: 1900. Year of latest death: 1905. No burial records are maintained and compiled by Anne Arundel Genealogical Society.

CLARK FAMILY CEMETERY
Location: Reece Road 1/4 mile from Severn RR Bridge toward Ft. Meade, 4th house on left (Evans) after crossing railroad tracks. [A.D.C. map location: 1989 Edition, page 6, grid coordinates J-8.] Year of earliest death: 1857. Year of latest death: 1935. No burial records are maintained. The gravemarkers were transcribed in 1983 and published by Anne Arundel Genealogical Society. Title: *Cemetery Inscriptions of Anne Arundel County, Maryland*, Vol. II (1987), p. 146.

CLARK STATION ROAD CEMETERY
Location: Off Clark Station Road at 1st, 2nd or 3rd Streets, 20' x 30' plot surrounded by iron fence. [A.D.C. map location: 1989 Edition, page 7, grid coordinates A-8/9.] Possible cemetery.

CLARK STATION ROAD CEMETERY
Location: Clark Station Road south of Donaldson Avenue. [A.D.C. map location: 1989 Edition, page 7, grid coordinates A-8.] Well kept. No burial records are maintained. 10 stones.

CLAYTOR FAMILY CEMETERY (BROWSLEY HALL CEMETERY)
Location: At #500 Polling House Road. [A.D.C. map location: 1989 Edition, page 28, grid coordinates F-5.] Overgrown. Year of earliest death: 1820. Year of latest death: 1851. No burial records are maintained. The gravemarkers were transcribed in 1968 by Daughters of the American Revolution. Title: *Tombstone Inscriptions of Southern Anne Arundel County* (1971), p. 298. Includes Anne Arundel Genealogical Society cemetery records.

CLEM MOORE GRAVE
Location: At Mary's Mount farm, about 45 minute walk from house near Tucker property. [A.D.C. map location: 1989 Edition, page 29, grid coordinates D-2.] Year of earliest death: 1853. Year of latest death: 1853. No burial records are maintained. The gravemarker was transcribed in 1991. Single elaborately carved inscribed stone to "servant."

COLLINS GRAVE
Location: In yard, exact location unknown. [A.D.C. map location: 1989 Edition, page 9, grid coordinates F-6/7.] No burial records maintained. Four or five stones, including a "Samuel Collins".

COOK FAMILY CEMETERY
Location: Alpine Beach Road just after 1st sharp left turn from Bayside Beach Road, on right side. [A.D.C. map location: 1989 Edition, page 10, grid coordinates E-6.] No burial records are maintained. Marked only with fieldstones, no tombstones.

COVE OF CORK MEMORIAL
Location: Between Route 50 and Cove of Cork, approximately 100 feet from Route 50 and 300 feet from bridge on wooded hillside. [A.D.C. map location: 1989 Edition, page 20, grid coordinates H-5.] Wooden cross in memoriam.

CRANDELL-SMITH CEMETERY
Location: At head of Broadwater Creek on boundary line between McWilliams and Phelps properties. [A.D.C. map location: 1989 Edition,

page 34, grid coordinates C-4?.] Year of earliest death: 1862. Year of latest death: 1910. No burial records are maintained. The gravemarkers were transcribed in 1964 by Anne Arundel Historical Society. Some graves moved to Quaker burying grounds.

CROMWELL GRAVE
Location: Between #307 and #309 Ferndale Road in Ferndale Farms between Belvidere and West Dale Roads. [A.D.C. map location: 1989 Edition, page 2, grid coordinates G-11.] Single grave of James Cromwell, died in 1880. No burial records are maintained. The gravemarker was transcribed and published by Anne Arundel Genealogical Society. Title: *Cemetery Inscriptions of Anne Arundel County, Maryland*, Vol. II (1987), p. 98.

CROWNSVILLE STATE HOSPITAL CEMETERY
Location: On State Hospital grounds, exact location unknown. [A.D.C. map location: 1989 Edition, page 19.] Approximately 1200 graves. Markers numbered; near bike path.

DAKER CEMETERY (THORNTON FAMILY BURYING GROUNDS)
Location: In Point Pleasant Community. [A.D.C. map location: 1989 Edition, page 3, grid coordinates EF-11/13.] Year of earliest death: 1812. Year of latest death: 1890. No burial records are maintained. Maintained by Anne Arundel Genealogical Society. 1 stone, possibly more.

DARNALL FAMILY CEMETERY (ST. JEROME'S FARM CEMETERY)
Location: Route 258 on Paddy Farm, owned by F. H. Darnall in 1923. [A.D.C. map location: 1989 Edition, page 32, grid coordinates C-5.] Year of earliest death: 1835. Year of latest death: 1873. No burial records are maintained. The gravemarkers were transcribed in 1967; published by Daughters of the American Revolution. Title: *Tombstone Inscriptions of Southern Anne Arundel County* (1971), p. 61.

DAWSON FAMILY CEMETERY
Location: Fenced off burial plot just before Camp Wabanna, at Dutchman Point. [A.D.C. map location: 1989 Edition, page 30, grid coordinates G-3.] Well-maintained. Year of earliest death: 1809. Year of latest death: 1865. Buried here is Capt. Joseph I. Dawson. No burial records are maintained by Anne Arundel Genealogical Society. The gravemarkers were transcribed in 1993.

DEFENSE HIGHWAY CEMETERY
Location: At #149 Defense Highway (Route 250). [A.D.C. map location: 1989 Edition, page 19, grid coordinates K-9.] No burial records are maintained. Possible mid-18th century gravesite, possibly a Dorsey family member.

DEICHGRAEBER FAMILY CEMETERY
Location: On east side of Quarterfield Road 2½ miles s.w. of Route 3, near #8060, on knoll. [A.D.C. map location: 1989 Edition, page 7, grid coordinates D-9.] Well-maintained. Year of earliest death: 1908. Year of latest death: 1969. No burial records are maintained. The gravemarkers were transcribed in 1974 and records held by Anne Arundel Genealogical Society.

DENNIS FAMILY CEMETERY
Location: Off Columbia Beach Road about 0.7 mile on right side of road in woods visible from road. [A.D.C. map location: 1989 Edition, page 30, grid coordinates H-12.] Stones legible, wooded area. Year of earliest death: 1873. Year of latest death: 1887. No burial records are maintained. The gravemarkers were transcribed in 1994 and records held by Anne Arundel Genealogical Society.

DISNEY FAMILY CEMETERY
Location: Off Route 554 and Jacobs Road in Stillmeadow Subdivision. [A.D.C. map location: 1989 Edition, page 6, grid coordinates F-11.] Year of earliest death: 1858. Year of latest death: 1910. No burial records are maintained. Transcribed by Anne Arundel Genealogical Society. Title: *Cemetery Inscriptions of Anne Arundel County, Maryland*, Vol. II (1987), p. 103. See also *Anne Arundel's Legacy*, p. 171.

DITTY TOMBSTONE
Location: At Mary's Mount Estate at end of Mary's Mount Road (inside house in 1991). [A.D.C. map location: 1989 Edition, page 29, grid coordinates D-2.] Maintained. No burial records are maintained. The gravemarker was transcribed in 1991 by Anne Arundel Genealogical Society. Portion of stone only, name but no date. Ditty supposedly owned adjoining property. Stone is inside home.

DORSETT CEMETERY
Location: On left of Queen Anne Branch Road (0.2 mile past Police Academy) 2000' south of road at west edge of property. [A.D.C. map location: 1989 Edition, page 23, grid coordinates F-10.] Fair. No burial

records are maintained. Transcribed by Davidsonville Area Civic Association. Maintained by Anne Arundel Genealogical Society.

DORSETT-DUVALL CEMETERY
Location: East side of road below Tanglewood Lane and above Kingmanor Drive, at #3843. [A.D.C. map location: 1989 Edition, page 23, grid coordinates E-12.] No burial records are maintained by Anne Arundel Genealogical Society. Published by DAR in *Tombstone Inscriptions of Southern Anne Arundel County*, p. 386. See also *Anne Arundel's Legacy*, p. 173. Anne Arundel Genealogical Society. Transcribed by Davidsonville Area Civic Association in 1985.

DORSEY ROAD CEMETERY
Location: Located right on Route 176 northwest of St. Marks Church. [A.D.C. map location: 1989 Edition, page 6, grid coordinates D-1.] No burial records are maintained. Possible cemetery.

DOWNS-WILHAM CEMETERY (DOWNS-WELLHAM CEMETERY)
Location: Ferndale-Hollins Ferry Roads on Cromwell property south of railroad trestle. [A.D.C. map location: 1989 Edition, page 2.] Year of earliest death: 1848. Year of latest death: 1911. No burial records are maintained by Anne Arundel Genealogical Society. Compiled and published by Anne Arundel Genealogical Society. Title: *Cemetery Inscriptions of Anne Arundel County, Maryland*, Vol. II (1987), p. 91.

DOWNS CEMETERY (FT. MEADE CEMETERY #8)
Location: On Applewood Golf Course, northwest of Post CSM Quarters. [A.D.C. map location: 1989 Edition.] Good condition. Year of earliest death: 1858. Year of latest death: 1925. Published by Anne Arundel Genealogical Society. Title: *Cemetery Inscriptions of Anne Arundel County, Maryland*, Vol. II (1987), p. 74. Copied by Ft. Meade BSA Troop 379, grid 4829.

DR. ROBERT FRANKLIN CEMETERY
Location: On Mallard Drive on right between #732 and #736 in Hardesty Estates on Rockhall Creek. [A.D.C. map location: 1989 Edition, page 34, grid coordinates A-5.] Badly overgrown, few stones visible. Year of earliest death: 1828. Year of latest death: 1893. No burial records are maintained by Anne Arundel Genealogical Society. The gravemarkers were compiled and published by Anne Arundel Genealogical Society. Title: *Cemetery Inscriptions of Anne Arundel County, Maryland*, Vol. I (1982), p. 38.

ANNE ARUNDEL COUNTY CEMETERIES - PRIVATE

DRURY FAMILY CEMETERY
Location: At Bristol, on farm of Mrs. M. Courtney and Mrs. W. Welch. [A.D.C. map location: 1989 Edition, page 32, grid coordinates C-5.] Year of earliest death: 1868. Year of latest death: 1919. No burial records are maintained. The gravemarkers were transcribed in 1968. Published Daughters of the American Revolution. Title: *Tombstone Inscriptions of Southern Anne Arundel County* (1971), p. 63.

DRURY-LYLES FAMILY CEMETERY
Location: On Route 258, 0.6 mile east of McKendree Road on Someday Farm owned by T. C. Wood, Jr. [A.D.C. map location: 1989 Edition, page 33, grid coordinates B-6.] Year of earliest death: 1826. Year of latest death: 1865. No burial records are maintained. The gravemarkers were transcribed in 1967. Published by Daughters of the American Revolution. Title: *Tombstone Inscriptions of Southern Anne Arundel County* (1971), p. 79.

DUBOIS CEMETERY
Location: Reached from Dubois Road, on north side of curve of Dubois Court. [A.D.C. map location: 1989 Edition, page 20, grid coordinates E-6.] Unable to locate.

DURNER FAMILY CEMETERY
Location: About 200 feet past end of Faulkner Road on top of hill. [A.D.C. map location: 1989 Edition, page 7, grid coordinates A-8.] No burial records are maintained. No tombstones; 2-3 fieldstones.

DUVALL CEMETERY (FT. MEADE CEMETERY #14, NATHAN JONES (DUVALL) CEMETERY)
Location: 50 meters east of Trainfire Road, next to Range 20, Range 14D impact area. [A.D.C. map location: 1989 Edition, page 11, grid coordinates G-9.] Fairly good condition, gate off, bullet holes in sign. Year of earliest death: 1892. Year of latest death: 1910. No burial records are maintained. Published by Anne Arundel Genealogical Society. Title: *Cemetery Inscriptions of Anne Arundel County, Maryland*, Vol. II (1987), p. 77. Copied by Ft. Meade BSA Troop 379, grid 4623.

DUVALL FAMILY CEMETERY
Location: Turn right on unnamed road after Hidden Point Road. Residence of Weems Duvall. [A.D.C. map location: 1989 Edition, page 21, grid coordinates F-5/DE-3.] Year of earliest death: 1833. Year of

latest death: 1925. No burial records are maintained. Records maintained by Anne Arundel Genealogical Society.

DUVALL GRAVE
Location: At end of unnamed road south off Rossback Road. [A.D.C. map location: 1989 Edition, page 18, grid coordinates F-12.] No burial records are maintained. Unmarked grave from late 17th/early 18th century.

DUVALL-MERRIKEN CEMETERY
Location: Off Pleasant Plains Road on Weems Duvall property. [A.D.C. map location: 1989 Edition, page 21, grid coordinates F-5.] Year of earliest death: 1836. Year of latest death: 1938. No burial records are maintained. The gravemarkers were transcribed in 1941 and published by Anne Arundel Genealogical Society. Title: *Cemetery Inscriptions of Anne Arundel County, Maryland*, Vol. II (1987), p. 5. Possibly several cemeteries grouped as one.

EAST PARK DRIVE CEMETERY
Location: East of Route 3 and southwest of East Park Drive across road from unmarked road. [A.D.C. map location: 1989 Edition, page 7, grid coordinates H-8.] Possible cemetery, same as unnamed cemetery at p. 7, G-5.

EDGEWATER CEMETERY
Location: Unknown. [A.D.C. map location: 1989 Edition, page 24, grid coordinates DE-13.] Possible cemetery. Same as Mill Swamp Cemetery?

EVANS FAMILY CEMETERY
Location: Deale, location unknown. [A.D.C. map location: 1989 Edition, page 33/34?.] Year of earliest death: 1829. Year of latest death: 1910. No burial records are maintained. The gravemarkers were transcribed in 1967 and published Daughters of the American Revolution. Title: *Tombstone Inscriptions of Southern Anne Arundel County* (1971), p. 124.

FAWCUETT AVENUE CEMETERY
Location: Between Fawcuett Avenue and Macnamara west of Daniel Court. [A.D.C. map location: 1989 Edition, page 7, grid coordinates G-5.] Possible cemetery.

ANNE ARUNDEL COUNTY CEMETERIES - PRIVATE

FOREST HAVEN TRAINING SCHOOL CEMETERY
Location: On River Road across from Park Avenue. [A.D.C. map location: 1989 Edition, page 5, grid coordinates F-13.] Maintained. The monument was transcribed in 1993 and maintained by Anne Arundel Genealogical Society. Large monument with names of mentally retarded patients who died there (DC residents). Also single grave marker in open field adjoining area.

FRIEDHOFER AND GARY CEMETERY (FT. MEADE CEMETERY #5)
Location: Located on Ernie Pyle Avenue behind Building #2849. [A.D.C. map location: 1989 Edition.] Fairly good condition. Year of earliest death: 1854. Year of latest death: 1946. No burial records are maintained. Published by Anne Arundel Genealogical Society. Title: *Cemetery Inscriptions of Anne Arundel County, Maryland*, Vol. II (1987), p. 74. Copied by Ft. Meade BSA Troop 379, grid 5030.

FRIENDSHIP SCHOOL CEMETERY
Location: Route 778 north from Friendship School, on east side of road. [A.D.C. map location: 1989 Edition, page 35, grid coordinates F-1.]

GARDNER-ANDERSON CEMETERY
Location: Jessup, MD. [A.D.C. map location: 1989 Edition, page 5.] Year of earliest death: 1883. Year of latest death: 1930. No burial records are maintained. The gravemarkers were transcribed in 1960 and held by Anne Arundel Genealogical Society.

GEIS FAMILY CEMETERY
Location: On McKinsey Road next to #157, just beyond Shelbourn Road, surrounded by black chain. [A.D.C. map location: 1989 Edition, page 15, grid coordinates D-5.] Well-maintained. Year of earliest death: 1969. Year of latest death: 1989. No burial records are maintained. Records transcribed in 1993 and maintained Anne Arundel Genealogical Society.

GEORGE SCHMIDT FARM CEMETERY
Location: On Mountain Road where Route 100 merges with Mountain Road. [A.D.C. map location: 1989 Edition, page 9, grid coordinates G-10.] Year of earliest death: 1850. Year of latest death: 1898. No burial records are maintained by Anne Arundel Genealogical Society. Published by Anne Arundel Genealogical Society. Title: *Cemetery Inscriptions of Anne Arundel County, Maryland*, Vol. II (1987), p. 14.

GEORGE FOX CEMETERY
Location: Between George Fox Middle School and 211th Street. [A.D.C. map location: 1989 Edition, page 9, grid coordinates A-7/8.] Possible cemetery.

GOVERNOR'S BRIDGE ROAD CEMETERY
Location: Governor's Bridge Road east past Conne Mara Drive, on Buck Walton Farm. [A.D.C. map location: 1989 Edition, page 23, grid coordinates J-2.] No longer exists; destroyed about 1974.

GREENBERRY FAMILY CEMETERY
Location: Due north of Byrant by road, north of pond, on restricted military property. [A.D.C. map location: 1989 Edition, page 21, grid coordinates D/E-7.] No longer exists. Year of earliest death: 1697. Year of latest death: 1704. Col. N. Greenberry was buried here. No burial records are maintained. See Helen W. Ridgely, *Historic Graves of Maryland and the District of Columbia* (1908), p. 5. Reprinted by Family Line Publications (1992).

GREENOCK ROAD CEMETERY
Location: Route 259 next to Chaney's Promise on left from Route 4, in cluster of trees on hill. [A.D.C. map location: 1989 Edition, page 32, grid coordinates H-1.] No burial records are maintained.

GREENS LANE CEMETERY
Location: West side of Race Road at Greens Lane. [A.D.C. map location: 1989 Edition, page 6, grid coordinates C-2.] Possible cemetery.

GRIFFITH-DAY CEMETERY
Location: At sharp corner of New Cut Road go north on unnamed road. [A.D.C. map location: 1989 Edition, page 7, grid coordinates C-12.] Year of earliest death: 1889. Year of latest death: 1889. No burial records are maintained. Many tombstones are no longer there.

GRIFFITH FAMILY CEMETERY
Location: 300 feet east of junction of Route 170 and Donaldson Avenue in Stewart Corner Subdivision. [A.D.C. map location: 1989 Edition, page 7, grid coordinates A-7.] Year of earliest death: 1879. Year of latest death: 1979. No burial records are maintained. Records transcribed and published by Anne Arundel Genealogical Society. Title: *Cemetery Inscriptions of Anne Arundel County, Maryland*, Vol. II (1987), p. 144.

ANNE ARUNDEL COUNTY CEMETERIES - PRIVATE 17

HALL TOMBSTONE
Location: In Lothian at *Lothian* at home of Mr. William Chaney.
[A.D.C. map location: 1989 Edition, page 29?.] Year of earliest death:
1948. Year of latest death: 1948. No burial records are maintained. The
gravemarkers were transcribed in 1968; published by Daughters of the
American Revolution. Title: *Tombstone Inscriptions of Southern Anne
Arundel County (1971)*, p. 142.

HALL VAULT (*VINEYARD* VAULT)
Location: East of Route 179 and north of Sherwood Forest Road at
Vineyard property. [A.D.C. map location: 1989 Edition, page 19, grid
coordinates H-3.] No burial records are maintained. Single burial vault.

HAMMOND CEMETERY (NAVAL ACADEMY DAIRY FARM
CEMETERY)
Location: On grounds of former Naval Academy Dairy Farm. [A.D.C.
map location: 1989 Edition, page 13, grid coordinates A-8.] Year of
earliest death: 1773. Year of latest death: 1870. No burial records are
maintained. Philip Hammond who served in Rev. War is buried here.
Transcribed and published by Anne Arundel Genealogical Society. Title:
Cemetery Inscriptions of Anne Arundel County, Maryland, Vol. II
(1987), p. 136. See *Anne Arundel's Legacy*, p. 84.

HANCOCK FAMILY CEMETERY (JUBES FAMILY CEMETERY,
ALSO LINSTID FAMILY CEMETERY, ALSO LINSTEAD FAMILY
CEMETERY)
Location: East of junction of Bayside Road and Point Lookout Court at
Hancock's Resolution. [A.D.C. map location: 1989 Edition, page 10,
grid coordinates G-7.] Year of earliest death: 1800. Year of latest death:
1954. No burial records maintained. Transcribed and published by
Anne Arundel Genealogical Society. Title: *Cemetery Inscriptions of
Anne Arundel County, Maryland*, Vol. II (1987), p. 21. One tombstone
inside *Hancock's Resolution*. Additional information unpublished in
Anne Arundel Genealogical Society records.

HANCOCK-WHITTEMORE CEMETERY
Location: #7923 Chesapeake Drive (vacant lot) off Cherry Lane,
Orchard Beach, next to 3rd house on left. [A.D.C. map location: 1989
Edition, page 9, grid coordinates E-1.] No longer exists. Year of earliest
death: 1866. Year of latest death: 1915. No burial records are maintained by Anne Arundel Genealogical Society. The gravemarkers were
transcribed in 1980 and published by Anne Arundel Genealogical

Society. Title: *Cemetery Inscriptions of Anne Arundel County, Maryland*, Vol. II (1987) p. 34. Area cleared.

HARDESTY FAMILY CEMETERY
Location: Friendship, on property of Miss Delma Leitch. [A.D.C. map location: 1989 Edition, page 35?.] Year of earliest death: 1826. Year of latest death: 1884. No burial records are maintained. The gravemarkers were transcribed in 1968 and published by Daughters of the American Revolution. Title: *Tombstone Inscriptions of Southern Anne Arundel County* (1971), p. 54.

HARMAN FAMILY CEMETERY
Location: Farm at Harman's Station, on top of hill with large fieldstones marking grave. [A.D.C. map location: 1989 Edition, page 6?, grid coordinates J-3?.] No longer exists. Reinterred at Glen Haven Cemetery. Year of earliest death: 1861. Year of latest death: 1933. The gravemarkers were transcribed in 1977 and maintained by Anne Arundel Genealogical Society.

HARMAN-DISNEY CEMETERY (CEMETERY AT WILDERNESS)
Location: South of Route 176 on unnamed road off commuter parking lot on Harman property, *The Wilderness*. [A.D.C. map location: 1989 Edition, page 6.] Badly littered and neglected. Year of earliest death: 1869. Year of latest death: 1902. No burial records are maintained. The gravemarkers were transcribed and records held by Anne Arundel Genealogical Society.

HARMAN CEMETERY
Location: North of Route 176 opposite the Parkway. Industrial site. [A.D.C. map location: 1989 Edition, page 1.] No longer exists. Reinterred at Holy Cross Cemetery. Year of earliest death: 1859. Year of latest death: 1969. No burial records are maintained. Records compiled and published by Anne Arundel Genealogical Society. Title: *Cemetery Inscriptions of Anne Arundel County, Maryland*, Vol. II (1987), p. 92.

HARMAN-LUCAS CEMETERY
Location: To Ridge Road past Hanover Road, go 2 more roads and turn left, on right side (rear of #7090 Drive). [A.D.C. map location: 1989 Edition, page 1, grid coordinates H-10.] Year of earliest death: 1856. Year of latest death: 1902. No burial records are maintained. The

gravemarkers were transcribed in 1982 and maintained by Anne Arundel Genealogical Society. About 15 stones.

HARMANS PARK CEMETERY
Location: Southeast edge of Harman's Park. [A.D.C. map location: 1989 Edition, page 6, grid coordinates G-4.] No burial records are maintained. Possible cemetery.

HARRISON FAMILY CEMETERY
Location: E. on Route 261 from Route 2 for 1 1/2 mile turn right onto drive across from Holly Hill marker. [A.D.C. map location: 1989 Edition, page 35, grid coordinates K-3.] Year of earliest death: 1844. Year of latest death: 1844. Col. Joseph G. Harrison is buried here. No burial records are maintained. The gravemarkers were transcribed in 1968 and published by Daughters of the American Revolution. Title: *Tombstone Inscriptions of Southern Anne Arundel County* (1971), p. 56. There is an interesting note in book regarding tombstones.

HARTGE FAMILY CEMETERY
Location: Off Hayes Road on left in Grove of trees. [A.D.C. map location: 1989 Edition, page 30, grid coordinates E-8.] Badly overgrown, sunken stones. Year of earliest death: 1858. Year of latest death: 1923. No burial records are maintained. The gravemarkers were transcribed in 1995 and maintained by Anne Arundel Genealogical Society.

HARVEY FAMILY CEMETERY (KING FAMILY PROPERTY)
Location: Approximately ½ mile from Route 424 on south side of Double Gate Road, 500 feet from road. [A.D.C. map location: 1989 Edition, page 23, grid coordinates D-5.] Deteriorated. Year of earliest death: 1860. Year of latest death: 1861. No burial records are maintained by Anne Arundel Genealogical Society. Transcribed by Davidsonville Area Civic Association.

HARWOOD CEMETERY
Location: See A.D.C. map location. [A.D.C. map location: 1989 Edition, page 28, grid coordinates EFG-2.] No burial records are maintained. Possible cemetery.

HARWOOD CEMETERY
Location: Near C&P microwave tower east of Route 2 between Route 2 and Warthen Knolls. [A.D.C. map location: 1989 Edition, page 29, grid

coordinates C-3.] No burial records are maintained. No longer exists. Has not been there since before 1940.

HARWOOD TOMBSTONE
Location: About 0.4 mile from Route 424 at Bittersweet Nursery off Governor's Bridge Road. [A.D.C. map location: 1989 Edition, page 23, grid coordinates F-2.] Year of earliest death: 1859. Year of latest death: 1859. No burial records are maintained. Two stones: one of James Henry Harwood who died in 1859; the other unrecorded. The gravemarkers were transcribed in 1985 by Davidsonville Area Civis Association. Moved from original location. Also, *Anne Arundel's Legacy*, p. 163.

HESSELIUS FAMILY CEMETERY (PRIMROSE HILL CEMETERY)
Location: Off Hilltop Lane in Truxton Park in wooded area east of softball field. [A.D.C. map location: 1989 Edition, page 20, grid coordinates H-13.] No burial records are maintained. Vault. No tombstones visible.

HIGHLANDS CEMETERY (ROBINSON FAMILY CEMETERY, ALSO FOREST HOME ACADEMY CEMETERY)
Location: Between Crownsway and Royal Arms Way (s. of Royal Arms cul-de-sac) in Southgate. [A.D.C. map location: 1989 Edition, page 8, grid coordinates A/B-7.] No longer exists. No burial records are maintained.

HINES FAMILY CEMETERY
Location: Ft. Smallwood Road, east to 1st unmarked road on right after old Nike Missle site road, ½ mile south. [A.D.C. map location: 1989 Edition, page 9, grid coordinates J-7.] Year of earliest death: 1854. Year of latest death: 1865. No burial records are maintained. Compiled and published by Anne Arundel Genealogical Society. Title: *Cemetery Inscriptions of Anne Arundel County, Maryland*, Vol. II (1987), p. 56.

HODGES FAMILY CEMETERY
Location: 1415 Hodges Avenue. [A.D.C. map location: 1989 Edition, page 3, grid coordinates F-13.] Year of earliest death: 1844. Year of latest death: 1945. No burial records are maintained by Anne Arundel Genealogical Society. Transcribed by Anne Arundel Historical Society. Published by Anne Arundel Genealogical Society. Title: *Cemetery Inscriptions of Anne Arundel County, Maryland*, Vol. II (1987), p. 10.

ANNE ARUNDEL COUNTY CEMETERIES - PRIVATE   21

Anne Arundel Genealogical Society cemetery record also has genealogy information on the Hodges family.

HOLLINS FAMILY CEMETERY
Location: On Hilltop overlooking southwest end of Martins Pond off Sleepy Hollow Road (now Porters Hill Road). [A.D.C. map location: 1989 Edition, page 20, grid coordinates F-4.] Civil War Veterans. No burial records are maintained. Approximately 2 stones.

HOLLY BEACH FARM ROAD CEMETERY
Location: Holly Beach Farm Road between Weedon Cemetery and *Goose Pond House*. [A.D.C. map location: 1989 Edition, page 21, grid coordinates K-8.] No longer exists. No burial records are maintained. It was a small African-American cemetery.

HOOD-HIGGS CEMETERY
Location: On Race Road past Green Lane, small fenced area in woods on Simms property. [A.D.C. map location: 1989 Edition, page 6, grid coordinates C-2.] Overgrown. No burial records are maintained. Possibly same as other p. 6, C-2 cemetery. No stones left, used at least 80 years. The cemetery was in use for over 60 years. Tombstones no longer exist.

HOPKINS CEMETERY (FT. MEADE CEMETERY #15)
Location: 20 meters north of South Road, intersection of Boundary and South Roads. [A.D.C. map location: 1989 Edition, grid coordinates A-11.] Year of earliest death: 1873. Year of latest death: 1915. Poor condition, gate off, sign has bullet holes, markers tilted. No burial records are maintained. Records held and published by Anne Arundel Genealogical Society. Title: *Cemetery Inscriptions of Anne Arundel County, Maryland*, Vol. II (1987), p. 77. Copied by Ft. Meade BSA Troop 379, grid 4822.

HOPKINS FAMILY CEMETERY (ROSE HILL CEMETERY)
Location: At end of unnamed road south of Bell Branch Road. [A.D.C. map location: 1989 Edition, page 18, grid coordinates E-9.] No burial records are maintained. See *Anne Arundel's Legacy*.

HOWARD FAMILY CEMETERY (ST. GEORGE BARBER CEMETERY)
Location: 1 mile east on Howard Grove Road on dirt road, 150 feet northwest of Howard Grove House at 660 Howard Grove Road. [A.D.C.

map location: 1989 Edition, page 18, grid coordinates H-12.] Few stones in original locations. Year of earliest death: 1832. Year of latest death: 1855. No burial records are maintained by Anne Arundel Genealogical Society. The gravemarkers were transcribed in 1983. Copied by Davidsonville Area Civic Assoc. See *Anne Arundel's Legacy*, p. 163.

INDIAN CREEK LANE CEMETERY
Location: Near Indian Creek Lane. [A.D.C. map location: 1989 Edition, page 14, grid coordinates B-7.] Possible cemetery.

INGLEHART CEMETERY
Location: South of junction of Route 178 and Sherwood Forest Road, next to Rudy's Tavern. [A.D.C. map location: 1989 Edition, page 19, grid coordinates H-3.] Year of earliest death: 1811. Year of latest death: 1860. No burial records are maintained by Anne Arundel Genealogical Society. The gravemarkers were transcribed in 1975 and published by Anne Arundel Genealogical Society. Title: *Cemetery Inscriptions of Anne Arundel County, Maryland*, Vol. I (1982), p. 2.

IVY NECK FARM CEMETERY
Location: Near Ivy Neck Farm past end of paved Cumberstone Road, onto dirt road. [A.D.C. map location: 1989 Edition, page 30, grid coordinates A-6.] No burial records are maintained. Same as Johns Cemetery?

JACOBS CEMETERY (FT. MEADE CEMETERY #13)
Location: 300 meters northeast of intersection of Trainfire and South Roads. [A.D.C. map location: 1989 Edition, page 11, grid coordinates G-7.] No burial records are maintained. Compiled and published by Anne Arundel Genealogical Society. Title: *Cemetery Inscriptions of Anne Arundel County, Maryland*, Vol. II (1987), p. 77. Gravestones obliterated. Copied by Ft. Meade BSA Troop 379, grid 4625.

JEFFREY FAMILY CEMETERY
Location: North of Watts Avenue, on Ridge Road. [A.D.C. map location: 1989 Edition, page 6, grid coordinates F-4.] No longer exists. See *Anne Arundel's Legacy*, p. 164. Reinterred at Holy Cross Cemetery.

JEFFREY ROAD CEMETERY
Location: Bargers Road to Jeffrey Drive to end, then through woods. [A.D.C. map location: 1989 Edition, page 17, grid coordinates K-2/3; or

page 18, grid coordinates A-2.] No burial records are maintained. African-American cemetery.

JOHN ARNOLD GRAVE
Location: Freshfield Lane near College Parkway on George W. Schriefer, Jr. property on e. side of dirt road. [A.D.C. map location: 1989 Edition, page 15, grid coordinates K-12.] Year of earliest death: 1857, single stone. Year of latest death: 1857. No burial records are maintained. The gravemarker record is held by Anne Arundel Genealogical Society and published by Anne Arundel Genealogical Society. Title: *Cemetery Inscriptions of Anne Arundel County, Maryland*, Vol. II (1987), p. 24. Single stone.

JOHN WORTHINGTON GRAVE (PENDENNIS CEMETERY)
Location: On Pendennis farm owned by Tilghman Brice c1908. About 100 feet north of house on hill. [A.D.C. map location: 1989 Edition, page 21, grid coordinates A/B-6/7.] No burial records are maintained. Compiled by Ridgely. Title: *Historic Graves of Maryland and the District of Columbia* (1908), p. 16.

JOHNS CEMETERY (SUDLEY CEMETERY)
Location: At Sudley, part of tract once known as *Cumberstone*. [A.D.C. map location: 1989 Edition, page 29/30?] Year of earliest death: 1867. Year of latest death: 1867. Kensey and Susannah Johns are buried here. No burial records are maintained. The gravemarkers were compiled and published by Daughters of the American Revolution. Title: *Tombstone Inscriptions Of Southern Anne Arundel County* (1971), p. 190. *Anne Arundel Legacy*, p. 53. Reinterred. Quakers, relatives of Johns Hopkins, prominent in Anne Arundel County.

JOHNSON CEMETERY
Location: On Locust Grove Road about .3 mile from Lombardee Beach Road on right side. [A.D.C. map location: 1989 Edition, page 9, grid coordinates A-3?.] Year of earliest death: 1979. Year of latest death: 1909. No burial records are maintained by Anne Arundel Genealogical Society. The gravemarker records were compiled and published by Anne Arundel Genealogical Society. Title: *Cemetery Inscriptions of Anne Arundel County, Maryland*, Vol. II (1987), p. 12.

JOHNSON FAMILY CEMETERY
Location: On hilltop close to southwest corner of Route 408 and Sands Road surrounded by white fence. [A.D.C. map location: 1989 Edition,

page 31, grid coordinates K-1.] Maintained. No burial records are maintained by Anne Arundel Genealogical Society. The gravemarkers were transcribed in 1993; published by Anne Arundel Genealogical Society. African-American Cemetery. Markers have names but no dates.

JOHNSON CEMETERY (LOOPER PROPERTY CEMETERY)
Location: In woods, southwest of junction of Route 177 and North Shore Road on Looper property known as *Eagle Hill*. [A.D.C. map location: 1989 Edition, page 15, grid coordinates K-?.] Year of earliest death: 1818. Year of latest death: 1818. No burial records are maintained by Anne Arundel Genealogical Society. Tombstone records were published by Anne Arundel Genealogical Society. Title: *Cemetery Inscriptions of Anne Arundel County, Maryland*, Vol. II (1987), p. 22. Location unknown, possibly vandlized.

JOHNSON GRAVE (ROYAL BEACH CEMETERY)
Location: Royal Beach Area. [A.D.C. map location: 1989 Edition, page 9, grid coordinates C-13.] No burial records are maintained. Single stone.

JOHNSON-FOREMAN CEMETERY
Location: Jumpers Hole Road north of Luthern Church on property of Mr. Reverdy Duvall. [A.D.C. map location: 1989 Edition, page 8, grid coordinates F-8.] Year of earliest death: 1825. Year of latest death: 1924. No burial records are maintained. The gravemarkers were transcribed in 1961 by Anne Arundel Historical Society. Published by Anne Arundel Genealogical Society. Title: *Cemetery Inscriptions of Anne Arundel County, Maryland*, Vol. II (1987), p. 54. Possibly same as unnamed cemetery at p. 8, E-10 location, supposedly some slave stones.

JONES ACRES
Location: Jones Station Road just southeast of Church Road onto gravel drive (Jones Acres Road). [A.D.C. map location: 1989 Edition, page 15, grid coordinates K-12/13.] No burial records are maintained. Unable to find cemetery.

JUMPERS HOLE ROAD CEMETERY
Location: Jumpers Hole Road between Waterford Road and Christ Church (Owner: Steinfort). [A.D.C. map location: 1989 Edition, page 8,

ANNE ARUNDEL COUNTY CEMETERIES - PRIVATE

grid coordinates E-10.] No burial records are maintained. Possibly same as Johnson Cemetery.

JUNE DRIVE/JUNE WAY CEMETERY
Location: In private yard near June Drive/June Way area in Riviera Isles. [A.D.C. map location: Edition 1989, page 9, grid coordinates F-6/7.] No burial records are maintained. Possible cemetery.

KINDER FAMILY CEMETERY (KINDER BROTHERS CATTLE FARM CEMETERY, KINDER PARK CEMETERY)
Location: North Park entrance off Jumpers Hole Road right to office. On left before house, chain-link fence. [A.D.C. map location: 1989 Edition, page 8, grid coordinates F-13.] Well-maintained. Year of earliest death: 1913. Year of latest death: 1952. No burial records are maintained by Anne Arundel Genealogical Society. The gravemarkers were transcribed in 1963 and published by Anne Arundel Genealogical Society. Title: *Cemetery Inscriptions of Anne Arundel County, Maryland*, Vol. II (1987), p. 20. Information published includes two cemetery locations.

KINDER PARK FAMILY PLOT (KINDER BROTHERS CATTLE FARM CEMETERY, ALSO KINDER PARK CEMETERY)
Location: N. Park entrance from Jumpers Hole right turn right to office. On left beside chain link fence. [A.D.C. map location: 1989 Edition, page 8, grid coordinates F-13.] No burial records are maintained. Two unmarked sandstones. Homestead was near Kinder Cemetery but different family.

KNOPP FAMILY CEMETERY
Location: Left on Drum Point Road to Owings Beach Road, on left. [A.D.C. map location: 1989 Edition, page 34, grid coordinates A-7.] Year of earliest death: 1906. Year of latest death: 1935. No burial records are maintained. The gravemarkers were transcribed in 1967. Published by Daughters of the American Revolution. Title: *Tombstone Inscriptions of Southern Anne Arundel County* (1971), p. 128.

LABROT FAMILY CEMETERY
Location: At #1800 Holly Beach Farm Road to right of main entrance to house, on bluff. [A.D.C. map location: 1989 Edition, page 21, grid coordinates K-6.] Maintained. Year of earliest death: 1915. Year of latest death: 1992. No burial records are maintained. The

gravemarkers were transcribed in 1993 and published by Anne Arundel Genealogical Society.

LANGLEY CEMETERY (LANGVILLE FAMILY CEMETERY)
Location: Between Dividing Creek Road and Dividing Creek. Formerly owned by T. H. Langley/D. C. Langley. [A.D.C. map location: 1989 Edition, page 15, grid coordinates F-8.] Year of earliest death: 1901. Year of latest death: 1969. No burial records are maintained. The gravemarkers were transcribed in 1995.

LANKFORD FAMILY CEMETERY
Location: At end of Lankford Road within traffic circle in front of family home. [A.D.C. map location: 1989 Edition, page 28, grid coordinates G-3.] No longer exists. No burial records are maintained.

LEE CEMETERY (SMITH FARM ROAD CEMETERY)
Location: [A.D.C. map location: 1989 Edition, page 1, grid coordinates FG-13.] Possible cemetery.

LIGHTHOUSE KEEPER'S CEMETERY
Location: Near powerlines, near Bodkin Point, lighthouse keeper's graves. [A.D.C. map location: 1989 Edition, page 10, grid coordinates J-8.] No burial records are maintained. Possibly Bodkin Point Cemetery. Lighthouse Keeper's graves, even though lighthouse was in a slightly different location.

LINSTID-HANSHAW BURIAL GROUND
Location: Swift Road off Lake Shore Drive near Cockey's Creek. [A.D.C. map location: 1989 Edition, page 15, grid coordinates G-1.] Year of earliest death: 1825. Year of latest death: 1826. No burial records are maintained. The gravemarkers were transcribed and published by Anne Arundel Genealogical Society. Title: *Cemetery Inscriptions of Anne Arundel County, Maryland*, Vol. II (1987), p. 12. About 40 graves, mostly unmarked fieldstones.

LINSTID-HEATH FAMILY CEMETERY
Location: In woods off Cypress Creek Road. [A.D.C. map location: 1989 Edition, page 15, grid coordinates C-6?.] Year of earliest death: 1819. Year of latest death: 1871. No burial records are maintained by Anne Arundel Genealogical Society. The gravemarkers were transcribed in 1961 and published by Anne Arundel Genealogical Society. Title:

ANNE ARUNDEL COUNTY CEMETERIES - PRIVATE

Cemetery Inscriptions of Anne Arundel County, Maryland, Vol. II (1987), p. 11.

LINTHICUM FAMILY CEMETERY
Location: On B.A. King Family farm near Gambrills. [A.D.C. map location: 1989 Edition, page 13-?.] Year of earliest death: 1847. Year of latest death: 1880. No burial records are maintained. Copied by owner of property at unknown time.

LINTHICUM-LEE CEMETERY
Location: 1 mile north of Route 2 and Route 214, intersection opposite (Dairy) building, near airstrip. [A.D.C. map location: 1989 Edition, page 24, grid coordinates HJ-5/6.] Year of earliest death: 1829. Year of latest death: 1910. No burial records are maintained. Compiled and published by Daughters of the American Revolution. Title: *Tombstone Inscriptions of Southern Anne Arundel County* (1971), p. 303.

LUSBY FAMILY CEMETERY
Location: East of Mackiebeth Road, 200 feet from Kansala Drive intersection in woods on hill. [A.D.C. map location: 1989 Edition, page 19, grid coordinates E-7.] Year of earliest death: 1831. Year of latest death: 1877. No burial records are maintained by Anne Arundel Genealogical Society. The gravemarkers were transcribed in 1994 and published by Anne Arundel Genealogical Society. Formerly many more tombstones. Located on old Lusby Farm in new subdivision.

LYNCH-WILLIAMS FAMILY CEMETERY
Location: Approximately 100 yards southwest of Greenhaven Firehouse on Cyril Avenue on Robert Holmes property. [A.D.C. map location: 1989 Edition, page 9, grid coordinates F-10.] Year of earliest death: 1814. Year of latest death: 1890. No burial records are maintained by Anne Arundel Genealogical Society. The gravemarkers were transcribed in 1979 and published by Anne Arundel Genealogical Society. Title: *Cemetery Inscriptions of Anne Arundel County, Maryland*, Vol. II (1987), p. 24.

MACKUBIN CEMETERY (BELLEFIELD CEMETERY)
Location: No location given. [A.D.C. map location: 1989 Edition, page 21, grid coordinates J-2.] Year of earliest death: 1793. Year of latest death: 1834. No burial records are maintained by Anne Arundel Genealogical Society. The gravemarkers were compiled and published by Anne Arundel Genealogical Society. Title: *Cemetery Inscriptions of*

Anne Arundel County, Maryland, Vol. II (1987), p. 42. Capt. Thomas Homewood and John Hesselius (portrait painter) buried there, unmarked graves.

MAJOR THOMAS FRANCIS TOMBSTONE (JAVA TOMBSTONE, ALSO WOODSTOCK TOMBSTONE)
Location: At *Woodstock* on Contees Wharf Road 0.5 mile from Route 468 intersection. [A.D.C. map location: 1989 Edition, page 24, grid coordinates K-11.] No longer exists. Year of death: 1685. No burial records are maintained. Records compiled by Ridgely and published in *Historic Graves of Maryland and the District of Columbia* (1908), p. 18. Also recorded in DAR's *Tombstone Inscriptions of Southern Anne Arundel County* (1971), p. 292. Single stone no longer there. Major Thomas Francis is buried here.

MARIOTT CEMETERY (FT. MEADE CEMETERY #18)
Location: 400 meters northeast from intersection of Patuxent and Telegraph Roads. [A.D.C. map location: 1989 Edition, page 12.] Published by Anne Arundel Genealogical Society. Title: *Cemetery Inscriptions of Anne Arundel County, Maryland*, Vol. II (1987), p. 79. Copied by Ft. Meade BSA Troop 379, grid 4724. Gravestones obliterated. No easy access.

MARLEY NECK ROAD CEMETERY
Location: Off Marley Neck Road near Dobrody Farm Road. [A.D.C. map location: 1989 Edition, page 8, grid coordinates G-2.] Possible cemetery.

MARTIN SPALDING CEMETERY
Location: West of Route 3 and east of New Cut Road, east of Martin Spalding H.S. [A.D.C. map location: 1989 Edition, page 7, grid coordinates H-9.] Possible cemetery.

MARYWOOD DRIVE GRAVE
Location: In Spring Lake Community, in front yard of #1054 Marywood Drive. [A.D.C. map location: 1989 Edition, page 19, grid coordinates A-13.] No burial records are maintained. Single grave, no stone, supposedly Civil War veteran brought back to homestead.

MARZOFF ROAD CEMETERY
Location: Off Marzoff Road in Rest Haven Community. At roads end walk across prop. into woods. [A.D.C. map location: 1989 Edition, page

ANNE ARUNDEL COUNTY CEMETERIES - PRIVATE

34, grid coordinates D-7.] No burial records are maintained. Supposedly 8-10 graves.

MATHIAS HARMAN CEMETERY
Location: Off Route 176 behind 84 Lumber Company at Route 170 on southwest side of road. [A.D.C. map location: 1989 Edition, page 6, grid coordinates J-3.] No burial records are maintained. See *Anne Arundel's Legacy*, p. 172.

MAXCY FAMILY CEMETERY (TULIP HILL CEMETERY)
Location: At Tulip Hill off Route 468 just north of Route 255 on east side of road, back in woods. [A.D.C. map location: 1989 Edition, page 29, grid coordinates K-6.] Overgrown, stones very legible. Year of earliest death: 1752. Year of latest death: 1891. No burial records are maintained by Anne Arundel Genealogical Society. The gravemarkers were transcribed in 1967 and published Daughters of the American Revolution. Title: *Tombstone Inscriptions of Southern Anne Arundel County* (1971), p. 295. See Ridgely, *Historic Graves of Maryland and the District of Columbia*, p. 18 (error in name spelling here).

MCKENDREE ROAD CEMETERY
Location: At #6368 McKendree Road about 300 yards behind house. [A.D.C. map location: 1989 Edition, page 32, grid coordinates K-10.] Overgrown. Year of earliest death: 1845. Year of latest death: 1853. No burial records are maintained by Anne Arundel Genealogical Society. The gravemarkers were transcribed in 1995.

MCKENDREE ROAD CEMETERY
Location: On McKendree Road on property of Thomas Lyons (1990). [A.D.C. map location: 1989 Edition, page 33, grid coordinates K-7/10.] No burial records are maintained. Slave graves, only small wooden post left.

MCKINSEY WOODS CEMETERY
Location: East of Route 2 on McKinsey Road, formerly in the middle of three dirt roads on south side. [A.D.C. map location: 1989 Edition, page 15, grid coordinates C-5.] No longer exists. No burial records are maintained. This area was developed in the Fall of 1993.

MERCER CEMETERY (CEDAR PARK CEMETERY)
Location: Straight at junction of Cumberstone/Bayfield Roads to Bridgeman property (1991) past Bayfields Road. [A.D.C. map location:

1989 Edition, page 30, grid coordinates D-3.] Year of earliest death: 1796. Year of latest death: 1913. No burial records are maintained. The gravemarkers were transcribed in 1967 and published by Daughters of the American Revolution. Title: *Tombstone Inscriptions of Southern Anne Arundel County* (1971), p. 290. See *Historic Graves of Maryland and the District of Columbia*, p. 18.

MERRITT FAMILY CEMETERY
Location: Within boundary of BWI Airport. [A.D.C. map location: 1989 Edition, page 2/7?.] No longer exists. No burial records are maintained. Compiled and published by Anne Arundel Genealogical Society. Title: *Cemetery Inscriptions of Anne Arundel County, Maryland*, Vol. II (1987), p. 81. Reinterred at Cedar Hill Cemetery in 1946.

MEWSHAW FAMILY CEMETERY
Location: Off Route 3 facing north. Lane 1/4 mile north of Quarterfield Road Underpass. [A.D.C. map location: 1989 Edition, page 7, grid coordinates G-5.] Year of earliest death: 1871. Year of latest death: 1915. No burial records are maintained. The gravemarkers were transcribed in 1979 and published by Anne Arundel Genealogical Society. Title: *Cemetery Inscriptions of Anne Arundel County, Maryland*, Vol. II (1987), p. 102.

MEYN FAMILY CEMETERY (KINDER BROS. CATTLE FARM CEMETERY, ALSO KINDER PARK CEMETERY)
Location: North Park entrance from Jumpers Hole Road make 1st right to office, behind barn in tree grove. [A.D.C. map location: 1989 Edition, page 8, grid coordinates F-13.] Overgrown. Year of earliest death: 1898. Year of latest death: 1941. No burial records are maintained. The gravemarkers were transcribed in 1993 and published by Anne Arundel Genealogical Society. Title: *Cemetery Inscriptions of Anne Arundel County, Maryland*, Vol. II (1987), p. 20. Published information shows two separate cemeteries as a single one.

MICHELLE COURT CEMETERY
Location: South of Elevaton Road at Michelle Court. [A.D.C. map location: 1989 Edition, page 8, grid coordinates B-9.] Possible cemetery.

MIDDLE PLANTATION CEMETERY
Location: At *Middle Plantation* on Route 424. [A.D.C. map location: 1989 Edition, page 18, grid coordinates E-12.] No longer exists. No burial records are maintained. Possibly Duvall Cemetery. Property, but

not cemetery, mentioned in *Anne Arundel's Legacy*. Destroyed by barn construction circa 1928.

MILBUR CEMETERY
Location: Cornfield Creek between Linthicum Farm and housing development. [A.D.C. map location: 1989 Edition, page 10, grid coordinates F/G-13.] No burial records are maintained. See *Anne Arundel's Legacy*, p. 171.

MILL SWAMP ROAD CEMETERY
Location: Mill Swamp Road next to house #385. [A.D.C. map location: 1989 Edition, page 29, grid coordinates G-1.] No burial records are maintained.

MILL CREEK CEMETERY
Location: St. Margaret's Road 1/2 mile southwest of St. Margaret's Church, near head of Mill Creek. [A.D.C. map location: 1989 Edition, page 21, grid coordinates C-3?.] No burial records are maintained.

MORGAN ROAD CEMETERY
Location: Between Odenton Road and next parallel road north. East of Morgan Road. [A.D.C. map location: 1989 Edition, page 12, grid coordinates H-3.] No tombstones remain.

MOSS FAMILY PLOT
Location: At end of Holly Beach Farm Road near Goose Pond at Hackett Point near water's edge. [A.D.C. map location: 1989 Edition, page 21, grid coordinates K-8.] No longer exists. Year of earliest death: 1859. Year of latest death: 1940. No burial records are maintained. The gravemarkers were transcribed in 1993 by Anne Arundel Genealogical Society. Reinterred at Cedar Bluffs. Ground plaque in original cemetery location.

MOUNTAIN ROAD CEMETERY
Location: On Mountain Road across from (school/firehouse?) between Routes 177 and 607 on north side of road. [A.D.C. map location: 1989 Edition, page 8/9, grid coordinates ?-3.] No burial records are maintained. Possibly same as George Schmidt Farm Cemetery.

MRS. HILL'S BURYING GROUND (EZEKIEL GILLIS' GRAVE)
Location: Probably near intersection of Harbor and Great Lakes Drive in Hillsmere Estates. [A.D.C. map location: 1989 Edition, page 25, grid

coordinates J-5.] No longer exists. Year of earliest death: 1749. Year of latest death: 1749. Capt. Ezekiel Gillis is buried here. See Ridgely, *Historic Graves of Maryland and District of Columbia*, p. 2; also see St. Anne's Parish Register (MD Archives M143, p. 168).

MULLIKAN CEMETERY (FT. MEADE CEMETERY #17)
Location: 1200 meters northwest of Range 12 entrance. [A.D.C. map location: 1989 Edition, page 12.] Fair condition, sign has bullet holes, no markers. Year of earliest death: 1885. Year of latest death: 1897. No burial records are maintained. Gravemarker records published by Anne Arundel Genealogical Society. Title: *Cemetery Inscriptions of Anne Arundel County, Maryland*, Vol. II (1987), p. 78. Copied by Ft. Meade BSA Troop 379, grid 4824.

MURRAY/BEVERLY CEMETERY
Location: Between Murray Road and Beverly Avenue near curve. [A.D.C. map location: 1989 Edition, page 12, grid coordinates J-3.] Possible cemetery.

MYERS CEMETERY
Location: From Quarterfield Road turn left onto Westphalia Court on the right a few houses from intersection. [A.D.C. map location: 1989 Edition, page 7, grid coordinates F-7.] No burial records are maintained. Probably same as Myers Cemetery at p. 7, F-6 location.

MYERS FAMILY CEMETERY
Location: Route 3 approx. 3/4 mile south of Glen Burnie near Phirne Road (Rippling Estates) near fire station. [A.D.C. map location: 1989 Edition, page 7, grid coordinates J-7.] Year of earliest death: 1891. Year of latest death: 1925. No burial records are maintained. The gravemarkers were transcribed in 1967 and published by Anne Arundel Genealogical Society. Title: Cemetery Inscriptions of Anne Arundel County, Maryland, Vol. II (1987), p. 17.

MYERS CEMETERY (OLD MYERS BURIAL GROUND)
Location: South of Quarterfield Road, west of Westphalia Drive, north of Kennan Road/Westphalia Court. [A.D.C. map location: 1989 Edition, page 7, grid coordinates F-6.] Year of earliest death: 1902. Year of latest death: 1956. No burial records are maintained. The gravemarkers were transcribed in 1992 and records held by Anne Arundel Genealogical Society. Probably same as Myers Cemetery at p. 7, F-7 location.

NORMAN CEMETERY
Location: Mimosa Cove subdivision, between Joe Road and Milton Avenue. [A.D.C. map location: 1989 Edition, page 34, grid coordinates B-6.] Year of earliest death: 1824. Year of latest death: 1889. Capt. Theophilus Norman is buried here. No burial records are maintained. The gravemarkers were transcribed in 1974. Records held by Anne Arundel Genealogical Society, which also has plat of location and a J. Nicholas Norman will dated 1758.

NORRIS CEMETERY (DENT ROAD CEMETERY)
Location: Dent Road to end of road. Garage is straight ahead at waters edge. A single stone, propped against the garage. [A.D.C. map location: 1989 Edition, page 34, grid coordinates G-1.] No longer exists. Year of death: 1854. No burial records are maintained. The gravemarker record is held by Anne Arundel Genealogical Society.

NUTWELL FAMILY CEMETERY
Location: Nutwell Road 0.9 mile north of intersection of Routes 2 and 258 on W. Bogley property in field 0.6 mile from main entrance. [A.D.C. map location: 1989 Edition, page 33-?.] Year of earliest death: 1825. Year of latest death: 1858. No burial records are maintained. The gravemarkers were transcribed in 1968. Records held by Anne Arundel Genealogical Society. Compiled by Daughters of the American Revolution. Title: *Tombstone Inscriptions of Southern Anne Arundel County* (1971), p. 81.

NUTWELL GRAVE
Location: A single stone on Route 258 east of Route 2 intersection on Nutwell property (1968) on wooded hill; has a wrought iron fence. [A.D.C. map location: 1989 Edition, page 33-?.] Year of death: 1857. No burial records are maintained. The gravemarkers were transcribed in 1968 and published by Daughters of the American Revolution. Records held by Anne Arundel Genealogical Society. Title: *Tombstone Inscriptions of Southern Anne Arundel County* (1971), p. 83.

OLD CROMWELL CEMETERY
Location: On east side of Hammonds Ferry Road between Ferndale and Maple Roads. May be the property of Beulah Clark. [A.D.C. map location: 1989 Edition, page 2, grid coordinates G-11.] Year of earliest death: 1813. Year of latest death: 1880. No burial records are maintained. The gravemarkers were compiled and published by Anne

Arundel Genealogical Society. Title: *Cemetery Inscriptions of Anne Arundel County, Maryland*, Vol. II (1987), p.93.

OLD PUMPHREY FAMILY CEMETERY
Location: On Olen Drive, next to George Cromwell Elementary School. [A.D.C. map location: 1989 Edition, page 2, grid coordinates J-11/12.] Year of earliest death: 1904. Year of latest death: 1937. No burial records are maintained. Transcribed and published by Anne Arundel Genealogical Society. Title: *Cemetery Inscriptions of Anne Arundel County, Maryland*, Vol. II (1987), p. 95. Same as Pumphrey Family Cemetery. Reinterred at Glen Haven.

OLD RIDOUT CEMETERY
Location: Whitehall Road in Whitehall; contact Orlando Ridout. [A.D.C. map location: 1989 Edition, page 21, grid coordinates J-2.] No burial records are maintained.

OUTING/205TH CEMETERY
Location: Near 205th and Outing Avenue in backyard. [A.D.C. map location: 1989 Edition, page 9, grid coordinates A-6.] No burial records are maintained. Contact Community Association Chairman for additional information.

OWENS FAMILY CEMETERY
Location: At Bristol, on Route 259 at property of Ashby Lee Shepherd, Jr. [A.D.C. map location: 1989 Edition, page 32?.] Year of earliest death: 1840. Year of latest death: 1864. No burial records are maintained. The gravemarker records held by Anne Arundel Genealogical Society. Transcribed and published by Daughters of the American Revolution. Title: *Tombstone Inscriptions of Southern Anne Arundel County* (1971), p. 73.

OWENS FAMILY CEMETERY
Location: On Route 259 in Bristol on property of Mrs. Eugene Chaney, Sr. (1967). [A.D.C. map location: 1989 Edition, page 32-?.] Year of earliest death: 1813. Year of latest death: 1869. No burial records are maintained. The gravemarkers were transcribed in 1967 by Daughters of the American Revolution. Held by Anne Arundel Genealogical Society. Compiled and published by Daughters of the American Revolution. Title: *Tombstone Inscriptions of Southern Anne Arundel County* (1971), p. 75.

ANNE ARUNDEL COUNTY CEMETERIES - PRIVATE 35

OWINGS CEMETERY
Location: At end of Samuel Owings Road in Heritage Harbor. [A.D.C. map location: 1989 Edition, page 36, grid coordinates C-4?.] Year of earliest death: 1822. Year of latest death: 1894. No burial records are maintained. The gravemarkers were transcribed and held by Anne Arundel Genealogical Society.

PARISH-MACE CEMETERY (IDLEWILDE CEMETERY)
Location: At #4891 Idlewilde Road face down in front yard. [A.D.C. map location: 1989 Edition, page 30, grid coordinates J-8.] No burial records are maintained. The gravemarkers were transcribed in 1995 by Anne Arundel Genealogical Society. Cemetery at least 31 years old (length of time owner has been there). No dates on stones.

PARKWAY/DORSEY CEMETERY
Location: Just southeast of ramp from Baltimore-Washington Parkway onto Route 176 about 10 feet off right of way. [A.D.C. map location: 1989 Edition, page 6, grid coordinates D-1.] No longer at this location. No burial records are maintained. Reinterred at Holy Cross Cemetery.

PATUXENT RIVER ROAD CEMETERY
Location: Located off Patuxent River Road. [A.D.C. map location: 1989 Edition, page 23, grid coordinates B-3.]

PEACH-GALLOWAY CEMETERY (RIVA ROAD CEMETERY, ALSO TAYLORSVILLE CHURCHYARD CEMETERY)
Location: Just west of South River Bridge on Riva Road on north side of road. [A.D.C. map location: 1989 Edition, page 24, grid coordinates G-1.] Maintained. Year of earliest death: 1891. Year of latest death: 1969. No burial records are maintained. The gravemarkers were transcribed in 1992 by Anne Arundel Genealogical Society.

PETTEBONE CEMETERY
Location: Bay Head Road (on Waring-Stinchcome property). [A.D.C. map location: 1989 Edition, page 16, grid coordinates K-11.] Year of earliest death: 1833. Year of latest death: 1888. No burial records are maintained. The gravemarkers were transcribed in 1965. Held by Anne Arundel Genealogical Society.

PHELPS CEMETERY (FT. MEADE CEMETERY #19)
Location: 100 meters northwest of Amtrak rails, off Boundary Road near landfill. [A.D.C. map location: 1989 Edition, page 12, grid coor-

dinates F-4.] Poor condition. Transient/youth party vandalism, no gate. Year of earliest death: 1861. Year of latest date: 1886. Published by: Anne Arundel Genealogical Society. Title: *Cemetery Inscriptions of Anne Arundel County, Maryland*, Vol. II (1987), p. 79. Copied by Ft. Meade BSA Troop 379, grid 5126.

PHIPPS CEMETERY
Location: Deale, location unknown. [A.D.C. map location: 1989 Edition, page 33-34?.] Year of death: 1904. No burial records are maintained. The gravemarker was transcribed in 1967. Held by Anne Arundel Genealogical Society. Compiled and published by Daughters of the American Revolution. Title: *Tombstone Inscriptions of Southern Anne Arundel County* (1971), p. 130.

PHIPPS CEMETERY
Location: At Mt. Zion, on Route 422 in thicket behind home of Mr. Roland Brady. [A.D.C. map location: 1989 Edition, page 28.] Year of death: 1850. No burial records are maintained. The gravemarker was transcribed in 1968 by Daughters of the American Revolution. Records held by Anne Arundel Genealogical Society. Published by Daughters of the American Revolution. Title: *Tombstone Inscriptions of Southern Anne Arundel County* (1971), p. 188.

PINDELL FAMILY CEMETERY
Location: On Route 2, 0.3 mile north of intersection with Route 408 on Fitzhugh property. [A.D.C. map location: 1989 Edition, page 29?.] Year of earliest death: 1853. Year of latest death: 1863. No burial records are maintained. The gravemarkers were transcribed in 1968 and published by Anne Arundel Genealogical Society. Compiled by Daughters of the American Revolution. Title: *Tombstone Inscriptions of Southern Anne Arundel County* (1971), p. 300.

PINDELL FAMILY CEMETERY
Location: Bristol, 0.5 mile from intersection of Lower Pindell Road and Route 408, under tree on right, concrete wall. [A.D.C. map location: 1989 Edition, page 32-?, grid coordinates .] Year of earliest death: 1935. Year of latest death: 1945. No burial records are maintained. The gravemarkers records are held by Anne Arundel Genealogical Society. Compiled and published by Daughters of the American Revolution. Title: *Tombstone Inscriptions of Southern Anne Arundel County* (1971), p. 77. Concrete wall mostly underground.

ANNE ARUNDEL COUNTY CEMETERIES - PRIVATE 37

PINDELL PROPERTY CEMETERY
Location: 1st or 2nd dirt road north of Lothian Post Office on west side of Route 2 behind Pindell farmhouse. [A.D.C. map location: 1989 Edition, page 29, grid coordinates B-10.] No burial records are maintained. Supposedly Civil War veteran who died at Gettysburg.

PLEASANT HILL FARM CEMETERY (ARMIGER CEMETERY, ALSO BAY HILLS GOLF CLUB CEMETERY)
Location: At 11th hole of Bay Hills Golf Club. A fence surrounds it. [A.D.C. map location: 1989 Edition, page 16, grid coordinates A-11.] Year of death: 1843. Gravemarkers transcribed in 1963. Compiled and published by Anne Arundel Genealogical Society. Title: *Cemetery Inscriptions of Anne Arundel County, Maryland*, Vol. II (1987), p.20. Two stones remain, one illegible.

POST CEMETERY (FT. MEADE CEMETERY #1)
Location: Rock Avenue across from Building 2250. [A.D.C. map location: 1989 Edition, page 12, grid coordinates E-3.] Well-maintained. Year of earliest death: 1934. Year of latest death: 1973. Published by Anne Arundel Genealogical Society. Title: *Cemetery Inscriptions of Anne Arundel County, Maryland*, Vol. II (1987), p. 57. Copied by Ft. Meade BSA Troop 379, grid 5027. Several German soldiers buried here.

PUMPHREY CEMETERY (MAX LOWMAN'S PLACE, ALSO OLD PUMPHREY CEMETERY)
Location: Off Route 170 on farm north of Old Severn Run in wooded area approximately 50-60 feet off road. [A.D.C. map location: 1989 Edition, page 6, grid coordinates K-13.] Year of earliest death: 1865. Year of latest death: 1909. No burial records are maintained. The gravemarkers were transcribed in 1992 and records held by Anne Arundel Genealogical Society. Hopkins Map of 1878 shows same families at this place.

PUMPHREY FAMILY CEMETERY
Location: Near junction of Jumpers Hole Road and Mountain Road. [A.D.C. map location: 1989 Edition, page 8, grid coordinates F-8.] The cemeterey no longer exists. Year of earliest death: 1877. Year of latest death: 1904. No burial records are maintained. The gravemarkers were transcribed in 1969 by Anne Arundel Genealogical Society. Records held by and published by Anne Arundel Genealogical Society. Title: *Cemetery Inscriptions of Anne Arundel County, Maryland*, Vol. II

(1987), p. 12. Reinterred at Glen Haven Memorial Park, Glen Burnie. Two burial grounds.

PUMPHREY FAMILY CEMETERY
Location: Olan Road, Olan Plaza. [A.D.C. map location: 1989 Edition, page 2, grid coordinates J-12.] Year of earliest death: 1904. Year of latest death: 1937. No burial records are maintained. The gravemarkers were transcribed and published by Anne Arundel Genealogical Society. Title: *Cemetery Inscriptions of Anne Arundel County, Maryland*, Vol. II (1987), p. 56. Same as Old Pumphrey Family Cemetery (both published). Reinterred at Glen Haven Memorial Park.

PUMPHREY FAMILY CEMETERY
Location: West of WB&A Road on Evergreen Road. [A.D.C. map location: 1989 Edition, page 6, grid coordinates K-11.] Overgrown. Year of earliest death: 1886. Year of latest death: 1936. No burial records are maintained. The gravemarkers were transcribed in 1991 by Anne Arundel Genealogical Society; Records held and published by Anne Arundel Genealogical Society. Title: *Cemetery Inscriptions of Anne Arundel County, Maryland*, Vol. II (1987), p. 146.

PUMPHREY FARM CEMETERY
Location: On little hill to east of Solley Road on right of unnamed road directly across from Solley store. [A.D.C. map location: 1987 Edition, page 8.] Year of death: 1818. Records held and published by Anne Arundel Genealogical Society. Title: *Cemetery Inscriptions of Anne Arunder County, Maryland*, Vol. II, (1987), p. 51. Evidence of other graves, but no other markers. Several stones, only one death date.

REDGRAVE-NOLEN FAMILY CEMETERY
Location: Deep Creek Avenue. Left at 2nd intersection (Hilltop), go to end of road, down dirt road on right. [A.D.C. map location: 1989 Edition, page 16, grid coordinates DE-10.] Badly overgrown. Year of earliest death: 1875. Year of latest death: 1888. No burial records are maintained. The gravemarkers were transcribed and records held by Anne Arundel Genealogical Society. Compiled and published by Anne Arundel Genealogical Society. Title: *Cemetery Inscriptions of Anne Arundel County, Maryland*, Vol. II (1987), p. 82.

REDMOND TOMBSTONE
Location: Behind Big Vanilla Tennis Club, southwest of intersection of Route 2 and College Pkwy and north of west Campus Drive. [A.D.C. map location: 1989 Edition, page 15, grid coordinates F-10.] The gravemarker was transcribed in 1993 by Anne Arundel Genealogical Society. One propped stone near wood's edge, possibly others.

REDMORE DRIVE/COURT CEMETERY
Location: South of Reece Road and east of railroad tracks near Redmore Drive and Redmore Court. [A.D.C. map location: 1989 Edition, page 6, grid coordinates J-8.]

RICHARDSON FAMILY CEMETERY
Location: 1.1 miles east of Route 256 and Mimosa Cove Road opposite red single story house on water. [A.D.C. map location: 1989 Edition, page 34, grid coordinates B-6.] Year of death: 1861. No burial records are maintained. The gravemarker was transcribed by Daughters of the American Revolution. Records held by Anne Arundel Genealogical Society. Compiled and published by Daughters of the American Revolution. Title: *Tombstone Inscriptions of Southern Anne Arundel County, Maryland* (1971), p. 191. Single headstone, different footstone.

RICHARDSON FAMILY CEMETERY
Location: On Route 2, 1 mile (west?) of intersection of Route 2 and Route 255. [A.D.C. map location: 1989 Edition, page 29?.] Year of earliest death: 1824. Year of latest death: 1858. No burial records are maintained. The gravemarkers were transcribed in 1968 by Daughters of the American Revolution. Records held by Anne Arundel Genealogical Society. Compiled and published by Daughters of the American Revolution. Title: *Tombstone Inscriptions of Southern Anne Arundel County, Maryland* (1971), p. 179.

RIDGELY-WORTHINGTON CEMETERY
Location: Probably off current Chesterfield Road. [A.D.C. map location: 1989 Edition, page 19, grid coordinates D/E-6/7.] No burial records are maintained. Was at site of family home (razed). Possibly single stone, 2 stones left in 1908.

RIDOUT FAMILY CEMETERY (WHITEHALL CEMETERY)
Location: On property of *Whitehall* in 1808. [A.D.C. map location: 1989 Edition, page 211?.] No longer exists. Year of earliest death: 1781. Year of latest death: 1808. No burial records are maintained. See *Historic*

Graves of Maryland and the District of Columbia, p. 8. Included unnamed indentured servant.

RIVIERA BEACH CEMETERY (THOMAS-WHEELER CEMETERY)
Location: At end of Main Street on Stoney Creek on south side of Carroll, on top of hill. [A.D.C. map location: 1989 Edition, page 9, grid coordinates F-1/2.] Year of earliest death: 1833. Year of latest death: 1906. No burial records are maintained. Gravemarkers transcribed and published by Anne Arundel Genealogical Society. Title: *Cemetery Inscriptions of Anne Arundel County, Maryland*, Vol. II (1987), p. 13. See *Anne Arundel's Legacy*, p. 167.

ROBINSON-GARDNER CEMETERY
Location: At #612 Randell Road in Round Bay Community. [A.D.C. map location: 1989 Edition, page 15, grid coordinates C-7?.] Year of earliest death: 1820. Year of latest death: 1849. No burial records are maintained. The gravemarkers were transcribed in 1975 and published by Anne Arundel Genealogical Society. Compiled by Anne Arundel Genealogical Society. Title: *Cemetery Inscriptions of Anne Arundel County, Maryland*, Vol. II (1987), p. 13.

ROBINSON GRAVE
Location: Chestnut Hill east of Solley Road and south of Nabbs Creek Road. [A.D.C. map location: 1989 Edition, page 8, grid coordinates J-2/3.]

ROCKVIEW BEACH CEMETERY
Location: Rockview Beach at end of East Road, in the woods. [A.D.C. map location: 1989 Edition, page 9, grid coordinates F-6.] Year of earliest death: 1813. Year of latest death: 1911. No burial records are maintained. The gravemarkers were transcribed in 1979 and published by Anne Arundel Genealogical Society. Title: *Cemetery Inscriptions of Anne Arundel County, Maryland*, Vol. II (1987), p. 55.

ROGERS FAMILY CEMETERY
Location: Deale, specific location unknown. [A.D.C. map location: p. 33/34.] Year of earliest death: 1838. Year of latest death: 1960. No burial records are maintained. The gravemarkers were transcribed in 1967 by Daughters of the American Revolution. Records held by Anne Arundel Genealogical Society. Compiled and published by Daughters of the American Revolution. Title: *Tombstone Inscriptions of Southern Anne Arundel County* (1971), p. 132.

ANNE ARUNDEL COUNTY CEMETERIES - PRIVATE

ROLLING KNOLLS CEMETERY
Location: Between Knollwood Road and Rolling Knolls Elementary School east of Valley Road. [A.D.C. map location: 1989 Edition, page p.19, grid coordinates K-6.] Overgrown. Possible landowner dispute re: if cemetery there.

ROUTE 3 CEMETERY
Location: Route 3 northbound lane 1/4 mile north of business Route 3 Junction. [A.D.C. map location: 1989 Edition, page 7, grid coordinates H-8.] Possibly same as Mewshaw Family Cemetery.

RUTLAND CEMETERY (BEARD HALL MEMORIAL CEMETERY)
Location: Rutland and Rossbach Rds. 300 yds. west of Rutland near end of Forest Trail Ct. [A.D.C. map location: 1989 Edition, page 18, grid coordinates H-11.] Year of earliest death: 1813. Year of latest death: 1875. Tombstone records are held by Anne Arundel Genealogical Society. The gravemarkers were transcribed and published by Anne Arundel Genealogical Society. Title: *Cemetery Inscriptions of Anne Arundel County, Maryland*, Vol. I (1982), p.163. Also published in *Anne Arundel's Legacy*, p. 5.

SCHEMINART FAMILY CEMETERY
Location: East of Marley Neck Road "in middle of street" on Cedar Avenue. [A.D.C. map location: 1989 Edition, page 8, grid coordinates E-4.] Year of death: 1884. No burial records are maintained. The gravemarkers were transcribed and published by Anne Arundel Genealogical Society. Title: *Cemetery Inscriptions of Anne Arundel County, Maryland*, Vol. II (1987), p. 33. Four or five graves, only 1 remains.

SCOTT FAMILY CEMETERY
Location: At end of Scott Town Road on far right corner. [A.D.C. map location: 1989 Edition, page 30, grid coordinates E-11.] Maintained. Year of earliest death: 1922. Year of latest death: 1982. WWII Veterans. No burial records are maintained. The gravemarkers were transcribed in 1994 by Anne Arundel Genealogical Society.

SELBY GROVE CEMETERY
Location: On Pasadena Road near Lake Waterford. [A.D.C. map location: 1989 Edition, page 8, grid coordinates H-11/12.] No burial records are maintained. Possible cemetery, shown on topo. map in Selby Grove Community.

SELLMAN CEMETERY (ELIZABETH'S FANCY CEMETERY)
Location: 3011 Patuxent River Road on east side approximately 1/2 mile from road and 1/2 mile south of Governor's Bridge Road. [A.D.C. map location: 1989 Edition, page 23, grid coordinates B-2.] Year of earliest death: 1812. Year of latest death: 1849. Mary Sellman, A.D., is buried here. No burial records are maintained. The gravemarkers were transcribed in 1985. Records held by Anne Arundel Genealogical Society. See *Anne Arundel's Legacy*, p. 163. Copied by Davidsonville Area Civic Association.

SEVERN ROAD CEMETERY
Location: Severn Road between Pines Court and Severn Station Road. [A.D.C. map location: 1989 Edition, page 6, grid coordinates J-7.] Possible cemetery.

SEVERN ROAD CEMETERY
Location: South of Severn Road between Disney Road and Severn Tree Road. [A.D.C. map location: 1989 Edition, page 6, grid coordinates GH-7.] Possible cemetery.

SEVIER-STEWART CEMETERY (CHARTWELL COUNTRY CLUB CEMETERY)
Location: Off Benfield Road near front entrance to country club. Plot within parking lot. [A.D.C. map location: 1989 Edition, page 14, grid coordinates C-1.] Year of earliest death: 1863. Year of latest death: 1885. Transcribed and published by Anne Arundel Genealogical Society. Title: *Cemetery Inscriptions of Anne Arundel County, Maryland*, Vol. II (1987), p. 42.

SHERBERTS CEMETERY
Location: Route 258 to Rockhold Creek Road, on right. [A.D.C. map location: 1989 Edition, page 33, grid coordinates J/K-5.] Well maintained. Year of earliest death: 1922. Year of latest death: 1989. WWI Veterans. No burial records are maintained. The gravemarkers were transcribed in 1967. Records held by Anne Arundel Genealogical Society. Compiled and published by Daughters of the American Revolution. Title: *Tombstone Inscriptions of Southern Anne Arundel County* (1971), p. 135.

SHESLEY ROAD CEMETERY
Location: Left off Mayo Road before Shesley Road in field between house and woods. [A.D.C. map location: 1989 Edition, page 30, grid

ANNE ARUNDEL COUNTY CEMETERIES - PRIVATE 43

coordinates H-1.] Overgrown. Year of death: 1942. No burial records are maintained. The gravemarkers were transcribed in 1993 by Anne Arundel Genealogical Society. Field submerges, mounds widely spread apart, possibly affiliated with St. Mark's Methodist Church, supposedly WWII graves.

SHIPLEY CEMETERY

Location: East side of Route 173, 1/2 mile north of junction with Route 176. [A.D.C. map location: 1989 Edition, page 6, grid coordinates G-2.] No longer at this location. Year of earliest death: 1826. Year of latest death: 1914. No burial records are maintained. The gravemarkers were transcribed and published by Anne Arundel Genealogical Society. Title: *Cemetery Inscriptions of Anne Arundel County, Maryland*, Vol. II (1987), p. 98. Most are reinterred at Holy Cross Cemetery.

SIMMONS FAMILY CEMETERY

Location: Route 2, 0.7 mile south of Route 2 and Route 258 intersection, east on Tracy's Lane to end of dirt road, field. [A.D.C. map location: 1989 Edition, page 33, grid coordinates F-6.] Stones uprooted, broken pieces. Year of earliest death: 1771. Year of latest death: 1881. No burial records are maintained. The gravemarkers were transcribed in 1993 and published by Anne Arundel Genealogical Society. Three known stones, only fragments left, barely legible, property owned by BG&E (under power lines).

SMITH CEMETERY

Location: East of Route 652 on Smith Avenue midway on road on left in Plummer's Pasture. [A.D.C. map location: 1989 Edition, page 7, grid coordinates B-4.] Year of earliest death: 1867. Year of latest death: 1960. No burial records are maintained. The gravemarkers held by Anne Arundel Genealogical Society. Two sets of inscriptions include major differences.

SMITH CEMETERY

Location: East of Route 2 and south of Jordan Taylor Road on Birdville Beech Road, at end. [A.D.C. map location: 1989 Edition, page 24, grid coordinates J12.] Year of death: 1850. No burial records are maintained. Not transcribed. Kitty Smith buried here. Single stone.

SMITH CEMETERY

Location: Furnace Branch Road West and Crain Highway. [A.D.C. map location: 1989 Edition, page 3, grid coordinates B-11.] Maintained. Year of earliest death: 1810. Year of latest death: 1865. No burial records are maintained. The gravemarkers were transcribed in 1987.

SMITH FAMILY BURYING GROUNDS
Location: In Marley Creek area. [A.D.C. map location: 1989 Edition, page 8]. Ann and Patrick Smith are buried here. Revolutionary War Veterans. No burial records are maintained. DAR markers there, two graves.

SMITH FAMILY CEMETERY
Location: Southwest of junction of Route 170 and Poplar Avenue. [A.D.C. map location: 1989 Edition, page 2, grid coordinates D-10.] No longer exists. Year of earliest death: 1877. Year of latest death: 1883. No burial records are maintained. Transcribed by Anne Arundel Genealogical Society. Title: *Cemetery Inscriptions of Anne Arundel County, Maryland*, Vol. II (1987), p. 96.

SNOWDEN CEMETERY (FT. MEADE CEMETERY #12)
Location: 200 meters from Switchboard Road Extension, west edge of T22. [A.D.C. map location: 1989 Edition, page 11, grid coordinates A-5.] Poor condition, sign shot full of bullet holes, markers deteriorated. Year of earliest death: 1748. Year of latest death: 1863. Records held and published by Anne Arundel Genealogical Society. Title: *Cemetery Inscriptions of Anne Arundel County, Maryland*, Vol. II (1987), p. 77. Copied by Ft. Meade BSA Troop 379, grid 4226.

SOLLEY CEMETERY
Location: Off Marley Neck Road near Marley. [A.D.C. map location: 1989 Edition, page 8.] Year of earliest death: 1816. Year of latest death: 1909. No burial records are maintained. The gravemarkers were transcribed and published by Anne Arundel Genealogical Society. Title: *Cemetery Inscriptions of Anne Arundel County, Maryland*, Vol. II (1987), p. 51.

SPCA AREA CEMETERY
Location: Near water's edge in vicinity of SPCA, in woods. [A.D.C. map location: 1989 Edition, page 26, grid coordinates A-1?.] Possible cemetery.

ST. DEMETRIOS GREEK ORTHODOX CEMETERY
Location: on Riva Road beside Parole Shopping Plaza on east side near West Street. [A.D.C. map location: 1989 Edition, page 20, grid coor-

dinates B-9.] Well-maintained. Greek cemetery; most inscriptions in Greek.

ST. STEPHENS CHURCH ROAD CEMETERY
Location: #1110 St. Stephens Church road. East side of St. Stephens Church Road; due to become part of Penderbrooke subdivision. [A.D.C. map location: 1989 Edition, page 18, grid coordinates H-2.] Approximatley 6 ironstone tombstones. Possibly African-American cemetery.

STALLINGS LANE CEMETERY
Location: Reached either west at end of Stallings Lane or east of unmarked hooked road east of intersection of Routes 607 and 173. [A.D.C. map location: 1989 Edition, page 9, grid coordinates G-8.]

STEWARD-NORMAN CEMETERY (*NORMAN'S RETREAT CEMETERY*)
Location: At *Norman's Retreat* at 670 Plantation Boulevard, exact site not yet known. [A.D.C. map location: 1989 Edition, page 30, grid coordinates B-11.]

STEWART FAMILY CEMETERY (STEUART FAMILY CEMETERY)
Location: 0.5 mile south of Lothian Post Office off Route 2 on dirt road between two schools on Lloyd Owen Farm. [A.D.C. map location: 1989 Edition, page 29, grid coordinates B-12.] Overgrown. Year of death: 1853. No burial records are maintained. Records held by Anne Arundel Genealogical Society. The gravemarkers were transcribed and published by Daughters of the American Revolution. Title: *Tombstone Inscriptions of Southern Anne Arundel County* (1971), p. 181. Supposedly Hall graves there as well.

STEWART FAMILY CEMETERY
Location: In Garland. East Ferndale between 4th and 5th Avenues. [A.D.C. map location: 1989 Edition, page 2, grid coordinates H-11.] Year of earliest death: 1817. Year of latest death: 1859. No burial records are maintained. Grvemarkers transcribed and published by Anne Arundel Genealogical Society. Title: *Cemetery Inscriptions of Anne Arundel County, Maryland,* Vol. II (1987), p. 93. Vandalized.

STINCHCOMB FAMILY CEMETERY
Location: 1 mile east of Route 3 on Brightview Road on south side. [A.D.C. map location: 1989 Edition, page 7, grid coordinates K-11.] Year of earliest death: 1889. Year of latest death: 1956. No burial records

are maintained. The gravemarkers were transcribed in 1981 and published by Anne Arundel Genealogical Society. Title: *Cemetery Inscriptions of Anne Arundel County, Maryland*, Vol. II (1987), p. 55.

STINCHCOMB FAMILY CEMETERY
Location: In Manhattan Beach Subdivision on property of Mrs. Nellie Sekinger. [A.D.C. map location: 1989 Edition, page 15, grid coordinates E-7?.] Year of earliest death: 1833. Year of latest death: 1851. No burial records are maintained. The gravemarkers were transcribed in 1932 and published by Anne Arundel Genealogical Society. Title: *Cemetery Inscriptions of Anne Arundel County, Maryland*, Vol. II (1987), p. 19. Article possibly from DAR Magazine (1932), p. 69. Area developed circa 1932.

STINCHCOMB GRAVE
Location: Persimmon Point, no exact location given. [A.D.C. map location: 1989 Edition, page 16.] No burial records are maintained. Mentioned in book: *Broadneck, Maryland's Historic Peninsula*.

STINCHCOMB-TYDINGS FAMILY CEMETERY
Location: Rive Bay Road and Little Magothy River on east side of road. On Swan Drive. Jordan property (1965). [A.D.C. map location: 1989 Edition, page 16, grid coordinates J-10/11.] Year of earliest death: 1878. Year of latest death: 1945. No burial records are maintained. The gravemarkers were transcribed in 1965 by Anne Arundel Historical Society. Published by Anne Arundel Genealogical Society. Title: *Cemetery Inscriptions of Anne Arundel County, Maryland*, Vol. II (1987), p. 19. Ten graves, supposedly contains unmarked slave graves.

STOCKETT FAMILY CEMETERY (*OBLIGATION* CEMETERY)
Location: 3.3 mile south of Route 214 on Route 2, right turn onto dirt road. [A.D.C. map location: 1989 Edition, page 24, grid coordinates D-13.] No longer exists. Reinterred at all Hallows Church Cemetery.

SULPHUR SPRINGS CEMETERY
Location: Located off Scott Circle behind Building #1912, close to housing area. [A.D.C. map location: 1989 Edition, page 6, grid coordinates E-11.] Fair condition. Date of earliest death: 1860. Date of latest death: 1977. Records held and published by Anne Arundel Genealogical Society. Title: *Cemetery Inscriptions of Anne Arundel County, Maryland*, Vol. II (1987), p. 73. Copied by Boy Scout Troop 379, grid 5030.

ANNE ARUNDEL COUNTY CEMETERIES - PRIVATE

SUNDERLAND-PROUT CEMETERY
Location: Route 423 opposite junction with Franklin-Gibson Road. [A.D.C. map location: 1989 Edition, page 33, grid coordinates G-12.] Year of earliest death: 1839. Year of latest death: 1845. No burial records are maintained. The gravemarkers were compiled and published by Anne Arundel Genealogical Society. Title: *Cemetery Inscriptions of Anne Arundel County, Maryland*, Vol. I (1982), p. 38. Original inscriptions not available.

SWEETSER CEMETERY
Location: Across from apartments "next to Dr. Ball's house" within wrought iron fence. [A.D.C. map location: 1989 Edition, page 2, grid coordinates E-7.] Year of earliest death: 1858. Year of latest death: 1966. No burial records are maintained. The gravemarkers were compiled and published by Anne Arundel Genealogical Society. Title: *Cemetery Inscriptions of Anne Arundel County, Maryland*, Vol. II (1987), p. 97.

THOMAS SOLLEY FARM CEMETERY
Location: At end of Marley Neck Road at end of unnamed road. [A.D.C. map location: 1989 Edition, page 8, grid coordinates H-1.] No burial records are maintained. See *Anne Arundel's Legacy*, p. 169. Large cemetery.

TUCKER FAMILY CEMETERY
Location: At #165 Fiddlers Hill Road (in 1968). [A.D.C. map location: 1989 Edition, page 24, grid coordinates G-12.] Year of earliest death: 1825. Year of latest death: 1873. No burial records are maintained. The gravemarkers were transcribed in 1968. Records held by Anne Arundel Genealogical Society. Compiled by Daughters of the American Revolution. Title: *Tombstone Inscriptions of Southern Anne Arundel County* (1971), p. 340. Unable to find cemetery in 1993.

TYDINGS-ROBOSSON CEMETERY
Location: Off Baltimore-Annapolis Boulevard north of Macey's Corner, near "old stone house." [A.D.C. map location: 1989 Edition, page 15, grid coordinates B-2.] Year of earliest death: 1815. Year of latest death: 1923. No burial records are maintained. The gravemarkers were transcribed in 1984 by Anne Arundel Co. Historical Society. Published by Anne Arundel Genealogical Society. Title: *Cemetery Inscriptions of Anne Arundel County, Maryland*, Vol. II (1987), p. 14.

UNNAMED ROAD CEMETERY
Location: On outside of south edge of circular unnamed road. [A.D.C. map location: 1989 Edition, page 9, grid coordinates H/J-7/8.] Possibly Lawton or Tracy families.

UNNAMED CEMETERY (FT. MEADE CEMETERY #7)
Location: On southeast corner of Sargent Road and Cooper Avenue. [A.D.C. map location: 1989 Edition, page 6, grid coordinates A-10.] No burial records are maintained. Gravestones obliterated. Copied by Boy Scout Troop 379, grid 4831.

VENTNOR/PINEHURST CEMETERY
Location: South of Ventnor Road right 1/2 mile before crossing Pinehurst Road, about 1/2 on north side of road. [A.D.C. map location: 1989 Edition, page 10?.] Same as Milbur Cemetery (at F/G-13 area)?

W. PASADENA ROAD CEMETERY
Location: Near end of West Pasadena Road east of intersection with Pasadena Road. [A.D.C. map location: 1989 Edition, page 8, grid coordinates E/F-13.] Possible cemetery.

WARD TOMBSTONE
Location: Mt. Zion, on Route 422 1 mile n. of intersection of Routes 408, 2 and 422 on John Wm. Ward property. [A.D.C. map location: 1989 Edition, page 28.] Year of death: 1854. No burial records are maintained. The gravemarker was transcribed in 1968 by Daughters of the American Revolution. Records held by Anne Arundel Genealogical Society. Published by Daughters of the American Revolution. Title: *Tombstone Inscriptions of Southern Anne Arundel County* (1971), p. 189. Single stone.

WARFIELD FAMILY CEMETERY
Location: Route 3 to St. Stephens Church Yard; go 1/4 mile then left on Brandy Farms Road go 02 mile, dirt road on right, within white cinderblock walls. [A.D.C. map location: 1989 Edition, page 13, grid coordinates D-11.] Well-maintained. Year of earliest death: 1828. Year of latest death: 1922. Rev. James Turner is buried here. No burial records are maintained. The gravemarkers were transcribed in 1993 and published by Anne Arundel Genealogical Society. Title: *Cemetery Inscriptions of Anne Arundel County, Maryland*, Vol. II (1987), p. 80. See *Anne Arundel's Legacy*, p.165.

ANNE ARUNDEL COUNTY CEMETERIES - PRIVATE 49

WARFIELD CEMETERY (FT. MEADE CEMETERY #6)
Location: Corner of "E" Street and 26th Street, west 150 meters. [A.D.C. map location: 1989 Edition, page 6, grid coordinates C-9.] Good condition, frequented by family. Year of earliest death: 1866. Year of latest death: 1977. Records held by Anne Arundel Genealogical Society. Title: *Cemetery Inscriptions of Anne Arundel County, Maryland*, Vol. II (1987), p. 74. Copied by Boy Scout Troop 379, grid 4931.

WATERS GRAVE
Location: St. Stephens Church Road at Chesterfield Road, old schoolhouse, 300 feet in field. [A.D.C. map location: 1989 Edition, page 18, grid coordinates K-6.] No longer exists. There was a single stone, possibly removed from field within last 10-20 years by owner.

WATERS FAMILY CEMETERY (CAMP BARRETT CEMETERY)
Location: At Elk's Camp Barrett off Crownsville Road at end of Hawkins Road. [A.D.C. map location: 1989 Edition, page 19, grid coordinates B-6.] Good condition, maintained. Year of earliest death: 1833. Year of latest death: 1902. No burial records are maintained. The gravemarkers were transcribed in 1990 and published by Anne Arundel Genealogical Society. Title: *Cemetery Inscriptions of Anne Arundel County, Maryland*, Vol. II (1987), p. 3. Some stones stored inside camp building near cemetery. (These were not included in Vol. II edition.)

WATERS CEMETERY (FT. MEADE CEMETERY #11)
Location: Off Road 834 west of edge of T33. [A.D.C. map location: Unknown.] Fair condition, gate off. Year of earliest death: 1899. Year of latest death: 1918. Records held by Anne Arundel Genealogical Society. Title: *Cemetery Inscriptions of Anne Arundel County, Maryland*, Vol. II (1987), p. 76. Copied by Ft. Meade BSA Troop 379, grid 4526.

WATTS CEMETERY
Location: At corner of Annapolis and Walker Drive between Buildings #1617 AND #1819. [A.D.C. map location: 1989 Edition, page 6, grid coordinates E-11.] No sign, no gate. Year of earliest death: 1904. Year of latest death: 1977. Records held and published by Anne Arundel Genealogical Society. Title: *Cemetery Inscriptions of Anne Arundel County, Maryland*, Vol. II (1987), p. 73. Copied by Boy Scout Troop 379, grid 5030. Two stones, only one date.

WAYSON PROPERTY CEMETERY
Location: On Mt. Airy Road on Wayson Property. [A.D.C. map location: 1989 Edition, page 23, grid coordinates ?-6.] Possibly single stone.

WEEDON FAMILY CEMETERY
Location: Just beyond #1741 Holly Beach Farm Road, southwest corner of property near water's edge. [A.D.C. map location: 1989 Edition, page 22, grid coordinates A-9.] Overgrown. Year of earliest death: 1841. Year of latest death: 1858. No burial records are maintained. The gravemarkers were transcribed in 1993 by Anne Arundel Genealogical Society.

WEEMS-SELLMAN FAMILY CEMETERY (BURRAGE'S END CEMETERY)
Location: Old Ridge Path to Burrage's End, on left. Cemetery is behind main house. [A.D.C. map location: 1989 Edition, page 33, grid coordinates D-3.] Badly overgrown. Year of earliest death: 1723. Year of latest death: 1900. Dr. Richard Weems and Thomas Sellman are buried here. No burial records are maintained. The gravemarkers were transcribed in 1967 by Daughters of the American Revolution. Records held by Anne Arundel Genealogical Society. Compiled and published by Daughters of the American Revolution. Title: *Tombstone Inscriptions of Southern Anne Arundel County* (1971), p. 115. See *Anne Arundel's Legacy*, p. 27. Also includes stones from "Coxby" residence of Weems.

WEEMS FAMILY CEMETERY (ST. MARK'S EPISCOPAL CHAPEL OF ST. JAMES PARISH)
Location: In Deale, off Route 256, 1.5 miles from Route 2 intersection close to Rockhold Creek Bridge. [A.D.C. map location: 1989 Edition, page 33, grid coordinates H-8.] Year of earliest death: 1779. Year of latest death: 1995. Buried here are Drs. J. B. and D. G. Weems. No burial records are maintained. The gravemarkers were transcribed in 1967 by Daughters of the American Revolution. Records held by Anne Arundel Genealogical Society. Compiled and published by Daughters of the American Revolution. Title: *Tombstone Inscriptions of Southern Anne Arundel County* (1971), p. 139.

WELCH FAMILY CEMETERY
Location: On Route 408, 0.4 mile west of intersection of Route 259 and Route 408 on Moreland farm. [A.D.C. map location: 1989 Edition, page 28, grid coordinates GH-13.] Year of earliest death: 1822. Year of latest death: 1829. No burial records are maintained. The gravemarkers were

transcribed in 1968 by Daughters of the American Revolution. Records held by Anne Arundel Genealogical Society. Published by Daughters of the American Revolution. Title: *Tombstone Inscriptions of Southern Anne Arundel County* (1971), p. 182.

WESLEY FAMILY CEMETERY
Location: Route 176, Burkytown subdivision, probably between Sawmill Creek and Fork Branch, Hiram Kelly's farm. [A.D.C. map location: 1989 Edition, page 7.] Year of earliest death: 1869. Year of latest death: 1897. No burial records are maintained. The gravemarkers were transcribed and published by Anne Arundel Genealogical Society. Title: *Cemetery Inscriptions of Anne Arundel County, Maryland*, Vol. II (1987), p. 94. Mrs. E. Wesley owned 250 acres in 1878 (Hopkins Map).

WEST RIVER ROAD CEMETERY
Location: Near shed and property line adjoining 1392 West River Road's *Red Top Farm* (house #1348 on opposite side of street). [A.D.C. map location: 1989 Edition, page 30, grid coordinates J-8.] Supposedly unmarked slave cemetery.

WHARF CREEK CEMETERY
Location: Ventnor Road. [A.D.C. map location: 1989 Edition, page 10, grid coordinates F-11.] No burial records are maintained. See Anne Arundel's Legacy, p.171.

WHITE-BARBER CEMETERY
Location: On farm formerly owned by Geo. F. White, now owned by Mr. Barton, on Great Fork of Patuxent. [A.D.C. map location: 1989 Edition, page 12?.] Year of earliest death: 1849. Year of latest death: 1919. No burial records are maintained. The gravemarkers were transcribed. Records held by Anne Arundel Genealogical Society.

WHITEHALL CREEK CEMETERY
Location: Northwest of Whitehall on Whitehall Creek. [A.D.C. map location: 1989 Edition, page 21?.] Mentioned in book, *Broadneck, Maryland's Historic Peninsula*.

WILLIAMS FAMILY CEMETERY
Location: At junction of Cedar Hill Lane and Snow Hill Road behind Motor Vehicle Admin. [A.D.C. map location: 1989 Edition, page 3, grid coordinates C-6.] No longer exists. Year of earliest death: 1890. Year of latest death: 1925. No burial records are maintained. The

gravemarkers were transcribed and published by Anne Arundel Genealogical Society. Title: *Cemetery Inscriptions of Anne Arundel County, Maryland,* Vol. II (1987), p. 109. See *Anne Arundel's Legacy,* p. 174.

WILLIAMS CEMETERY
Location: Route 177 near Tick Neck Road near C&P Telephone Building. [A.D.C. map location: 1989 Edition, page 9, grid coordinates D-9.] No burial records are maintained. The gravemarkers were transcribed and published by Anne Arundel Genealogical Society. Title: *Cemetery Inscriptions of Anne Arundel County, Maryland,* Vol. II (1987), p. 22. Seven stones, no dates given on any; information from granddaughter.

WOOD FAMILY CEMETERY
Location: North side of Elvaton Road east of Northway Drive. [A.D.C. map location: 1989 Edition, page 8, grid coordinates D-9.] Year of earliest death: 1908. Year of latest death: 1967. No burial records are maintained. The gravemarkers were transcribed in 1985 and published by Anne Arundel Genealogical Society. Compiled by Anne Arundel Genealogical Society. Title: *Cemetery Inscriptions of Anne Arundel County, Maryland,* Vol. II (1987), p. 103.

WOOD FAMILY CEMETERY
Location: At Jewell, on McKendree Road 2 mile from Route 258 on Jas. F. Armiger, Jr. farm. [A.D.C. map location: 1989 Edition, page 33, grid coordinates A-11.] Year of earliest death: 1845. Year of latest death: 1853. No burial records are maintained. The gravemarkers were transcribed in 1968 by Daughters of the American Revolution. Records maintained by Anne Arundel Genealogical Society. Published by Daughters of the American Revolution. Title: *Tombstone Inscriptions of Southern Anne Arundel County* (1971), p. 58.

WOODFIELD-RIDGELY CEMETERY
Location: Rutland Road at Bell Branch Road opposite Bell Bridge Road about 50 feet off rod. [A.D.C. map location: 1989 Edition, page 18, grid coordinates H-10/11.] Year of earliest death: 1813. Year of latest death: 1875. No burial records are maintained. Records of gravemarkers held and published by Anne Arundel Genealogical Society. Title: *Cemetery Inscriptions of Anne Arundel County, Maryland,* Vol. I (1982), p. 5. See also *Anne Arundel's Legacy,* p. 163. Copied by Davidsonville Area Civic Assoc.

ANNE ARUNDEL COUNTY CEMETERIES - PRIVATE

WOODWARD CEMETERY (FT. MEADE CEMETERY #16)
Location: Off Boundary Road south of Range No. 9. 500 meters northwest of entrance to Range 12. [A.D.C. map location: 1989 Edition, page 12, grid coordinates B-9.] Fair condition, gate off, sign has bullet holes. Year of earliest death: 1871. Year of latest death: 1914. Records of gravemarkers published by Anne Arundel Genealogical Society, Vol. II (1987), p.78. Copied by Ft. Meade BSA Troop 379, grid 4924.

WORTHINGTON FAMILY CEMETERY (SUMMER HILL ESTATE CEMETERY)
Location: On west side of Honeysuckle Lane at point where road heads due north. [A.D.C. map location: 1989 Edition, page 19, grid coordinates F-4/5.] Badly overgrown. Year of earliest death: 1773. Year of latest death: 1851. Revolutionary War Veterans. No burial records are maintained. The gravemarkers were transcribed in 1993; records held by Anne Arundel Genealogical Society. Marked by Daughters of the American Revolution. Confederate Surgeon Dr. Gantt, and Col. Nicholas Worthing, are buried here. Information provided by Thomas C. Worthington, DAR marker.

WRIGHT ROAD CEMETERY
Location: Near end of Wright Road on north or west side of road. [A.D.C. map location: 1989 Edition, page 6, grid coordinates C/D-2.]

Church Cemeteries

ADAMS UNITED METHODIST CHURCH CEMETERY
Location: South side of Route 422. [A.D.C. map location: 1989 Edition, page 28, grid coordinates B-8.] No burial records are maintained.

ALL HALLOWS EPISCOPAL CHAPEL CEMETERY
Location: Route 214 approximately 1/4 mile west of Route 424. [A.D.C. map location: 1989 Edition, page 23, grid coordinates J-7.] Maintained. Year of earliest death: 1816. Year of latest death: 1967. Civil War, WWI and WWII Veterans. No burial records are maintained. The gravemarkers were transcribed and published by Daughters of the American Revolution. Title: *Tombstone Inscriptions of Southern Anne Arundel County* (1971), p. 342.

ALL HALLOWS EPISCOPAL CHURCH CEMETERY
Location: Route 2 at South River Clubhouse Road and Brick Church Road. [A.D.C. map location: 1989 Edition, page 24, grid coordinates G-9.] Well-maintained. Year of earliest death: 1686. Year of latest death: 1965. Revolutionary War and Civil War Veterans. No burial records are maintained. The gravemarkers were transcribed in 1967 by Anne Arundel Genealogical Society; records maintained by Anne Arundel Genealogical Society. Records compiled and published by Daughters of the American Revolution. Title: *Tombstone Inscriptions of Southern Anne Arundel County* (1971), p. 323. See also *Anne Arundel's Legacy*, p. 25 and *Historic Graves of Maryland*, p. 20. Burgess and Sellman families reinterred.

ANNAPOLIS HEBREW CEMETERY (KNESETH ISRAEL CONGREGATIONAL CEMETERY)
Location: Junction of Route 178 and Route 450 at Threemile Oak Corner. [A.D.C. map location: 1989 Edition, page p.20, grid coordinates A-8.] Well-maintained. Hebrew cemetery.

ARNOLD ASBURY METHODIST CHURCH CEMETERY
Location: On north side of Church Road between Joyce Lane and Sheridan Road. [A.D.C. map location: 1989 Edition, page 15, grid coordinates J-13.] Maintained. Year of earliest death: 1814. Year of latest death: 1963. No burial records are maintained. The gravemarkers were transcribed in 1963 Anne Arundel County Historical Society. Records held by Anne Arundel Genealogical Society.

ASBURY UNITED METHODIST CHURCH CEMETERY
Location: At end of South Villa Avenue behind Bates High School on right, enclosed in locked chainlink fence. [A.D.C. map location: 1989 Edition, page 20, grid coordinates G-10.] Maintained. No burial records are maintained. African-American cemetery.

ASBURY TOWN-NECK UNITED METHODIST CHURCH CEMETERY
Location: #429 Baltimore-Annapolis Boulevard. Between Berrywood South and Berrywood Communities on east side of Route 648. [A.D.C. map location: 1989 Edition, page 15, grid coordinates A-3.] Year of earliest death: 1807. Year of latest death: 1978. Rev. Horace A. Johnson is buried here. WWI and WWII Veterans. No burial records are maintained. The gravemarkers were transcribed in 1979 and published by Anne Arundel Genealogical Society. Title: *Cemetery*

Inscriptions of Anne Arundel County, Maryland, Vol. II (1987), p. 48. African-American cemetery.

ASBURY UNITED METHODIST CHURCH CEMETERY
Location: At southern end of Broadneck Road (visible but not reachable from Route 50). [A.D.C. map location: 1989 Edition, page 21, grid coordinates F-1.] Maintained. Year of earliest death: 1910. Year of latest death: 1969. WWI and WWII Veterans. No burial records are maintained. Records held by Anne Arundel Genealogical Society. African-American cemetery.

BALDWIN MEMORIAL METHODIST CHURCH CEMETERY
(CROSS ROADS CHURCH CEMETERY)
Location: #921 General's Highway. At south corner of Route 178 and Indian Landing Road. [A.D.C. map location: 1989 Edition, page 13, grid coordinates K-8.] Maintained. Year of earliest death: 1830. Year of latest death: 1978. Buried here are Col. H. Baldwin Gantt, Jr. M.D. and WWI and WWII Veterans. No burial records are maintained. The gravemarkers were transcribed in 1979 and published by Anne Arundel Genealogical Society. Title: *Cemetery Inscriptions of Anne Arundel County, Maryland*, Vol. II (1987), p. 12. See also *Historic Graves of Maryland*, p. 24 and *Anne Arundel's Legacy*, p. 141.

BALDWIN MEMORIAL METHODIST CHURCH CEMETERY
Location: Unknown. Year of earliest death: 1744. Year of latest death: 1865. No burial records are maintained. The gravemarkers were transcribed in by Anne Arundel Genealogical Society. Compiled and published by Ridgely. Title: *Historic Graves of Maryland and the District of Columbia* (1908), p. 24. Not same as other Baldwin Methodist Church at p. 13, K-8 location.

BELLE GROVE ROAD CEMETERY
Location: North of Belle Grove Road near corner of Gibbons Avenue and Bishop Avenue. [A.D.C. map location: 1989 Edition, page 2, grid coordinates H-5.] Possible cemetery.

BIRKHEAD'S MEADOW CEMETERY
Location: On tract belonging to Christopher Birkhead in 1666 near St. James Church. [A.D.C. map location: 1989 Edition, page 33?.] No burial records are maintained. See *Historic Graves*, p. 23. Supposedly reinterred at St. James Parish Church in 1888. Not in DAR record of St. James Parish.

BROCK BRIDGE ROAD CEMETERY
Location: 0.3 mile south of Route 175 on Brock Bridge Road on right.
[A.D.C. map location: 1989 Edition, page 5, grid coordinates J-6.]

BROOKLYN CEMETERY (HILLCREST CEMETERY)
Location: 4117 Audrey Avenue. 0.6 mile east of Route 2, approximately 1 block west of Baltimore City line. [A.D.C. map location: 1989 Edition, page 3, grid coordinates C-3.] Year of earliest death: 1912. Year of latest death: 1976. Korean War Veterans. No burial records are maintained. The gravemarkers were transcribed and published by Anne Arundel Genealogical Society. Title: *Cemetery Inscriptions of Anne Arundel County, Maryland*, Vol. II (1987), p. 101. Numerous markers with no information.

CARROLL GARDENS CEMETERY (CARROLL HOUSE CEMETERY)
Location: South off Duke of Gloucester Street behind St. Mary's, bordered by Spa Creek. [A.D.C. map location: 1989 Edition, page 20, grid coordinates K-10.] Year of earliest death: 1696. Year of latest death: 1855. Charles Carroll, and other prominent persons are buried here. Carroll Family reinterred here as well as redemptionist priests.

CENTENARY UNITED METHODIST CHURCH CEMETERY
(SHADY SIDE METHODIST CHURCH CEMETERY)
Location: #6248 Shady Side Road. On West Side of Route 468 just north of St. Matthews Methodist Church. [A.D.C. map location: 1989 Edition, page 30, grid coordinates FG-10.] Maintained. Year of earliest death: 1874. Year of latest death: 1988. WWI, WWII and Korean Veterans. No burial records are maintained. The gravemarkers were transcribed in 1994 and records held by Anne Arundel Genealogical Society. Gravemarkers compiled and published by Daughters of the American Revolution. Title: *Tombstone Inscriptions of Southern Anne Arundel County* (1971), p. 196. Caucasian cemetery (St. Matthew's Methodist down the street is African-American cemetery).

CHEWS UNITED METHODIST CHURCH CEMETERY
Location: #492 Owensville Road. Route 255 about 2.5 miles from Route 2 on left side of road. [A.D.C. map location: 1989 Edition, page 29, grid coordinates H-6.] Maintained. The gravemarkers were transcribed in 1995 and records held by Anne Arundel Genealogical Society. Large African-American cemetery.

CHRIST EPISCOPAL CHURCH CEMETERY (OLD CHRIST CHURCH CEMETERY, ALSO ST. JAMES THE LESS CEMETERY)

Location: On left side of Route 255 about a mile from Route 2. [A.D.C. map location: 1989 Edition, page 29?, grid coordinates .] Year of earliest death: 1820. Year of latest death: 1948. Civil War and WWII Veterans. No burial records are maintained. The gravemarkers were transcribed in 1949 by Daughters of the American Revolution. Records held by Anne Arundel Genealogical Society. Compiled and published by Daughters of the American Revolution. Title: *Tombstone Inscriptions of Southern Anne Arundel County* (1971), p. 252. DAR information published alphabetically.

CHURCH OF GOD CEMETERY

Location: North side of Route 175 east of Arundel High School. [A.D.C. map location: 1989 Edition, page 13, grid coordinates C-6?.] Year of earliest death: 1921. Year of latest death: 1978.
WWII Veterans. No burial records are maintained. The gravemarkers were transcribed in 1979 and published by Anne Arundel Genealogical Society. Title: *Cemetery Inscriptions of Anne Arundel County, Maryland*, Vol. II (1987), p. 118. Church is now a Boy Scout hall.

DAVIDSONVILLE UNITED METHODIST CHURCH CEMETERY

Location: Southeast corner of Route 214 and Route 424. [A.D.C. map location: 1989 Edition, page 23, grid coordinates J-7.] Maintained. Year of earliest death: 1836. Year of latest death: 1967. Dr. William P. Bird is buried here. No burial records are maintained. The gravemarkers were transcribed in 1968 by Daughters of the American Revolution. Records maintained by Anne Arundel Genealogical Society. Compiled and pubished by Daughters of the American Revolution. Title: *Tombstone Inscriptions of Southern Anne Arundel County* (1971), p. 364.

DEALE EPISCOPAL CHURCH CEMETERY

Location: At Route 256. [A.D.C. map location: 1989 Edition, page 30/34?.]

EBENEZER A.M.E. ST. PAUL'S CEMETERY

Location: Off Route 468 across from fire department at end of dirt road. [A.D.C. map location: 1989 Edition, page 30, grid coordinates G-9.] Maintained, some destruction by vandals. Year of earliest death: 1912. Year of latest death: 1993. No burial records are maintained. The gravemarkers were transcribed in 1994 and records held by Anne

Arundel Genealogical Society. African-American cemetery?; at least 8 markers with no identifying information.

EPIPHANY EPISCOPAL CHURCH CEMETERY (ST. PETER'S PARISH CEMETERY)
Location: 1419 Odenton Road. Route 175 south of Morgan Road to end at Odenton Road across street behind church. [A.D.C. map location: 1989 Edition, page 12, grid coordinates H-3.] Year of earliest death: 1886. Year of latest death: 1960. No burial records are maintained. Some data copied.

FOWLER UNITED METHODIST CHURCH
Location: 816 Bestgate Road. On north side of Bestgate Road east of Route 178 near Annapolis Mall. [A.D.C. map location: 1989 Edition, page 20, grid coordinates C-7.] Well-maintained. No burial records are maintained. The gravemarkers were transcribed in 1994 and records held by Anne Arundel Genealogical Society. African-American church cemetery.

FRANKLIN CHURCH CEMETERY
Location: Across from Deale Elementary School on Masons Beach Road. [A.D.C. map location: 1987 Edition, page 34, grid coordinates A-7.]

FRIENDSHIP CEMETERY (BWI CEMETERY)
Location: 1 mile northwest of junction of Route 176 and Ft. Meade Roads on airport grounds. [A.D.C. map location: 1989 Edition, page 7, grid coordinates B-2.] No longer there. Year of earliest death: 1865. Year of latest death: 1977. WWI Veterans. No burial records are maintained. The gravemarkers were compiled and published by Anne Arundel Genealogical Society. Title: *Cemetery Inscriptions of Anne Arundel County, Maryland*, Vol. II (1987), p. 122.

FRIENDSHIP UNITED METHODIST CHURCH CEMETERY
Location: Friendship off Route 2. [A.D.C. map location: 1989 Edition, page 35, grid coordinates E-2.] Year of earliest death: 1832. Year of latest death: 1966. Rev. Frank T. Griffith is buried here; also Civil War, WWI and WWII Veterans. No burial records are maintained. The gravemarkers were transcribed in 1967 by Daughters of the American Revolution. Records held by Anne Arundel Genealogical Society. Compiled and published by Daughters of the American Revolution.

Title: *Tombstone Inscriptions of Southern Anne Arundel County* (1971), p. 1.

GALESVILLE METHODIST CHURCH CEMETERY
Location: Unknown. [A.D.C. map location: 1989 Edition, page 30-?.] Year of earliest death: 1888. Year of latest death: 1955. No burial records are maintained. The gravemarkers were transcribed in 1968 by Anne Arundel County Historical Society. Records held by Anne Arundel Genealogical Society. Compiled and published by Daughters of the American Revolution. Title: *Tombstone Inscriptions of Southern Anne Arundel County* (1971), p. 199.

HALL UNITED METHODIST CHURCH CEMETERY
Location: 7780 Solley Road. Southwest corner of junction of Solley Road and Nabbs Creek Road. [A.D.C. map location: 1989 Edition, page 8, grid coordinates J-2.] Year of earliest death: 1905. Year of latest death: 1978. WWII Veterans. No burial records are maintained. The gravemarkers were transcribed in 1979, compiled and published by Anne Arundel Genealogical Society. Title: *Cemetery Inscriptions of Anne Arundel County, Maryland*, Vol. II (1987), p. 35.

HOLY CROSS CEMETERY
Location: Route 2 approximately 1000 feet northwest of junction of Route 2 and Route 695 (Baltimore Beltway) and south of Hammonds Lane. [A.D.C. map location: 1989 Edition, page 3, grid coordinates A-7.] Maintained. WWI Veterans. Partial records held by Anne Arundel Genealogical Society. Older section copied. Some Polish and German inscriptions. Reports of stone destruction by cemetery personnel.

HOPE METHODIST CHURCH CEMETERY
Location: 3672 Muddy Creek Road. South on Route 468 just below intersection with Route 214 on west side of road. [A.D.C. map location: 1989 Edition, page 25, grid coordinates A-9.] Maintained. Year of earliest death: 1942. Year of latest death: 1958. No burial records are maintained. The gravemarkers were transcribed in 1968. Compiled and published by Daughters of the American Revolution. Title: *Tombstone Inscriptions of Southern Anne Arundel County* (1971), p. 293. African-American cemetery.

HOPE METHODIST CHURCH CEMETERY
Location: North and 0.5 mile east of Route 214 and Route 248 intersection (behind liquor store, on hill). [A.D.C. map location: 1989 Edition,

page 25, grid coordinates B-8.] Well-maintained. Year of earliest death: 1890. Year of latest death: 1978. No burial records are maintained. The gravemarkers were transcribed and published by Anne Arundel Genealogical Society. Title: *Cemetery Inscriptions of Anne Arundel County, Maryland*, Vol. II (1987), p. 82. See also *Anne Arundel's Legacy*, p. 176.

JOHN WESLEY UNITED METHODIST CHURCH
Location: 6922 Ritchie Highway. Between Route 2 and Route 3, 200 yards northwest of intersection with Furnace Branch Road. [A.D.C. map location: 1989 Edition, page 3, grid coordinates B-11.] Maintained. Year of earliest death: 1898. Year of latest death: 1940. No burial records are maintained. The gravemarkers were transcribed and published by Anne Arundel Genealogical Society. Title: *Cemetery Inscriptions of Anne Arundel County, Maryland*, Vol. II (1987), p. 99. Vandalized, possibly relocated.

JOHN WESLEY WATERBURY M.E. CHURCH
Location: On south side of Route 178 0.2 mile north of Sunrise Beach Road, near Waterbury Road. [A.D.C. map location: 1989 Edition, page 14, grid coordinates A-9.] Year of earliest death: 1881. Year of latest death: 1979. WWI, WWII and Korean Veterans. The gravemarkers were transcribed in 1979 and published by Anne Arundel Genealogical Society. Title: *Cemetery Inscriptions of Anne Arundel County, Maryland*, Vol. II (1987), p. 1. African-American cemetery, includes two slave graves.

JOY CIRCLE CEMETERY
Location: West of Elizabeth Road near southernmost part of Joy Circle between those roads and bypass. [A.D.C. map location: 1989 Edition, page 7, grid coordinates G-7.]

KOCH ROAD CEMETERY
Location: Between Camp Meade Road and Baltimore-Annapolis Boulevard, near Koch Road. [A.D.C. map location: 1989 Edition, page 2, grid coordinates G-6.] Possible cemetery.

LILY OF THE VALLEY TABERNACLE CEMETERY
Location: South on Route 408 on both sides of Sands Road. [A.D.C. map location: 1989 Edition, page 31, grid coordinates K-2.] Well-maintained. No burial records are maintained. African-American cemetery. No trespassing except through contact person.

LINTHICUM WALKS CEMETERY

Location: Off Route 424 beside Crofton Middle School at white building. (Used by Anne Arundel Co. Hist. Trust.) [A.D.C. map location: 1989 Edition, page 18, grid coordinates C-6.] Year of earliest death: 1828. Year of latest death: 1866. No burial records are maintained. The gravemarkers are held by Anne Arundel Genealogical Society. See *Anne Arundel's Legacy, The Historic Properties of Anne Arundel County* (1990), p. 145.

LUCE CREEK CEMETERY (EVANGELICAL PRESBYTERIAN CHURCH CEMETERY)

Location: 710 Ridgely Avenue. Junction of Ridgely Avenue and Bestgate Roads on northeast corner. [A.D.C. map location: 1989 Edition, page 20, grid coordinates F-6.] Maintained. Year of earliest death: 1914. Year of latest death: 1973. No burial records are maintained. The gravemarkers were transcribed in 1975 and published by Anne Arundel Genealogical Society. Title: *Cemetery Inscriptions of Anne Arundel County, Maryland*, Vol. I (1982), p. 11.

LUTHER A. PALMER MEMORIAL CEMETERY (EDWARDS M.E. CHAPEL CEMETERY)

Location: Junction of Riva Road and Route 450 within triangle formed by Riva Road split. [A.D.C. map location: 1989 Edition, page 20, grid coordinates C-9.] Well-maintained. Year of earliest death: 1879. Year of latest death: 1975. WWI and WWII Veterans. No burial records are maintained. The gravemarkers were transcribed in 1975 and published by Anne Arundel Genealogical Society. Title: *Cemetery Inscriptions of Anne Arundel County, Maryland*, Vol. I (1982), p. 6.

MACEDONIA UNITED METHODIST CHURCH CEMETERY

Location: 1567 Sappington Station Road. Junction of Route 32 and Route 175. [A.D.C. map location: 1989 Edition, page 13, grid coordinates A-5.] Year of earliest death: 1911. Year of latest death: 1974. No burial records are maintained. The gravemarkers were transcribed in 1979 and published by Anne Arundel Genealogical Society. Title: *Cemetery Inscriptions of Anne Arundel County, Maryland*, Vol. II (1987), p. 101. African-American cemetery.

MAGOTHY UNITED METHODIST CHURCH CEMETERY

Location: Route 177 approximately 200 yards west of junction with Route 607. [A.D.C. map location: 1989 Edition, page 9, grid coordinates E-9.] Year of earliest death: 1830. Year of latest death: 1974. No burial records are maintained. The gravemarkers were transcribed in 1975 and published by Anne Arundel Genealogical Society. Title: *Cemetery Inscriptions of Anne Arundel County, Maryland*, Vol. II (1987), p. 25. See also *Anne Arundel's Legacy*, p. 175.

MARKET PLACE CEMETERY
Location: At end of Market Place. [A.D.C. map location: 1989] Edition, page 5, grid coordinates F-10.] Possible cemetery.

MAYO UNITED METHODIST CHURCH CEMETERY
Location: 1005 Old Turkey Point Road at Turkey Point Road. [A.D.C. map location: 1989 Edition, page 25, grid coordinates G-11.] Well-maintained. Year of earliest death: 1887. Year of latest death: 1966. WWI and WWII Veterans. The gravemarkers were transcribed in 1993 and records held by Anne Arundel Genealogical Society. Compiled and published by Daughters of the American Revolution. Title: *Tombstone Inscriptions of Southern Anne Arundel County* (1971), p. 304.

MT. CALVARY CEMETERY
Location: Cedar Hill Lane approximately 1/2 mile east of Route 2. [A.D.C. map location: 1989 Edition, page 3, grid coordinates A-6.]

MT. CALVARY CHAPEL CEMETERY (OLD ST. MARK'S CHURCH CEMETERY)
Location: West side of Ridge Road across from northwest corner of Baltimore Commons Business Park. [A.D.C. map location: 1989 Edition, page 1, grid coordinates G-13.] Year of earliest death: 1897. Year of latest death: 1974. WWII and Korean Veterans. No burial records are maintained. The gravemarkers were transcribed and published by Anne Arundel Genealogical Society. Title: Cemetery Inscriptions of Anne Arundel County, Maryland, Vol. 2 (1987), p.86.

MT. CALVARY METHODIST CHURCH CEMETERY
Location: 1236 Jones Station Road, south side of road between College Parkway and Shore Acres Road. [A.D.C. map location: 1989 Edition, page 15, grid coordinates J-12.] Maintained. Year of earliest death: 1923. Year of latest death: 1984. WWI, WWII and Korean Veterans. No burial records are maintained. The gravemarkers were transcribed in 1985. Records held by Anne Arundel Genealogical Society. African-American cemetery.

ANNE ARUNDEL COUNTY CEMETERIES - CHURCH

MT. CALVARY METHODIST CHURCH CEMETERY
Location: At Bristol, 2.4 mile east of Wayson's Corner on Route 2.
[A.D.C. map location: 1989 Edition, page 32-?.] Year of earliest death: 1850. Year of latest death: 1967. No burial records are maintained. The gravemarkers were transcribed in 1967 by Daughters of the American Revolution. Records held by Anne Arundel Genealogical Society. Compiled by Daughters of the American Revolution. Title: *Tombstone Inscriptions of Southern Anne Arundel County* (1971), p. 65.

MT. CALVARY UNITED METHODIST CHURCH CEMETERY
Location: On northwest side of intersection of Route 408 and Ed Prout Road. [A.D.C. map location: 1989 Edition, page 28, grid coordinates D-12.]

MT. CARMEL UNITED METHODIST CEMETERY
Location: Route 177 west of Ventnor Road and east of Long Point Road. [A.D.C. map location: 1989 Edition, page 10, grid coordinates E-12.] Maintained. Year of earliest death: 1881. Year of latest death: 1974. Interment records are held by church. Gravemarkers transcribed and published by Anne Arundel Genealogical Society. Title: *Cemetery Inscriptions of Anne Arundel County, Maryland*, Vol. II (1987), p. 43. The Church also has agreement with the State of Maryland to bury bodies washing up from bay.

MT. PILGRIM BAPTIST CHURCH CEMETERY
Location: On Route 176, 0.2 mile west of Route 713. [A.D.C. map location: 1989 Edition, page 6, grid coordinates F-2?.] No longer exists. Year of earliest death: 1861. Year of latest death: 1963. No burial records are maintained. Gravemarker records compiled and published by Anne Arundel Genealogical Society. Title: *Cemetery Inscriptions of Anne Arundel County, Maryland*, Vol. II (1987), p. 99. Reinterred at Holy Cross Cemetery.

MT. TABOR UNITED METHODIST CHURCH CEMETERY
Location: 1421 St. Stephens Church Road. On St. Stephens Church Road about 1 mile north of Chesterfield subdivision, on right. [A.D.C. map location: 1989 Edition, page 18, grid coordinates J-4.] No burial records are maintained. 60-70 stones at ground level.

MT. ZION METHODIST CHURCH CEMETERY
Location: 122 Bayard Road. At intersections of Route 408, Route 2, and Route 422. [A.D.C. map location: 1989 Edition, page 29, grid coor-

dinates A-10.] Year of earliest death: 1838. Year of latest death: 1965. WWI and WWII Veterans. No burial records are maintained. The gravemarkers were transcribed in 1968 by DAR; records held by Anne Arundel Genealogical Society. Compiled and published by Daughters of the American Revolution. Title: *Tombstone Inscriptions of Southern Anne Arundel County* (1971), p. 143.

MT. ZION UNITED METHODIST CHURCH CEMETERY
Location: On Artic Drive between Route 100 and Route 177 just west of Magothy Beach Road. [A.D.C. map location: 1989 Edition, page 9, grid coordinates F-10.] Maintained. Year of earliest death: 1863. Year of latest death: 1978. WWI and WWII Veterans. No burial records are maintained. The gravemarkers were transcribed and published by Anne Arundel Genealogical Society. Title: *Cemetery Inscriptions of Anne Arundel County, Maryland,* Vol. II (1987), p. 37. African-American cemetery.

MT. ZION UNITED METHODIST CHURCH CEMETERY
Location: 41 Ark Road, past the church on the opposite side of the road. [A.D.C. map location: 1989 Edition, page 29, grid coordinates Bc-10/11.] Well-maintained. Year of earliest death: 1886. Year of latest death: 1986. WWI, WWII and Korean Veterans. No burial records are maintained. The gravemarkers were transcribed and records held by Anne Arundel Genealogical Society. African-American cemetery.

NICHOLS ROAD CEMETERY
Location: At end of Nichols Road. [A.D.C. map location: 1989 Edition, page 19, grid coordinates K-9.] Possible cemetery.

OLD BETHEL METHODIST CHURCH CEMETERY
Location: Route 175 and Lokus Road on northwest corner. [A.D.C. map location: 1989 Edition, page 12, grid coordinates H-2.] Year of earliest death: 1868. Year of latest death: 1976. Rev. John R. Nichols is buried here. WWII Veterans. No burial records are maintained. The gravemarkers were transcribed in 1979 and published by Anne Arundel Genealogical Society. Title: *Cemetery Inscriptions of Anne Arundel County, Maryland,* Vol. II (1987), p. 110.

OUR LADY OF SORROWS ROMAN CATHOLIC CHURCH CEMETERY
Location: 101 Owensville Road. Route 255 about 0.5 mile east of Route 2, on right side of road. Older stones in rear. [A.D.C. map location:

ANNE ARUNDEL COUNTY CEMETERIES - CHURCH 65

1989 Edition, page 29, grid coordinates D-8.] Well-maintained. Year of earliest death: 1884. Year of latest death: 1966. No burial records are maintained. The gravemarkers were transcribed in 1968 by Daughters of the American Revolution. Records held by Anne Arundel Genealogical Society. Compiled and published by Daughters of the American Revolution. Title: *Tombstone Inscriptions of Southern Anne Arundel County* (1971), p. 281.

OUR LADY OF THE FIELDS CHURCH CEMETERY (ROMAN CATHOLIC CHURCH CEMETERY)
Location: Cecil Avenue and William Road in Baldwin Hills. [A.D.C. map location: 1989 Edition, page 13, grid coordinates F-10.] Year of earliest death: 1900. Year of latest death: 1978. WWI, WWII and Korean Veterans. No burial records are maintained. The gravemarkers records were transcribed and published by Anne Arundel Genealogical Society. Title: *Cemetery Inscriptions of Anne Arundel County, Maryland*, Vol. II (1987), p. 104.

PINEY GROVE METHODIST CHURCH CEMETERY
Location: Southeast of junction of Benfield Road and Jumpers Hole Road. [A.D.C. map location: 1989 Edition, page 14, grid coordinates F-4.] No longer exists. Year of earliest death: 1878. Year of latest death: 1921. No burial records are maintained. The gravemarkers were transcribed in 1962 and published by Anne Arundel Genealogical Society. Title: *Cemetery Inscriptions of Anne Arundel County, Maryland*, Vol. II (1987), p. 15. Reinterred in 1967 at Glen Haven Memorial Park/Cedar Hill Cemetery.

POINT PLEASANT CEMETERY
Location: In Point Pleasant Community near Point Pleasant Elem. School. [A.D.C. map location: 1989 Edition, page 3, grid coordinates E-13.] No burial records are maintained.

QUAKER BURIAL GROUNDS (WEST RIVER QUAKER BURYING GROUNDS)
Location: Route 468 at intersection with Route 255 on northeast corner. [A.D.C. map location: 1989 Edition, page 29, grid coordinates K-7.] Maintained. Year of earliest death: 1822. Year of latest death:

1965. WWI and WWII Veterans. No burial records are maintained. The gravemarkers were transcribed in 1968; records held by Anne Arundel Genealogical Society. Compiled and published by Daughters of the American Revolution. Title: *Tombstone Inscriptions of Southern Anne Arundel County* (1971), p. 201. See also *Anne Arundel's Legacy*, p. 143. Oldest Quaker Cemetery in Anne Arundel Co.

RACE ROAD CEMETERY
Location: East side of Race Road south of unnamed road. [A.D.C. map location: 1989 Edition, page 6, grid coordinates C-2.] Possible cemetery.

RING FAMILY CEMETERY (WHITE AVENUE CEMETERY)
Location: Off Andover Road between White Avenue and Main Avenue in Linthicum Heights. [A.D.C. map location: 1989 Edition, page 2, grid coordinates C-9.] Year of earliest death: 1819. Year of latest death: 1905. No burial records are maintained. Gravemarkers transcribed and published by Anne Arundel Genealogical Society. Title: *Cemetery Inscriptions of Anne Arundel County, Maryland*, Vol. II (1987), p. 99. See *Anne Arundel's Legacy*, p. 173.

SILAS FIRST BAPTIST CHURCH CEMETERY
Location: East of Earleigh Heights Road and north of Early Spring Hill Avenue. [A.D.C. map location: 1989 Edition, page 14, grid coordinates H-2.] Possible cemetery.

SOLLERS UNITED METHODIST CHURCH CEMETERY
Location: 1219 Wrighton Road. On southwest corner of Plummers Lane and Wrighton Road. [A.D.C. map location: 1989 Edition, page 32, grid coordinates A-4.] MAINTAINED. Year of earliest death: 1910. Year of latest death: 1949. No burial records are maintained. The gravemarkers were transcribed in 1993 and records held by Anne Arundel Genealogical Society. African-American cemetery.

SOLLEY CEMETERY (OLD MARLEY METHODIST CHURCH CEMETERY)
Location: Marley Neck Road between Freeman Shores Road and Greenlawn Shores (Tanyard Cove). [A.D.C. map location: 1989 Edition, page 3, grid coordinates HJ-13.] Year of earliest death: 1827. Year of latest death: 1945. No burial records are maintained. The gravemarkers were transcribed in 1975. Records are held by Anne Arundel Genealogical Society. Not the same as Solley Cemetery.

ANNE ARUNDEL COUNTY CEMETERIES - CHURCH

SOLLEY ROAD CEMETERY
Location: West of Solley Road and North of Solley Elementary School.
[A.D.C. map location: 1989 Edition, page 4, grid coordinates A-13.]

ST. GEORGE BARBER CEMETERY (HOWARD CEMETERY)
Location: 1 mile east on Howard Grove Road to #660, several yards north of the house. [A.D.C. map location: 1989 Edition, page 18, grid coordinates H-12.] Some stones broken and scattered. Some legible. Year of earliest death: 1832. Year of latest death: 1855. No burial records are maintained. The tombstones were transcribed in 1983; records held by Anne Arundel Genealogical Society. See *Anne Arundel's Legacy*, p. 163. Copied by Davidsonville Area Civic Association.

ST. STEPHENS EPISCOPAL CHURCH CEMETERY
Location: On St. Stephens Church Road, on hill overlooking church. [A.D.C. map location: 1989 Edition, page 13, grid coordinates E-12.] Maintained. Year of earliest death: 1857. Year of latest death: 1962. Dr. Walter S. Phillips is buried here. The following records are maintained: Deed and Plat, Interment, Tombstone and Maps. The cemetery book records copied by Anne Arundel County Historical Society. 200-300 stones. See *Historic Graves of Maryland*, p. 24. Possibly two churches with same name.

ST. MARGARET'S EPISCOPAL CHURCH CEMETERY
Location: On southeast corner of St. Margaret's Road and Pleasant Plains Road. [A.D.C. map location: 1989 Edition, page 21, grid coordinates D-2.] Maintained. Year of earliest death: 1837. Year of latest death: 1983. No burial records are maintained. The gravemarkers were transcribed in 1984 and published by Anne Arundel Genealogical Society. Title: *Cemetery Inscriptions of Anne Arundel County, Maryland*, Vol. II (1987), p. 137. Published records incomplete. Ten Greek tombstones also transcribed but not published.

ST. MATTHEWS METHODIST CHURCH CEMETERY
Location: On west side of Route 468 south of Centenary United Methodist Church. [A.D.C. map location: 1989 Edition, page 30, grid coordinates F-10.] Well-maintained. Year of earliest death: 1925. Year of latest death: 1988. WWI, WWII and Korean Veterans. No burial records are maintained. The gravemarkers were transcribed in 1994. Records held by Anne Arundel Genealogical Society. African-American cemetery.

ST. PAUL'S EPISCOPAL CHURCH CEMETERY
Location: 1505 Crownsville Road. Off Route 178 at junction with Marbury Drive. [A.D.C. map location: 1989 Edition, page 19, grid coordinates D-1.] Maintained. Year of earliest death: 1801. Year of latest death: 1965. Interment records are maintained. The gravemarkers were transcribed in 1964 and published by Anne Arundel Genealogical Society. Title: *Cemetery Inscriptions of Anne Arundel County, Maryland*, Vol. II (1987), p. 4. Records at St. Stephens Episcopal Church, Millersville.

ST. MATTHEWS UNITED METHODIST CHURCH CEMETERY
Location: On Masons Beach Road across from Deale Elementary School. [A.D.C. map location: 1989 Edition, page 34, grid coordinates A-7.] No burial records are maintained.

ST. LUKE'S CHAPEL CEMETERY
Location: North side of Route 422. [A.D.C. map location: 1989 Edition, page 28, grid coordinates F-8.] Year of earliest death: 1947. Year of latest death: 1964. No burial records are maintained. The gravemarkers were transcribed in 1968 by DAR; records held by Anne Arundel Genealogical Society. Compiled and published by Daughters of the American Revolution. Title: *Tombstone Inscriptions of Southern Anne Arundel County*, p.186. Church closed (by 1995).

ST. LAWRENCE ROMAN CATHOLIC CEMETERY
Location: On Route 175 at southwest junction of Baltimore-Washington Parkway and Route 32. [A.D.C. map location: 1989 Edition, page 5, grid coordinates K-6.] Maintained. Year of earliest death: 1878. Year of latest death: 1975. Rev. Eistert and Rev. Albert are buried here. Gravemarkers were transcribed and published by Anne Arundel Genealogical Society. Title: *Cemetery Inscriptions of Anne Arundel County, Maryland*, Vol. II (1987), p. 119.

ST. DEMETRIOS GREEK ORTHODOX CEMETERY
Location: On Riva Road beside Parole Shopping Plaza on east side near West Street. [A.D.C. map location: 1989 Edition, page 20, grid coordinates B-9.] Well-maintained. Greek cemetery. Most inscriptions in Greek.

ST. JAMES EPISCOPAL PARISH CHURCH CEMETERY (OLD HERRING CREEK CEMETERY)

Location: On Route 2, 0.8 mile north of intersection with Route 258. [A.D.C. map location: 1989 Edition, page 33, grid coordinates D-5.] Well-maintained. Year of earliest death: 1665. Year of latest death: 1965. Many famous persons buried here. WWI Veterans. The gravemarkers were transcribed in 1967 by Daughters of the American Revolution. Records held by Anne Arundel Genealogical Society. Compiled and published by Daughters of the American Revolution. Title: *Tombstone Inscriptions of Southern Anne Arundel County* (1971), p. 84. See also *Historic Graves*, p. 22. and *Anne Arundel's Legacy*, p. 49. Supposedly oldest stone in state is here.

ST. JOHN A.M.E. ZION CHURCH CEMETERY

Location: In Forks, on Conway Road at end of paved roadway. [A.D.C. map location: 1989 Edition, page p.12, grid coordinates B-12.] Maintained. Year of earliest death: 1922. Year of latest death: 1992. WWII Veterans. No burial records are maintained. The gravemarkers were transcribed in 1993 and records held by Anne Arundel Genealogical Society. African-American cemetery. Many unmarked graves, object of vandalism/satanic rituals, about 1/4 stones left.

ST. ANNE'S CEMETERY

Location: Northwest Street bordered by Rowe Boulevard and College Creek. [A.D.C. map location: 1989 Edition, page 20, grid coordinates J-9.] Maintained. Year of earliest death: 1697. Year of latest death: 1974. Many famous persons buried here. The gravemarkers were transcribed and published by Anne Arundel Genealogical Society. Title: *Cemetery Inscriptions of Anne Arundel County, Maryland*, Vol. I (1982), p. 88.

ST. ANDREW THE FISHERMAN EPISCOPAL CEMETERY

Location: Central Avenue at Carrs Wharf Road across from Mayo Elementary School. [A.D.C. map location: 1989 Edition, page 25, grid coordinates G-12.] Well-maintained. Year of earliest death: 1839. Year of latest death: 1955. No burial records are maintained. The records are held by Anne Arundel Genealogical Society. Compiled and published by Daughters of the American Revolution. Title: *Tombstone Inscriptions of Southern Anne Arundel County* (1971), p. 319.

ST. MARY'S CEMETERY
Location: West Street on north side, across from Brewer Hill Cemetery, bordered by Spa Road. [A.D.C. map location: 1989 Edition, page 20, grid coordinates H-10.] Maintained. Year of earliest death: 1832. Year of latest death: 1978. War of 1812, Spanish-American War, Revolutionary War, WWI, WWII and Korean Veterans. The gravemarkers were transcribed and published by Anne Arundel Genealogical Society. Title: *Cemetery Inscriptions of Anne Arundel County, Maryland*, Vol. I (1982), p. 39.

ST. JOHNS EPISCOPAL CHURCH CEMETERY
Location: Snug Harbor Road, first brick church on right. [A.D.C. map location: 1989 Edition, page 30, grid coordinates G-9.] Well-maintained. Year of earliest death: 1896. Year of latest death: 1959. WWI Veterans. No burial records are maintained. The gravemarkers were transcribed in 1994 and records held by Anne Arundel Genealogical Society. Compiled and published by Daughters of the American Revolution. Title: *Tombstone Inscriptions of Southern Anne Arundel County* (1971), p. 192.

ST. JACOB'S LODGE AT MT. ZION CHURCH
Location: At Mt. Zion Church south of Whiskey Bottom Road at Old Stage Coach Road. [A.D.C. map location: 1989 Edition, page 5, grid coordinates A-12.] Freed African-American cemetery.

STUART HILL CEMETERY (FT. MEADE CEMETERY #9, ALSO ST. PETERS P.E. CHURCH CEMETERY, ALSO STEWART/STEWERT HILL CEMETERY/DUVALL CEMETERY/NATHAN JONES)
Location: 100 meters south off Patterson Trail, across from Tipton Army Airfield. [A.D.C. map location: 1989 Edition, page 11, grid coordinates K-4.] Fair condition. Year of earliest death: 1890. Year of latest death: 1957. Historical marker. Gravemarker records held and published by Anne Arundel Genealogical Society. Title: *Cemetery Inscriptions of Anne Arundel County, Maryland*, Vol. II (1987), p. 75. Copied by Ft. Meade BSA Troop 379, grid 4727. Also Ellicott's Episcopal Chapel, Queen Caroline Parish.

SYCAMORE/CIRCLE ROADS CEMETERY
Location: In woods near Sycamore Road and Circle Road. [A.D.C. map location: 1989 Edition, page 4, grid coordinates A-11.] Possible stone or cemetery.

TULIP OAK/GOLDEN OAK CEMETERY
Location: Off Tulip Oak at Golden Oak. [A.D.C. map location: 1989 Edition, page 2, grid coordinates F/G-8.] Possible cemetery.

UNION MEMORIAL CHURCH CEMETERY
Location: Route 424 on east side of road, 500 feet south of junction with Mt. Airy Road. [A.D.C. map location: 1989 Edition, page 23, grid coordinates J-6.] Maintained. No burial records are maintained. The gravemarkers were transcribed in 1994; records held by Anne Arundel Genealogical Society. African-American cemetery, many hand carved tombstones, many illegible.

UNNAMED CEMETERY
Location: Near Lindale Jr. High School, east of Baltimore-Annapolis Boulevard. [A.D.C. map location: 1989 Edition, page 2, grid coordinates H-10.] Possible cemetery. Possibly same as Stewart Family Cemetery.

UNNAMED CEMETERY
Location: Topo. map shows cemetery in upper right quadrant of square. [A.D.C. map location: 1989 Edition, page 7, grid coordinates B/C-7.]

WARD OF FAITH CENTER CHURCH CEMETERY
Location: [A.D.C. map location: 1989 Edition, page 1, grid coordinates G-13.]

WAUGH CHAPEL CEMETERY
Location: Waugh Chapel Road East near Francis Station Road. [A.D.C. map location: 1989 Edition, page 12, grid coordinates H-7.] Maintained. Year of earliest death: 1854. Year of latest death: 1963. No burial records are maintained. The gravemarkers were transcribed in 1978. Records held by Anne Arundel Genealogical Society. See *Anne Arundel's Legacy*, p. 171. Records provided to Maryland Genealogical Society 3 June 1971, source unknown.

WESLEY GROVE UNITED METHODIST CHURCH CEMETERY
Location: On Route 176, east of Ashton Road. [A.D.C. map location: 1989 Edition, page 6, grid coordinates H-3.] Possible cemetery.

WILSON MEMORIAL UNITED METHODIST CHURCH CEMETERY
Location: Northbound Route 3 between Carver Road and Lee Street.
[A.D.C. map location: 1989 Edition, page 17, grid coordinates K-1.] No burial records are maintained.

YIELDHALL FAMILY CEMETERY
Location: On Linwood Avenue between Broadview and Lotus Avenue.
[A.D.C. map location: 1989 Edition, page 2, grid coordinates EF-9/10.]

Public Cemeteries

ANNAPOLIS NATIONAL CEMETERY
Location: 800 block of West Street just east of Brewer Hill Cemetery, near Taylor Avenue. [A.D.C. map location: 1989 Edition, page 20, grid coordinates H-10.] Well-maintained. Military cemetery.

CEDAR HILL CEMETERY
Location: Route 2 north of juncton of Route 695 (Balt. Beltway) on east side before Hammonds Lane. [A.D.C. map location: 1989 Edition, page 3, grid coordinates B-5.] Well-maintained. Burial records are maintained including deed and plat, interment, tombstone and maps. Records are held at Cedar Hill. The gravemarkers were transcribed in 1995 by DAR; the records will be published by Anne Arundel Genealogical Society sometime in the near future.

DEALE BEACH ROAD CEMETERY
Location: North of Route 256 intersection on Deale Beach Road, 0.1 mile from intersection, on north before #5905. [A.D.C. map location: 1989 Edition, page 34, grid coordinates B-4.] Fairly well-maintained; some stones outside maintained area. Year of earliest death: 1891. Year of latest death: 1966. No burial records are maintained. The gravemarkers were transcribed by Daughters of the American Revolution. Records are maintained by Anne Arundel Genealogical Society. Compiled and published by Daughters of the American Revolution. Title: *Tombstone Inscriptions of Southern Anne Arundel County* (1971), p. 120. Published information incomplete.

DUVALL FAMILY CEMETERY
Location: Inside General's Highway Corridor Park (Co. park) just south of Honeysuckle Lane. [A.D.C. map location: 1989 Edition, page 19, grid coordinates E-5.] Good condition. A white fence surrounds it, main-

tained by county. Year of earliest death: 1853. Year of latest death: 1903. Samuel Duvall is buried here. Civil War Veterans. No burial records are maintained. The gravemarkers were transcribed in 1992 and records maintained by Anne Arundel Genealogical Society. Samuel Duvall, Confederate soldier died at Gettysburg, buried here.

FERDINAND DUVALL GRAVE
Location: On Harrow Avenue. [A.D.C. map location: 1989 Edition, page 18, grid coordinates A-5.] Ferdinand Duvall is buried here. Listed in Ware, D.M. Title: *Anne Arundel's Legacy, The Historic Properties of Anne Arundel County* (1990), p. 166. Single grave.

GLEN HAVEN MEMORIAL PARK
Location: #7215 Ritchie Highway. Route 2 between 7th Avenue NE and 8th Avenue NE in Glen Burnie. [A.D.C. map location: 1989 Edition, page 3, grid coordinates A/B-13.] Well-maintained. Burial records maintained by Glen Haven. Maryland Historical Society has records on microfilm.

HILLCREST MEMORIAL CEMETERY
Location: #1911 Forest Drive near Chiquapin Round Road. [A.D.C. map location: 1989 Edition, page 20, grid coordinates D-10.] Well-maintained. Year of earliest death: 1830. Established in 1911; some from 19th century reinterred there. Computer update to be done there in 1992.

LAKEMONT MEMORIAL GARDENS
Location: Route 214 west of Route 424 on north side of road. [A.D.C. map location: 1989 Edition, page 23, grid coordinates H-7.] Well-maintained.

MARYLAND VETERANS CEMETERY
Location: Off Route 178 onto Sunrise Beach Road then left between Evergreen Roadand Whitneys Landing Road. [A.D.C. map location: 1989 Edition, page 14, grid coordinates DE-7.] Well-maintained. Small private cemetery within grounds. Military cemetery.

MIDSHIPMEN MEMORIAL (SCENIC OVERLOOK MEMORIAL)
Location: Just below Scenic Overlook on Route 450 near Severn River Bridge within median strip. [A.D.C. map location: 1989 Edition, page 21, grid coordinates A-6.] Maintained. No burial records are maintained. Memorial To U.S.N.A. Midshipmen killed in auto accident.

OLD SALEM CEMETERY/M.E. CHURCH CEMETERY (ANNAPOLIS JUNIOR HIGH SCHOOL CEMETERY, ALSO DUVALL FAMILY CHAPEL)
Location: 0.3 mile east of junction of Spa Road and Forest Drive northeast of school and west of Old Forest Drive in small grove. [A.D.C. map location: 1989 Edition, page 20, grid coordinates G-13.] Overgrown. Year of earliest death: 1832. Year of latest death: 1973. School clean-up project 1994. Gravemarker records compiled and published by Anne Arundel Genealogical Society. Title: *Cemetery Inscriptions of Anne Arundel County, Maryland*, Vol. I (1982), p. 1. School clean-up project in 1994. The school is actively working to restore cemetery.

U.S. NAVAL ACADEMY CEMETERY
Location: At Strawberry Hill, in front of former Naval Hospital, bordered by College Creek and Severn River. [A.D.C. map location: 1989 Edition, page 20, grid coordinates K-8.] Maintained. Military and civilian graves.

WOODFIELD CEMETERY
Location: Route 468 at intersection with Route 255 on southeast corner. [A.D.C. map location: 1989 Edition, page 29, grid coordinates K-7.] Well-maintained. Year of earliest death: 1806. Year of latest death: 1967. WWI and WWII Veterans. No burial records are maintained. The gravemarkers were transcribed in 1968 by Daughters of the American Revolution. Records held by Anne Arundel Genealogical Society. Compiled and published by Daughters of the American Revolution. Title: *Tombstone Inscriptions of Southern Anne Arundel County* (1971), p. 239.

CARROLL COUNTY

Private Cemeteries

ADAM SHIPLEY FAMILY CEMETERY
Location: On the grounds of Springfield State Hospital. [A.D.C. map location: 10th Edition, page 35, grid coordinates 1B.] The original cemetery is gone (stones existed in 1916; a monument was placed by descendants of A. Shipley in 1984). There is information at the Carroll County Public Library, 50 Main Street, Westminster, MD 21157. Some

information on the cemetery and family was published in Carroll County Genealogical Society, *Carroll County Cemeteries*, Volume 1, Carroll County Genealogical Society, P.O. Box 1752, Westminster, MD 21158 (1989).

ALLGIRE FAMILY (JOHN ALLGIRE) CEMETERY (ALSO CALLED HOUCK FAMILY CEMETERY)
Location: North of Carrollton Road and west of Houcksville Road. [A.D.C. map location: 10th Edition, page 21, grid coordinates 7D.] The cemetery has disappeared; only native stones remain. The property was owned by Fred'k Basler (1870). The cemetery is discussed in Carroll County Genealogical Society, *Carroll County Cemeteries*, Volume 2, Carroll County Genealogical Society, P.O. Box 1752, Westminster, MD 21158 (1990).
It is presumed that John Allgire and wife Ruth were buried here. This is the site of an early meeting house.

BAILE FAMILY CEMETERY
Location: West side of Bowersox Road at sharp bend, opposite Overbrook Lane. [A.D.C. map location: 10th Edition, page 23, grid coordinates 2E.] The stone fence was falling down in 1987, groundhog damage. Year of earliest known death: 1819. Year of most recent death: 1862. The gravemarkers were transcribed in 1987. Location of transcribed records: Carroll County Public Library, 50 Main Street, Westminster, MD 21157. The transcribed records (6 names) were published in Jacob Mehrling Holdcraft's *Names in Stone, 75,000 Cemetery Inscriptions From Frederick County, Maryland*. The Monocacy Book Company, Redwood City, CA (2nd printing, 1972). Data were transcribed in 1963 by Dr. B.F.M. MacPherson. All six graves have surname Baile.

BARNES FAMILY CEMETERY
Location: West side of Greens Mill Road about half way between Deer Park and Old Westminster Roads. [A.D.C. map location: 10th Edition, page 25, grid coordinates 3G.] Cemetery abandoned. Gravemarkers were transcribed in 1990. Location of transcribed records: Carroll County Public Library, 50 Main Street, Westminster, MD 21157. The transcribed records were published in Carroll County Genealogical Society, *Carroll County Cemeteries*, Volume 2, Carroll County Genealogical Society, P.O. Box 1752, Westminster, MD 21158 (1990).

BARNES FAMILY CEMETERY
Location: Reputed to be just east of Taylorsville, along Route 26 (Liberty

Road) east of Taylorsville. [A.D.C. map location: 10th Edition, page 23, grid coordinates 13E.] No other information.

BEASMAN FAMILY (THOMAS BEASMAN) CEMETERY (BASEMAN FAMILY CEMETERY)
Location: Off Pouder Road; follow fire trail in Liberty Reservoir property about 1 mile on right. [A.D.C. map location: 10th Edition, page 30, grid coordinates 2D.] Abandoned, periwinkle as ground cover, surrounded by pines, 100 feet square. Year of earliest known death: 1833. Year of most recent death: 1879. The gravemarkers were transcribed in 1988. Location of transcribed records: Carroll County Public Library, 50 Main Street, Westminster, MD 21157. The transcribed records were published in Carroll County Genealogical Society, *Carroll County Cemeteries*, Volume 1, Carroll County Genealogical Society, P.O. Box 1752, Westminster, MD 21158 (1989). Surnames: Beasman, Bennett, Murray.

BEAVER FAMILY CEMETERY
Location: Behind Maryland State Police Barracks on Route 140 east of Westminster. [A.D.C. map location: 10th Edition, page 20, grid coordinates 8C.] Abandoned. Year of earliest known death: 182? Year of most recent death: 1839. The gravemarkers were transcribed in 1978. Location of transcribed records: Carroll County Public Library, 50 Main Street, Westminster, MD 21157. These records were published in Carroll County Genealogical Society, *Carroll County Cemeteries*, Volume 2, Carroll County Genealogical Society, P.O. Box 1752, Westminster, MD 21158 (1990). Additional comments: Martin Beaver, Rev. War Soldier is buried here. Other surnames: Robertson, Riley.

BEGGS CHAPEL CEMETERY (BEGGS FAMILY CEMETERY)
Location: Between Beggs and Sullivan Roads near intersection with Old Fridinger Road. [A.D.C. map location: 10th Edition, page 13, grid coordinates 8B.] The cemetery is in very bad condition; most stones knocked over; the small chapel has disappeared. Year of earliest known death: 1877. Year of most recent death: 1973. No burial records are kept. The gravemarkers were transcribed in 1982. Location of transcribed records: Carroll County Public Library, 50 Main Street, Westminster, MD 21157. The transcribed records were published in Jacob Mehrling Holdcraft's *Names in Stone, 75,000 Cemetery Inscriptions From Frederick County, Maryland*. The Monocacy Book Company, Redwood City, CA (2nd printing, 1972). Data were transcribed between 1959 and 1962. Surnames include Beggs, Royer, Leese, Mower, Riegel, Cole, Bankert, etc.

CARROLL COUNTY CEMETERIES - PRIVATE 77

BENNETT CEMETERY (SAM AND TEVIS BENNETT) CEMETERY
Location: East side of Oklahoma Road near Mineral Hill Road intersection. [A.D.C. map location: 10th Edition, page 30, grid coordinates 8J.] The cemetery has disappeared; the stones were carried away in the 1940s or 1950s. The cemetery is discussed in Carroll County Genealogical Society, *Carroll County Cemeteries*, Volume 1, Carroll County Genealogical Society, P.O. Box 1752, Westminster, MD 21158 (1989). Additional comments: The site was pinpointed by Carroll Phillips, a descendant.

BENNETT FAMILY CEMETERY
Location: Between Oakland Road and Lakeview Drive in southeast part of county called "Oakland." [A.D.C. map location: 10th Edition, page 31, grid coordinates 8A.] Well-maintained with fence. Year of earliest known death: 1786. Year of most recent death: 1885. The gravemarkers were transcribed in 1989. Location of transcribed records: Carroll County Public Library, 50 Main Street, Westminster, MD 21157. The transcribed records were published in Carroll County Genealogical Society, *Carroll County Cemeteries*, Volume 1, Carroll County Genealogical Society, P.O. Box 1752, Westminster, MD 21158 (1989). Surnames: Tevis, Bennett, Hewett.

BENNETT FAMILY (PERRY BENNETT) CEMETERY
Location: Between Bennett and Liberty Roads east of Route 32. [A.D.C. map location: 10th Edition, page 30, grid coordinates 8F.] Abandoned. Year of earliest known death: 1848. Year of most recent death: 1867. The gravemarkers were transcribed in 1977. Location of transcribed records: Carroll County Public Library, 50 Main Street, Westminster, MD 21157. The transcribed records were published in Carroll County Genealogical Society, *Carroll County Cemeteries*, Volume 1, Carroll County Genealogical Society, P.O. Box 1752, Westminster, MD 21158 (1989). Additional comments: Four stones with some footstones.

BOND FAMILY CEMETERY
Location: 2805 Sam's Creek Road near Franklinville Road. [A.D.C. map location: 10th Edition, page 23, grid coordinates 9B.] The cemetery is well-maintained, fenced. Year of earliest known death: 1814. Year of most recent death: 1853. The gravemarkers were transcribed in 1988. Location of transcribed records: Carroll County Public Library, 50 Main Street, Westminster, MD 21157. Copied by Charles L. Manahan, photo included.

BOONE FAMILY CEMETERY
Location: At intersection between Pine Knob and Mineral Hill Roads near Liberty Watershed. Originally it was part of the tract, *Conaway Venture Improved* (1769). [A.D.C. map location: 10th Edition, page 30, grid coordinates 5H.] The cemetery was in existence in the 1940s; tombstones were on side of hill. It had disappeared by 1983. A brief discussion of the cemetery was published in Carroll County Genealogical Society, *Carroll County Cemeteries*, Volume 1, Carroll County Genealogical Society, P.O. Box 1752, Westminster, MD 21158 (1989).

BROTHERS FAMILY CEMETERY
Location: Between Don Avenue and Bollinger Road off Deer Park Road. [A.D.C. map location: 10th Edition, page 25, grid coordinates 2A.] Year of earliest known death: 1852. Year of most recent death: 1852. Gravemarkers were transcribed in 1982. Location of transcribed records: Carroll County Public Library, 50 E. Main Street, Westminster. The transcribed records were published in Carroll County Genealogical Society, *Carroll County Cemeteries*, Volume 2, Carroll County Genealogical Society, P.O. Box 1752, Westminster, MD 21158 (1990). Additional comments: Two stones only.

BROWN/OWINGS FAMILIES CEMETERY
Location: West side of intersection of Ridge and Marriottsville Roads. [A.D.C. map location: 10th Edition, page 35, grid coordinates 1J.] Earliest tombstone: 1897. Cemetery was reported in *Maryland Genealogical Society Bulletin*, Vol. 19, No. 1, by E. McCallahan. Eleven tombstones were recorded in 1897. See MGS Bulletin article or Carroll County Genealogical Society, *Carroll County Cemeteries*, Volume 1, Carroll County Genealogical Society, P.O. Box 1752, Westminster, MD 21158 (1989). Surnames: Brown, Perry and Baseman.

BUCKINGHAM FAMILY CEMETERY
Location: East side of Hodges Road. The cemetery has disappeared. A local resident recalled seeing fieldstones in 1920s. [A.D.C. map location: 10th Edition, page 30, grid coordinates 6C.] The transcribed records were published in Carroll County Genealogical Society, *Carroll County Cemeteries*, Volume 1, Carroll County Genealogical Society, P.O. Box 1752, Westminster, MD 21158 (1989). In 1850 the tract belonged to P. Buckingham.

BUCKINGHAM FAMILY CEMETERY
Location: West side of Fleming Road between Gillis and Braddock Roads.

CARROLL COUNTY CEMETERIES - PRIVATE

[A.D.C. map location: 10th Edition, page 28, grid coordinates 4D.] Abandoned. Year of earliest known death: 1829. Year of most recent death: 1833. The gravemarkers (two tombstones) were transcribed in 1982. Location of transcribed records: Carroll County Public Library, 50 E. Main Street, Westminster, MD 21157. The transcribed records were published by Carroll County Genealogical Society, *Carroll County Cemeteries*, Volume 3, Carroll County Genealogical Society, P.O. Box 1752, Westminster, MD 21158 (1992).

CAPLE FAMILY CEMETERY
Location: Between Constellation Way and Kay's Mill Road off Deer Park Road, Starview Estates. [A.D.C. map location: 10th Edition, page 25, grid coordinates 6G.] Year of earliest known death: 1836. Year of most recent death: 1861. The gravemarkers were transcribed in 1984. Location of transcribed records: Carroll County Public Library, 50 Main Street, Westminster, MD 21157. The transcribed records were published in Carroll County Genealogical Society, *Carroll County Cemeteries*, Volume 2, Carroll County Genealogical Society, P.O. Box 1752, Westminster, MD 21158 (1990). Surnames: Caple, Blizzard and Arnold.

CASSELL FAMILY CEMETERY
Location: Adam's Mill Road off Route 31 between Westminster and New Windsor. [A.D.C. map location: 10th Edition, page 18, grid coordinates 7J.] Moderately well kept, walled, subject to some vandalism at times. Earliest known death: 1800. Most recent death: 1950. No burial records are kept. The tombstones were transcribed in 1982; these transcribed records are held by Carroll County Public Library, 50 E. Main St. Westminster. The records have not been published. Comments: An article appeared in *Carroll County Times* in 1980s or 1990s on vandalism at this cemetery.

COLD SATURDAY FARM CEMETERY
Location: South of Cold Saturday Drive and east of Route 91 (Gamber Road). [A.D.C. map location: 10th Edition, page 26, grid coordinates 8A.] A cemetery was reputed to be here but was gone in 1984. A farm worker stated that it had contained the grave of a Gittings youngster. For brief discussion see Carroll County Genealogical Society, *Carroll County Cemeteries*, Volume 2, Carroll County Genealogical Society, P.O. Box 1752, Westminster, MD 21158 (1990).

CONDON FAMILY CEMETERY
Location: North side of Bethel Road just before intersection with

Woodbine Road. [A.D.C. map location: 10th Edition, page 28, grid coordinates 6H.] Abandoned. Year of earliest known death: 1872. The gravemarkers were transcribed in 1982. Location of transcribed records: Carroll County Public Library, 50 Main Street, Westminster, MD 21157. The transcribed records were published in Carroll County Genealogical Society, *Carroll County Cemeteries*, Volume 3, Carroll County Genealogical Society, P.O. Box 1752, Westminster, MD 21158 (1992). There are three inscribed stones and scattered fieldstones.

CONOWAY FAMILY CEMETERY
Location: South of Bollinger Mill Road and east of intersection with Mineral Hill Road. [A.D.C. map location: 10th Edition, page 30, grid coordinates 2H.] Year of earliest known death: 1848. The gravemarkers were transcribed in 1995. Location of transcribed records: Carroll County Public Library, 50 Main Street, Westminster, MD 21157. A single stone was found (1995) in an area where the Conoway Family owned land. Name: Zachariah Conoway.

COOK FAMILY CEMETERY
Location: North side of Old Washington Road as it turns southwest to meet Bushey Road near Route 26. [A.D.C. map location: 10th Edition, page 29, grid coordinates 4E.] This may have been the property of Andrew Cook. Abandoned. Year of earliest known death: 1858. The gravemarkers were transcribed in 1991. Location of transcribed records: Carroll County Public Library, 50 Main Street, Westminster, MD 21157. The transcribed records were published in Carroll County Genealogical Society, *Carroll County Cemeteries*, Volume 3, Carroll County Genealogical Society, P.O. Box 1752, Westminster, MD 21158 (1992). Surnames: Coleman, Shipley.

CRAWFORD/GOSNELL FAMILIES CEMETERY
Location: Across from Crawford homestead on Iroquois Drive and Sam's Creek Road near Taylorsville. [A.D.C. map location: 10th Edition, page 23, grid coordinates 12E.] Abandoned. There were tombstone fragments but no stones seen intact. The site visit report is held at Carroll County Public Library, 50 Main Street, Westminster, MD. 21157. Information on births and deaths have been recorded from family Bible; two reinterred at Taylorsville U.M.

DAVIS FAMILY CEMETERY #1
Location: East side of Cabbage Spring Road south of Zack Drive intersection, in the field of a farm. [A.D.C. map location: 10th Edition, page 28,

grid coordinates 8B.] Year of earliest known death: 1906. Year of most recent death: 1936. The gravemarkers were transcribed in 1991. Location of transcribed records: Carroll County Public Library, 50 Main Street, Westminster, MD 21157. The transcribed records were published in Carroll County Genealogical Society, *Carroll County Cemeteries*, Volume 3, Carroll County Genealogical Society, P.O. Box 1752, Westminster, MD 21158 (1992). Surnames: Davis.

DAVIS FAMILY CEMETERY #2
Location: North of Mt. Airy and east of Route 27 (Ridge Road). [A.D.C. map location: 10th Edition, page 27, grid coordinates 13F.] The cemetery had disappeared by 1971. It was on Zachariah Davis Farm, later owned by S. England. It was near the Joseph Spurrier Family Cemetery.

DAVIS/WATERS FAMILIES CEMETERY
Location: West side of Watersville Road south of intersection with Flag Marsh Road. [A.D.C. map location: 10th Edition, page 32, grid coordinates 2K.] The cemetery was restored about 1990. It is fenced with a large modern stone plus old stones. Year of earliest known death: 1837. Year of most recent death: 1909. The gravemarkers were transcribed in 1991. Location of transcribed records: Carroll County Public Library, 50 Main Street, Westminster, MD 21157. The transcribed records were published in Carroll County Genealogical Society, *Carroll County Cemeteries*, Volume 3, Carroll County Genealogical Society, P.O. Box 1752, Westminster, MD 21158 (1992). There were nine original stones plus a modern stone erected to memory of family members.

DEVILBISS FAMILY CEMETERY
Location: Southwest of Sam's Creek Road between Oak Orchard and New Windsor Roads. [A.D.C. map location: 10th Edition, page 22, grid coordinates 4H?.] Abandoned, overgrown, groundhog damage; stones are in good condition. Year of earliest known death: 1830. Year of most recent death: 1855. The gravemarkers were transcribed in 1987. The transcribed records were published in Jacob Mehrling Holdcraft's *Names in Stone, 75,000 Cemetery Inscriptions From Frederick County, Maryland*. The Monocacy Book Company, Redwood City, CA (2nd printing, 1972). Data were transcribed between 1959 and 1962. Surnames: Naill, Devilbiss.

DODS/BROOKE/SCOTT FAMILIES CEMETERY
Location: Just west of Route 194 (FSK Highway) and south of Keysville-Bruceville Road intersection. [A.D.C. map location: 10th Edition, page 8, grid coordinates 11A.] Fenced off but abandoned with badly broken

stones. Year of earliest known death: 1806. Year of most recent death: 1841. Robert Dods who was born in Scotland is buried here. The gravemarkers were transcribed in 1991. Location of transcribed records: Carroll County Public Library, 50 Main Street, Westminster, MD 21157. The transcribed records were published in Jacob Mehrling Holdcraft's *Names in Stone, 75,000 Cemetery Inscriptions From Frederick County, Maryland*. The Monocacy Book Company, Redwood City, CA (2nd printing, 1972). Data were transcribed between 1959 and 1962. Additional information can be found in J. Thomas Scharf's *History of Western Maryland* and Holdcraft's *Names in Stone*.

DORSEY FAMILY CEMETERY
Location: At terminus of Long Meadow Drive off Route 26 east of intersection with Route 32. [A.D.C. map location: 10th Edition, page 30, grid coordinates 9E.] Abandoned. Year of earliest known death: 1814. Year of most recent death: 1862. The gravemarkers were transcribed in 1978. Location of transcribed records: Carroll County Public Library, 50 Main Street, Westminster, MD 21157. The records were published in Carroll County Genealogical Society, *Carroll County Cemeteries*, Volume 1, Carroll County Genealogical Society, P.O. Box 1752, Westminster, MD 21158 (1989). There are six stones with surnames: Warfield, Norris (or Morris) and Dorsey.

DORSEY FAMILY (JONATHAN DORSEY) CEMETERY
Location: Between Route 97 (Old Washington Road) and Streaker Road in southeast quarter. [A.D.C. map location: 10th Edition, page 29, grid coordinates 9D.] Year of earliest known death: 1837. Year of most recent death: 1856. There were five tombstones. The gravemarkers were transcribed in 1982 and are held by Carroll County Public Library, 50 E. Main Street, Westminster, MD 21157. See Carroll County Genealogical Society, *Carroll County Cemeteries*, Volume 3, Carroll County Genealogical Society, P.O. Box 1752, Westminster, MD 21158 (1992).

DOUTY FAMILY CEMETERY
Location: South side of Old West Falls Road just east of intersection with Buffalo Road. [A.D.C. map location: 10th Edition, page 27, grid coordinates 6F.] Abandoned, in terrible disrepair (1992). Year of earliest known death: 1850. Year of most recent death: 1929. The gravemarkers were transcribed in 1957 by Holdcraft. Location of transcribed records: Carroll County Public Library, 50 Main Street, Westminster, MD 21157. The transcribed records were published in Jacob Mehrling Holdcraft's *Names in Stone, 75,000 Cemetery Inscriptions From Frederick County,*

Maryland. The Monocacy Book Company, Redwood City, CA (2nd printing, 1972). Data were transcribed between 1959 and 1962. Surnames: Douty, Haines, Harn, Keefer.

EVANS FAMILY CEMETERY
Location: Southwest corner of intersection between Marston Road and Route 27. [A.D.C. map location: 10th Edition, page 23, grid coordinates 8F.] Fair condition with iron fence around it. Year of earliest known death: 1803. Year of most recent death: 1862. John Evans, Methodist, and other members of the Evans family are buried here. No burial records are kept. The gravemarkers were transcribed in 1982. Location of transcribed records: Carroll County Public Library, 50 E. Main Street, Westminster, MD 21157. The transcribed records were published in Jacob Mehrling Holdcraft's *Names in Stone, 75,000 Cemetery Inscriptions From Frederick County, Maryland*. The Monocacy Book Company, Redwood City, CA (2nd printing, 1972). Data were transcribed between 1959 and 1962.

FARQUHAR/SHEPHERD/WEBB FAMILIES CEMETERY
Location: Near intersection of Good Intent Road and Bucher John Road west of Union Bridge. [A.D.C. map location: 10th Edition, page 16, grid coordinates 5H.] It was being restored in 1991; it had been in very poor condition prior to that time. Year of earliest known death: 1792. Year of most recent death: 1855. The gravemarkers were transcribed in 1991. Location of transcribed records: Carroll County Public Library, 50 Main Street, Westminster, MD 21157. The transcribed records were published in Jacob Mehrling Holdcraft's *Names in Stone, 75,000 Cemetery Inscriptions From Frederick County, Maryland*. The Monocacy Book Company, Redwood City, CA (2nd printing, 1972). Data were transcribed between 1959 and 1962. SURNAMES: Buser, Shepherd, Cox, Webb.

FRANKLIN FAMILY #1 CEMETERY
Location: On south side of Gilbert Road between Perry Road and Route 27 (Ridge Road). [A.D.C. map location: 10th Edition, page 28, grid coordinates 2B.] Abandoned. Tombstones are scattered and broken. There appears to be a right-of-way in development. Year of earliest known death: 1801. Year of most recent death: 1869. The gravemarkers were transcribed in 1987. Location of transcribed records: Carroll County Public Library, 50 Main Street, Westminster, MD 21157. The transcribed records were published in Carroll County Genealogical Society, *Carroll County Cemeteries*, Volume 3, Carroll County Genealogical Society, P.O. Box 1752, Westminster, MD 21158 (1992). Surnames: Condon, Buckingham, Franklin, Barnes.

FRANKLIN FAMILY #2 CEMETERY
Location: West side of Franklinville Road south of Sam's Creek Road, first road to right. [A.D.C. map location: 10th Edition, page 23, grid coordinates 10B.] The cemetery is reasonably well maintained. Year of earliest known death: 1814. Year of most recent death: 1899. The gravemarkers were transcribed in 1992. Location of transcribed records: Carroll County Public Library, 50 Main Street, Westminster, MD 21157. Surnames: Franklin, Demmit, Bond, Evans and Williams.

GARNER FAMILY (FLINN GARNER) CEMETERY
Location: Between Cedarhurst and Emory Roads about 500 feet from Route 140. [A.D.C. map location: 10th Edition, page 26, grid coordinates 6C.] This cemetery was reported to exist in the 1980s but the land owner stated that it was gone by 1990. The F. Garner Graveyard was mentioned in Scharf's *History of Western Maryland*. The transcribed records were published in Carroll County Genealogical Society, *Carroll County Cemeteries*, Volume 2, Carroll County Genealogical Society, P.O. Box 1752, Westminster, MD 21158 (1990).

GARRISON FAMILY CEMETERY
Location: North side of Deer Park Road between Kay's Mill Road and Route 91. [A.D.C. map location: 10th Edition, page 25, grid coordinates 8H.] Abandoned. The gravemarkers were transcribed in 1982. There are broken pieces of stone with partial inscriptions. Location of transcribed records: Carroll County Public Library, 50 E. Main Street, Westminster, MD 21157. These records have been published in Carroll County Genealogical Society, *Carroll County Cemeteries*, Volume 2, P.O. Box 1752, Westminster, MD 21158 (1990).

GEIMAN FAMILY (CHRISTIAN GEIMAN) CEMETERY
Location: On the northwest side of Hoover Mill Road off New Bachman Valley Road. Part of stone wall remains; stones were relocated to a nearby church in Pennsylvania. [A.D.C. map location: 10th Edition, page 5, grid coordinates 12G.] Information on the property of C. Geiman is available at the Carroll County Public Library, 50 Main Street, Westminster, MD 21157.

GEIMAN FAMILY (DAVID GEIMAN) CEMETERY
Location: East side of Old Bachman Valley Road between Lemmon and Fridinger Roads. [A.D.C. map location: 10th Edition, page 12, grid coordinates 9K.] Surrounded by a wall in 1963 when seen by Holdcraft. Year of earliest known death: 1811. Year of most recent death: 1899. The

gravemarkers were transcribed in 1982. Location of transcribed records: Carroll County Public Library, 50 Main Street, Westminster, MD 21157. The transcribed records were published in Jacob Mehrling Holdcraft's *Names in Stone, 75,000 Cemetery Inscriptions From Frederick County, Maryland*. The Monocacy Book Company, Redwood City, CA (2nd printing, 1972). Data were transcribed between 1959 and 1962. Additional comments: Approx. 35 gravestones. Surnames: Geiman, Myers.

GIST FAMILY CEMETERY
Location: Off Hook Road near intersection with Gist Road south of Westminster. [A.D.C. map location: 10th Edition, page 19, grid coordinates 9F.] The cemetery is fenced and well-maintained. Year of earliest known death: 1816. Year of most recent death: 1980. Gist family members are buried here. Veterans interred: Revolutionary War, Civil War and WWII. No burial records are kept. The gravemarkers were transcribed in 1983. Location of transcribed records: Carroll County Public Library, 50 Main Street, Westminster, MD 21157. Surnames include Gist, Eckenrode, Dorsey, Smith, Beatty, Pickens, etc.

GORSUCH FAMILY CEMETERY
Location: West side of Ridge Road (Route 27 south of Westminster), 3115 Ridge Road, on a farm. [A.D.C. map location: 10th Edition, page 23, grid coordinates 7G.] Abandoned, walled. Year of earliest known death: 1815. Year of most recent death: 1860. The gravemarkers were transcribed in 1982. Location of transcribed records: Carroll County Public Library, 50 Main Street, Westminster, MD 21157. There are five stones all with Gorsuch surname.

GORSUCH FAMILY CEMETERY
Location: Was located along Poole Road near village of Gamber. [A.D.C. map location: 10th Edition, page 25, grid coordinates 12E.] The stones were moved to Gamber, probably to Mt. Pleasant Methodist Cemetery. For more details see Carroll County Genealogical Society, *Carroll County Cemeteries*, Volume 2, Carroll County Genealogical Society, P.O. Box 1752, Westminster, MD 21158 (1990).

GREEN/GARDSON FAMILIES CEMETERY
Location: On Mineral Hill Road off Bollinger Road near Liberty Reservoir property. [A.D.C. map location: 10th Edition, page 30, grid coordinates 2H.] The cemetery is discussed in Carroll County Genealogical Society, *Carroll County Cemeteries*, Volume 1, Carroll County Genealogical Society, P.O. Box 1752, Westminster, MD 21158 (1989). According to

William Breeding, Zachariah Green's daughter told him that she used to come to visit the site "years ago" and that Freeborn Gardson was buried next to her father Zachariah Green.

HAINES FAMILY CEMETERY
Location: Off Uniontown Road about 3 miles west of Westminster. [A.D.C. map location: 10th Edition, page 18, grid coordinates 2G.] An effort was made to find it in 1991 but never located. The cemetery's existence was reported by Karen Dattilio.

HAINES FAMILY CEMETERY
Location: East side of John Hyde Road near intersection with Roop's Mill Road. [A.D.C. map location: 10th Edition, page 18, grid coordinates 6F.] It was walled in 1957 when seen by Holdcraft. Year of earliest known death: 1829. Year of most recent death: 1882. No burial records are kept. The gravemarkers were transcribed in 1983. Location of transcribed records: Carroll County Public Library, 50 Main Street, Westminster, MD 21157. The transcribed records were published in Jacob Mehrling Holdcraft's *Names in Stone, 75,000 Cemetery Inscriptions From Frederick County, Maryland*. The Monocacy Book Company, Redwood City, CA (2nd printing, 1972). Data were transcribed between 1959 and 1962. Surnames: Haines, Shaffer, Williams, Matthews, Smith, Ensor.

HAINES FAMILY CEMETERY (MORDICA HAINES GRAVE)
Location: On Olin Grimes property, southwest side of Deer Park Road west of Route 91. [A.D.C. map location: 10th Edition, page 25, grid coordinates 7G.] An isolated stone was found under the porch of Olin Grimes' property. Year of earliest known death: 1856. The gravemarkers were transcribed in 1978. Location of transcribed records: Carroll County Public Library, 50 Main Street, Westminster, MD 21157. The transcribed records were published in Carroll County Genealogical Society, *Carroll County Cemeteries*, Volume 2, Carroll County Genealogical Society, P.O. Box 1752, Westminster, MD 21158 (1990). Additional comments: A stone probably belonging in Haines Family Cemetery located at corner of Deer Park Road and Route 91.

HAINES FAMILY (MICHAEL HAINES) CEMETERY
Location: Off Marston Road between Marston and New Windsor, on unoccupied Snader Farm. [A.D.C. map location: 10th Edition, page 23, grid coordinates 2A.] The cemetery is run down; a partial stone wall remains. There is groundhog damage. Year of earliest known death: 1818. Year of most recent death: 1835. The gravemarkers were transcribed in

CARROLL COUNTY CEMETERIES - PRIVATE 87

1987. Location of transcribed records: Carroll County Public Library, 50 Main Street, Westminster, MD 21157. Surnames: Haines, Hooper, Baile.

HALL FAMILY CEMETERY
Location: Off West Falls and Old West Falls Roads between Buffalo Road and Route 27. [A.D.C. map location: 10th Edition, page 27, grid coordinates 5J.] The cemetery had disappeared in 1992. Several isolated stones reported. Year of earliest known death: 1819. The gravemarkers were transcribed in 1992. Location of transcribed records: Carroll County Public Library, 50 Main Street, Westminster, MD 21157. The transcribed records were published in Carroll County Genealogical Society, *Carroll County Cemeteries*, Volume 3, Carroll County Genealogical Society, P.O. Box 1752, Westminster, MD 21158 (1992). The tombstone of Mary Hall was reported here but never seen. Other surname: Douty.

HARDIN/HARDEN FAMILY CEMETERY (ALSO DAY FAMILY CEMETERY?)
Location: East side of Hodges Road off Bartholow Road. [A.D.C. map location: 10th Edition, page 30, grid coordinates 6C.] Cemetery no longer exists. The transcribed records were published in Carroll County Genealogical Society, *Carroll County Cemeteries*, Volume 1, Carroll County Genealogical Society, P.O. Box 1752, Westminster, MD 21158 (1989). A local resident recalled the cemetery; there was no evidence of one in 1979.

HARRIS FAMILY CEMETERY
Location: Off St. Paul Road between Houcksville and Lees Mill Roads. [A.D.C. map location: 10th Edition, page 21, grid coordinates 5G.] Abandoned. Year of earliest known death: 1846. Year of most recent death: 1875. The gravemarkers were transcribed in 1980. Location of transcribed records: Carroll County Public Library, 50 E. Main Street, Westminster, MD 21157. The transcribed records were published by Carroll County Genealogical Society, *Carroll County Cemeteries*, Volume 2, Carroll County Genealogical Society, P.O. Box 1752, Westminster, MD 21158 (1990). There are fewer than 10 tombstones.

HILTABIDEL FAMILY CEMETERY
Location: South side of Old Liberty Road (Route 850) east of Freter Road intersection. [A.D.C. map location: 10th Edition, page 29, grid coordinates 4C.] Abandoned. The gravemarkers were transcribed in 1982. Location of transcribed records: Carroll County Public Library, 50 E. Main Street, Westminster, MD 21157. These records were published in Carroll County

Genealogical Society, *Carroll County Cemeteries*, Volume 3, Carroll County Genealogical Society, P.O. Box 1752, Westminster, MD 21158 (1992). There are two footstones with initials J.H. (Jacob Hiltabidel?) and R.H.

HORN (ELIZABETH HORN) TOMBSTONE
Location: A stone was found on Arter's Mill Road near Flickinger Road, lying beside the road. Location of stone unknown in 1995. The gravemarker was transcribed in 1991. The inscription says "Elizabeth Horn, a faithful slave, 1865," possibly a hoax.

JACOBS FAMILY CEMETERY
Location: Between Slaysmans Road and Day Drive off Deer Park Road. [A.D.C. map location: 10th Edition, page 25, grid coordinates 7F.] Abandoned. Year of earliest known death: 1818. Year of most recent death: 1843. No burial records are kept. The gravemarkers were transcribed in 1984. Location of transcribed records: Carroll County Public Library, 50 Main Street, Westminster, MD 21157. The transcribed records were published in Carroll County Genealogical Society, *Carroll County Cemeteries*, Volume 2, Carroll County Genealogical Society, P.O. Box 1752, Westminster, MD 21158 (1990). There are numerous pieces of headstones. Stones were moved for plowing, then destroyed.

JOHN WILLIAMS FAMILY CEMETERY
Location: Somewhere along Emory Church Road. [A.D.C. map location: 10th Edition, page 21, grid coordinates 11F.] Additional comments: Several tombstones were reported but none located.

JONES FAMILY CEMETERY
Location: Was located along Emory Road southwest of intersection with Emory Church Road. [A.D.C. map location: 10th Edition, page 21, grid coordinates 13G.] The stones were moved to Emory Church Cemetery in 1951.

JORDAN FAMILY CEMETERY
Location: East side of Route 32 (Sykesville Road) near intersection with Nicodemus Road. [A.D.C. map location: 10th Edition, page 24, grid coordinates 7K.] Abandoned. Year of earliest known death: 1855. Year of most recent death: 1872. The gravemarkers were transcribed in 1982. Location of transcribed records: Carroll County Public Library, 50 Main Street, Westminster, MD 21157. The transcribed records were published in Carroll County Genealogical Society, *Carroll County Cemeteries*,

Volume 2, Carroll County Genealogical Society, P.O. Box 1752, Westminster, MD 21158 (1990). Additional comments: 3 Stones, only 2 are readable. Holdcraft also reported this cemetery.

KEY SLAVE CEMETERY
Location: At "Terra Rubra" on Keysville-Bruceville Road. Marked by a permanent memorial stone. [A.D.C. map location: 10th Edition, page 8, grid coordinates 7H.] No inscriptions, only fieldstones, a permanent marker now erected. Information at Carroll County Public Library, 50 Main Street, Westminster, MD. A marker was donated by F. Kale Mathias; a plot is maintained by Silver Fancy Garden Club.

KURTZ FAMILY CEMETERY
Location: West side of Old Bachman Valley Road on Myers farm property. [A.D.C. map location: 10th Edition, page 12, grid coordinates 10J.] Year of earliest known death: 1813. Year of most recent death: 1827. The gravemarkers were transcribed in 1982. Location of transcribed records: Carroll County Public Library, 50 Main Street, Westminster, MD 21157. Additional comments: Three stones, all of children.

LANDIS FAMILY CEMETERY
Location: Sam's Creek Road just north of New Windsor Road, 200 yards east of road; faces creek. [A.D.C. map location: 10th Edition, page 22, grid coordinates 3G.] Enclosed by stone wall but very overgrown. Year of earliest known death: 1831. Year of most recent death: 1855. The gravemarkers were transcribed in 1982. Location of transcribed records: Carroll County Public Library, 50 Main Street, Westminster, MD 21157. The transcribed records were published in Jacob Mehrling Holdcraft's *Names in Stone, 75,000 Cemetery Inscriptions From Frederick County, Maryland*. The Monocacy Book Company, Redwood City, CA (2nd printing, 1972). Data were transcribed between 1959 and 1962. Copied by Holdcraft, Robert Barnes and Bellinger/Manzer.

LANDIS SLAVE CEMETERY
Location: Approx. 1/4 mi. north of Landis Family Cemetery, off Sam's Creek Road. [A.D.C. map location: 10th Edition, page 22, grid coordinates 2G.] Abandoned. No grave markers have been transcribed. Additional information is available at the Carroll County Public Library, 50 Main Street, Westminster, MD 21157. Stones have been located but there are no names inscribed on them, mostly shaped fieldstones.

LEATHERWOOD FAMILY (SAMUEL LEATHERWOOD) CEMETERY

90 DIRECTORY OF MARYLAND'S BURIAL GROUNDS

(LEATHERWOOD/GUNN/FLEMING FAMILIES)
Location: On the northeast corner of intersection of Gillis Road with Route 27 (Ridge Road). [A.D.C. map location: 10th Edition, page 28, grid coordinates 3A.] The cemetery is gone; one stone in 1991. A new home was later built on the site. The cemetery (with one inscription) is described in Carroll County Genealogical Society, *Carroll County Cemeteries*, Volume 3, Carroll County Genealogical Society, P.O. Box 1752, Westminster, MD 21158 (1992). This may have been cemetery for Leatherwood, Gunn, Fleming, Warfield and Gillis families.

LEISTER FAMILY CEMETERY
Location: Off Uniontown Road east of Springdale Road, never precisely located in 1991. [A.D.C. map location: 10th Edition, page 18, grid coordinates 2G.] It was reported by Spencer Leister and Karen Dattilio.

LEMMON FAMILY CEMETERY
Location: In northern portion of triangle between Schalk Road #1 and Alesia-Lineboro Road. [A.D.C. map location: 10th Edition, page 7, grid coordinates 8A.] Abandoned. Year of earliest known death: 1814. Year of most recent death: 1823. The gravemarkers were transcribed in 1982. Location of transcribed records: Carroll County Public Library, 50 Main Street, Westminster, MD 21157. The transcribed records were published in Carroll County Genealogical Society, *Carroll County Cemeteries*, Volume 4, Carroll County Genealogical Society, P.O. Box 1752, Westminster, MD 21158 (1995). There are two stones with surnames Lemmon and Koltrider.

LINDSAY FAMILY CEMETERY
Location: Between Route 27 and Bloom Road north of Baker Road. [A.D.C. map location: 10th Edition, page 23, grid coordinates 9H.] In 1982 it was fenced and well-maintained. Year of earliest known death: 1819. Year of most recent death: 1891. There are approximately 8 stones, copied by several individuals. The gravemarkers were transcribed in 1982. Location of transcribed records: Carroll County Public Library, 50 E. Main Street, Westminster, MD 21157. The transcribed records were published in Jacob Mehrling Holdcraft's *Names in Stone, 75,000 Cemetery Inscriptions From Frederick County, Maryland*. The Monocacy Book Company, Redwood City, CA (2nd printing, 1972). Data were transcribed between 1959 and 1962.

LOGHOUSE CEMETERY
Location: Between Davis Road and Woodbine Road north of Gillis Falls

Road. [A.D.C. map location: 10th Edition, page 28, grid coordinates 9E?.] The cemetery has disappeared; it was on Lot #3 of the tract, *Batchelor's Refuge*, patented in 1813. It was reported to have 4 stones; located in Gillis Falls watershed.

LYNN FAMILY CEMETERY
Location: South side of Middleburg Road directly opposite Bowling Brook/Walden Farm. [A.D.C. map location: 10th Edition, page 16, grid coordinates 1E.] Year of earliest known death: 1827. Year of most recent death: 1895. The transcribed records were published in Jacob Mehrling Holdcraft's *Names in Stone, 75,000 Cemetery Inscriptions From Frederick County, Maryland*. The Monocacy Book Company, Redwood City, CA (2nd printing, 1972). Data were transcribed between 1959 and 1962. Surnames: Koons, Lynn.

MANRO/CONNER FAMILIES CEMETERY
Location: On Strawbridge Terrace off Route 32 (Sykesville Road), in Strawbridge Estates Development. [A.D.C. map location: 10th Edition, page 30, grid coordinates 7C.] The cemetery has disappeared; there are two stones that have been relocated to Trinity Episcopal Cemetery. Year of earliest known death: 1845. The gravemarkers were transcribed in 1991. Location of transcribed records: Carroll County Public Library, 50 Main Street, Westminster, MD 21157. The records have not been published. Two stones were rescued from the construction site in Strawbridge Estates. Both surnames were Manro.

MILLER FAMILY CEMETERY
Location: Near #4001 London Bridge Road off Route 32 (Sykesville Road). [A.D.C. map location: 10th Edition, page 25, grid coordinates 12C.] Abandoned. Year of earliest known death: 1855. No burial records are kept. The gravemarkers were transcribed in 1982. Location of transcribed records: Carroll County Public Library, 50 E. Main Street, Westminster, MD 21157. The transcribed records were published by Carroll County Genealogical Society, *Carroll County Cemeteries*, Volume 2, Carroll County Genealogical Society, P.O. Box 1752, Westminster, MD 21158 (1990). There are supposedly 12 graves. Only one was found; it was the grave of Thomas Miller.

MYERS FAMILY (ANDREW MYERS) CEMETERY
Location: Off Frizzellburg Road about 3/4 mi. south of Frizzellburg and 1/2 mi. east of road. [A.D.C. map location: 10th Edition, page 11, grid coordinates 12F?.] Abandoned. Stones have fallen. Year of earliest known

death: 1828. Year of most recent death: 1883. The gravemarkers were transcribed in 1987. Location of transcribed records: Carroll County Public Library, 50 Main Street, Westminster, MD 21157. Cemetery appears on topography map. Surnames: Myers, Huntz.

NICODEMUS FAMILY CEMETERY
Location: Southwest corner of Bowersox and Nicodemus Roads. [A.D.C. map location: 10th Edition, page 18, grid coordinates 13H.] Abandoned. Year of earliest known death: 1801. Year of most recent death: 1879. Gravemarkers were transcribed in 1959. Location of transcribed records: Carroll County Public Library, 50 Main Street, Westminster, MD 21157. The transcribed records were published in Jacob Mehrling Holdcraft's *Names in Stone, 75,000 Cemetery Inscriptions From Frederick County, Maryland*. The Monocacy Book Company, Redwood City, CA (2nd printing, 1972). Data were transcribed between 1959 and 1962. Corrections to Holdcraft have been made.

NUSBAUM CEMETERY (RUNNYMEADE CEMETERY (?))
Location: East side of Baust Church Road off Route 832 near Tyrone. [A.D.C. map location: 10th Edition, page 11, grid coordinates 9A.] Abandoned. Some of the same names appear in Runnymeade and Nusbaum Cemeteries. Year of earliest known death: 1797. Year of most recent death: 1853. No burial records are kept. The gravemarkers were transcribed in 1983. Location of transcribed records: Carroll County Public Library, 50 Main Street, Westminster, MD 21157. The records were published by Mary Baumgardner in *Bulletin of the Seattle Genealogical Society*, Volume: 15-3, Seattle Genealogical Society, Seattle, Washington (1955). Surnames include Babylon, Foutz, Youn, Kitzmiller (may be same as Runnymeade Cemetery).

NUSBAUM/NICODEMUS FAMILIES CEMETERY
Location: South side of New Windsor on hill above railroad tracks and north of road. [A.D.C. map location: 10th Edition, page 18, grid coordinates 11A.] Year of earliest known death: 1837. Year of most recent death: 1857. The gravemarkers were transcribed in 1958. Location of transcribed records: Carroll County Public Library, 50 Main Street, Westminster, MD 21157. The transcribed records were published in Jacob Mehrling Holdcraft's *Names in Stone, 75,000 Cemetery Inscriptions From Frederick County, Maryland*. The Monocacy Book Company, Redwood City, CA (2nd printing, 1972). Data were transcribed between 1959 and 1962. Surnames: Nicodemus and Nusbaum.

CARROLL COUNTY CEMETERIES - PRIVATE   93

OGG FAMILY CEMETERY
Location: On northwest side of Bird View Road near Holliday Lane; cemetery has now disappeared. [A.D.C. map location: 10th Edition, page 25, grid coordinates 6C.] Relocated to Deer Park U.M. Church Cemetery. Year of earliest known death: 1856. Year of most recent death: 1888. The gravemarkers were transcribed in 1990. Location of transcribed records: Carroll County Public Library, 50 Main Street, Westminster, MD 21157. The transcribed records were published in Carroll County Genealogical Society, *Carroll County Cemeteries*, Volume 2, Carroll County Genealogical Society, P.O. Box 1752, Westminster, MD 21158 (1990). The land was sold by the Ogg family in 1887 but had been in family's possession over 100 yrs.

OKLAHOMA ROAD CEMETERY
Location: On Oklahoma Road just north of Route 26. The cemetery has disappeared. [A.D.C. map location: 10th Edition, page 30, grid coordinates 10G.] The site is mentioned in Carroll County Genealogical Society, *Carroll County Cemeteries*, Volume 1, Carroll County Genealogical Society, P.O. Box 1752, Westminster, MD 21158 (1989). There was some evidence unearthed in 1982.

OWINGS FAMILY CEMETERY
Location: Northwest side of the intersection between Nicodemus and Salem Bottom Roads. [A.D.C. map location: 10th Edition, page 24, grid coordinates 5C.] Year of earliest known death: 1845. Year of most recent death: 1955. No burial records are kept. The gravemarkers were transcribed in 1982. Location of transcribed records: Carroll County Public Library, 50 E. Main Street, Westminster, MD 21157. The records have not been published.

OWINGS FAMILY CEMETERY
Location: Off Warfieldsburg Road near Bertie Avenue. [A.D.C. map location: 10th Edition, page 24, grid coordinates 1E.] Condition/description of cemetery: Abandoned. Year of earliest known death: 1845. Year of most recent death: 1889. No burial records are kept. The gravemarkers were transcribed in 1982. Location of transcribed records: Carroll County Public Library, 50 E. Main Street, Westminster. The records have not been published. Five stones have been found.

OWINGS SLAVE CEMETERY
Location: East of Ridge Road and west of Marriottsville Road in southeast Carroll County. [A.D.C. map location: 10th Edition, page 30, grid

coordinates 12H.] Except for the location nothing is known about this cemetery.

PATTERSON FAMILY CEMETERY (SUNNYSIDE CEMETERY)
Location: On Springfield State Hospital grounds. [A.D.C. map location: 10th Edition, page 35, grid coordinates 1C.] The cemetery has disappeared. The graveyard was mentioned in Tracey records of Historical Society of Carroll County. The transcribed records were published in Carroll County Genealogical Society, *Carroll County Cemeteries*, Volume 1, Carroll County Genealogical Society, P.O. Box 1752, Westminster, MD 21158 (1989).

PHILLIPS FAMILY CEMETERY (ELIZABETH J. AND IDA M. PHILLIPS FAMILY CEMETERY)
Location: East side of Mineral Hill Road opposite the intersection of Oklahoma Road. [A.D.C. map location: 10th Edition, page 30, grid coordinates 7J.] The cemetery is referenced in land records, Liber 112, Folio 391. The site is discussed in Carroll County Genealogical Society, *Carroll County Cemeteries*, Volume 1, Carroll County Genealogical Society, P.O. Box 1752, Westminster, MD 21158 (1989). Carroll Phillips stated that a sister and some slaves were buried here. The property now belongs to the Catholic Archdiocese of Baltimore.

PICKETT FAMILY CEMETERY #1
Location: South side of Gillis Road as it intersects Route 27 (Ridge Road) [A.D.C. map location: 10th Edition, page 28, grid coordinates 3A.] Cemetery has disappeared; it stood on the tract, *Peter's Garden Enlarged*, which was patented in 1795.

PICKETT FAMILY CEMETERY #2
Location: South side of Gillis Road between Bethel and Woodbine Roads. It was located on the tract of Lot #2 of *Batchelor's Refuge*, patented in 1813. [A.D.C. map location: 10th Edition, page 28, grid coordinates 9G.] The cemetery was owned by W. Pickett in 1862. Annie Pickett was buried here in 1924.

PLOWMAN FAMILY CEMETERY
Location: Between Coon Club and Leister's Church Roads just east of Gorsuch Road. [A.D.C. map location: 10th Edition, page 20, grid coordinates 2G.] By 1993 the cemetery had disappeared. There is information at Carroll County Public Library, 50 Main Street, Westminster, MD 21157.

CARROLL COUNTY CEMETERIES - PRIVATE 95

POOL/FLEMING FAMILIES CEMETERY (ALSO FLEMING/GOSNELL CEMETERY (BY HOLDCRAFT, 5 STONES))
Location: At the "Y" where Gillis Falls and Cabbage Spring Roads join. [D.C. map location: 10th Edition, page 28, grid coordinates 9A.] Abandoned. Year of earliest known death: 1870. Year of most recent death: 1911. The gravemarkers were transcribed in 1991. Location of transcribed records: Carroll County Public Library, 50 Main Street, Westminster, MD 21157. The transcribed records were published in Carroll County Genealogical Society, *Carroll County Cemeteries*, Volume 3, Carroll County Genealogical Society, P.O. Box 1752, Westminster, MD 21158 (1992) including those found by Holdcraft but no longer in evidence.

POULSON FAMILY CEMETERY
Location: Off Nicodemus Road near intersection with Brick Church Road. [A.D.C. map location: 10th Edition, page 18, grid coordinates 11G.] The cemetery was relocated to Stone Chapel U.M. Cemetery with stones laid flat. Year of earliest known death: 1781. Year of most recent death: 1850. The gravemarkers were transcribed in 1983. Location of transcribed records: Carroll County Public Library, 50 Main Street, Westminster, MD 21157. Surnames: Poulson, Leaming, Franklin, Durbin, Dell.

RICHARDS FAMILY (DANIEL RICHARDS) CEMETERY
Location: Between Houcksville Road and Route 30 north of St. Paul Road. [A.D.C. map location: 10th Edition, page 21, grid coordinates 4G.] Abandoned. Year of earliest known death: 1855. The gravemarkers were transcribed in 1981. Location of transcribed records: Carroll County Public Library, 50 Main Street, Westminster, MD 21157. The transcribed records were published in Carroll County Genealogical Society, *Carroll County Cemeteries*, Volume 4, Carroll County Genealogical Society, P.O. Box 1752, Westminster, MD 21158 (1995). Additional comments: A few stones, some native stones with no inscriptions. A founding family of the area.

RICHARDS FAMILY (GEORGE RICHARDS) CEMETERY
Location: West of Highfield Drive near Shiloh Road in Hampstead. [A.D.C. map location: 10th Edition, page 14, grid coordinates 12G.] Abandoned. Year of earliest known death: 1835. Year of most recent death: 186? George Richards is buried here. No burial records are kept. The gravemarkers were transcribed in 1981. Location of transcribed records: Carroll County Public Library, 50 E. Main Street, Westminster, MD 21157. These records were published in Carroll County Genealogical Society, *Carroll County Cemeteries*, Volume 4, Carroll County

Genealogical Society, P.O. Box 1752, Westminster, MD 21158 (1995). Additional comments: To be restored in 1995-96.

RUNNYMEADE CEMETERY (NUSBAUM CEMETERY (?))
Location: East side of Baust Church Road off Route 832 near Tyrone. [A.D.C. map location: 10th Edition, page 10, grid coordinates 9K.] Abandoned. Tombstones are widely scattered on farm. Year of earliest known death: 1785. Year of most recent death: 1852. The gravemarkers were transcribed in 1987. Location of transcribed records: Carroll County Public Library, 50 Main Street, Westminster, MD 21157. The records were published by Mary Baumgardner in *Bulletin of the Seattle Genealogical Society*, Volume: 15-3, published by Seattle Genealogical Society, Seattle, Washington (1966). Surnames: Foutz, Babylon, Yon, Barnhard, etc.

SATER FAMILY CEMETERY
Location: On Schalk Road #2 just west of where it crosses railroad tracks, near pond. [A.D.C. map location: 10th Edition, page 6, grid coordinates 11J.] Abandoned. Year of earliest known death: 1830. Year of most recent death: 1864. The gravemarkers were transcribed in 1982. Location of transcribed records: Carroll County Public Library, 50 Main Street, Westminster, MD 21157. The transcribed records were published in Carroll County Genealogical Society, *Carroll County Cemeteries*, Volume 4, Carroll County Genealogical Society, P.O. Box 1752, Westminster, MD 21158 (1995). Two stones. Surnames: Sater and Shuman.

SENSENEY FAMILY CEMETERY
Location: Junction of Priestland and McKinstry's Mill Roads, directly adjoining the road. [A.D.C. map location: 10th Edition, page 17, grid coordinates 9C.] Year of earliest known death: 1801. Year of most recent death: 1860. The gravemarkers were transcribed in 1959. Location of transcribed records: Carroll County Public Library, 50 Main Street, Westminster, MD 21157. The transcribed records were published in Jacob Mehrling Holdcraft's *Names in Stone, 75,000 Cemetery Inscriptions From Frederick County, Maryland*. The Monocacy Book Company, Redwood City, CA (2nd printing, 1972). Data were transcribed between 1959 and 1962. Surnames: Senseney, Swigart(?), Carroll, Cook.

SHIPLEY CEMETERY (PETER SHIPLEY) CEMETERY
Location: Off Church Street near intersection with Flohr Avenue in Sykesville/Flohrville. [A.D.C. map location: 10th Edition, page 30, grid

coordinates 11A.] There is a single stone in an old barn, "J. Cary," year of death: 1823. The gravemarker was transcribed in 1982. Location of transcribed records: Carroll County Public Library, 50 Main Street, Westminster, MD 21157 and published in Carroll County Genealogical Society, *Carroll County Cemeteries*, Volume 1, Carroll County Genealogical Society, P.O. Box 1752, Westminster, MD 21158 (1989). Peter Shipley, who died c1756, is thought to be buried here.

SHIPLEY FAMILY (HENRY BASKUM SHIPLEY) CEMETERY (LEWIS SHIPLEY FAMILY CEMETERY)
Location: East side of Gorsuch Switch Road south of Arrington Road. [A.D.C. map location: 10th Edition, page 35, grid coordinates 3F.] It was mentioned in a deed of 1865, Liber 32, Folio 106 (Carroll County) The site is discussed in Carroll County Genealogical Society, *Carroll County Cemeteries*, Volume 1, Carroll County Genealogical Society, P.O. Box 1752, Westminster, MD 21158 (1989).

SHIPLEY FAMILY (JOHN SHIPLEY) CEMETERY
Location: This cemetery was formerly located on north side of Bethel Road west of Woodbine Road. [A.D.C. map location: 10th Edition, page 28, grid coordinates 6G.] The cemetery was part of John Gillis' estate, deeded to Aramina Shipley in 1813.

SHRIVER FAMILY CEMETERY
Location: Old New Windsor Pike off Route 31 before Luther Drive. [A.D.C. map location: 10th Edition, page 18, grid coordinates 7K.] Walled cemetery, well maintained in 1982. Year of earliest known death: 1812. Year of most recent death: 1902. No burial records are kept. Gravemarkers were transcribed in 1982. Location of transcribed records: Carroll County Public Library, 50 E. Main St, Westminster. The transcribed records were published in Jacob Mehrling Holdcraft's *Names in Stone, 75,000 Cemetery Inscriptions From Frederick County, Maryland*. The Monocacy Book Company, Redwood City, CA (2nd printing, 1972). Data were transcribed between 1959 and 1962.

SHUE FAMILY CEMETERY
Location: Along St. Paul's Road northwest of intersection with Shaffer Mill Road. [A.D.C. map location: 10th Edition, page 7, grid coordinates 4G.] Abandoned. Year of earliest known death: 1818. Year of most recent death: 1903. The gravemarkers were transcribed in 1982. Location of transcribed records: Carroll County Public Library, 50 Main Street, Westminster, MD 21157. The transcribed records were published in

Carroll County Genealogical Society, *Carroll County Cemeteries*, Volume 4, Carroll County Genealogical Society, P.O. Box 1752, Westminster, MD 21158 (1995). Surnames include Shue, Williams, Zimmerman, Fisher, Steffey

SIXES BRIDGE AREA CEMETERY
Location: Just east of the point where Sixes Bridge Road crosses Monocacy River. [A.D.C. map location: 10th Edition, page 8, grid coordinates 7C.] It was reputed to be here 100 years ago. There is some information on the cemetery at Carroll County Public Library, 50 Main Street, Westminster, MD 21157. M. Helen Six stated that there were two cemeteries in this general area. Neither was visible in 1990s.

SLAVE CEMETERY
Location: 1000 feet east of Route 32 along London Town Boulevard at the site of London Fog Building. The cemetery no longer exists. [A.D.C. map location: 10th Edition, page 30, grid coordinates 9D.] This cemetery is discussed in Carroll County Genealogical Society, *Carroll County Cemeteries*, Volume 1, Carroll County Genealogical Society, P.O. Box 1752, Westminster, MD 21158 (1989). There were some fieldstones among the fruit trees on the site that was once the Bevard Farm.

SNOWDEN FAMILY CEMETERY
Location: North of Liberty Road, south of Barnes Lane and east of Oakland Mills Road. [A.D.C. map location: 10th Edition, page 30, grid coordinates 10K.] The cemetery was mentioned in an old deed as the family cemetery on the land of F. Snowden. The site is discussed in Carroll County Genealogical Society, *Carroll County Cemeteries*, Volume 1, Carroll County Genealogical Society, P.O. Box 1752, Westminster, MD 21158 (1989).

SPENCER FAMILY CEMETERY
Location: West side of Brown Road (off Route 140) near Roaring Run Creek. [A.D.C. map location: 10th Edition, page 26, grid coordinates 2A.] The site is in the middle of a field. For more details see Carroll County Genealogical Society, *Carroll County Cemeteries*, Volume 2, Carroll County Genealogical Society, P.O. Box 1752, Westminster, MD 21158 (1990). Carl R. Spencer of Finksburg stated (c1990) that there were originally three gravestones, but that they were plowed over many years earlier. The site is in the middle of a field.

CARROLL COUNTY CEMETERIES - PRIVATE

SPURRIER FAMILY CEMETERY
Location: North of Boteler Road between Ridge and Runkles Roads on Joseph Spurrier farm. [A.D.C. map location: 10th Edition, page 27, grid coordinates 12G ?.] The cemetery has disappeared. Greenbury Spurrier was buried here in 1866, a War of 1812 veteran (See *Democratic Advocate*).

STANSBURY FAMILY CEMETERY (ALSO LAWSON FAMILY CEMETERY)
Location: East side of Young Road northwest of Village of Millers. [A.D.C. map location: 10th Edition, page 6, grid coordinates 12H.] A row of stones standing on the edge of a field. Year of earliest known death: 1809. Year of most recent death: 1889. The gravemarkers were transcribed in 1982. Location of transcribed records: Carroll County Public Library, 50 Main Street, Westminster, MD 21157. The transcribed records were published in Carroll County Genealogical Society, *Carroll County Cemeteries*, Volume 4, Carroll County Genealogical Society, P.O. Box 1752, Westminster, MD 21158 (1995). Surnames include Lawson, Stansbury, Face and Miller.

STEVENSON FAMILY CEMETERY
Location: East side of Route 27 (south of Westminster) between Spring Mills and Kate Wagner Roads, on the farm of Carl Hoff (1995). [A.D.C. map location: 10th Edition, page 19, grid coordinates 9D.] Walled cemetery still exists but the stones have been removed to Krider's Cemetery. Year of earliest known death: 1841. Year of most recent death: 1893. The gravemarkers were transcribed in 1995. Location of transcribed records: Carroll County Public Library, 50 E. Main Street, Westminster, MD 21157. The records have not been published.

STOCKSDALE FAMILY CEMETERY
Location: North side of Deer Park Road between Kay's Mill Road and Route 91. [A.D.C. map location: 10th Edition, page 25, grid coordinates 9J.] Abandoned. Year of earliest known death: 1854. The gravemarker (one gravestone) was transcribed in 1982. Location of transcribed records: Carroll County Public Library, 50 E. Main St. Westminster, MD 21157. The transcribed records were published by Carroll County Genealogical Society, in *Carroll County Cemeteries*, Volume 2, Carroll County Genealogical Society, P.O. Box 1752, Westminster, MD 21158 (1990).

STORMS FAMILY CEMETERY
Location: Northeast corner of intersection of Coon Club Road with

Gorsuch Road. [A.D.C. map location: 10th Edition, page 20, grid coordinates 2G.]. The land belonged to Jacob Storm(s). Abandoned. Only three headstones, two footstones. Year of earliest known death: 1816. Year of most recent death: 1853. The gravemarkers were transcribed in 1991. Location of transcribed records: Carroll County Public Library, 50 Main Street, Westminster, MD 21157. The transcribed records were published in Carroll County Genealogical Society, *Carroll County Cemeteries*, Volume 4, Carroll County Genealogical Society, P.O. Box 1752, Westminster, MD 21158 (1995).

STREVIG FAMILY CEMETERY
Location: About 2.2 miles east of Route 30 on south side of Tracey's Mill Road. [A.D.C. map location: 10th Edition, page 6, grid coordinates 6E.] Abandoned; cemetery difficult to locate without help; partially walled. Year of earliest known death: 1844. Year of most recent death: 1854. The gravemarkers were transcribed in 1994. Location of transcribed records: Carroll County Public Library, 50 Main Street, Westminster, MD 21157. The transcribed records were published in Carroll County Genealogical Society, *Carroll County Cemeteries*, Volume 4, Carroll County Genealogical Society, P.O. Box 1752, Westminster, MD 21158 (1995). There are three graves, one tombstone is inscribed in German.

TAYLOR/ULRICH FAMILIES CEMETERY
Location: South side of Ridge Road between Patapsco and Carrollton Roads. [A.D.C. map location: 10th Edition, page 21, grid coordinates 9B.] Abandoned. Year of earliest known death: 1858. The gravemarkers were transcribed in 1982. Location of transcribed records: Carroll County Public Library, 50 Main Street, Westminster, MD 21157. The transcribed records were published in Carroll County Genealogical Society, *Carroll County Cemeteries*, Volume 2, Carroll County Genealogical Society, P.O. Box 1752, Westminster, MD 21158 (1990). Includes native stones plus carved stones. A Taylor married an Ulrich.

TENER/HOOPER FAMILY CEMETERY
Location: South side of Old Liberty Road west of Skidmore Road intersection, near Taylorsville. [A.D.C. map location: 10th Edition, page 28, grid coordinates 1E.] Abandoned. Year of earliest known death: 1804. Year of most recent death: 1904. The gravemarkers were transcribed in 1982. Location of transcribed records: Carroll County Public Library, 50 Main Street, Westminster, MD 21157. The records were published in Jacob Mehrling Holdcraft's *Names in Stone, 75,000 Cemetery Inscriptions From Frederick County, Maryland*. The Monocacy Book Company,

Redwood City, CA (2nd printing, 1972). Data were transcribed between 1959 and 1962. Surnames: Hooper, Tener, Zile.

TEVIS/ROBOSSON AND SHIPLEY FAMILIES CEMETERY
Location: East of Marriottsville Road and west of western fork of Liberty Reservoir. [A.D.C. map location: 10th Edition, page 30, grid coordinates 12J.] The will of M.A. Shipley (1890) mentions a family graveyard (Book 6, page 377). The site is discussed in Carroll County Genealogical Society, *Carroll County Cemeteries*, Volume 1, Carroll County Genealogical Society, P.O. Box 1752, Westminster, MD 21158 (1989).

TOOP'S CEMETERY
Location: Disappeared. It was located where Route 31 (New Windsor Road) and Fenby Farm Road intersected. [A.D.C. map location: 10th Edition, page 19, grid coordinates 6C.] Most stones were relocated to Strawbridge U.M. Church Cemetery near New Windsor. Year of earliest known death: 1859. Year of most recent death: 1883. Location of transcribed records: Carroll County Public Library, 50 Main Street, Westminster, MD 21157. The records have not been published.
This is a African-American cemetery. Surnames: Pye, Snowden, Woodyard, Brown, Clark, Hollingsworth.

WAREHIME FAMILY CEMETERY
Location: This cemetery has not been located; it is supposedly between Bell and Rockland Roads on the land belonging to B. Bryson (1990s). [A.D.C. map location: 10th Edition, page 18, grid coordinates 6J.]

WARNER FAMILY (JOHN WARNER) CEMETERY
Location: On south side of Uniontown Road across from intersection of Morelock Schoolhouse Road. [A.D.C. map location: 10th Edition, page 18, grid coordinates 3G.] Abandoned. Year of earliest known death: 1811. Year of most recent death: 1827. The gravemarkers were transcribed in 1991. Location of transcribed records: Carroll County Public Library, 50 Main Street, Westminster, MD 21157. The records have not been published. Surnames: John Warner and Rebecca Warner.

WAYS FAMILY CEMETERY
Location: West side of Woodbine Road south of intersection with Gillis Falls Road. [A.D.C. map location: 10th Edition, page 33, grid coordinates 1G.] The cemetery has disappeared; it was shown on the 1949 map. In 1877 John Ways owned land here.

WELLS FAMILY CEMETERY

Location: West side of Route 27 (Ridge Road) between Chapel Road and Rolling Ridge Drive. [A.D.C. map location: 10th Edition, page 19, grid coordinates 11C.] Abandoned. Year of earliest known death: 1769. Year of most recent death: 1828. Location of transcribed records: Carroll County Public Library, 50 Main Street, Westminster, MD 21157. The transcribed records were published in Jacob Mehrling Holdcraft's *Names in Stone, 75,000 Cemetery Inscriptions From Frederick County, Maryland*. The Monocacy Book Company, Redwood City, CA (2nd printing, 1972). Data were transcribed between 1959 and 1962. Surnames: Wells, Turfell. The Wells stone at Krider's Cemetery was supposedly brought from Stevenson Family Cemetery.

WELSH/PENN/BARNES FAMILIES CEMETERY

Location: Between Streaker and Fannie Dorsey Roads east of Woodbine Road. [A.D.C. map location: 10th Edition, page 28, grid coordinates 8K.] Abandoned. Year of earliest known death: 1831. Year of most recent death: 1883. The gravemarkers were transcribed in 1983. Location of transcribed records: Carroll County Public Library, 50 Main Street, Westminster, MD 21157. The transcribed records were published in Carroll County Genealogical Society, *Carroll County Cemeteries*, Volume 3, Carroll County Genealogical Society, P.O. Box 1752, Westminster, MD 21158 (1992). Additional comments: It is widely known that there are many more people buried here than 5 graves as recorded.

WIGHT FAMILY (RICHARD WIGHT) CEMETERY

Location: Southeast side of Slacks Road off Ridge Road in southeastern part of county [A.D.C. map location: 10th Edition, page 30, grid coordinates 12F.] Abandoned. Year of earliest known death: 1819. Year of most recent death: 1865. The gravemarkers were transcribed in 1983. Location of transcribed records: Carroll County Public Library, 50 Main Street, Westminster, MD 21157. The transcribed records were published in Carroll County Genealogical Society, *Carroll County Cemeteries*, Volume 1, Carroll County Genealogical Society, P.O. Box 1752, Westminster, MD 21158 (1989). Surnames: Wight, Gelley And McCullough; 3 stones.

WILSON FAMILY (NICHOLAS WILSON) CEMETERY

Location: West side of Klees Mill Road just north of Liberty Road in Industrial Park. [A.D.C. map location: 10th Edition, page 29, grid coordinates 5G.] The cemetery no longer exists but Wilson Family members recall tombstones. The transcribed records were published in

CARROLL COUNTY CEMETERIES - PRIVATE

Carroll County Genealogical Society, *Carroll County Cemeteries*, Volume 1, Carroll County Genealogical Society, P.O. Box 1752, Westminster, MD 21158 (1989).

WISNER FAMILY CEMETERY
Location: Between Lake Drive and Bankard Road near Pennsylvania line. [A.D.C. map location: 10th Edition, page 4, grid coordinates 7J.] Abandoned. Year of earliest known death: 1794. Year of most recent death: 1890. The gravemarkers were transcribed in 1983. Location of transcribed records: Carroll County Public Library, 50 Main Street, Westminster, MD 21157. There is one stone (Christopher Wisner) plus broken fieldstone with date 1794.

YOHN FAMILY CEMETERY
Location : On south side of Baker Road between Bloom Road and Ridge Road (Route 27) [A.D.C. map location: 10th Edition, page 23, grid coordinates 10H.] Abandoned. There were two stones in 1991, but there had been more. Year of earliest known death: 1847. Year of most recent death: 1871. The gravemarkers were transcribed in 1991. Location of transcribed records: Carroll County Public Library, 50 Main Street, Westminster, MD 21157. The records have not been published. Surnames: Yohn. The land was given by L. Wampler to daughter Mary W. Yohn (relict of John).

Church Cemeteries

ALESIA FREE METHODIST CEMETERY
Location: At the "Y" where Schalk Road #1 and the Alesia-Lineboro Road intersect. [A.D.C. map location: 10th Edition, page 6, grid coordinates 9K.] The cemetery is well-maintained. The gravemarkers were transcribed in 1989. Location of transcribed records: Carroll County Public Library, 50 Main Street, Westminster, MD 21157. The transcribed records were published in Carroll County Genealogical Society, *Carroll County Cemeteries*, Volume 4, Carroll County Genealogical Society, P.O. Box 1752, Westminster, MD 21158 (1995). There are about 40 Inscriptions - Surnames: Whalen, Yelton, Frederick, Gouge, and others.

ASCENSION EPISCOPAL CHURCH CEMETERY
Location: Behind church on N. Court Street in Westminster. [A.D.C. map location: 10th Edition, page 19, grid coordinates 5H.] This is a very small, well-maintained cemetery. Year of earliest known death: 1796. Year of

most recent death: 1937. Leigh Masters is buried here. The gravemarkers were transcribed in 1983. Location of transcribed records: Carroll County Public Library, 50 Main Street, Westminster, MD 21157. A partial listing is included in Scharf's *History of Western Maryland*. Includes confederate soldier grave. Mailing address: Ascension Episcopal Church, 23 N. Court Street, Westminster, MD 21157-0000.

BAPTIST ROAD CEMETERY
Location: East side of Baptist Road at intersection with Route 140 (Taneytown Pike) [A.D.C. map location: 10th Edition, page 1, grid coordinates 13F.] It was well-maintained in 1980s when last visited. Year of earliest known death: 1802. Year of most recent death: 1921. The gravemarkers were transcribed in 1982. Location of transcribed records: Carroll County Public Library, 50 E. Main Street, Westminster MD 21157. The transcribed records were published in Jacob Mehrling Holdcraft's *Names in Stone, 75,000 Cemetery Inscriptions From Frederick County, Maryland*. The Monocacy Book Company, Redwood City, CA (2nd printing, 1972). Data were transcribed between 1959 and 1962.

BAUST UNITED CHURCH OF CHRIST CEMETERY (EMMANUEL (BAUST) U.C. OF C.)
Location: On Old Taneytown Road (Route 832) About 1/2 mile west of Village of Tyrone. [A.D.C. map location: 10th Edition, page 11, grid coordinates 9A.] This cemetery is well-maintained. One section with very old stones, some in German. Year of earliest known death: 1790. Veterans interred: Revolutionary War and Civil War. The gravemarkers were transcribed in 1983. Location of transcribed records: Carroll County Public Library, 50 Main Street, Westminster, MD 21157. Some old burials were included in Scharf's *History of Western Maryland* from 1882. Cemetery's mailing address: Baust United Church of Christ, 2950 Old Taneytown Road, Taneytown, MD 21787-0000.

BETH JACOB CONGREGATION CEMETERY
Location: On South side of Route 140 Just west of intersection with Gamber Road (Route 91) [A.D.C. map location: 10th Edition, page 26, grid coordinates 6B.] Cemetery is well-maintained. Year of earliest known death: 1959. Burials of Baltimore Hebrew Community. Mailing address: Beth Jacob Congregation, 5713 Park Heights Avenue, Baltimore, MD 21215-0000.

BETHANY METHODIST EPISCOPAL CHURCH CEMETERY
Location: West side of Hooper Road about 600 feet north of Route 26

(Liberty Road) [A.D.C. map location: 10th Edition, page 23, grid coordinates 11A.] This is a moderately well-maintained cemetery on hill top; the church is gone. Year of earliest known death: circa 1870. No burial records are kept. The gravemarkers were transcribed in 1957. The transcribed records were published in Jacob Mehrling Holdcraft's *Names in Stone, 75,000 Cemetery Inscriptions From Frederick County, Maryland*. The Monocacy Book Company, Redwood City, CA (2nd printing, 1972). Data were transcribed between 1959 and 1962. Holdcraft recorded 189 names.

BETHEL-CARROLLTON CHURCH OF GOD CEMETERY (UNION BETHEL CHURCH)
Location: At intersection of Bethel, Carrollton and Patapsco Roads. [A.D.C. map location: 10th Edition, page 20, grid coordinates 10J.] Cemetery is well-maintained. Year of earliest known death: 1867. The gravemarkers were transcribed in 1990. Location of transcribed records: Carroll County Public Library, 50 Main Street, Westminster, MD 21157. The transcribed records were published in Carroll County Genealogical Society, *Carroll County Cemeteries*, Volume 2, Carroll County Genealogical Society, P.O. Box 1752, Westminster, MD 21158 (1990).

BETHEL UNITED METHODIST CHURCH CEMETERY
Location: At intersection of Sam's Creek and Hooper Roads near Frederick County line. [A.D.C. map location: 10th Edition, page 22, grid coordinates 6K.] The cemetery needs some attention, some interesting old stones. Year of earliest known death: 1810. The gravemarkers were transcribed in 1957. The transcribed records were published in Jacob Mehrling Holdcraft's *Names in Stone, 75,000 Cemetery Inscriptions From Frederick County, Maryland*. The Monocacy Book Company, Redwood City, CA (2nd printing, 1972). Data were transcribed between 1959 and 1962. Holdcraft copied 405 names. Mailing address: 3001 Hooper Road, New Windsor, MD 21776-0000.

BETHESDA UNITED METHODIST CHURCH CEMETERY
Location: On Klees Mill Road just southwest of intersection of Cherry Tree Lane [A.D.C. map location: 10th Edition, page 24, grid coordinates 13J.] Cemetery is well-maintained. Year of earliest known death: 1837 The gravemarkers were transcribed in 1984. Location of transcribed records: Carroll County Public Library, 50 Main Street, Westminster, MD 21157. The transcribed records were published in Carroll County Genealogical Society, *Carroll County Cemeteries*, Volume 2, Carroll County Genealogical Society, P.O. Box 1752, Westminster, MD 21158

(1990). A parsonage is located next to church and the caretaker has burial records.

BIXLER'S UNITED METHODIST CHURCH CEMETERY (UNITED BRETHREN)
Location: On Bixler's Church Road off Bachman's Valley Road (Route 496), cemetery beside church. [A.D.C. map location: 10th Edition, page 13, grid coordinates 1C.] The cemetery is well-maintained. Year of earliest known death: 1853. The gravemarkers were transcribed in 1992. Location of transcribed records: Carroll County Public Library, 50 Main Street, Westminster, MD 21157. The transcribed records were published in Carroll County Genealogical Society, *Carroll County Cemeteries*, Volume 4, Carroll County Genealogical Society, P.O. Box 1752, Westminster, MD 21158 (1995). Additional comments: May have originally been Bixler Family Cemetery. Approx. 100 stones with inscriptions. Mailing address: Bixler's U.M. Church, 3282 Charmil Drive, Manchester, MD 21102-0000.

BRANDENBURG UNITED METHODIST CHURCH CEMETERY
Location: On Old Washington Road at intersection with Streaker Road in the town of Berrett. [A.D.C. map location: 10th Edition, page 29, grid coordinates 9D.] Cemetery is well-maintained. Year of earliest known death: 1878. The gravemarkers were transcribed in 1991. Location of transcribed records: Carroll County Public Library, 50 Main Street, Westminster, MD 21157. The transcribed records were published in Carroll County Genealogical Society, *Carroll County Cemeteries*, Volume 3, Carroll County Genealogical Society, P.O. Box 1752, Westminster, MD 21158 (1992). Mailing Address: Brandenburg U.M. Church, 6050 Old Washington Road, Sykesville, MD 21784-0000.

CHARITY MEETING HOUSE CEMETERY
Location: Between Old Westminster Pike and Route 140 (Baltimore Boulevard) opposite Bollinger Road. [A.D.C. map location: 10th Edition, page 20, grid coordinates 12G.] Cemetery abandoned. Year of earliest known death: 1811. The gravemarkers were transcribed in 1982. Location of transcribed records: Carroll County Public Library, 50 Main Street, Westminster, MD 21157. The transcribed records were published in Carroll County Genealogical Society, *Carroll County Cemeteries*, Volume 2, Carroll County Genealogical Society, P.O. Box 1752, Westminster, MD 21158 (1990). Surname: Oursler (Rachel). One stone remains, others were relocated at Sandymount U.M. Cemetery.

"COLORED" CEMETERY ON BRICK CHURCH ROAD
Location: Across from cemetery assoc. with Pipe Creek (Brick) Methodist. [A.D.C. map location: 10th Edition, page 18, grid coordinates 11F.] The cemetery has disappeared; no evidence remains. The records have not been published. See 1877 Atlas Map of Carroll County for this district. This African-American cemetery is shown on the 1877 map.

DEER PARK UNITED METHODIST CHURCH CEMETERY
Location: At intersection of Sykesville Road (Route 32) and Deer Park Road. [A.D.C. map location: 10th Edition, page 24, grid coordinates 3K.] Cemetery is well-maintained. Year of earliest known death: 1854. Burial records held by Harold Robertson, 2332 Sykesville Road, Westminster, MD The gravemarkers were transcribed in 1985. Location of transcribed records: Carroll County Public Library, 50 Main Street, Westminster, MD 21157. The transcribed records were published in Carroll County Genealogical Society, *Carroll County Cemeteries*, Volume 2, Carroll County Genealogical Society, P.O. Box 1752, Westminster, MD 21158 (1990). Mailing address: Deer Park Cemetery, c/o Harold Robertson, 2332 Sykesville Road, Westminster, MD 21157-0000. Some tombstones from Ogg and Nelson families have been relocated here.

DETOUR METHODIST PROTESTANT CHURCH CEMETERY
Location: 1/4 mile south of Detour. The stone church and cemetery were in ruins in 1955, and the cemetery is now gone. [A.D.C. map location: 10th Edition, page 8, grid coordinates 12F.] The gravemarkers were transcribed in 1955. Transcribed records were published in: *Gravestones of Frederick County, Maryland* by Jacob M. Holdcraft. Fifty-five names were recorded.

EBENEZER UNITED METHODIST CHURCH CEMETERY
Location: On Woodbine Road about 1/2 mile south of Route 26 (Liberty Road) and village of Winfield. [A.D.C. map location: 10th Edition, page 28, grid coordinates 3H.] Cemetery is well-maintained. Year of earliest known death: 1806. The gravemarkers were transcribed in 1987. Location of transcribed records: Carroll County Public Library, 50 Main Street, Westminster, MD 21157. The transcribed records were published in Carroll County Genealogical Society, *Carroll County Cemeteries*, Volume 3, Carroll County Genealogical Society, P.O. Box 1752, Westminster, MD 21158 (1992). Mailing address: Ebenezer U.M. Church, Woodbine Road, Sykesville, MD 21784-0000.

ELLSWORTH CEMETERY
Location: On Leidy Road just off Route 140 east of Westminster. [A.D.C. map location: 10th Edition, page 20, grid coordinates 7A.] Restoration was in progress in 1990, not consistently maintained. Year of earliest known death: 1862. Year of most recent death: 1981. The gravemarkers were transcribed in 1982. Transcribed records and list of lot owners held at Carroll County Public Library, 50 Main Street, Westminster, MD 21157. The transcribed tombstone records were published in Carroll County Genealogical Society, *Carroll County Cemeteries*, Volume 2, Carroll County Genealogical Society, P.O. Box 1752, Westminster, MD 21158 (1990). African-American cemetery.

EMORY UNITED METHODIST CHURCH CEMETERY (BROWN'S MEETING HOUSE)
Location: At intersection of Emory and Emory Church Roads on Baltimore County Line [A.D.C. map location: 10th Edition, page 21, grid coordinates 12G.] Cemetery is well-maintained. Year of earliest known death: 1851. The gravemarkers were transcribed in 1989. Location of transcribed records: Carroll County Public Library, 50 Main Street, Westminster, MD 21157. The transcribed records were published in Carroll County Genealogical Society, *Carroll County Cemeteries*, Volume 2, Carroll County Genealogical Society, P.O. Box 1752, Westminster, MD 21158 (1990). Tombstones relocated from nearby Jones Family Cemetery date to 1812. Mailing address: Emory U.M. Church, 1600 Emory Road, Upperco, MD 21155-0000.

FAIR VIEW UNITED METHODIST CHURCH CEMETERY
Location: On the south side of Route 26 (Liberty Road) at Frederick County line near Buffalo Road. [A.D.C. map location: 10th Edition, page 22, grid coordinates 12J.] The cemetery is moderately well maintained. Year of earliest known death: 1862. The gravemarkers were transcribed in 1991. An incomplete set of transcribed records is held by Carroll County Public Library, 50 Main Street, Westminster, MD 21157. This is an African-American cemetery.

FINKSBURG METHODIST CHURCH CEMETERY (MT. ZION U.M. CHURCH, ZION METHODIST PROTESTANT CHURCH)
Location: On north side of Route 140 just east of intersection with Cedarhurst Road. [A.D.C. map location: 10th Edition, page 26, grid coordinates 6C.] Cemetery is well-maintained. Year of earliest known death: 1824. The gravemarkers were transcribed in 1989. Location of transcribed records: Carroll County Public Library, 50 Main Street,

Westminster, MD 21157. The transcribed records were published in Carroll County Genealogical Society, *Carroll County Cemeteries*, Volume 2, Carroll County Genealogical Society, P.O. Box 1752, Westminster, MD 21158 (1990). Some stones were mentioned in Scharf's *History of Western Maryland*. Mailing address: Mt. Zion U.M. Church, 3006 Old Westminster Pike, Finksburg, MD 21048-0000.

FINKSBURG METHODIST EPISCOPAL CHURCH SOUTH CEMETERY
Location: Not found. [A.D.C. map location: 10th Edition, page 26, grid coordinates 7C.] Relocated. The transcribed records were published in Carroll County Genealogical Society, *Carroll County Cemeteries*, Volume 2, Carroll County Genealogical Society, P.O. Box 1752, Westminster, MD 21158 (1990). The stones were probably placed in Finksburg Methodist Church Cemetery.

FRIZZELLBURG CHURCH OF GOD CEMETERY
Location: Frizzellburg Road near Old Taneytown Road in town of Frizzellburg. [A.D.C. map location: 10th Edition, page 11, grid coordinates 12G.] This is a very small, well-maintained cemetery. Year of earliest known death: 1852. Year of most recent death: 1977. The gravemarkers were transcribed in 1983. Location of transcribed records: Carroll County Public Library, 50 Main Street, Westminster, MD 21157.

GREENMOUNT UNITED METHODIST CHURCH CEMETERY (GREENMOUNT UNITED BRETHREN IN CHRIST)
Location: East side of Hanover Pike (Route 30) in village of Greenmount, north of Hampstead. [A.D.C. map location: 10th Edition, page 14, grid coordinates 7G.] The cemetery is well-maintained. Year of earliest known death: 1818. The gravemarkers were transcribed in 1993. Location of transcribed records: Carroll County Public Library, 50 Main Street, Westminster, MD 21157. The transcribed records were published in Carroll County Genealogical Society, *Carroll County Cemeteries*, Volume 4, Carroll County Genealogical Society, P.O. Box 1752, Westminster, MD 21158 (1995). A small portion contains some very old graves. Cemetery's mailing address: Greenmount U.M. Church, 2001 Hanover Pike, Hampstead, MD 21074-0000.

GREENWOOD CHURCH CEMETERY
Location: East side of Greenwood Church Road, southwest of the town of New Windsor. [A.D.C. map location: 10th Edition, page 17, grid coordinates 13G.] The cemetery is well-maintained. Year of earliest known

death: 1825. The gravemarkers were transcribed in 1958. The transcribed records were published in Jacob Mehrling Holdcraft's *Names in Stone, 75,000 Cemetery Inscriptions From Frederick County, Maryland*. The Monocacy Book Company, Redwood City, CA (2nd printing, 1972). Data were transcribed between 1959 and 1962. Additional information may be found at the Carroll County Public Library, Westminster.

HAMPSTEAD CEMETERY (ST. JOHN'S U.M. CHURCH CEMETERY)
Location: On Black Rock Road at intersection of Gill Avenue on east side of Hampstead. [A.D.C. map location: 10th Edition, page 14, grid coordinates 12J.] Cemetery is well-maintained. Year of earliest known death: 1848. The gravemarkers were transcribed in 1993. Location of transcribed records: Carroll County Public Library, 50 Main Street, Westminster, MD 21157. The transcribed records were published in Carroll County Genealogical Society, *Carroll County Cemeteries*, Volume 4, Carroll County Genealogical Society, P.O. Box 1752, Westminster, MD 21158 (1995). Cemetery's mailing address: St. John's U.M. Church, 1205 N. Main Street, Hampstead, MD : 21074-0000.

HARMONY GROVE METHODIST CHURCH CEMETERY (METHODIST PROTESTANT CHURCH AT PLEASANT GAP)
Location: West side of Klees Mill Road at intersection with Bartholow Road. [A.D.C. map location: 10th Edition, page 29, grid coordinates 1H.] The cemetery is well-maintained. Year of earliest known death: 1872. The gravemarkers were transcribed in 1984. Location of transcribed records: Carroll County Public Library, 50 Main Street, Westminster, MD 21157. The transcribed records were published in Carroll County Genealogical Society, *Carroll County Cemeteries*, Volume 1, Carroll County Genealogical Society, P.O. Box 1752, Westminster, MD 21158 (1989). The church is no longer active but someone still cares for the cemetery.

HERITAGE BAPTIST CHURCH CEMETERY (WARFIELDSBURG CHURCH OF GOD)
Location: On Old Westminster Road just north of intersection with Stone Chapel Road. [A.D.C. map location: 10th Edition, page 19, grid coordinates 13A.] This cemetery is well-maintained. Year of earliest known death: 1875. The gravemarkers were transcribed in 1982. Location of transcribed records: Carroll County Public Library, 50 Main Street, Westminster, MD 21157. The church has had many different names over the years. Mailing address: Liberty Church of Maryland, 1641 Old Westminster Road, Westminster, MD 21157-0000.

HIGHLAND VIEW CEMETERY (MESSIAH LUTHERAN CHURCH)
Location: West side of Old Washington Road (Route 97) about 1 mile south of Route 26 intersection. [A.D.C. map location: 10th Edition, page 29, grid coordinates 6F.] Cemetery is well-maintained. Year of earliest known death: 1869. The gravemarkers were transcribed in 1990. Location of transcribed records: Carroll County Public Library, 50 Main Street, Westminster, MD 21157. The transcribed records were published in Carroll County Genealogical Society, *Carroll County Cemeteries*, Volume 3, Carroll County Genealogical Society, P.O. Box 1752, Westminster, MD 21158 (1992). Cemetery's mailing address: Messiah Lutheran Church, Route 97 (Old Washington Road), Sykesville, MD 21784-0000.

HOLY TRINITY EPISCOPAL CEMETERY
Location: Southwest corner of the intersection of Routes 32 and 26, about 200 yards from the corner. [A.D.C. map location: 10th Edition, page 30, grid coordinates 9C.] Cemetery is currently well-maintained but had been abandoned for many years. Year of earliest known death: 1826. Year of most recent death: 1922. Buried here is Susanna Warfield. The gravemarkers were transcribed in 1989. Location of transcribed records: Carroll County Public Library, 50 Main Street, Westminster, MD 21157. The transcribed records were published in Carroll County Genealogical Society, *Carroll County Cemeteries*, Volume 1, Carroll County Genealogical Society, P.O. Box 1752, Westminster, MD 21158 (1989). The stones have been transcribed by several people including J. M. Holdcraft in his, *More Names in Stone*. Mailing address: c/o James Purman, 5034 S. Klees Mill Road, Eldersburg, MD, 21784-0000.

JERUSALEM LUTHERAN CHURCH CEMETERY (BAUER'S CHURCH, BACHMAN'S CHURCH, BOWER'S CHURCH)
Location: On Bachman's Valley Road (Route 496) at intersection with Bixler's Church Road. [A.D.C. map location: 10th Edition, page 13, grid coordinates 1D.] Cemetery well-maintained. Year of earliest known death: 1786. Year of most recent death: 1939. The gravemarkers were transcribed in 1983. Location of transcribed records: Carroll County Public Library, 50 Main Street, Westminster, MD 21157. The transcribed records were published in Carroll County Genealogical Society, *Carroll County Cemeteries*, Volume 4, Carroll County Genealogical Society, P.O. Box 1752, Westminster, MD 21158 (1995). Modern burials are being made at John Luther Miller Cemetery. Cemetery's mailing address: Jerusalem Lutheran Church, P.O. Box 69, Lineboro, MD 21088-0000.

JOHN LUTHER MILLER MEMORIAL CEMETERY
Location: On Bachman's Valley Road (Route 496) west of Bixler's Church Road. [A.D.C. map location: 10th Edition, page 13, grid coordinates 2C.] The cemetery well-maintained. Year of earliest known death: 1890. The gravemarkers were transcribed in 1992. Location of transcribed records: Carroll County Public Library, 50 Main Street, Westminster, MD 21157. The transcribed records were published in Carroll County Genealogical Society, *Carroll County Cemeteries*, Volume 4, Carroll County Genealogical Society, P.O. Box 1752, Westminster, MD 21158 (1995). A list of lot owners is available at Carroll County Public Library, Westminster, MD.

JOHNSVILLE UNITED METHODIST CHURCH CEMETERY
Location: At the corner of Johnsville Road and Bartholow Road. [A.D.C. map location: 10th Edition, page 30, grid coordinates 8C.] The cemetery is well-maintained. Year of earliest known death: 1922. The gravemarkers were transcribed in 1985. Location of transcribed records: Carroll County Public Library, 50 Main Street, Westminster, MD 21157. The transcribed records were published in Carroll County Genealogical Society, *Carroll County Cemeteries*, Volume 1, Carroll County Genealogical Society, P.O. Box 1752, Westminster, MD 21158 (1989). Mailing address: Johnsville U.M. Church, 1124 Johnsville Road, Eldersburg, MD, 21784-0000. African-American Church dating from about 1919.

KEYSVILLE UNION CEMETERY
Location: In center of Community of Keysville in western part of county. [A.D.C. map location: 10th Edition, page 8, grid coordinates 7H.] The cemetery is well-maintained. Year of earliest known death: 1880. The gravemarkers were transcribed in 1959. Holdcraft reported 601 names. The transcribed records were published in Jacob Mehrling Holdcraft's *Names in Stone, 75,000 Cemetery Inscriptions From Frederick County, Maryland*. The Monocacy Book Company, Redwood City, CA (2nd printing, 1972). Data were transcribed between 1959 and 1962.

KIRKRIDGE PRESBYTERIAN CHURCH CEMETERY
Location: On Old Fort Schoolhouse Road east of Route 27 (Manchester Road), beside the church. [A.D.C. map location: 10th Edition, page 13, grid coordinates 5J.] Cemetery is well-maintained. Year of earliest known death: 1966. The gravemarkers were transcribed in 1994. Location of transcribed records: Carroll County Public Library, 50 Main Street, Westminster, MD 21157. The transcribed records were published in Carroll County Genealogical Society, *Carroll County Cemeteries*, Volume

4, Carroll County Genealogical Society, P.O. Box 1752, Westminster, MD 21158 (1995). There are about 50 inscriptions. Surnames: Yelton, Hearn, Etc. Mailing address: Kirkridge Asso. Reformed Presbyterian Church, 2236 Old Fort Schoolhouse Road, Manchester, MD 21102-0000.

LAZARUS LUTHERAN CHURCH CEMETERY (LAZARUS UNITED CHURCH of CHRIST)
Location: On Church St. in Lineboro east of Main St. [A.D.C. map location: 10th Edition, page 6, grid coordinates 5J.] The cemetery is well-maintained. Year of earliest known death: 1852. The gravemarkers were transcribed in 1979. Location of transcribed records: Carroll County Public Library, 50 Main Street, Westminster, MD 21157. The transcribed records were published in Carroll County Genealogical Society, *Carroll County Cemeteries*, Volume 4, Carroll County Genealogical Society, P.O. Box 1752, Westminster, MD 21158 (1995). Inscriptions are incomplete - not in row order. Cemetery's mailing address: Lazarus Lutheran Church, 5101 S. Church Street, Lineboro, MD 21088-0000.

MANCHESTER BETHEL CHURCH CEMETERY (BORING'S MEETING HOUSE)
Location: On south side of High Street in town of Manchester behind converted church. [A.D.C. map location: 10th Edition, page 14, grid coordinates 2C.] The cemetery well-maintained, fenced. Year of earliest known death: 1827. Year of most recent death: 1988. The gravemarkers were transcribed in 1991. Location of transcribed records: Carroll County Public Library, 50 Main Street, Westminster, MD 21157. The transcribed records were published in Carroll County Genealogical Society, *Carroll County Cemeteries*, Volume 4, Carroll County Genealogical Society, P.O. Box 1752, Westminster, MD 21158 (1995). Surnames: Boring, Little, Simpers, Lynerd, Dienst, etc.

MANCHESTER CEMETERY (TRINITY U.C.C. CEMETERY, IMMANUEL LUTHERAN CHURCH CEMETERY, "UNION" CEMETERY)
Location: On York and Church Streets in town of Manchester, annex on Locust Street. [A.D.C. map location: 10th Edition, page 14, grid coordinates 2D, 1E.] The cemetery is well-maintained. Year of earliest known death: 1780. The gravemarkers were transcribed in 1993. Location of transcribed records: Carroll County Public Library, 50 Main Street, Westminster, MD 21157. The transcribed records were published in Carroll County Genealogical Society, *Carroll County Cemeteries*, Volume 4, Carroll County Genealogical Society, P.O. Box 1752, Westminster, MD 21158 (1995). Over 3000 inscriptions in this very large, old cemetery.

Cemetery's mailing address: Immanuel Evangelical Lutheran Church, P.O. Box 739, Manchester, MD 21102-0000.

MAYBERRY CHURCH OF GOD CEMETERY
Location: In village of Mayberry on Mayberry Road about 1 mile north of Route 140 [A.D.C. map location: 10th Edition, page 11, grid coordinates 5B.] The cemetery is well-maintained. Year of earliest known death: 1851. Burial records maintained. The gravemarkers were transcribed in 1982. Location of transcribed records: Carroll County Public Library, 50 Main Street, Westminster, MD 21157. Mailing address: Mayberry First Church of God, 2428 Mayberry Road, Westminster, MD 21158-0000.

MEADOW BRANCH CHURCH OF THE BRETHREN CEMETERY
Location: At western city limits of Westminster on Old Taneytown Road off Route 140. [A.D.C. map location: 10th Edition, page 19, grid coordinates 2B.] The cemetery is well-maintained. Year of earliest known death: 1826. The gravemarkers were transcribed in 1983. Location of transcribed records: Carroll County Public Library, 50 Main Street, Westminster, MD 21157. Some old stones were published in Scharf's *History of Western Maryland*. Mailing address: Meadow Branch Church of the Brethren, 818 Old Taneytown Road, Westminster, MD 21158-0000.

MIDDLEBURG UNITED METHODIST CHURCH CEMETERY
Location: On Johnsville Road just south of intersection with Mt. Union/Middleburg Road. [A.D.C. map location: 10th Edition, page 16, grid coordinates 1D.] The cemetery is well-maintained. Year of earliest known death: 1850. The gravemarkers were transcribed in 1983. Location of transcribed records: Carroll County Public Library, 50 Main Street, Westminster, MD 21157. The transcribed records were published in Jacob Mehrling Holdcraft's *Names in Stone, 75,000 Cemetery Inscriptions From Frederick County, Maryland*. The Monocacy Book Company, Redwood City, CA (2nd printing, 1972). Data were transcribed between 1959 and 1962. Inscriptions were copied by several individuals, also see Scharf's *History of Western Maryland*. Mailing address: Middleburg U.M. Church, Johnsville Road, Middleburg, MD 21768-0000.

MILLERS UNITED METHODIST CHURCH CEMETERY (MILLERS UNITED BRETHREN CHURCH)
Location: On Warehime Road near the intersection with Miller Station Road. [A.D.C. map location: 10th Edition, page 6, grid coordinates 13J.] The cemetery is well-maintained. Year of earliest known death: 1854. Location of records: Phyllis and Roy Redding caretakers in 1993. The

CARROLL COUNTY CEMETERIES - CHURCH   115

gravemarkers were transcribed in 1993. Location of transcribed records: Carroll County Public Library, 50 Main Street, Westminster, MD 21157. The transcribed records were published in Carroll County Genealogical Society, *Carroll County Cemeteries*, Volume 4, Carroll County Genealogical Society, P.O. Box 1752, Westminster, MD 21158 (1995). Between 150-200 inscriptions were transcribed.

MORGAN'S CHAPEL UNITED METHODIST CHURCH CEMETERY
Location: At intersection of Gillis Falls Road and Woodbine Road. [A.D.C. map location: 10th Edition, page 28, grid coordinates 13H.] Cemetery is well-maintained. Year of earliest known death: 1853. The gravemarkers were transcribed in 1991. Location of transcribed records: Carroll County Public Library, 50 Main Street, Westminster, MD 21157. The transcribed records were published in Carroll County Genealogical Society, *Carroll County Cemeteries*, Volume 3, Carroll County Genealogical Society, P.O. Box 1752, Westminster, MD 21158 (1992). Most burials date from 1870s to present, very few prior to 1871. Mailing address: Morgan's Chapel, Woodbine Road, Woodbine, MD 21797-0000.

MOUNTAIN VIEW LUTHERAN CEMETERY (ST. PAUL'S LUTHERAN CEMETERY)
Location: West side of Harney Road (Route 134) at Pennsylvania state line. [A.D.C. map location: 10th Edition, page 1, grid coordinates 4E.] The cemetery is well-maintained. The gravemarkers were transcribed in 1961. The transcribed records were published in Jacob Mehrling Holdcraft's *Names in Stone, 75,000 Cemetery Inscriptions From Frederick County, Maryland*. The Monocacy Book Company, Redwood City, CA (2nd printing, 1972). Data were transcribed between 1959 and 1962; there were over 247 surnames.

MT. JOY METHODIST CHURCH CEMETERY
Location: On Middleburg Road about 1/2 mile west of Uniontown, south side. [A.D.C. map location: 10th Edition, page 17, grid coordinates 1G.] The cemetery is well-maintained. The church was erected about 1859 but gone by 1980. Year of earliest known death: 1853. The gravemarkers were transcribed in 1983. Location of transcribed records: Carroll County Public Library, 50 Main Street, Westminster, MD 21157. African-American church has been torn down, burials still take place here.

MT. OLIVE UNITED METHODIST CHURCH CEMETERY
Location: On Gillis Falls Road near intersection with Cabbage Spring Road. [A.D.C. map location: 10th Edition, page 28, grid coordinates 10A.]

Cemetery is well-maintained; the caretaker was R.W. Frederickson. Year of earliest known death: 1872. The gravemarkers were transcribed in 1991. Location of transcribed records: Carroll County Public Library, 50 Main Street, Westminster, MD 21157. The transcribed records were published in Carroll County Genealogical Society, *Carroll County Cemeteries*, Volume 3, Carroll County Genealogical Society, P.O. Box 1752, Westminster, MD 21158 (1992). Mailing address: Mt. Olive U.M. Church, 2809 Gillis Falls Road, Woodbine, MD 21797-0000.

MT. PLEASANT METHODIST CHURCH CEMETERY (EMMANUEL BAPTIST CHURCH)
Location: On Sykesville Road (Route 32) About 1/3 mile south of intersection with Gamber Road. [A.D.C. map location: 10th Edition, page 25, grid coordinates 12F.] Cemetery is well-maintained. Year of earliest known death: 1814. The gravemarkers were transcribed in 1989. Location of transcribed records: Carroll County Public Library, 50 Main Street, Westminster, MD 21157. The transcribed records were published in Carroll County Genealogical Society, *Carroll County Cemeteries*, Volume 2, Carroll County Genealogical Society, P.O. Box 1752, Westminster, MD 21158 (1990). This church is Baptist, but it is thought that the cemetery bears the name "Mt. Pleasant." Mailing address: Emmanuel Baptist Church, 4150 Sykesville Road, Finksburg, MD 21048-0000.

MT. UNION BRETHREN CHURCH CEMETERY
Location: On west side of Gorsuch Road north of intersection of Shiloh Road. [A.D.C. map location: 10th Edition, page 13, grid coordinates 12K.] The cemetery poorly maintained but not abandoned. Year of earliest known death: 1854. Year of most recent death: 1962. The records were maintained by Parke Leister until 1989. The gravemarkers were transcribed in 1993. Location of transcribed records: Carroll County Public Library, 50 Main Street, Westminster, MD 21157. The transcribed records were published in Carroll County Genealogical Society, *Carroll County Cemeteries*, Volume 4, Carroll County Genealogical Society, P.O. Box 1752, Westminster, MD 21158 (1995). The church was torn down in 1930s.

MT. UNION LUTHERAN CHURCH CEMETERY
Location: On Middleburg Road east of Village of Middleburg. [A.D.C. map location: 10th Edition, page 16, grid coordinates 1H?.] The cemetery is well-maintained. Year of earliest known death: 1856. The gravemarkers were transcribed in 1983. Location of transcribed records: Carroll County Public Library, 50 Main Street, Westminster, MD 21157.

CARROLL COUNTY CEMETERIES - CHURCH 117

MT. ZION METHODIST CEMETERY
Location: On the north side of Harrisville Road about 100 yards west of Route 27 (Ridge Road). The church has disappeared. [A.D.C. map location: 10th Edition, page 27, grid coordinates 8G.] The cemetery is well maintained, but many graves marked only with temporary markers. Year of earliest known death: 1887. The gravemarkers were transcribed in 1987. Location of transcribed records: Carroll County Public Library, 50 Main Street, Westminster, MD 21157. The transcribed records were published in Carroll County Genealogical Society, *Carroll County Cemeteries*, Volume 3, Carroll County Genealogical Society, P.O. Box 1752, Westminster, MD 21158 (1992). There are about 88 inscriptions. This is an African-American cemetery.

NEW OAKLAND METHODIST CHURCH CEMETERY
(NEW OAKLAND METHODIST EPISCOPAL CHURCH SOUTH)
Location: 5901 Mineral Hill Road in Eldersburg. [A.D.C. map location: 10th Edition, page 30, grid coordinates 8K.] Cemetery well-maintained. Year of earliest known death: 1908. The gravemarkers were transcribed in 1984. Location of transcribed records: Carroll County Public Library, 50 Main Street, Westminster, MD 21157. The transcribed records were published in Carroll County Genealogical Society, *Carroll County Cemeteries*, Volume 1, Carroll County Genealogical Society, P.O. Box 1752, Westminster, MD 21158 (1989). Mailing address: New Oakland Methodist Church, 5901 Mineral Hill Road, Eldersburg, MD 21784-0000.

NEW WINDSOR PRESBYTERIAN CHURCH CEMETERY
Location: In center of New Windsor next to church. [A.D.C. map location: 10th Edition, page 17, grid coordinates 10K.] This cemetery is well-maintained. The gravemarkers were transcribed in 1882. The transcribed records were published in Jacob Mehrling Holdcraft's *Names in Stone, 75,000 Cemetery Inscriptions From Frederick County, Maryland*. The Monocacy Book Company, Redwood City, CA (2nd printing, 1972). Data were transcribed between 1959 and 1962. Holdcraft repeated Scharf's listing in 1882 of 76 names. Holdcraft's list is just a partial one; see Holdcraft's, *More Names in Stone*. Mailing address: New Windsor Assoc. Reformed Presbyterian Church, Church and High Streets, New Windsor, MD 21776-0000.

OLD GERMAN CEMETERY
Location: At corner of Leister's Church and Coon Club Roads in woods near modern house. [A.D.C. map location: 10th Edition, page 20, grid coordinates 2G.] Abandoned. Year of earliest known death: 1888. Year of

most recent death: 1937. The gravemarkers were transcribed in ?. Location of transcribed records: Carroll County Public Library, 50 Main Street, Westminster, MD 21157. The transcribed records were published in Carroll County Genealogical Society, *Carroll County Cemeteries*, Volume 4, Carroll County Genealogical Society, P.O. Box 1752, Westminster, MD 21158 (1995). The church was built about 1880, sold in 1905 and moved to Patapsco, German-speaking.

OLD OAKLAND METHODIST CHURCH CEMETERY
Location: At the corner of Oakland Road and Mineral Hill Road. [A.D.C. map location: 10th Edition, page 31, grid coordinates 8A.] Cemetery well-maintained. There are 342 inscriptions. Year of earliest known death: 1846. The gravemarkers were transcribed in 1983. Location of transcribed records: Carroll County Public Library, 50 Main Street, Westminster, MD 21157. The transcribed records were published in Carroll County Genealogical Society, *Carroll County Cemeteries*, Volume 1, Carroll County Genealogical Society, P.O. Box 1752, Westminster, MD 21158 (1989). See also New Oakland Methodist Church Cemetery.

PATAPSCO BAPTIST CHURCH CEMETERY
Location: Old Liberty Road near Panorama and Marriottsville Road intersections. [A.D.C. map location: 10th Edition, page 31, grid coordinates 11A.] The cemetery has disappeared. Year of earliest known death: 1834. Year of most recent death: 1848. The gravemarkers were transcribed in 1982. Location of transcribed records: Carroll County Public Library, 50 Main Street, Westminster, MD 21157. The transcribed records were published in Carroll County Genealogical Society, *Carroll County Cemeteries*, Volume 1, Carroll County Genealogical Society, P.O. Box 1752, Westminster, MD 21158 (1989). Surnames: Choate, Odell, Fite. There are isolated stones left in the yard. The church was converted to apartments.

PATAPSCO UNITED METHODIST CHURCH CEMETERY
Location: At intersection of Patapsco and Ridge Roads in Village of Patapsco. [A.D.C. map location: 10th Edition, page 21, grid coordinates 10B.]. The cemetery is well-maintained. Year of earliest known death: 1884. The gravemarkers were transcribed in 1989. Location of transcribed records: Carroll County Public Library, 50 Main Street, Westminster, MD 21157. The transcribed records were published in Carroll County Genealogical Society, *Carroll County Cemeteries*, Volume 2, Carroll County Genealogical Society, P.O. Box 1752, Westminster, MD 21158 (1990).

PINEY CREEK CHURCH OF THE BRETHREN CEMETERY
Location: At intersection of Ruggles and Teeter Roads north of Taneytown. [A.D.C. map location: 10th Edition, page 2, grid coordinates 7C.] This cemetery is well-maintained. Additional comments: Graves may date to late 1700s. Mailing address: Piney Creek Church of the Brethren, 4699 Teeter Road, Taneytown, MD 21787-0000.

PINEY CREEK PRESBYTERIAN CEMETERY
Location: At the intersection of Harney and Piney Creek Roads in the northwest part of the county. [A.D.C. map location: 10th Edition, page 1, grid coordinates 8G.] The cemetery is well-maintained. The gravemarkers were transcribed in 1961. The transcribed records were published in Jacob Mehrling Holdcraft's *Names in Stone, 75,000 Cemetery Inscriptions From Frederick County, Maryland*. The Monocacy Book Company, Redwood City, CA (2nd printing, 1972). Data were transcribed between 1959 and 1962. Over 444 surnames. Mailing address: Piney Creek Associate-Reformed Presbyterian Church, Harney Road, Taneytown, MD 21787-0000.

PIPE CREEK FRIENDS (QUAKER) MEETING CEMETERY
Location: West side of Quaker Hill Road just outside the city limits of Union Bridge. [A.D.C. map location: 10th Edition, page 17, grid coordinates 6A.] The cemetery is well-maintained. The earliest known death: 1790. The gravemarkers were transcribed in 1957. The transcribed records were published in Jacob Mehrling Holdcraft's *Names in Stone, 75,000 Cemetery Inscriptions From Frederick County, Maryland*. The Monocacy Book Company, Redwood City, CA (2nd printing, 1972). Data were transcribed between 1959 and 1962. About 188 names were recorded. The tombstones are very plain, quite old, some with only initials.

PIPE CREEK CHURCH OF THE BRETHREN CEMETERY (GERMAN BAPTIST CEMETERY)
Location: West side of Clear Ridge Road (Route 84) About 2 miles south of Uniontown. [A.D.C. map location: 10th Edition, page 17, grid coordinates 4G.] The cemetery is well-maintained. Year of earliest known death: 1790. Some gravemarkers were transcribed in 1959. Holdcraft added a few names to Scharf's 1882 list. The transcribed records were published in Jacob Mehrling Holdcraft's *Names in Stone, 75,000 Cemetery Inscriptions From Frederick County, Maryland*. The Monocacy Book Company, Redwood City, CA (2nd printing, 1972). Data were transcribed between 1959 and 1962. See also *More Names in Stone* plus 1889/90

Democratic Advocate list. Cemetery's mailing address: Pipe Creek Church of The Brethren, Pipe Creek Road, Linwood, MD 21764-0000.

PIPE CREEK UNITED METHODIST CHURCH CEMETERY (BRICK METHODIST CHURCH CEMETERY)
Location: North side of Brick Church Road between Wakefield Valley and Nicodemus Roads. [A.D.C. map location: 10th Edition, page 18, grid coordinates 10F.] This cemetery is well-maintained. Year of earliest known death: 1833. Some Durbin Family members are buried here. The gravemarkers were transcribed in 1982. Location of transcribed records: Carroll County Public Library, 50 Main Street, Westminster, MD 21157. Mailing address: Pipe Creek U.M. Church, Brick Church Road, New Windsor, MD 21776-0000.

PLEASANT GROVE METHODIST CHURCH CEMETERY (PLEASANT GROVE METHODIST EPISCOPAL CHURCH)
Location: On Old Westminster Pike between Sandymount Road and Greens Mill Road. [A.D.C. map location: 10th Edition, page 25, grid coordinates 1H.] Cemetery is well-maintained. Year of earliest known death: 1825. Year of most recent death: 1970. The gravemarkers were transcribed in 1987. Location of transcribed records: Carroll County Public Library, 50 Main Street, Westminster, MD 21157. The transcribed records were published in Carroll County Genealogical Society, *Carroll County Cemeteries*, Volume 2, Carroll County Genealogical Society, P.O. Box 1752, Westminster, MD 21158 (1990). Some early interments were listed in an 11 Jan 1890 issue of *Democratic Advocate*. A private corporation holds an incomplete set of records. Behind a private dwelling which was once the church.

PLEASANT RIDGE CEMETERY (WINFIELD BIBLE CHURCH CEMETERY, PLEASANT RIDGE CHURCH OF GOD)
Location: On Woodbine Road at intersection with Bethel Road. Cemetery on both sides of road. [A.D.C. map location: 10th Edition, page 28, grid coordinates 6H.] Cemetery is well-maintained. Year of earliest known death: 1857. The gravemarkers were transcribed in 1987. Location of transcribed records: Carroll County Public Library, 50 Main Street, Westminster, MD 21157. The transcribed records were published in Carroll County Genealogical Society, *Carroll County Cemeteries*, Volume 3, Carroll County Genealogical Society, P.O. Box 1752, Westminster, MD 21158 (1992). Most tombstones date from 1870s and later. Cemetery's mailing address: Winfield Bible Chapel, 5407 Woodbine Road, Woodbine, MD 21797-0000.

POOL'S CHURCH CEMETERY
Location: On the southeast side of Sykesville Road (Route 32) About 1/2 mile south of Gamber Road. [A.D.C. map location: 10th Edition, page 25, grid coordinates 13G.] Year of earliest known death: 1885. Year of most recent death: 1908. The gravemarkers were transcribed in 1985. Location of transcribed records: Carroll County Public Library, 50 Main Street, Westminster, MD 21157. The transcribed records were published in Carroll County Genealogical Society, *Carroll County Cemeteries*, Volume 2, Carroll County Genealogical Society, P.O. Box 1752, Westminster, MD 21158 (1990). There are inscribed stones plus fieldstones; the last interment was prior to 1940. It is cared for by owners of neighboring property. This is a African-American church.

PROVIDENCE METHODIST CHURCH CEMETERY (CALVARY U.M. CHURCH)
Location: Southeast side of Gamber Road (Route 91) Near Gamber [A.D.C. map location: 10th Edition, page 25, grid coordinates 11G.] Cemetery is well-maintained. Year of earliest known death: 1844. The gravemarkers were transcribed in 1990. Location of transcribed records: Carroll County Public Library, 50 Main Street, Westminster, MD 21157. The transcribed records were published in Carroll County Genealogical Society, *Carroll County Cemeteries*, Volume 2, Carroll County Genealogical Society, P.O. Box 1752, Westminster, MD 21158 (1990). Mailing address: Calvary U.M. Church, 3939 Gamber Road, Finksburg, MD 21048-0000.

SALEM UNITED METHODIST CHURCH CEMETERY
Location: East side of Salem Bottom Road near the intersection with Muller Road. [A.D.C. map location: 10th Edition, page 24, grid coordinates 9B.] The cemetery is well-maintained. Year of earliest known death: 1834. The gravemarkers were transcribed in 1983. Location of transcribed records: Carroll County Public Library, 50 Main Street, Westminster, MD 21157. Mailing address: Salem United Methodist Church, 3500 Salem Bottom Road, Westminster, MD 21157-0000.

SAM'S CREEK CHURCH OF THE BRETHREN CEMETERY
Location: On Marston Road about 1/2 mile east of Bowersox Road intersection, next to the church. [A.D.C. map location: 10th Edition, page 23, grid coordinates 5D.] The cemetery is well-maintained. Year of earliest known death: 1834. The gravemarkers were transcribed in 1983. Location of transcribed records: Carroll County Public Library, 50 Main Street, Westminster, MD 21157. Mailing address: Sam's Creek Church of The

Brethren, 2736 Marston Road, New Windsor, MD 21776-0000.

SANDYMOUNT UNITED METHODIST CHURCH CEMETERY
Location: On Old Westminster Pike just east of intersection with Sandymount Road. [A.D.C. map location: 10th Edition, page 25, grid coordinates 1A.] Cemetery is well-maintained. Year of earliest known death: 1825. The gravemarkers were transcribed in 1989. Location of transcribed records: Carroll County Public Library, 50 Main Street, Westminster, MD 21157. The transcribed records were published in Carroll County Genealogical Society, *Carroll County Cemeteries*, Volume 2, Carroll County Genealogical Society, P.O. Box 1752, Westminster, MD 21158 (1990). There are 658 inscriptions plus church history (1827-1984) Mailing address: Sandymount United Methodist Church, 2101 Old Westminster Pike, Finksburg, MD 21048-0000.

SHILOH BAPTIST CEMETERY
Location: At the "Y" where Braddock Road joins Woodbine Road. [A.D.C. map location: 10th Edition, page 28, grid coordinates 5H.] The cemetery and church, established about 1886, have since disappeared. The information was published in Carroll County Genealogical Society, *Carroll County Cemeteries*, Volume 3, Carroll County Genealogical Society, P.O. Box 1752, Westminster, MD 21158 (1992). This African-American cemetery served the community in "Picadillo" west of Defiance. Permission to visit the site is required.

SHILOH UNITED METHODIST CHURCH CEMETERY (SHILOH PARK M.E. CHURCH)
Location: On Shiloh Road west of Hampstead and west of Brobeck Road intersection. [A.D.C. map location: 10th Edition, page 14, grid coordinates 13C.] Cemetery is well-maintained. Year of earliest known death: 1888. The gravemarkers were transcribed in 1984. Location of transcribed records: Carroll County Public Library, 50 Main Street, Westminster, MD 21157. The transcribed records were published in Carroll County Genealogical Society, *Carroll County Cemeteries*, Volume 4, Carroll County Genealogical Society, P.O. Box 1752, Westminster, MD 21158 (1995). Additional comments: Cemetery's mailing address: Shiloh U.M. Church, 3100 Shiloh Road, Hampstead, MD 21074-0000.

SPRINGFIELD CEMETERY
Location: Spout Hill Road off Third Avenue in Sykesville. [A.D.C. map location: 10th Edition, page 34, grid coordinates 2K.] It is well-maintained. Year of earliest known death: 1845. The gravemarkers were transcribed

in 1988. Location of transcribed records: Carroll County Public Library, 50 Main Street, Westminster, MD 21157. The transcribed records were published in Carroll County Genealogical Society, *Carroll County Cemeteries*, Volume 1, Carroll County Genealogical Society, P.O. Box 1752, Westminster, MD 21158 (1989). Additional comments: The cemetery is a private company. Mailing address: Springfield Presbyterian Church, 7300 Spout Hill Road, Sykesville, MD 21784-0000.

ST. BARTHOLOMEW'S ROMAN CATHOLIC CHURCH CEMETERY
Location: On Park Avenue in town of Manchester. [A.D.C. map location: 10th Edition, page 14, grid coordinates 2C.] The cemetery is well-maintained. Year of earliest known death: 1866. The gravemarkers were transcribed in 1989. Location of transcribed records: Carroll County Public Library, 50 Main Street, Westminster, MD 21157. The transcribed records were published in Carroll County Genealogical Society, *Carroll County Cemeteries*, Volume 4, Carroll County Genealogical Society, P.O. Box 1752, Westminster, MD 21158 (1995). About 30 persons are buried here. Mailing address: St. Bartholomew's R.C., Church, 3071 Park Avenue, Manchester, MD 21102-0000.

ST. BENJAMIN'S (KRIDERS) CHURCH CEMETERY
(ST. BENJAMIN'S LUTHERAN CHURCH/BENJAMIN'S U.C. OF C.)
Location: On Krider's Church Road About 1/2 Mile west off Route 97-North of Westminster. [A.D.C. map location: 10th Edition, page 19, grid coordinates 1E.] The cemetery well-maintained. Year of earliest known death: 1760. The gravemarkers were transcribed in 1965. Location of transcribed records: Historical Society of Carroll County, 210 E. Main Street, Westminster, MD 21157. The tombstones were copied in 1960s by Wm. Winchester Chapter of DAR, recopied 1995-96. Cemetery's mailing address: St. Benjamin's Lutheran church, 700 Krider's Church Road, Westminster, MD 21158-0000.

ST. JAMES UNITED METHODIST CHURCH CEMETERY
Location: West side of Marston Road about 1.5 miles form the intersection with Route 27. [A.D.C. map location: 10th Edition, page 23, grid coordinates 6E.] The cemetery is well-maintained. Year of earliest known death: 1885. The gravemarkers were transcribed in 1983. Location of transcribed records: Carroll County Public Library, 50 Main Street, Westminster, MD 21157. One tombstone dated to 1837; most of the rest from 1880 to present. Mailing address: St. James U.M. Church, 2900 Marston Road, New Windsor, MD 21776-0000.

124 DIRECTORY OF MARYLAND'S BURIAL GROUNDS

ST. JOHN'S ROMAN CATHOLIC CHURCH CEMETERY
Location: On East Main St. in Westminster, behind Carroll County Public Library. [A.D.C. map location: 10th Edition, page 19, grid coordinates 4G.] The cemetery is well-maintained. Year of earliest known death: 1790. The gravemarkers were transcribed in 1988. Location of transcribed records: Carroll County Public Library, 50 Main Street, Westminster, MD 21157. A partial list was included in Scharf's *History of Western Maryland*. Mailing address: St. John's R.C. Church, 43 Monroe Street, Westminster, MD 21157-0000.

ST. JOHN'S (LEISTER'S) EVANGELICAL LUTHERAN CEMETERY (LEISTER'S CHURCH)
Location: On Leister's Church Road just east of intersection with Route 482 (Hampstead-Mexico Road). [A.D.C. map location: 10th Edition, page 13, grid coordinates 13F.] The cemetery well-maintained. Year of earliest known death: 1845. The gravemarkers were transcribed in 1991. Location of transcribed records: Carroll County Public Library, 50 Main Street, Westminster, MD 21157. The transcribed records were published in Carroll County Genealogical Society, *Carroll County Cemeteries*, Volume 4, Carroll County Genealogical Society, P.O. Box 1752, Westminster, MD 21158 (1995). Cemetery's mailing address: St. John's Lutheran Church, Leister's Church Road, Westminster, MD 21157-0000.

ST. JOSEPH'S ROMAN CATHOLIC CHURCH CEMETERY
Location: Beside and behind church on Frederick Street in Taneytown. [A.D.C. map location: 10th Edition, page 9, grid coordinates 2K.] This cemetery contains tombstones from the early 1800s; it is well-maintained. Year of earliest known death: 1800. Location of transcribed records: See *Names In Stone*. The transcribed records were published in Jacob Mehrling Holdcraft's *Names in Stone, 75,000 Cemetery Inscriptions From Frederick County, Maryland*. The Monocacy Book Company, Redwood City, CA (2nd printing, 1972). Data were transcribed between 1959 and 1962. Mailing address: St. Joseph's R.C. Church, Frederick Street, Taneytown, MD 21787-0000.

ST. JOSEPH'S ROMAN CATHOLIC CHURCH CEMETERY
Location: Mellor Avenue in the heart of Sykesville. [A.D.C. map location: 10th Edition, page 35, grid coordinates 4A.] Cemetery well-maintained. Approximately 35-40 burials. Year of earliest known death: 1868. Year of most recent death: 1951. The gravemarkers were transcribed in 1985. Location of transcribed records: Carroll County Public Library, 50 Main Street, Westminster, MD 21157. The transcribed records were published

in Carroll County Genealogical Society, *Carroll County Cemeteries,* Volume 1, Carroll County Genealogical Society, P.O. Box 1752, Westminster, MD 21158 (1989).

ST. LUKE'S (WINTERS) LUTHERAN CHURCH CEMETERY
Location: On Route 75 between New Windsor and Union Bridge, about 1½ miles west of New Windsor. [A.D.C. map location: 10th Edition, page 17, grid coordinates 8H.] This cemetery is well-maintained. Year of earliest known death: 1780. The transcribed records were published in Jacob Mehrling Holdcraft's *Names in Stone, 75,000 Cemetery Inscriptions From Frederick County, Maryland.* The Monocacy Book Company, Redwood City, CA (2nd printing, 1972). Data were transcribed between 1959 and 1962. Holdcraft copied 140 names from Scharf's 1882 list in *History of Western Maryland.* Mailing address: St. Luke's Lutheran Church, Route 75, New Windsor, MD 21776-0000.

ST. MARK'S LUTHERAN AND REFORMED CHURCH CEMETERY
Location: On west side of Cape Horn Road north of village of Snydersburg. [A.D.C. map location: 10th Edition, page 14, grid coordinates 9B.] The cemetery well-maintained. Year of earliest known death: 1878. The gravemarkers were transcribed in 1992. Location of transcribed records: Carroll County Public Library, 50 Main Street, Westminster, MD 21157. The transcribed records were published in Carroll County Genealogical Society, *Carroll County Cemeteries,* Volume 4, Carroll County Genealogical Society, P.O. Box 1752, Westminster, MD 21158 (1995). Mailing address: St. Mark's Lutheran Church, 2812 Snydersburg, Road, Westminster, MD 21157-0000.

ST. MARY'S LUTHERAN AND REFORMED CHURCH CEMETERY (ST. MARY'S UNITED CHURCH OF CHRIST, ST. MARY'S EVANGELICAL LUTHERAN CHURCH)
Location: In town of Silver Run on Mayberry Road, about 1/8 mile off Littlestown Pike. [A.D.C. map location: 10th Edition, page 3, grid coordinates 10J.] The cemetery is well-maintained. Year of earliest known death: 1760. The gravemarkers were transcribed in 1987. Location of transcribed records: Carroll County Public Library, 50 Main Street, Westminster, MD 21157. A partial list of oldest burials is available; the entire cemetery was not transcribed. Cemetery's mailing address: St. Mary's U.C.C., 1441 E. Mayberry Road, Westminster, MD 21158-0000.

ST. PAUL'S LUTHERAN CHURCH CEMETERY
Location: At intersection of Clear Ridge Road and Middleburg Road at

west end of Uniontown. [A.D.C. map location: 10th Edition, page 17, grid coordinates 1H.] The cemetery is well-maintained. The gravemarkers were transcribed in 1959. The transcribed records were published in Jacob Mehrling Holdcraft's *Names in Stone, 75,000 Cemetery Inscriptions From Frederick County, Maryland*. The Monocacy Book Company, Redwood City, CA (2nd printing, 1972). Data were transcribed between 1959 and 1962. The 110 names found in Holdcraft represent only a small portion of this cemetery. Mailing address: St. Paul's Lutheran Church, 3330 Uniontown Road, Uniontown, MD 21158-0000.

ST. THOMAS ROMAN CATHOLIC CHURCH CEMETERY
Location: East side of Springdale Avenue before intersection of Rowe Road, on the edge of New Windsor. [A.D.C. map location: 10th Edition, page 18, grid coordinates 10A.] The cemetery has disappeared. Year of earliest known death: 1869. The gravemarkers were transcribed in 1995. Location of transcribed records: Carroll County Public Library, 50 Main Street, Westminster, MD 21157. There are only two loose stones in neighbor's barn; stones were carted away about 1930. The land belongs to Baltimore Archdiocese. Surnames: Dobbyn, Conway.

STONE CHAPEL UNITED METHODIST CHURCH CEMETERY
Location: At intersection of Stone Chapel and Bowersox Roads. [A.D.C. map location: 10th Edition, page 18, grid coordinates 12J.] This cemetery is well-maintained. Year of earliest known death: 1830. Poulson Family members are buried here. The gravemarkers were transcribed in 1982. Location of transcribed records: Carroll County Public Library, 50 Main Street, Westminster, MD 21157.

STRAWBRIDGE UNITED METHODIST CHURCH CEMETERY
Location: South of New Windsor on the east side of Route 31, about 2 miles. [A.D.C. map location: 10th Edition, page 18, grid coordinates 12A.] The cemetery is well-maintained. Year of earliest known death: 1859. The gravemarkers were transcribed in 1990. A partial list of transcribed records is held by Carroll County Public Library, 50 E. Main Street, Westminster, MD, 21157. The oldest stones are those relocated from Toop's Cemetery. The other stones are quite modern. Mailing address: Strawbridge U.M. Church, Route 3, New Windsor, MD 21776-0000.

SUNRISE CEMETERY
Location: West side of Bowers Road southeast of the village of Harney. [A.D.C. map location: 10th Edition, page 1, grid coordinates 5F.] The transcribed records were published in Jacob Mehrling Holdcraft's *Names*

in Stone, 75,000 Cemetery Inscriptions From Frederick County, Maryland. The Monocacy Book Company, Redwood City, CA (2nd printing, 1972). Data were transcribed between 1959 and 1962.

TANEYTOWN REFORMED CEMETERY (GRACE UNITED CHURCH OF CHRIST CEMETERY)
Location: On Memorial Drive (lane parallel to W. Baltimore St.) behind church in Taneytown. [A.D.C. map location: 10th Edition, page 9, grid coordinates 2J.] Cemetery well-maintained. Year of earliest known death: 1770. Location of transcribed records: See *Names In Stone.* Holdcraft added a few names to Scharf's List of 1882. The transcribed records were published in Jacob Mehrling Holdcraft's *Names in Stone, 75,000 Cemetery Inscriptions From Frederick County, Maryland.* The Monocacy Book Company, Redwood City, CA (2nd printing, 1972). Data were transcribed between 1959 and 1962. Additional comments: Holdcraft's inscriptions incomplete. Church established about 1760. Cemetery's mailing address: Grace United Church of Christ, 49 W. Baltimore Street, Taneytown, MD 21787-0000.

TAYLORSVILLE UNITED METHODIST CHURCH CEMETERY (MOUNTAIN VIEW METHODIST CHURCH)
Location: About 1/4 mile south of Route 26 and Route 27 intersection on Ridge Road. [A.D.C. map location: 10th Edition, page 23, grid coordinates 13C.] This cemetery is well-maintained. Holdcraft referred to it as "Mountain View." Year of earliest known death: 1850. The gravemarkers were transcribed in 1963. The transcribed records were published in Jacob Mehrling Holdcraft's *Names in Stone, 75,000 Cemetery Inscriptions From Frederick County, Maryland.* The Monocacy Book Company, Redwood City, CA (2nd printing, 1972). Holdcraft recorded 613 names. Mailing address: Taylorsville U.M. Church, 4356 Ridge Road, Mt. Airy, MD 21771-0000.

TRINITY LUTHERAN CHURCH CEMETERY (TRINITY EVANGELICAL LUTHERAN CHURCH CEMETERY)
Location: On Deer Park Road about 1/2 mile east of Sykesville Road intersection. [A.D.C. map location: 10th Edition, page 25, grid coordinates 2B.] Cemetery is well-maintained. Year of earliest known death: 1851. The gravemarkers were transcribed in 1986. Location of transcribed records: Carroll County Public Library, 50 Main Street, Westminster, MD 21157. The transcribed records were published in Carroll County Genealogical Society, *Carroll County Cemeteries,* Volume 2, Carroll County Genealogical Society, P.O. Box 1752, Westminster, MD 21158

(1990). Inscriptions were copied by Kyle Alexander for Eagle Scout Project in 1986. Mailing address: Trinity Lutheran Church, 833 Deer Park Road, Westminster, MD 21157-0000.

TRINITY LUTHERAN CHURCH CEMETERY
Location: About 2 blocks north of West Baltimore Street behind the church in Taneytown. [A.D.C. map location: 10th Edition, page 9, grid coordinates 1K.] This cemetery is well-maintained. Year of earliest known death: 1780. The gravemarkers were transcribed in 1959. Location of transcribed records: See Holdcraft's *Names In Stone*. Holdcraft added a few names to Scharf's list of 1882. The transcribed records were published in Jacob Mehrling Holdcraft's *Names in Stone, 75,000 Cemetery Inscriptions From Frederick County, Maryland*. However these inscriptions are incomplete; only 290 names are listed. The Monocacy Book Company, Redwood City, CA (2nd printing, 1972). Data were transcribed between 1959 and 1962. Mailing address: Trinity Evangelical Lutheran Church, 38 W. Baltimore Street, Taneytown, MD 21787-0000.

UNIONTOWN CHURCH OF GOD CEMETERY
Location: East side of Trevanion Road Just north of intersection with Uniontown Road. [A.D.C. map location: 10th Edition, page 17, grid coordinates 1J.] The cemetery is well-maintained. Year of earliest known death: 1830. The gravemarkers were transcribed in 1959. 125 names recorded, Holdcraft added randomly to 1882 Scharf's list. The transcribed records were published in Jacob Mehrling Holdcraft's *Names in Stone, 75,000 Cemetery Inscriptions From Frederick County, Maryland*. The Monocacy Book Company, Redwood City, CA (2nd printing, 1972). Data were transcribed between 1959 and 1962. The church burned about 1976; the cemetery is still in use.

UNIONTOWN METHODIST CHURCH CEMETERY
Location: On north side of Uniontown Road in Village of Uniontown. [A.D.C. map location: 10th Edition, page 17, grid coordinates 1J.] This cemetery is well-maintained. Year of earliest known death: 1830. Mailing address: Uniontown Methodist Church, 3405 Uniontown Road, Westminster, MD 21158-0000.

UNITED BRETHREN IN CHRIST CEMETERY
Location: Was located on west side of Route 32 (Sykesville Road) south of village of Smallwood. [A.D.C. map location: 10th Edition, page 24, grid coordinates 3K.] The cemetery has disappeared. The transcribed records were published in Carroll County Genealogical Society, *Carroll County*

Cemeteries, Volume 2, Carroll County Genealogical Society, P.O. Box 1752, Westminster, MD 21158 (1990). Stones and remains were removed in early 1900s, majority to Deer Park U.M. Cemetery.

WATERSVILLE M.E. CHURCH CEMETERY
Location: West side of Watersville Road just north of railroad in Watersville [A.D.C. map location: 10th Edition, page 33, grid coordinates 3A.] Church still exists but no stones visible, some periwinkle groundcover. The transcribed records were published in Carroll County Genealogical Society, *Carroll County Cemeteries*, Volume 3, Carroll County Genealogical Society, P.O. Box 1752, Westminster, MD 21158 (1992). Burials of Emma Hatfield Smith and 2 children were reported, no dates.

WESLEY CHAPEL CEMETERY
Location: North side of Route 26 (Liberty Road) just west of the intersection with the Johnsville Road. [A.D.C. map location: 10th Edition, page 30, grid coordinates 9B.] The cemetery is well-maintained. Year of earliest known death: 1807. The gravemarkers were transcribed in 1980. Location of transcribed records: Carroll County Public Library, 50 Main Street, Westminster, MD 21157. The transcribed records were published in Carroll County Genealogical Society, *Carroll County Cemeteries*, Volume 1, Carroll County Genealogical Society, P.O. Box 1752, Westminster, MD 21158 (1989). Stones were also transcribed by J.M. Holdcraft in *Names in Stone*.

WESLEY FREEDOM METHODIST CHURCH CEMETERY (FREEDOM METHODIST EPISCOPAL CHURCH SOUTH)
Location: Southeast side of the intersection between Johnsville Road and Route 26 (Liberty Road) [A.D.C. map location: 10th Edition, page 30, grid coordinates 9B.] The cemetery is well-maintained. Year of earliest known death: 1826. Included are some stones relocated from family cemeteries and burials of Springfield Hospital patients. The gravemarkers were transcribed in 1985. Location of transcribed records: Carroll County Public Library, 50 Main Street, Westminster, MD 21157. The transcribed records were published in Carroll County Genealogical Society, *Carroll County Cemeteries*, Volume 1, Carroll County Genealogical Society, P.O. Box 1752, Westminster, MD 21158 (1989). Mailing address: Wesley Freedom U.M. Church, 961 Johnsville, Road, Sykesville, MD 21784-0000.

WESLEY UNITED METHODIST CHURCH CEMETERY
Location: Corner of Wesley and Carrollton Roads southwest of

Hampstead. [A.D.C. map location: 10th Edition, page 21, grid coordinates 8D.] Cemetery is well-maintained. Year of earliest known death: 1829. The gravemarkers were transcribed in 1983. Location of transcribed records: Carroll County Public Library, 50 Main Street, Westminster, MD 21157. The transcribed records were published in Carroll County Genealogical Society, *Carroll County Cemeteries*, Volume 2, Carroll County Genealogical Society, P.O. Box 1752, Westminster, MD 21158 (1990). 1082 names were transcribed. Mailing address: Wesley U.M. Church, Wesley and Carrollton Roads., Hampstead, MD 21074-0000.

WESTERN CHAPEL CEMETERY
Location: East side of Western Chapel Road about 1/2 mile from Stone Chapel intersection. [A.D.C. map location: 10th Edition, page 19, grid coordinates 11A.] This cemetery is in very poor condition. Year of earliest known death: 1871. Burial records are maintained. The gravemarkers were transcribed in 1984. Location of transcribed records: Carroll County Public Library, 50 Main Street, Westminster, MD 21157. This is an African-American cemetery. There are some very old gravestones and some modern ones, often just funeral home markers.

WHITE ROCK METHODIST CHURCH CEMETERY
Location: West side of White Rock Road between Liberty Road (Route 26) and Streaker Road. [A.D.C. map location: 10th Edition, page 29, grid coordinates 10F.] Cemetery well-maintained. Year of earliest known death: 1880. The gravemarkers were transcribed in 1988. Location of transcribed records: Carroll County Public Library, 50 Main Street, Westminster, MD 21157. The transcribed records were published in Carroll County Genealogical Society, *Carroll County Cemeteries*, Volume 1, Carroll County Genealogical Society, P.O. Box 1752, Westminster, MD 21158 (1989). An African-American congregation.

ZIMMERMAN'S MENNONITE CEMETERY
Location: In field behind Zimmerman's Church on Grave Run Road near Shaffer Mill Road. [A.D.C. map location: 10th Edition, page 7, grid coordinates 7E.] The cemetery is fenced but badly overgrown. The gravemarkers were transcribed in 1986. Location of transcribed records: Carroll County Public Library, 50 Main Street, Westminster, MD 21157. The transcribed records were published in Carroll County Genealogical Society, *Carroll County Cemeteries*, Volume 4, Carroll County Genealogical Society, P.O. Box 1752, Westminster, MD 21158 (1995). About 45 inscriptions. Surnames: Zimmerman, Lammott, Grogg, Jones, Hoffacker.

ZION UNITED METHODIST CHURCH CEMETERY.
Location: West side of Old Washington Road between Nicodemus and Salem Bottom Roads. [A.D.C. map location: 10th Edition, page 24, grid coordinates 5F.] The cemetery is well-maintained. Year of earliest known death: 1880. The gravemarkers were transcribed in 1984. Location of transcribed records: Carroll County Public Library, 50 Main Street, Westminster, MD 21157. Mailing address: Zion U.M. Church, 2716 Old Washington Road, Westminster, MD 21157-0000.

Public Cemeteries

ALMSHOUSE CEMETERY (POTTERS FIELD)
Location: At intersection of Gist Road and Center Street near Landon Burns Park on the Farm Museum property. [A.D.C. map location: 10th Edition, page 19, grid coordinates 8G.] Well-maintained. Year of earliest known death: 1909. Year of most recent death: 1934. The gravemarkers were transcribed in 1982. Location of transcribed records: Carroll County Public Library, 50 Main Street, Westminster, MD 21157. The transcribed records were published in Carroll County Genealogical Society, *Carroll County Cemeteries*, Volume 2, Carroll County Genealogical Society, P.O. Box 1752, Westminster, MD 21158 (1990). Many people were buried at the Almshouse beginning in the 1850s. Cemetery's mailing address: Carroll County Farm Museum, Center Street extended, Westminster, MD 21157-0000.

EVERGREEN MEMORIAL GARDENS CEMETERY
Location: On section of Old Westminster Pike, parallel to Route 140, opposite Kay's Mill Road. [A.D.C. map location: 10th Edition, page 26, grid coordinates 4B.] The cemetery is well-maintained. Year of earliest known death: 1955. Veterans interred: WWII and other wars. Records are held at the Cemetery Office. Mailing address: Evergreen Memorial Gardens, 2800 Old Westminster Pike, Finksburg, MD 21048-0000.

GARDENS OF ETERNAL HOPE CEMETERY (DEER PARK MEMORIAL GARDENS, CARROLL MEMORIAL GARDENS)
Location: On Deer Park Road between Greens Mill Road and Davinda Drive. [A.D.C. map location: 10th Edition, page 25, grid coordinates 5E.] Information on this modern cemetery has been difficult to find. Year of earliest known death: 1959. Location of records: Unknown. Some information (not inscriptions) was published in Carroll County Genealogical Society, *Carroll County Cemeteries*, Volume 2, Carroll

County Genealogical Society, P.O. Box 1752, Westminster, MD 21158 (1990). The cemetery was established circa 1959. Mailing address: Carroll Memorial Gardens, Inc., c/o Paul J. Duclos, Washington, DC 20020-0000.

LAKEVIEW MEMORIAL PARK CEMETERY
Location: North side of Liberty Road near Baltimore County line. [A.D.C. map location: 10th Edition, page 31, grid coordinates 10A.] The cemetery is well-maintained. Year of earliest known death: 1959. (It was established circa 1959.) Records are held in the cemetery office. Mailing address: Lakeview Memorial Park, 2724 Liberty Road, Eldersburg, MD 21784-0000.

LINEBORO CEMETERY
Location: On Church St. in the village of Lineboro, east of Main Street. [A.D.C. map location: 10th Edition, page 6, grid coordinates 5J.] The cemetery is well-maintained. Year of earliest known death: 1931. The gravemarkers were transcribed in 1979. Location of transcribed records: Carroll County Public Library, 50 Main Street, Westminster, MD 21157. The transcribed records were published in Carroll County Genealogical Society, *Carroll County Cemeteries*, Volume 4, Carroll County Genealogical Society, P.O. Box 1752, Westminster, MD 21158 (1995). Lineboro Cemetery Corporation was established in 1928, next to Lazarus Cemetery.

MOREHEAD MEMORIAL CEMETERY (UNION MILLS CEMETERY (?))
Location: On east side of Route 97 (Littlestown Pike) in Union Mills at Cemetery Lane. [A.D.C. map location: 10th Edition, page 4, grid coordinates 13B.] The cemetery is well-maintained. Year of earliest known death: 1876. The gravemarkers were transcribed in 1985. Location of transcribed records: Carroll County Public Library, 50 Main Street, Westminster, MD 21157.

MOUNTAIN VIEW CEMETERY
Location: South end of Main Street in Union Bridge, on the east side of the street. [A.D.C. map location: 10th Edition, page 16, grid coordinates 6K.] The cemetery is well-maintained. Year of earliest known death: 1860. The gravemarkers were transcribed in 1961. The transcribed records were published in Jacob Mehrling Holdcraft's *Names in Stone, 75,000 Cemetery Inscriptions From Frederick County, Maryland*. The Monocacy Book Company, Redwood City, CA (2nd printing, 1972). Data were transcribed between 1959 and 1962. Holdcraft recorded 782 names, some

badly eroded. Some inscriptions were mentioned in Scharf's *History of Western Maryland*.

MT. PLEASANT CEMETERY
Location: About 1/2 mile east of Taneytown on Route 832 (Old Taneytown Road) [A.D.C. map location: 10th Edition, page 10, grid coordinates 4D.] The cemetery is well-maintained. The records have not been published. Details on this cemetery's affiliation and ownership are unknown; it is relatively modern.

NEW LAUREL CEMETERY (FORMERLY LAUREL CEMETERY ON BELAIR ROAD IN BALTIMORE)
Location: West side of Hodges Road about 3/4 mile from intersection with Bartholow Road. [A.D.C. map location: 10th Edition, page 30, grid coordinates 6C.] Location of transcribed records: Carroll County Public Library, 50 Main Street, Westminster, MD 21157. See Agnes Kane Callum, "Partial List of Interments at Laurel Cemetery," published by *Flower of The Forest* Black Genealogical Journal, Baltimore, MD (1984). A portion of the tombstones from this African-American cemetery were moved from Laurel Cemetery on Belair Road in Baltimore County to Carroll County.

NEW PORT CEMETERY
Location: Vacant lot adjacent to 2149 Flag Marsh Road (south side) [A.D.C. map location: 10th Edition, page 33, grid coordinates 3E.] Although many persons are reported buried here only two tombstones are visible. Year of earliest known death: 1915. Year of most recent death: 1923. The gravemarkers were transcribed in 1991. Location of transcribed records: Carroll County Public Library, 50 Main Street, Westminster, MD 21157. The transcribed records were published in Carroll County Genealogical Society, *Carroll County Cemeteries*, Volume 3, Carroll County Genealogical Society, P.O. Box 1752, Westminster, MD 21158 (1992). The land was donated for burials of less affluent persons. Surnames: Woodward, Evans.

PINE GROVE CEMETERY (RIDGE PRESBYTERIAN CHURCH)
Location: South end of Main Street in the town of Mt. Airy. [A.D.C. map location: 10th Edition, page 32, grid coordinates 2B.] This is a well-maintained large cemetery. Year of earliest known death: 1839. The gravemarkers were transcribed in 1991. Location of transcribed records: Carroll County Public Library, 50 Main Street, Westminster, MD 21157. The transcribed records were published in Carroll County Genealogical

Society, *Carroll County Cemeteries,* Volume 3, Carroll County Genealogical Society, P.O. Box 1752, Westminster, MD 21158 (1992). Approximately 1600 inscriptions were transcribed.

PLEASANT VALLEY CEMETERY
Location: On Pleasant Valley Road South, about 2 miles from Route 140 intersection. [A.D.C. map location: 10th Edition, page 11, grid coordinates 8J.] The cemetery is well-maintained. Year of earliest known death: 1871. The gravemarkers were transcribed in 1994. Location of transcribed records: Carroll County Public Library, 50 Main Street, Westminster, MD 21157. There is a large memorial to WWI and WWII veterans.

SPRINGFIELD STATE HOSPITAL CEMETERY (SUNNYSIDE CEMETERY)
Location: On grounds of Springfield State Hospital off Route 32 in Sykesville [A.D.C. map location: 10th Edition, page 35, grid coordinates 1B.] These are numbered markers (no names), unknown condition. Year of earliest known death: 1899. Year of most recent death: 1961. The gravemarkers were transcribed in 1984 and held by Carroll County Public Library, 50 Main Street, Westminster, MD 21157. The transcribed records were published in Carroll County Genealogical Society, *Carroll County Cemeteries,* Volume 1, Carroll County Genealogical Society, P.O. Box 1752, Westminster, MD 21158 (1989). There are 955 recorded burials of patients from Maryland and other states. See burial record books of State Hospital.

WESTMINSTER CEMETERY
Location: In the city of Westminster, off North Church Street. [A.D.C. map location: 10th Edition, page 19, grid coordinates 5H.] The cemetery is well-maintained. Year of earliest known death: 1790. A partial list of inscriptions is in Scharf's *History of Western Maryland.* Some old inscriptions are listed in 1889/1890 issues of the *Democratic Advocate.* Cemetery's mailing address: Westminster Cemetery, Westminster, MD 21157-0000; 410-848-7240.

WOLF (WOLFE) CEMETERY
Location: West side of Quaker Hill Road about halfway between Union Bridge and Priestland Road. [A.D.C. map location: 10th Edition, page 17, grid coordinates 8B.] The cemetery is well-maintained. Year of earliest known death: 1770. Year of most recent death: 1855. The gravemarkers were transcribed in 1957. Location of transcribed records: Carroll County Public Library, 50 Main Street, Westminster, MD 21157. The transcribed

records were published in Jacob Mehrling Holdcraft's *Names in Stone, 75,000 Cemetery Inscriptions From Frederick County, Maryland*. The Monocacy Book Company, Redwood City, CA (2nd printing, 1972). Data were transcribed between 1959 and 1962.

MONTGOMERY COUNTY

Private Cemeteries

ALLNUTT-AYTON-BOWMAN FAMILY BURYING GROUND AT CLAYSVILLE
Directions: From Laytonsville, Route 108 southeast, Olney-Laytonsville Road, Claysville on left. [A.D.C. Map: Montgomery, page 15, grid coordinates D-6.] Located in middle of actively cultivated field, exact location unknown. This cemetery is non-extant. Records not transcribed. Comments: Field stone markers only.

ASH MEMORIAL CEMETERY AT SANDY SPRING
Directions: Route 97 North, right on Route 108, left on Brook Road, left on Chandlee Mill Road, cemetery on left. [A.D.C. Map: Montgomery, page 16, grid coordinates G-12.] Condition of cemetery: Well kept. Active cemetery. Earliest known death: 1918. Most recent death: Present. Veterans interred: WWI, WWII and other wars vets. Location of burial records: Ash Memorial Cemetery office. Date transcribed: 1983. Location of transcribed records: Montgomery County Historical Society Library, 42 West Middle Lane, Rockville, Maryland 20850. Comments: Over 400 marked graves, African-American cemetery.

ASPIN HILL MEMORIAL PARK AND COMPANION CEMETERY
Directions: From Silver Spring, Route 97 North, Georgia Avenue. [A.D.C. Map: Montgomery, page 33, grid coordinates B-1.] Condition of cemetery: Well kept. Active cemetery. Most recent death: Present. Location of burial records: Aspin Hill Memorial Park and Companion Cemetery office. Records not transcribed. Comments: Pet cemetery, contains remains of about 40 humans who wished to be buried with their pets.

AUD FAMILY BURYING GROUND NEAR POOLESVILLE
Directions: West of Willard Road, Poolesville. No markers extant at site. [A.D.C. Map: Montgomery, page 19.] Condition of cemetery: Overgrown.

Formerly located about 100 yards south of barn. This cemetery is nonextant. Earliest known death: 1818. Most recent death: 1916. Records not transcribed, information obtained from family records. Author: Kathleen L. and Susan E. Aud. Title: *Our Ancestors (Aud, Veirs, Hickman, Lucas, Harriss, Spates, Granger, etc.)*, Kathleen L. and Susan E. Aud, 700 Copley Lane, Silver Spring, MD 20904, 1972. Comments: Seven interments from family records, tenant farmer removed grave markers about 1929.

AWKARD FAMILY BURYING GROUND AT BIG WOODS
Directions: West side of Beallsville Road in Big Woods community. [A.D.C. Map: Montgomery, page 11, grid coordinates B-6.] Condition of cemetery: Neglected, only 5 marked graves. Maryland Historic Trust site survey information 1979. Inactive cemetery. Earliest known death: 1880. Most recent death: 1883. Date transcribed: 1979. Location of transcribed records: Montgomery County Historical Society Library, 42 West Middle Lane, Rockville, Maryland 20850. Comments: African-American cemetery, 1/4 acre was reserved for family cemetery, Mt. Zion Church once located here.

BATSON FAMILY BURYING GROUND NEAR TRIADELPHIA
Directions: Route 97 North, Georgia Avenue, right on Triadelphia Lake Road. [A.D.C. Map: Montgomery, page 8, grid coordinates F-12.] Condition of cemetery: Well kept. Inactive cemetery. Earliest known death: 1883. Most recent death: 1883. Date transcribed: 1989. Location of transcribed records: Montgomery County Historical Society Library, 42 West Middle Lane, Rockville, Maryland 20850. Comments: Only 3 marked graves, Pigtail/Dutton's Fields.

BEALL FAMILY BURYING GROUND NEAR LAYHILL
Directions: Route 97 North, right on Bel Pre Road, right on Beaverwood Lane, right on Beechvue Lane, cemetery on left. [A.D.C. Map: Montgomery, page 25, grid coordinates C-13.] Condition of cemetery: In 1981, all but one stone toppled, it is located between 14121 and 14125 in Spruce trees. Inactive cemetery. Earliest known death: 1831. Most recent death: 1895. Date transcribed: 1981. Location of transcribed records: Montgomery County Historical Society Library, 42 West Middle Lane, Rockville, Maryland 20850. Comments: Historic site 27/15, community cleaned up cemetery in April 1993.

BONIFANT FAMILY BURYING GROUND NEAR LAYHILL
Directions: Route 182 North, Layhill Road, right on Bonifant Road, road leading to Bonifant home. [A.D.C. Map: Montgomery, page 25, grid coordinates F-12.] Condition of cemetery: Well kept. Inactive cemetery. Earliest known death: 1810. Most recent death: 1978. Famous person interred: Samuel Bonifant. Veterans interred: Revolutionary Vets. Date transcribed: 1982. Location of transcribed records: Montgomery County Historical Society Library, 42 West Middle Lane, Rockville, Maryland 20850. Comments: Historic site 28/21, contains at least 25 marked graves.

BREADY FAMILY BURYING GROUND NEAR LAYHILL
Directions: Route 182 North, Layhill Road, in Northwest Branch Park on golf course. [A.D.C. Map: Montgomery, page 25, grid coordinates G-9.] Condition of cemetery: Unknown. Inactive cemetery. Earliest known death: 1850. Most recent death: 1878. Location of transcribed records: Montgomery County Historical Society Library, 42 West Middle Lane, Rockville, Maryland 20850. Comments: Four marked graves, on farm land recently owned by Maj. E. Brook Lee.

BROWN (JAMES) FAMILY BURYING GROUND NEAR ETCHISON
Directions: Off Sunshine Road between *Gittings HaHa* and *Far View*, now in backyard of home. Condition of cemetery: Unknown. Inactive cemetery. Earliest known death: 1833. Most recent death: 1912. Veterans interred: Revolutionary Vets. Date transcribed: 1968. Location of transcribed records: Montgomery County Historical Society Library, 42 West Middle Lane, Rockville, Maryland 20850. Comments: 14 marked graves.

BROWN (OWEN) NICHOLAS WATKINS FAMILY BURYING GROUND NEAR DAMASCUS
Directions: Route 27 north, Ridge Road, through Damascus, right on Browns Church Road, cemetery on right. [A.D.C. Map: Montgomery, page 2, grid coordinates D-8.] Condition of cemetery: Overgrown, but clean up in progress, no inscribed markers. Inactive cemetery. Location of burial records: Montgomery United Methodist Church has unpublished manuscript with names of probable interments. Comments: Cemetery now located on part of Patuxent River State Park.

BURGESS FAMILY BURYING GROUND AT CABIN JOHN
Directions: West on MacArthur Boulevard, right on Seven Locks Road, right on Tomlinson Terrace and Avenue, left on Arden Road. [A.D.C. Map: Montgomery, page 37, grid coordinates J-7.] Condition of cemetery:

Unknown. This cemetery is non-extant. Earliest known death: 1841. Date transcribed: 1941. Location of transcribed records: Montgomery County Historical Society Library, 42 West Middle Lane, Rockville, Maryland 20850. Comments: Photograph taken 1941, one marked grave, many unmarked graves.

BURTON FAMILY BURYING GROUND NEAR PATUXENT RIVER
Directions: Route 29 North, left on Bell Road, cemetery on right at dead end. [A.D.C. Map: Montgomery, page 27, grid coordinates A-5.] Condition of cemetery: Well kept. Inactive cemetery. Earliest known death: 1832. Most recent death: 1873. Location of transcribed records: Montgomery County Historical Society Library, 42 West Middle Lane, Rockville, Maryland 20850. Comments: Historic site 15/64, Wilcox Farm, at least 8 marked graves.

BYRD FAMILY BURYING GROUND NEAR DAWSONVILLE
Directions: On Edward Byrd farm near Dawsonville. [A.D.C. Map: Montgomery, page 21, grid coordinates A-5.] Condition of cemetery: Unknown. Inactive cemetery. Earliest known death: 1834. Most recent death: 1885. Location of transcribed records: Montgomery County Historical Society Library, 42 West Middle Lane, Rockville, Maryland 20850. Comments: Historic site, at least 5 marked graves.

CARR FAMILY BURYING GROUND AT BURTONSVILLE
Directions: Route 29 North, Columbia Pike, left on Route 198, Spencerville-Sandy Spring Road, cemetery on left. [A.D.C. Map: Montgomery, page 27, grid coordinates B-8.] Condition of cemetery: Unknown. Inactive cemetery. Earliest known death: 1832. Most recent death: 1903. Date transcribed: 1974. Location of transcribed records: Montgomery County Historical Society Library, 42 West Middle Lane, Rockville, Maryland 20850. Comments: Historic site 15/63, Thomas Waters House, at least 13 marked graves.

CASHELL FAMILY BURYING GROUND NEAR LAYHILL
Directions: Cemetery located on property now owned by Leisure World. [A.D.C. Map: Montgomery, page 25, grid coordinates B-9.] Condition of cemetery: Unknown. This cemetery is non-extant. The cemetery has been relocated. Earliest known death: 1859. Most recent death: 1916. Location of transcribed records: Montgomery County Historical Society Library, 42 West Middle Lane, Rockville, Maryland 20850. At least 39 bodies moved to Rockville Cemetery, list exists of known people buried in Cashell family cemetery.

CISSEL-TRUNDLE FAMILY BURYING GROUND NEAR POOLESVILLE

Directions: Route 28 Northwest to Dawsonville, left on Route 107, Whites Ferry Road to Humphrey Cissel farm. [A.D.C. Map: Montgomery, page 20.] Condition of cemetery: Abandoned. Inactive cemetery. Earliest known death: 1822. Most recent death: 1885. Location of transcribed records: Montgomery County Historical Society Library, 42 West Middle Lane, Rockville, Maryland 20850. Comments: All Cissell stones moved to Monocacy Cemetery, 16 bodies left behind in this burial ground.

CLARK FAMILY BURYING GROUND AT CLARKSBURG

Directions: Route 355 North, right on Route 121, Clarksburg Road, to Kings Community Pond. [A.D.C. Map: Montgomery, page 5, grid coordinates A-10.] Condition of cemetery: Destroyed. This cemetery is nonextant. Earliest known death: 1803. Most recent death: 1817. Famous person interred: John Clark. Location of transcribed records: Montgomery County Historical Society Library, 42 West Middle Lane, Rockville, Maryland 20850. Author: J. Thomas Scharf, A.M. Title: *History of Western Maryland*, page 720, Regional Publishing Company [reprinted 1968], Baltimore, MD [originally printed in Philadelphia, 1882]. Comments: Reportedly two markers found in field bordering park by Norman Meese several years before 1995

COOKE (NATHAN) FAMILY BURYING GROUND AT REDLAND

Directions: On *Cooke's Range*, now Carson Pope farm, on Muncaster Mill Road, near Redland. [A.D.C. Map: Montgomery, page 24, grid coordinates A-2.] Condition of cemetery: Unknown, land now owned by Maryland National Capital Park and Planning Commission. Inactive cemetery. Earliest known death: 1805. Most recent death: 1904. Date transcribed: 1983. Location of transcribed records: Montgomery County Historical Society Library, 42 West Middle Lane, Rockville, Maryland 20850. Comments: Historic site 22/22, at least 21 marked graves.

CRABB FAMILY BURYING GROUND AT DERWOOD

[A.D.C. Map: Montgomery, page 23, grid coordinates H-8.] Condition of cemetery: Unknown. Inactive cemetery. Earliest known death: 1800. Most recent death: 1925. Famous person interred: General Jeremiah Crabb. Veterans interred: Revolutionary Vets. Date transcribed: 1968. Location of transcribed records: Montgomery County Historical Society Library, 42 West Middle Lane, Rockville, Maryland 20850. Comments: At least 12 marked graves.

DARNALL FAMILY BURYING GROUND AT DAWSONVILLE
Directions: Route 28 West, Darnestown Road, to Dawsonville, on tract of land called *Darnall's*. [A.D.C. Map: Montgomery, page 21, grid coordinates A-5.] Condition of cemetery: Unknown. Inactive cemetery. Earliest known death: 1830. Most recent death: 1857. Date transcribed: 1978. Location of transcribed records: Montgomery County Historical Society Library, 42 West Middle Lane, Rockville, Maryland 20850. Comments: Historic site 18/21, four graves, data from photographs taken in 1978, by Mary Ann Kephart.

DAVIS FAMILY BURYING GROUND AT BROOKEVILLE [THE HOME IS CALLED "GREENWOOD"]
Directions: Route 97 North, Georgia Avenue, 21315 Georgia Avenue, Brookeville, southwestern section of yard. [A.D.C. Map: Montgomery, page 16, grid coordinates C-4.] Condition of cemetery: Stone wall enclosure, protected but neglected, endowed by Miss Mary Davis. Inactive cemetery. Earliest known death: 1769. Most recent death: 1939. Famous person interred: Thomas Davis III. Veterans interred: other wars vets. Date transcribed: 1975. Location of transcribed records: Montgomery County Historical Society Library, 42 West Middle Lane, Rockville, Maryland 20850. Author: Helen W. Ridgely. Title: *Historic Graves of Maryland and the District of Columbia*, pages 178-179. Publisher: Family Line Publications [Grafton Press original publisher, 1908], Westminster, MD [reprinted 1992]. Comments: At least 21 marked graves, slave cemetery on hill about 300 feet east of barn, no markers.

DAVIS FAMILY BURYING GROUND ON CECIL PLANTATION, TAKOMA PARK (CECIL PLANTATION)
Directions: 901 Prospect Avenue at corner of Greenwood Avenue, at extreme North end of Takoma Park. [A.D.C. Map: Montgomery, page 40, grid coordinates B-4.] Condition of cemetery: Well kept in 1937. Inactive cemetery. Location of transcribed records: Montgomery County Historical Society Library, 42 West Middle Lane, Rockville, Maryland 20850. Comments: Over 125 interments, information from 8 Aug 1937 newspaper article.

DERWOOD CEMETERY (FAITH CHAPEL METHODIST EPISCOPAL CHURCH SOUTH, BAPTIST CHURCH CEMETERY AT DERWOOD)
Directions: Route 355 North, right on Yellowstone Way, left on Chieftan Avenue, cemetery on right. [A.D.C. Map: Montgomery, page 23, grid coordinates H-7.] Condition of cemetery: Well kept, located behind Derwood Bible Church. Active cemetery. Earliest known death: 1871. Most recent

death: Present. Veterans interred: WWI and WWII Vets. Date transcribed: 1981. Location of transcribed records: Montgomery County Historical Society Library, 42 West Middle Lane, Rockville, Maryland 20850. Comments: At least 56 marked graves.

DESELLUM FAMILY BURYING GROUND AT GAITHERSBURG
Directions: Route 355 North, to Gaithersburg, 510 South Frederick Avenue, cemetery on left. [A.D.C. Map: Montgomery, page 23, grid coordinates C-4.] Condition of cemetery: Well kept, has been restored and enclosed. Inactive cemetery. Earliest known death: 1847. Most recent death: 1891. Date transcribed: 1978. Location of transcribed records: Montgomery County Historical Society Library, 42 West Middle Lane, Rockville, Maryland 20850. Comments: Historic site 21/3, four marked graves.

DORSEY (JOSHUA) FAMILY BURYING GROUND NEAR GOSHEN
Directions: Goshen Road North to Wightman Road, Trundle Farm at intersection. [A.D.C. Map: Montgomery, page 14, grid coordinates D-7.] Condition of cemetery: Two marked graves. This cemetery is non-extant. Relocated: Moved by Kettler Bros to Forest Oak Cemetery in 1970. Earliest known death: 1843. Most recent death: 1848. Location of transcribed records: Montgomery County Historical Society Library, 42 West Middle Lane, Rockville, Maryland 20850. Author: Helen W. Ridgely. Title: *Historic Graves of Maryland and the District of Columbia*, page 177. Publisher: Family Line Publications [Grafton Press original publisher, 1908], Westminster, MD, [reprinted 1992]. Comments: Historic site 23/6, two stones and several bodies moved to Forest Oak Cemetery in Gaithersburg.

DORSEY (SAMUEL) FAMILY BURYING GROUND NEAR ETCHISON
Directions: Route 650, Damascus Road, on right side of road from Unity to Damascus. [A.D.C. Map: Montgomery, page 8, grid coordinates A-13.] Condition of cemetery: Unknown, on Howes farm. Inactive cemetery. Earliest known death: 1862. Most recent death: 1927. Date transcribed: 1970. Location of transcribed records: Montgomery County Historical Society Library, 42 West Middle Lane, Rockville, Maryland 20850. Comments: Historic site 23/6, at least 5 marked graves.

EDWARD'S FERRY CEMETERY, HICKMAN FAMILY BURYING GROUND
Directions: Exact location kept confidential to protect it. [A.D.C. Map: Montgomery, page 19, grid coordinates: B-10.] Condition of cemetery:

Unknown. Inactive cemetery. Earliest known death: 1766. Location of transcribed records: Montgomery County Historical Society Library, 42 West Middle Lane, Rockville, Maryland 20850. Comments: Oldest existing cemetery in Montgomery County, data from Historic sites study and Evening Star article, 4 marked graves.

FLETCHALL FAMILY BURYING GROUND AT MT. NEBO, POOLESVILLE (MOUNT NEBO CEMETERY)
Directions: Route 190 West, River Road, north on Mt. Nebo Road to *Mt. Nebo* land tract. [A.D.C. Map: Montgomery, page 19, grid coordinates E-10.] Condition of cemetery: Stones removed from original location and found on a creek or river bank. Inactive cemetery. Earliest known death: 1777. Most recent death: 1878. Date transcribed: 1982. Location of transcribed records: Montgomery County Historical Society Library, 42 West Middle Lane, Rockville, Maryland 20850. Comments: "Joche" was attempting to determine original location and return stones to the nine sites.

FOREST OAK CEMETERY AT GAITHERSBURG (FOREST CHAPEL METHODIST EPISCOPAL CHURCH)
Directions: Route 355 North, Frederick Road, to Gaithersburg, cemetery on left. [A.D.C. Map: Montgomery, page 23, grid coordinates B-2.] Condition of cemetery: Well kept. Active cemetery. Earliest known death: 1869. Most recent death: Present. Veterans interred: Civil War, WWI Vet, WWII Vet, and other wars vets. Some records exist. Date transcribed: 1974. Location of transcribed records: Montgomery County Historical Society Library, 42 West Middle Lane, Rockville, Maryland 20850. Author: J. Thomas Scharf, A.M. Title: *History of Western Maryland*, page 786, Vol. I. Publisher: Regional Publishing Company [reprinted 1968], Baltimore, MD [originally printed in Philadelphia, 1882]. Comments: Over 1800 marked graves, more that 150 unmarked graves, Forest Oak Cemetery established in 1879.

GAITHER (BENJAMIN) FAMILY BURYING GROUND AT GAITHERSBURG
Directions: Brookes Avenue, Gaithersburg, on private property. [A.D.C. Map: Montgomery, page 23, grid coordinates C-2.] Located in backyard of a residence, but reserved as a cemetery. This cemetery is non-extant. The records have not been transcribed. Comments: No stones in 1978, however resident remembers four stones in early 1900s.

GAITHER (HENRY CHEW) FAMILY BURYING GROUND AT UNITY

Directions: Route 650 Northwest, New Hampshire Avenue, left on Sundown Road, near Unity. [A.D.C. Map: Montgomery, page 16, grid coordinates A-1.] Condition of cemetery: Unknown. This cemetery is non-extant. Earliest known death: 1845. Most recent death: 1858. Famous person interred: William Lingan Gaither. Date transcribed: 1959. Location of transcribed records: Montgomery County Historical Society Library, 42 West Middle Lane, Rockville, Maryland 20850. Author: Helen W. Ridgely. Title: *Historic Graves of Maryland and the District of Columbia*, pages 182-183. Publisher: Family Line Publications [Grafton Press original publisher, 1908], Westminster, MD [reprinted 1992]. Comments: At least 4 marked graves, cemetery located on the tract of land called *Pleasant Fields*.

GARRETT FAMILY BURYING GROUND NEAR SHADY GROVE

Directions: Muddy Branch Road (Water Street) Gaithersburg. [A.D.C. Map: Montgomery, page 23, grid coordinates B-3.] Condition of cemetery: Became part of Washingtonian Gulf Course, later sold to a developer, no stones. This cemetery is non-extant. Records have not been transcribed. Comments: Bodies and markers moved to Forest Oak Cemetery in Gaithersburg, historic site 20/23.

GRAFF-MUSSER FAMILY BURYING GROUND NEAR GERMANTOWN

Directions: Route 117 south, Clopper Road and Mateney Roads on Weis Market parking lot. [A.D.C. Map: Montgomery, page 13, grid coordinates B-13.] Condition of cemetery: Unknown. This cemetery is non-extant. Earliest known death: 1823. Location of transcribed records: Montgomery County Historical Society Library, 42 West Middle Lane, Rockville, Maryland 20850. Comments: Only one marker engraved, other sites marked with fieldstones, 23 names appear on memorial plaque.

GRIFFITH FAMILY BURYING GROUND AT EDGEHILL

Directions: Off road from Unity to Etchison on "Edgehill," Vestus Wilcox farm, near Laytonsville. [A.D.C. Map: Montgomery, page 15, grid coordinates E-1.] Condition of cemetery: Unknown, monument moved to Laytonsville Cemetery. This cemetery is non-extant. Relocated. Earliest known death: 1803. Most recent death: 1906. Famous person interred: Henry Griffith of Orlando. Veterans interred: Revolutionary Vets. Date transcribed: 1959. Location of transcribed records: Montgomery County Historical Society Library, 42 West Middle Lane, Rockville, Maryland 20850. Author: Helen W. Ridgely. Title: *Historic Graves of Maryland and* the *District of Columbia,* pages 180-181. Publisher: Family Line Publications [Grafton Press original publisher, 1908], Westminster, MD [reprinted 1992].

GRIFFITH (LYDE) FAMILY BURYING ON WARFIELD FARM
Condition of cemetery: Unknown. Inactive cemetery. Earliest known death: 1864. Most recent death: 1898. Date transcribed: 1970. Location of transcribed records: Montgomery County Historical Society Library, 42 West Middle Lane, Rockville, Maryland 20850. Comments: At least 2 marked graves.

HAITI CEMETERY AT ROCKVILLE
Directions: Rockville, North Washington Street North, left on Martin's Lane, right on Bickford Avenue. [A.D.C. Map: Montgomery, page 23, grid coordinates J-12.] Condition of cemetery: Well kept. Active cemetery. Earliest known death: 1886. Most recent death: 1983. Date transcribed: 1986. Location of transcribed records: Montgomery County Historical Society Library, 42 West Middle Lane, Rockville, Maryland 20850. Comments: Over 35 marked graves, African-American cemetery located at end of Bickford Avenue, behind last house on left.

HARDING (ANDREW JACKSON) FAMILY BURYING GROUND AT CLOVERLY
Directions: Route 650 North, New Hampshire Avenue, right on Briggs Chaney Road, cemetery on left. [A.D.C. Map: Montgomery, page 26, grid coordinates C-9.] Condition of cemetery: Well kept, enclosed with fence. Inactive cemetery. Earliest known death: 1882. Most recent death: 1907. Date transcribed: 1987. Location of transcribed records: Montgomery County Historical Society Library, 42 West Middle Lane, Rockville, Maryland 20850. Comments: At least 2 marked graves, cemetery located next to Cloverly Elementary School.

HARDING (JOSEPH) FAMILY BURYING GROUND NEAR CLOVERLY
Directions: Route 650 North, New Hampshire Avenue, right on Harding Lane, cemetery on left at end. [A.D.C. Map: Montgomery, page 26, grid coordinates E-8.] Condition of cemetery: Well kept, enclosed with fence. Active cemetery. Earliest known death: 1852. Most recent death: Present. Location of transcribed records: Montgomery County Historical Society Library, 42 West Middle Lane, Rockville, Maryland 20850. Comments: At least 20 marked graves.

MONTGOMERY COUNTY CEMETERIES - PRIVATE 145

HAYES FAMILY BURYING GROUND AT BARNESVILLE
Directions: Route 355 North, left on Route 109, Old Hundred Road, to Barnesville. [A.D.C. Map: Montgomery, page 11, grid coordinates F-1.] Condition of cemetery: Unknown. Location: In 1880 was located on land owned by John W. Brown. Inactive cemetery. Earliest known death: 1822. Most recent death: 1857. Date transcribed: 1880. Location of transcribed records: Montgomery County Historical Society Library, 42 West Middle Lane, Rockville, Maryland 20850. Author: J. Thomas Scharf, A.M. Title: *History of Western Maryland*, page 731, Vol. I. Publisher: Regional Publishing Company [reprinted 1968], Baltimore, MD [originally printed in Philadelphia, 1882]

HERSHEY FAMILY BURYING GROUND AT COMUS
Directions: Route 109 South, Old Hundred Road, to Comus. [A.D.C. Map: Montgomery, page 3, grid coordinates K-10.] Condition of cemetery: Unknown. Inactive cemetery. Earliest known death: 1837. Most recent death: 1901. Date transcribed: 1960. Location of transcribed records: Montgomery County Historical Society Library, 42 West Middle Lane, Rockville, Maryland 20850. Comments: At least 9 marked graves.

HIGGINS (JAMES) FAMILY BURYING GROUND AT PARKLAWN
Directions: From Parklawn, right on Washington St, right on Arundel Avenue at end of street on left. [A.D.C. Map: Montgomery, page 32, grid coordinates E-5.] Condition of cemetery: Well kept, in park near Parklawn Building. Inactive cemetery. Earliest known death: 1816. Most recent death: 1891. Date transcribed: 1981. Location of transcribed records: Montgomery County Historical Society Library, 42 West Middle Lane, Rockville, Maryland 20850. Comments: Cemetery located in Old Springlake Park, at least 10 marked grave sites, plus at least two others.

HOLLAND FAMILY BURYING GROUND AT PROSPECT HILL
Directions: Route 97 North, Georgia Avenue, right on Brighton Dam Road. [A.D.C. Map: Montgomery, page 16, grid coordinates E-8.] Condition of cemetery: Poor, many stones destroyed, property overlooks Hawlings River. Inactive cemetery. Earliest known death: 1858. Most recent death: 1911. Date transcribed: 1968. Location of transcribed records: Montgomery County Historical Society Library, 42 West Middle Lane, Rockville, Maryland 20850. Comments: Historic site 23/72, cemetery located at Prospect Hill.

HOPKINS FAMILY BURYING GROUND NEAR WHITE OAK
Directions: Located on part of land tract called *Exchange* in the White Oak area of Silver Spring. [A.D.C. Map: Montgomery, page 34, grid coordinates C-7.] This cemetery is non-extant. Comments: Graveyard in 1873 property survey by Joseph Hopkins who purchased land in 1848.

HOSKINSON FAMILY BURYING GROUND AT POOLESVILLE
Directions: One grave on Edward's Ferry Road near Poolesville. [A.D.C. Map: Montgomery, page 19, grid coordinates D-1.] Condition of cemetery: Unknown. Inactive cemetery. Earliest known death: 1855. Most recent death: 1855. Date transcribed: 1970. Location of transcribed records: Montgomery County Historical Society Library, 42 West Middle Lane, Rockville, Maryland 20850. Comments: One marked grave for Hilleary Hoskinson, born 6 July 1799, died 16 July 1855, age 56.

HOWES (LEVEN) FAMILY BURYING GROUND NEAR MIDDLEBROOK
Directions: Route 355 North, right on Blunt Road, in housing development. [A.D.C. Map: Montgomery, page 13, grid coordinates G-8.] Condition of cemetery: Unknown. Inactive cemetery. Location of transcribed records: Montgomery County Historical Society Library, 42 West Middle Lane. Rockville, Maryland 20850. Comments: Only one marked grave.

JONES FAMILY BURYING GROUND AT MT. ZION
Directions: Route 108 North, right on Mt. Zion Road to Stanley Stabler farm. [A.D.C. Map: Montgomery, page 15, grid coordinates G-8.] Condition of cemetery: Unknown. Inactive cemetery. Earliest known death: 1853. Most recent death: 1889. Location of transcribed records: Montgomery County Historical Society Library, 42 West Middle Lane, Rockville, Maryland 20850. Comments: At least 4 marked graves.

JONES FAMILY BURYING GROUND ON BLUNT ROAD NEAR GREAT SENECA PARK
Directions: On Blunt Road, enclosed by a brick wall with no entrance, there are steps on the inside. [A.D.C. Map: Montgomery, page 14, grid coordinates A-4.] Condition of cemetery: Terribly overgrown over 14 marked graves. Inactive cemetery. Earliest known death: 1847. Most recent death: 1914. Famous person interred: W.J. Jones, M.D. Location of transcribed records: Montgomery County Historical Society Library, 42 West Middle Lane, Rockville, Maryland 20850. Comments: Emma Jones, wife of Reuben Riggs was last family member to own the property.

MONTGOMERY COUNTY CEMETERIES - PRIVATE 147

JUDEAN MEMORIAL GARDENS NEAR OLNEY
Directions: Route 97, Georgia Avenue, one mile north of Rossmoor-Leisure World, right on Bachellors Forest Road. [A.D.C. Map: Montgomery, page 25, grid coordinates A-6.] Condition of cemetery: Well kept. Active cemetery. Earliest known death: 1975. Most recent death: Present. Location of burial records: Cemetery office. Location of transcribed records: Montgomery Cemetery Limited Partnership, 16225 Batchellors Forest Road and Georgia Avenue, Olney. Comments: Judean Memorial Gardens adjoins Norbeck Memorial Park, over 900 marked graves.

KEMP FAMILY BURYING GROUND NEAR LAYHILL
Directions: No longer exists, originally on present Indian Springs County Club Golf Course. [A.D.C. Map: Montgomery, page 33, grid coordinates G-1.] Condition of cemetery: One marker found in fence row of neighbor. Inactive cemetery. Comments: Kenneth Wheatley kept stone found in 1977 in his garage to protect it.

KING (JOHN DUCKETT) FAMILY BURYING GROUND NEAR DAMASCUS
Directions: Route 355 North, Route 121 East, right on Burnt Hill Road, right on Kingstead Road. [A.D.C. Map: Montgomery, page 5, grid coordinates F-6.] Condition of cemetery: Neglected, for years cows were allowed to roam in the grave yard. Inactive cemetery. Earliest known death: 1861. Most recent death: 1909. Date transcribed: 1994. Location of transcribed records: Montgomery County Historical Society Library, 42 West Middle Lane, Rockville, Maryland 20850. Comments: Over 30 interments, 17 markers remain.

KING (MIDDLETON) FAMILY BURYING GROUND NEAR PURDUM
Directions: Route 355 West, right on Route 121, right on Burnt Hill Road, left on Prices Distillery Road, house on right. [A.D.C. Map: Montgomery, page 5, grid coordinates E-4.] Condition of cemetery: Well kept. Active cemetery. Earliest known death: 1872. Most recent death: 1995. Records not transcribed. Comments: At least 5 marked graves.

LEWIS FAMILY BURYING GROUND AT LEWISDALE
Directions: Route 355 West, right on 121, right on Burnt Hill Road, left on Prices Distillery Road, cemetery on right. [A.D.C. Map: Montgomery, page 5, grid coordinates C-2.] Condition of cemetery: Neglected, over grown. Inactive cemetery. Records not transcribed. Comments: A few marked graves and some unmarked.

LINCOLN PARK CEMETERY AT ROCKVILLE

Directions: Route 355, Hungerford Drive North, right on Frederick Avenue, to North Horners Lane. [A.D.C. Map: Montgomery, page 24, grid coordinates A-12.] Condition of cemetery: Well kept. Active cemetery. Earliest known death: 1922. Most recent death: Present. Veterans interred: WWI Vet, WWII Vet, and other wars vets. Location of burial records: Cemetery office. Date transcribed: 1983. Location of transcribed records: Montgomery County Historical Society Library, 42 West Middle Lane, Rockville, Maryland 20850. Comments: Over 370 marked graves, African-American cemetery.

MAGRUDER (ROBERT POTTINGER) FAMILY BURYING GROUND AT THE RIDGE

Directions: Remains in this cemetery were moved to Laytonsville Cemetery in 1966. [A.D.C. Map: Montgomery, page 23, grid coordinates J-1.] Condition of cemetery: Originally located on land tract called *The Ridge*, which is now part of Mill Creek Towne. This cemetery is non-extant. Has been relocated. Earliest known death: 1822. Most recent death: 1833. Author: Helen W. Ridgely. Title: *Historic Graves of Maryland and the District of Columbia*. Publisher: Family Line Publications [Grafton Press original publisher, 1908], Westminster, MD [reprinted in 1992]. Comments: Original stones were not moved to Laytonsville Cemetery, a common stone was erected listing 9 names.

MAGRUDER (WALTER) FAMILY BURYING GROUND NEAR LAYTONSVILLE

Directions: Behind Stadler Nursery near Laytonsville on Sam Riggs property. [A.D.C. Map: Montgomery, page 15, grid coordinates B-5.] Condition of cemetery: Unknown, may now be part of the Montgomery Golf Club. This cemetery is non-extant. Earliest known death: 1832. Most recent death: 1874. Location of transcribed records: Montgomery County Historical Society Library, 42 West Middle Lane, Rockville, Maryland 20850. Comments: Three readable markers, others on ground face down.

MCELFRESH FAMILY BURYING GROUND AT HYATTSTOWN

Directions: Route 355 North, left on Firetower Road, in a cultivated field on county boundary. [A.D.C. Map: Montgomery, page 4, grid coordinates E-3.] Condition of cemetery: Unknown. Inactive cemetery. Earliest known death: 1808. Most recent death: 1948. Veterans interred: WWI Vets. Date transcribed: 1987. Location of transcribed records: Montgomery County Historical Society Library, 42 West Middle Lane, Rockville, Maryland 20850. Author: Jacob Mehrling Holdcraft. Title: *Names In Stone, 75,000*

Cemetery Inscriptions From Frederick County Maryland, Vol. I and II. Publisher: The Monocacy Book Company [second printing 1972], Redwood City, California [printed Ann Arbor, Michigan, 1966]. Comments: Over 28 marked graves, another 4 known burials.

MERSON FAMILY BURYING GROUND NEAR BURTONSVILLE
Directions: Old Columbia Pike North to Spencerville Road, cemetery at intersection. [A.D.C. Map: Montgomery, page 27, grid coordinates A-9.] Condition of cemetery: Unknown. Inactive cemetery. Earliest known death: 1872. Most recent death: 1940. Date transcribed: 1982. Location of transcribed records: Montgomery County Historical Society Library, 42 West Middle Lane, Rockville, Maryland 20850. Comments: At least 16 marked graves.

MILLER FAMILY BURYING GROUND AT ALLOWAY
Directions: Intersection of Route 650, New Hampshire Avenue and Route 198, Spencerville Road. [A.D.C. Map: Montgomery, page 26, grid coordinates D-6.] Condition of cemetery: No longer exists, graves moved to Friends' Meeting House, Sandy Spring. This cemetery is non-extant. Relocated. Earliest known death: 1876. Most recent death: 1878. Author: Roger Brooke Farquhar. Title: *Old Homes and History of Montgomery County, Maryland*, pages 92-93, American History Research Associates, Brookeville, MD [1952]. Comments: Listed as 15/49 in locational atlas and index of historical sites in Montgomery County.

MOBLEY-MAGERS-ARNOLD FAMILY BURYING GROUND AT GERMANTOWN (MAGERS FAMILY BURYING GROUND)
Directions: Behind last house on right side of Clopper Road just before intersecting with Route 118. [A.D.C. Map: Montgomery, page 12, grid coordinates K-12.] Condition of cemetery: Unknown. Inactive cemetery. Earliest known death: 1893. Most recent death: 1904. Date transcribed: 1976. Location of transcribed records: Montgomery County Historical Society Library, 42 West Middle Lane, Rockville, Maryland 20850. Comments: Only 3 markers with names, many stones missing, in 1976 property belonged to Herman Rabbitt.

MONOCACY CEMETERY COMPANY AT BEALLSVILLE (MONOCACY CEMETERY SOCIETY OF MONTGOMERY COUNTY)
Directions: Route 28 Northwest, Darnestown Road, to West Hunter Drive, entrance on left off Route 28. [A.D.C. Map: Montgomery, page 11, grid coordinates K-9.] Condition of cemetery: Well kept, over 3500 marked graves. Active cemetery. Earliest known death: 1748. Most recent

death: Present. Veterans interred: Civil War, WWI, WWII and other wars vets. Location of burial records: Cemetery Office. Location of transcribed records: Montgomery County Historical Society Library, 42 West Middle Lane, Rockville, Maryland 20850. Author: J. Thomas Scharf, A.M. Title: *History of Western Maryland*, pages 736 and 737, Vol. I, Regional Publishing Company [reprinted 1968], Baltimore, MD [originally printed in Philadelphia, 1882]. Comments: Cemetery established by 1747 and surrounded Old St. Peter's Church also known as Old Monocacy Chapel.

MOSES LODGE CEMETERY NEAR CABIN JOHN
Directions: Off Seven Locks Road behind house at 7947 Cypress Grove Lane, near Cabin John. [A.D.C. Map: Montgomery, page 37, grid coordinates H-6.] Condition of cemetery: Neglected, very overgrown. Inactive cemetery. Earliest known death: 1921. Date transcribed: 1983. Location of transcribed records: Montgomery County Historical Society Library, 42 West Middle Lane, Rockville, Maryland 20850. Comments: At least 7 marked graves, African-American cemetery, Moses Lodge now located in Baltimore.

MUTUAL MEMORIAL CEMETERY AT SANDY SPRING
Directions: Route 650 North, New Hampshire Avenue, left on Brooke Road. [A.D.C. Map: Montgomery, page 16, grid coordinates K-11.] Condition of cemetery: Well kept. Active cemetery. Earliest known death: 1873. Most recent death: Present. Veterans interred: WWI, WWII and other wars vets. Date transcribed: 1982. Location of transcribed records: Montgomery County Historical Society Library, 42 West Middle Lane, Rockville, Maryland 20850. Comments: Over 235 marked graves, African-American cemetery.

NORBECK MEMORIAL PARK NEAR OLNEY
Directions: Route 97 North, Georgia Avenue, located at corner of Batchellors Forest Road and Georgia Avenue. [A.D.C. Map: Montgomery, page 25, grid coordinates A-6.] Condition of cemetery: Well kept. Active cemetery. Earliest known death: 1976. Most recent death: Present. Location of burial records: Cemetery office. Comments: Over 200 marked graves.

OFFUTT (ANDREW) FAMILY BURYING GROUND AT DAWSONVILLE
Directions: Route 28 North, between Darnestown and Dawsonville on property. [A.D.C. Map: Montgomery, page 21.] Condition: A number of graves marked with uninscribed field stones. Inactive cemetery. Earliest

known death: 1863. Most recent death: 1875. Location of transcribed records: Montgomery County Historical Society Library, 42 West Middle Lane, Rockville, Maryland 20850. Comments: Historic site 24/3. Gretchen Minners photographed four stone markers during the 1970s.

OFFUTT (JAMES) FAMILY BURYING GROUND AT WOODBYRNE
Directions: Route 28 North, Darnestown Road, left on Seneca Road, on tract of land called *Woodbyrne* on private property. [A.D.C. Map: Montgomery, page 21.] Condition of cemetery: Unknown. Inactive cemetery. Earliest known death: 1855. Most recent death: 1876. Location of transcribed records: Montgomery County Historical Society Library, 42 West Middle Lane, Rockville, Maryland 20850. Comments: Historic site 24/30, 3 grave markers.

OWEN FAMILY BURYING GROUND AT NORBECK
Directions: Route 115 West, Muncaster Mill Road, right on Bowie Mill Road, right on Cashell Road. [A.D.C. Map: Montgomery, page 24, grid coordinates H-3.] Condition of cemetery: Neglected and overgrown in 1970, may no longer exist. Inactive cemetery. Earliest known death: 1840. Most recent death: 1894. Date transcribed: 1970. Location of transcribed records: Montgomery County Historical Society Library, 42 West Middle Lane, Rockville, Maryland 20850. Comments: At least 5 marked graves, located near the tennis courts at Norbeck Country Club.

OWEN (EDWARD) FAMILY BURYING GROUND AT BROOKEVILLE
Directions: Route 97 North, Georgia Avenue, left on Gregg Road. [A.D.C. Map: Montgomery, page 15, grid coordinates J-4.] Condition of cemetery: Unknown. Inactive cemetery. Earliest known death: 1838. Most recent death: 1911. Famous person interred: Col. Gustavus W. Dorsey. Veterans interred: Civil War. Location of transcribed records: Montgomery County Historical Society Library, 42 West Middle Lane, Rockville, Maryland 20850. Comments: Historic site 23/49, at least 8 marked graves.

OWENS FAMILY BURYING GROUND AT TRIADELPHIA
Directions: Route 97 North, Georgia Avenue, Supples Lane recreation area. [A.D.C. Map: Montgomery, page 8, grid coordinates F-13.] Condition of cemetery: Well kept. Inactive cemetery. Date transcribed: 1989. Location of transcribed records: Montgomery County Historical Society Library, 42 West Middle Lane, Rockville, Maryland 20850. Comments: Only 1 marked grave.

PARKLAWN MEMORIAL PARK AT ROCKVILLE
Directions: Route 586 South, Veirs Mill Road, cemetery on right. [A.D.C. Map: Montgomery, page 32, grid coordinates G-3.] Condition of cemetery: Well kept. Active cemetery. Earliest known death: 1952. Most recent death: Present. Location of burial records: Cemetery office. Records are not transcribed. Comments: Over 1,000 marked graves, moved 12 graves from other side of Indian Spring County Club near Layhill.

PEARRE FAMILY BURYING GROUND NEAR COMUS
Directions: Near Comus, on old Pearre farm property, located off Comus Road. [A.D.C. Map: Montgomery, page 4, grid coordinates C-11.] Condition of cemetery: Unknown. Inactive cemetery. Earliest known death: 1864. Most recent death: 1900. Location of transcribed records: Montgomery County Historical Society Library, 42 West Middle Lane, Rockville, Maryland 20850. Comments: Only partially transcribed.

PETER FAMILY CEMETERY ON MONTEVIDEO
Directions: Near Seneca, on tract of land called *Montevideo*. [A.D.C. Map: Montgomery, page 29, grid coordinates D-1.] Condition of cemetery: Unknown, on property of Martha Custis Peter, descendant of George Washington's wife. Inactive cemetery. Earliest known death: 1821. Most recent death: 1854. Famous person interred: John Parke Custis Peter. Location of transcribed records: Montgomery County Historical Society Library, 42 West Middle Lane, Rockville, Maryland 20850. Author: Roger Brooke Farquhar. Title: *Old Homes and History of Montgomery County, Maryland*, pages 219-220. Publisher: American History Research Associates, Brookeville, MD, 1952. Comments: At least 5 marked graves, appears to be an iron fence enclosed.

PRATHER FAMILY BURYING GROUND AT REDLAND
Directions: Located next to Lathrop Smith Educational Center at Meadowside off Muncaster Mill Road. [A.D.C. Map: Montgomery.] Condition of cemetery: Unknown, 14 names transcribed. Inactive cemetery. Date transcribed: 1983. Location of transcribed records: Montgomery County Historical Society Library, 42 West Middle Lane, Rockville, Maryland 20850. Comments: One monument erected 1866 by survivors, lists grandparents, parents, sisters and brother, 11 names.

QUERY FAMILY BURYING GROUND AT DARNESTOWN
Directions: Route 90 West, River Road, right on Esworthy Road, right on Query Mill Road, on private land. [A.D.C. Map: Montgomery, page 29, grid coordinates J-2.] Condition of cemetery: Poor, land was being

MONTGOMERY COUNTY CEMETERIES - PRIVATE 153

developed during the 1980s. Inactive cemetery. Earliest known death: 1788. Most recent death: 1826. Location of transcribed records: Montgomery County Historical Society Library, 42 West Middle Lane, Rockville, Maryland 20850. Comments: Farm was developed in 1980s, at least 2 inscribed stones and others not inscribed.

RESERVOIR ROAD CEMETERY SITE NEAR PATUXENT RIVER
Directions: Route 97 North, Georgia Avenue. [A.D.C. Map: Montgomery, page 8, grid coordinates F-12.] Condition of cemetery: Well kept. Inactive cemetery. Earliest known death: 1808. Most recent death: 1853. Date transcribed: 1989. Location of transcribed records: Montgomery County Historical Society Library, 42 West Middle Lane, Rockville, Maryland 20850. Comments: Between 6 and 10 marked graves, only initials inscribed, possibly a slave cemetery.

RICHARDSON FAMILY BURYING GROUND AT MT. AIRY AT SANDY SPRING
On land tract called *Mt. Airy at Sandy Spring*. [A.D.C. Map: Montgomery, page 25, grid coordinates K-1.] Condition of cemetery: Unknown. This cemetery is non-extant. Location of transcribed records: Montgomery County Historical Society Library, 42 West Middle Lane, Rockville, Maryland 20850. Author: Roger Brooke Farquhar. Title: *Old Homes and History of Montgomery County, Maryland*, pages 223-224. Publisher: American History Research Associates, Brookeville, MD, 1952. Comments: Only 1 marker left, other markers thrown into pond.

RICKETTS FAMILY BURYING GROUND NEAR MIDDLEBROOK
Directions: Located at Middlebrook in a housing development. [A.D.C. Map: Montgomery, page 13, grid coordinates F-9.] Condition of cemetery: Unknown. Inactive cemetery. Date transcribed: 1978. Location of transcribed records: Montgomery County Historical Society Library, 42 West Middle Lane, Rockville, Maryland 20850. Comments: No inscribed stones, only field stones for markers.

RIGGS (JOHN HAMMOND) BURYING GROUND AT LOCUST GROVE
Directions: *Locust Grove*, 3415 Brookeville Road, Brookeville. [A.D.C. Map: Montgomery, page 16, grid coordinates A-9.] Condition of cemetery: Poor, surrounded by fence. Inactive cemetery. Earliest known death: 1788. Most recent death: 1884. Famous person interred: Col. John Hammond Riggs. Veterans interred: Other Wars Vet. Records not transcribed. Author: John Beverley Riggs. Title: *The Riggs Family of Maryland*, page 413. Publisher: The Lord Baltimore Press, Baltimore,

MD, 1939. Comments: Cemetery owned by the descendants of Mrs. Kate Riggs Griffith.

RIGGS (SAMUEL) FAMILY BURYING GROUND AT PLEASANT HILL, BROOKEVILLE
Directions: Route 97 North, Georgia Avenue. [A.D.C. Map: Montgomery, page 16, grid coordinates C-7.] Condition of cemetery: Unknown. Inactive cemetery. Earliest known death: 1807. Most recent death: 1906. Famous person interred: Samuel Riggs. Veterans interred: Revolutionary Vet and other wars vets. Records not transcribed. Author: John Beverley Riggs. Title: *The Riggs Family of Maryland*, pages 158-159. Publisher: The Lord Baltimore Press, Baltimore, MD, 1939. Comments: Orndorff family removed and reinterred at Rockville Cemetery before 1912.

RIGGS FAMILY BURYING GROUND
Directions: Adjoins the Central Union Mission Farm, located among a grove of tall spruce trees. [A.D.C. Map: Montgomery.] Condition of cemetery: Overgrown and vandalized. Inactive cemetery. Earliest known death: 1829. Most recent death: 1893. Records not transcribed.

ROBERTSON (SAM)-COUNSELMAN FAMILY BURYING GROUND AT GOSHEN
Directions: Route 27 North, right on Brink Road East to Goshen, right on Goshen Road, *Fertile Meadows* on left. [A.D.C. Map: Montgomery, page 14, grid coordinates D-5.] Condition of cemetery: Unknown. Inactive cemetery. Earliest known death: 1816. Most recent death: 1980. Famous person interred: Brita Dyberg Counselman. Markers not transcribed. Author: Ardith Gunderman Boggs. Title: *Goshen, Maryland, A History and Its People*, page 37, Heritage Books, Inc., 1540-E Pointer Ridge Place, Bowie, MD 20716, 1994; *Roger Brooke Farquhar's Old Homes and History of Montgomery County, MD*, page 156.

ROCKVILLE CEMETERY ASSOCIATION (ROCKVILLE PROTESTANT EPISCOPAL CHURCH CEMETERY, ROCKVILLE UNION CEMETERY)
Directions: Route 28 East, right on Baltimore Road, cemetery on left. [A.D.C. Map: Montgomery, page 24, grid coordinates D-13.] Condition of cemetery: Well kept. Active cemetery. Earliest known death: 1752. Most recent death: Present. Famous person interred: Brooke Beall. Veterans interred: WWI Vet, WWII Vet, other wars vets. Location of burial records: Rockville Cemetery Association. Location of transcribed records: Montgomery County Historical Society Library, 42 West Middle Lane,

Rockville, Maryland 20850. Author: J. Thomas Scharf, A.M. Title: *History of Western Maryland*, page 749, Vol. I. Publisher: Regional Publishing Company [reprinted 1968], Baltimore, MD [originally printed in Philadelphia, 1882]. Comments: Originally part of Rock Creek Chapel Episcopal Church property.

SEAL'S FARM FAMILY BURYING GROUND
Directions: Route 650 West, Damascus Road, near Etchison, about the 5700 block. [A.D.C. Map: Montgomery, page 7.] Condition of cemetery: Not well kept, must have a Seal Family Tennessee connection for burial in this cemetery. Active cemetery. Earliest known death: 1946. Most recent death: Present. Date transcribed: 1982. Location of transcribed records: Montgomery County Historical Society Library, 42 West Middle Lane, Rockville, Maryland 20850. Comments: Over 55 marked and 12 unmarked graves, cemetery originated by Abijah and Amanda Seal.

SHAW FAMILY BURYING GROUND AT CLARKSBURG, GUE FAMILY CEMETERY
Directions: Near Clarksburg. [A.D.C. Map: Montgomery, page 4.] Condition of cemetery: Unknown. Inactive cemetery. Earliest known death: 1855. Most recent death: 1881. Date transcribed: 1990. Location of transcribed records: Montgomery County Historical Society Library, 42 West Middle Lane, Rockville, Maryland 20850. Comments: At least 8 marked graves, on historic sites list it is called Gue Family Cemetery.

SHAW (LEMUEL) FAMILY BURYING GROUND NEAR LAYTONSVILLE
Directions: Route 108 South, in backyard of farm house at 20300 Laytonsville Road. [A.D.C. Map: Montgomery, page 15, grid coordinates A-5.] Condition of cemetery: Unknown, land being developed in 1980s, graves moved in 1989. Inactive cemetery. Has been relocated. Earliest known death: 1818. Most recent death: 1818. Date transcribed: 1986. Location of transcribed records: Montgomery County Historical Society Library, 42 West Middle Lane, Rockville, Maryland 20850. Comments: Historic site 20/3, 2 marked graves.

SHOEMAKER FAMILY BURYING GROUND NEAR WESTMORELAND HILLS
Directions: In backyard of 4907 Jamestown Court in Westmoreland Hills area. [A.D.C. Map: Montgomery, page 38, grid coordinates G-11.] Condition of cemetery: Poor, fence enclosed with locked gate, no access, transcribed from outside fence. Inactive cemetery. Date transcribed: 1985.

Location of transcribed records: Montgomery County Historical Society Library, 42 West Middle Lane, Rockville, Maryland 20850. Comments: Historic site 35/33, 10 names transcribed.

SPENCER FAMILY BURYING GROUND AT DICKERSON
Directions: Dickerson, east of Big Woods Road. [A.D.C. Map: Montgomery, page 10, grid coordinates J-2.] Condition of cemetery: Neglected, surrounded by rail fence, one of the few surviving antebellum free African-American cemetery. Inactive cemetery. Markers not transcribed. Comments: 12 or more markers, markers are carved wooden slabs in shape of rounded top tombstones with no information inscribed. Spencers, an antebellum free African-American family, founded the Black Big Woods community.

SPRINGBROOK FOREST CITIZENS ASSOCIATION
Directions: One stone for James Lee 1790-1856, found in backyard of home on Grays Lane. [A.D.C. Map: Montgomery, page 33, grid coordinates K-6.] Condition of cemetery: Stone has been placed in Springbrook Forest, exact location not known. This cemetery is non-extant. Has been relocated. Comments: May have been found on property owned by Bailey family in 1979.

SUMMERS FAMILY BURYING GROUND AT ROCKVILLE, WILLOW TREE GRAVEYARD
Directions: Located on wooded lot near Broome J.H.S., path next to 502 Linthicum Street. [A.D.C. Map: Montgomery, page 32, grid coordinates E-1.] Condition of cemetery: Unknown. Inactive cemetery. Earliest known death: 1802. Most recent death: 1816. Date transcribed: 1986. Location of transcribed records: Montgomery County Historical Society Library, 42 West Middle Lane, Rockville, Maryland 20850. Author: Helen W. Ridgely. Title: *Historic Graves of Maryland and the District of Columbia*. Publisher: Family Line Publications [Grafton Press original publisher, 1908], Westminster, MD [reprint 1992]. Comments: Four names, only 1 inscribed stone in 1986.

UNION CEMETERY ASSOCIATION AT BURTONSVILLE (CARR FAMILY CEMETERY)
Directions: Route 650 North, New Hampshire Avenue, right at Route 198 East, Spencerville Road, cemetery on right. [A.D.C. Map: Montgomery, page 26, grid coordinates K-8.] Condition of cemetery: Well kept, organized about 1862. Active cemetery. Earliest known death: 1858. Most recent death: Present. Veterans interred: WWI Vet, WWII Vet, and other

wars vets. Date transcribed: 1984. Location of transcribed records: Montgomery County Historical Society Library, 42 West Middle Lane, Rockville, Maryland 20850. Author: J. Thomas Scharf, A.M. Title: *History of Western Maryland*, page 757, Vol. I. Publisher: Regional Publishing Company [reprinted 1968], Baltimore, MD [originally printed in Philadelphia, 1882]. Comments: Over 2000 marked graves. Thomas Dickerson reportedly first person interred.

WARD FAMILY BURYING GROUND AT HUNTING HILLS
Directions: Route 28 West, Darnestown Road, left on Muddy Branch Road, cemetery in field on left. [A.D.C. Map: Montgomery, page 22, grid coordinates J-11.] Condition of cemetery: Poor, located in overgrown clump of trees, dilapidated gated, wrought iron fence enclosure. Inactive cemetery. Has been relocated. Earliest known death: 1843. Most recent death: 1935. Date transcribed: 1983. Location of transcribed records: Montgomery County Historical Society Library, 42 West Middle Lane, Rockville, Maryland 20850. Comments: Historic site 25/3, some graves moved to Forest Oak Cemetery, Gaithersburg, 9 marked graves remain.

WATERS (RICHARD) WATERS FAMILY BURYING GROUND NEAR LAYTONSVILLE
Directions: Located on Hadley Farms Dairy property off Laytonsville Road, near or under power lines. [A.D.C. Map: Montgomery.] Condition of cemetery: Overgrown and neglected, long distance from road. Inactive cemetery. Veterans interred: Revolutionary Vets. Date transcribed: 1978. Location of transcribed records: Montgomery County Historical Society Library, 42 West Middle Lane, Rockville, Maryland 20850. Comments: Two marked graves remained in 1978 when photos taken.

WATERS FAMILY BURYING GROUND AT BELMONT
Directions: Located on tract of land called *Belmont*, off Georgia Avenue, between Olney and Brookeville. [A.D.C. Map: Montgomery.] Condition of cemetery: Unknown. Inactive cemetery. Has been relocated. Location of transcribed records: Montgomery County Historical Society Library, 42 West Middle Lane, Rockville, Maryland 20850. Comments: Some graves moved to St. John's Episcopal Church at Olney.

WATERS (WASHINGTON) FAMILY BURYING GROUND NEAR GOSHEN
Directions: On Davis Mill Road behind an old house. [A.D.C. Map: Montgomery.] Condition of cemetery: Unknown. Inactive cemetery. Date transcribed: 1970. Location of transcribed records: Montgomery County

Historical Society Library, 42 West Middle Lane, Rockville, Maryland 20850. Comments: At least seven marked graves.

WATERS (ZACHARIAH) FAMILY BURYING GROUND AT GERMANTOWN
Directions: Route 118 South, left on Aircraft Drive, right on Century Boulevard, right on Waters Road. [A.D.C. Map: Montgomery, page 13, grid coordinates B-6.] Condition of cemetery: Neglected, overgrown, vandalized. Inactive cemetery. Earliest known death: 1824. Most recent death: 1864. Date transcribed: 1994. Location of transcribed records: Montgomery County Historical Society Library, 42 West Middle Lane, Rockville, Maryland 20850. Comments: Over 4 marked graves, located on Century XXI Golf Course.

WELLING FAMILY BURYING GROUND AT COMUS, COMUS CEMETERY
Directions: Route 109 South, Old Hundred Road, on right side of road from Comus to Barnesville. [A.D.C. Map: Montgomery, page 3, grid coordinates K-10.] Condition of cemetery: Well kept. Inactive cemetery. Earliest known death: 1945. Most recent death: 1981. Date transcribed: 1985. Location of transcribed records: Montgomery County Historical Society Library, 42 West Middle Lane, Rockville, Maryland 20850.

WILSON FAMILY BURYING GROUND AT EDNOR
Directions: Route 650 North, right on Ednor Road, right on Link Road, cemetery in back of first house. [A.D.C. Map: Montgomery, page 26, grid coordinates G-3.] Condition of cemetery: Unknown. Inactive cemetery. Location of transcribed records: Montgomery County Historical Society Library, 42 West Middle Lane, Rockville, Maryland 20850. Comments: At least 2 marked graves.

WOOD FAMILY BURYING GROUND NEAR POOLESVILLE
Directions: Route. 28 West, to Dawsonville, left on Route 107, Whites Ferry Road. [A.D.C. Map: Montgomery, page 19, grid coordinates B-3.] Condition of cemetery: Unknown. Inactive cemetery. Earliest known death: 1830. Most recent death: 1850. Date transcribed: 1972. Location of transcribed records: Montgomery County Historical Society Library, 42 West Middle Lane, Rockville, Maryland 20850. Comments: At least 4 marked graves, in 1972 property known as Reddick Farm.

MONTGOMERY COUNTY CEMETERIES - PRIVATE 159

WOODSIDE CEMETERY AT BRINKLOW, LEA FAMILY CEMETERY
Directions: Route 650 North, right on Haviland Mill Road, cemetery on right. [A.D.C. Map: Montgomery, page 17, grid coordinates A-10.] Condition of cemetery: Well kept. Active cemetery. Earliest known death: 1829. Most recent death: Present. Date transcribed: 1975. Location of transcribed records: Montgomery County Historical Society Library, 42 West Middle Lane, Rockville, Maryland 20850. Comments: Over 310 marked graves, originally established by Edward and Deborah Pierce Lea.

YOUNG (LODOWICK) FAMILY BURYING GROUND AT POOLESVILLE
Directions: Route 28 Northwest, left on Route 107, Whites Ferry Road, to Edwards Ferry Road intersection. [A.D.C. Map: Montgomery, page 10, grid coordinates E-13.] Condition of cemetery: Unknown, cemetery located in grove of Locust trees. Inactive cemetery. Earliest known death: 1825. Most recent death: 1904. Location of transcribed records: Montgomery County Historical Society Library, 42 West Middle Lane, Rockville, Maryland 20850.

YOUNG (RICHARD) FAMILY BURYING GROUND NEAR DAMASCUS
Directions: Route 27 North, right on Sweepstakes Road near Upper Magruder Branch on right. [A.D.C. Map: Montgomery, page 5, grid coordinates K-7.] Condition of cemetery: Unknown. Inactive cemetery. Location of transcribed records: Montgomery County Historical Society Library, 42 West Middle Lane, Rockville, Maryland 20850. Comments: At least 3 marked graves remained in 1970s when photographs taken.

Church Cemeteries

ALLEN CHAPEL AFRICAN METHODIST EPISCOPAL CHURCH CEMETERY AT WHEATON
Directions: Route 193 East, University Boulevard, right on Dayton Street, left on Dodson Lane, church at end. [A.D.C. Map: Montgomery, page 33, grid coordinates F-9.] Condition of cemetery: Well kept. Active cemetery. Earliest known death: 1894. Most recent death: Present. Date transcribed: 1987. Location of transcribed records: Montgomery County Historical Society Library, 42 West Middle Lane, Rockville, Maryland 20850. Comments: Over 37 marked graves, African-American congregation, church organized in 1870.

ASBURY UNITED METHODIST CHURCH CEMETERY AT GERMANTOWN (ASBURY METHODIST EPISCOPAL CHURCH CEMETERY)
Directions: Route 28 West to Route 118, turn right, to Black Rock Road, turn left church and cemetery on left. [A.D.C. Map: Montgomery, page 21, grid coordinates H-3.] Condition of cemetery: Well kept. Active cemetery. Earliest known death: 1902. Most recent death: Present. Veterans interred: WWII Vets. In 1936, the WPA survey team was told that no church records were ever kept. Date transcribed: 1988. Location of transcribed records: Montgomery County Historical Society Library, 42 West Middle Lane, Rockville, Maryland 20850. Comments: Over 46 marked graves, African-American congregation, church organized in 1878, building erected in 1885.

ASHTON METHODIST EPISCOPAL CHURCH CEMETERY NEAR ASHTON, BOWEN CEMETERY
Directions: Route 650 North, New Hampshire Avenue, right on Route 108, Olney-Sandy Spring Road, cemetery on right. [A.D.C. Map: Montgomery, page 26, grid coordinates A-1.] Condition of cemetery: Unknown. Inactive cemetery. Earliest known death: 1893. Most recent death: 1966. In 1936, 3 volumes of records 1887-1937, located at M.E. Parsonage, Burtonsville. Date transcribed: 1980. Location of transcribed records: Montgomery County Historical Society Library, 42 West Middle Lane, Rockville, Maryland 20850. Comments: Over 15 marked graves, African-American cemetery, church organized 1887.

BARNESVILLE METHODIST EPISCOPAL CHURCH CEMETERY
Directions: No longer exists, church was two-story frame edifice built in 1843. [A.D.C. Map: Montgomery, page 11, grid coordinates F-1.] Condition of cemetery: In 1936 no evidence left of building, graveyard very neglected, and now no longer exists. This cemetery is non-extant. Earliest known death: 1845. Most recent death: 1874. Famous person interred: Hatton Browne. Veterans interred: Civil War. In 1936, records from 1857-1890 found in parts of two volumes at Clarksburg parsonage. Records only partially transcribed. Author: J. Thomas Scharf, A.M. Title: *History of Western Maryland*, page 731, Vol. I. Publisher: Regional Publishing Company [reprinted 1968], Baltimore, MD [originally printed in Philadelphia, 1882]. Comments: Was still active in July 1899 per Montgomery County Sentinel, page 3.

MONTGOMERY COUNTY CEMETERIES - CHURCH

BETHEL METHODIST EPISCOPAL CHURCH CEMETERY AT MT. ZION (MT. ZION CHURCH)
Directions: Route 108 Northwest, Olney-Laytonsville Road, right on Zion Road, church on left. [A.D.C. Map: Montgomery, page 15, grid coordinates G-8.] Condition of cemetery: Unknown. In 1936, small cemetery, very few inscribed grave markers. Records not transcribed. Comments: Records from 1934 in one volume, previous records lost, admitted to Washington Conference in 1875.

BETHESDA MEETING HOUSE CEMETERY AT BETHESDA (CAPTAIN JOHN PRESBYTERIAN CHURCH, CABIN JOHN PRESBYTERIAN CHURCH)
Directions: Route 355 West through Bethesda, past NIH, church and cemetery on left. [A.D.C. Map: Montgomery, page 38, grid coordinates H-1.] Condition of cemetery: Well kept, 109 marked graves. Active cemetery. Earliest known death: 1820. Most recent death: Present. Date transcribed: 1981. Location of transcribed records: Montgomery County Historical Society Library, 42 West Middle Lane, Rockville, Maryland 20850. Author: J. Thomas Scharf, A.M. Title: *History of Western Maryland*, page 768, Vol. I. Publisher: Regional Publishing Company [reprinted 1968], Baltimore, MD [originally printed in Philadelphia, 1882]. Comments: Original Presbyterian church built 1820, sold church to Baptists in 1950, but cemetery retained.

BETHESDA UNITED METHODIST CHURCH CEMETERY AT BROWNINGSVILLE (BETHESDA METHODIST EPISCOPAL CHURCH CEMETERY)
Directions: Route 27 North to Damascus, left on Bethesda Church Road cemetery on left across from church. [A.D.C. Map: Montgomery, page 1, grid coordinates E-11.] Condition of cemetery: Well kept. Active cemetery. Earliest known death: 1826. Most recent death: Present. Famous person interred: George W.W. Walker. Veterans interred: WWII and other wars vets. In 1936, 6 volumes of records 1860-1937, were located at Clarksburg parsonage. Location of burial records: Church office. Date transcribed: 1987. Location of transcribed records: Montgomery County Historical Society Library, 42 West Middle Lane, Rockville, Maryland 20850. Author: Jacob Mehrling Holdcraft. Title: *Names In Stone, 75000 Cemetery Inscriptions From Frederick County, Maryland*, Vol. I and II. Publisher: The Monocacy Book Company [second printing 1972], Redwood City, California, 1966.

162   DIRECTORY OF MARYLAND'S BURIAL GROUNDS

BOYDS PRESBYTERIAN CHURCH CEMETERY
Directions: Route 355 North to Route 121, turn left, at Boyds turn right after viaduct, church and cemetery on left. [A.D.C. Map: Montgomery, page 12, grid coordinates E-8.] Condition of cemetery: Well kept. Active cemetery. Earliest known death: 1879. Most recent death: Present. Famous person interred: Edward Lewis. Veterans interred: WWI, WWII, and other wars vets. Date transcribed: 1981. Location of transcribed records: Montgomery County Historical Society Library, 42 West Middle Lane, Rockville, Maryland 20850. Author: J. Thomas Scharf, A.M. Title: *History of Western Maryland*, page 724, Vol. I. Publisher: Regional Publishing Company [reprinted 1968], Baltimore, MD [originally printed in Philadelphia, 1882]. Comments: Over 250 marked graves.

BROOKE GROVE UNITED METHODIST CHURCH CEMETERY NEAR LAYTONSVILLE
Directions: From Gaithersburg, Route 124 North to Brink Road, turn right, cemetery on right. [A.D.C. Map: Montgomery, page 14, grid coordinates J-3.] Condition of cemetery: Well kept. Active cemetery. Earliest known death: 1890. Most recent death: Present. Famous person interred: Mattie B. Simpson. Veterans interred: WWI, WWII and other wars vets. Church organized 1871, records before 1893 missing, 1 volume of records 1893-1937 at parsonage in 1936. Date transcribed: 1982. Location of transcribed records: Montgomery County Historical Society Library, 42 West Middle Lane, Rockville, Maryland 20850. Comments: Over 300 marked graves, African-American cemetery.

BROOKEVILLE METHODIST EPISCOPAL CHURCH CEMETERY
Directions: Church was located about 200 feet beyond cross roads at Brookeville. [A.D.C. Map: Montgomery, page 16, grid coordinates C-9.] Condition of cemetery: Was a stone building church which burned in 1890, was never rebuilt or re-organized. Inactive cemetery. In 1936, 4 volumes of records, 1856-1877 with Rockville Circuit, 1888-1890 with Laytonsville Circuit. Records not transcribed.

CLARKSBURG UNITED METHODIST CHURCH CEMETERY (CLARKSBURG METHODIST EPISCOPAL CHURCH CEMETERY)
Directions: Route 355 North to Clarksburg, right on Church Spire Street, church and cemetery on right. [A.D.C. Map: Montgomery, page 4, grid coordinates K-11.] Condition of cemetery: Well kept. Active cemetery. Earliest known death: 1811. Most recent death: Present. Famous person interred: Dr. Horace Willson. Veterans interred: WWI and WWII vets. In 1937, 1 volume of class lists 1857-1937, Rockville Circuit, 6 volumes at

Clarksburg parsonage. Date transcribed: 1988. Location of transcribed records: Montgomery County Historical Society Library, 42 West Middle Lane, Rockville, Maryland 20850. Author: J. Thomas Scharf, A.M. Title: *History of Western Maryland*, page 720, Vol. I. Publisher: Regional Publishing Company [reprinted 1968], Baltimore, MD [originally printed in Philadelphia, 1882]. Comments: Over 470 marked graves.

COLESVILLE UNITED METHODIST CHURCH CEMETERY (COLESVILLE METHODIST EPISCOPAL CHURCH SOUTH, ANDREW CHAPEL METHODIST EPISCOPAL CHURCH SOUTH, FEDERAL METHODIST EPISCOPAL CHURCH)
Directions: Route 650 North, New Hampshire Avenue, left on Randolph Road, church on left, cemetery on right. [A.D.C. Map: Montgomery, page 34, grid coordinates A-2.] Condition of cemetery: Well kept, records for 1880-1894 were missing in 1937, over 650 marked graves. Active cemetery. Earliest known death: 1852. Most recent death: Present. Famous person interred: Benjamin Fawcett. Veterans interred: WWI, WWII and other wars vets. In 1937 records 1878-1903 Hyattsville Circuit, 1903-1909 Beltsville Circuit, 1935-1937 Colesville. Date transcribed: 1980. Location of transcribed records: Montgomery County Historical Society Library, 42 West Middle Lane, Rockville, Maryland 20850. Author: J. Thomas Scharf, A.M. Title: *History of Western Maryland*, page 759, Vol. I. Publisher: Regional Publishing Company [reprinted 1968], Baltimore, MD [originally printed in Philadelphia, 1882]. Comments: Cemetery originally next to Andrew's Methodist Episcopal Church, razed 1965, historic site 33/3.

COLUMBIA PRIMITIVE BAPTIST CHURCH CEMETERY AT BURTONSVILLE
Directions: Route 29 North, Columbia Pike, past Burtonsville, church and cemetery on left. [A.D.C. Map: Montgomery, page 27, grid coordinates B-7.] Condition of cemetery: Well kept, cemetery directly behind small white frame church, may be a Waters Family cemetery. Active cemetery. Earliest known death: 1848. Most recent death: 1939. WPA Survey states church incorporated in 1903. Date transcribed: 1987. Location of transcribed records: Montgomery County Historical Society Library, 42 West Middle Lane, Rockville, Maryland 20850. Comments: Over 19 marked graves, church originally built in 1855, rebuilt in 1880.

CONCORD METHODIST EPISCOPAL CHURCH CEMETERY AT BETHESDA (ST. MARK ORTHODOX CHURCH, 7126 RIVER ROAD, BETHESDA)
Directions: Concord M.E. Church was located near Cabin John, on road leading to Offutt's Crossroads. [A.D.C. Map: Montgomery, page 38, grid coordinates D-7.] Condition of cemetery: Neglected. Concord established 1851, early records 1856-1900. Inactive cemetery. Earliest known death: 1881. Most recent death: 1954. Cabin John Methodist Episcopal Church built as sister church of Concord M.E. Church in 1920. Date transcribed: 1983. Location of transcribed records: Montgomery County Historical Society Library, 42 West Middle Lane, Rockville, Maryland 20850. Comments: Over 17 marked graves, one volume of records 1920-1937 for Concord and Cabin John M.E. Churches.

DAMASCUS UNITED METHODIST CHURCH CEMETERY (MOUNT LEBANON CHURCH, PLEASANT PLAINS OF DAMASCUS CHURCH)
Directions: Route 355 North, right on Route 27, right on Route 108, right on Route 124, Woodfield Road, entrance on right. [A.D.C. Map: Montgomery, page 6, grid coordinates B-3.] Condition of cemetery: Well kept. Active cemetery. Earliest known death: 1865. Most recent death: Present. Famous person interred: Dr. Benjamin F. Lansdale. Veterans interred: WWI, WWII and other wars vets. 3 volumes records in 1936, 1858-1910, at Clarksburg, 3 volumes, 1910-1922, at Laytonsville. Location of burial records: Church office. Date transcribed: 1976. Location of transcribed records: Montgomery County Historical Society Library, 42 West Middle Lane, Rockville, Maryland 20850. Author: J. Thomas Scharf, A.M. Title: *History of Western Maryland*, page 725, Vol. I. Publisher: Regional Publishing Company [reprinted 1968], Baltimore, MD (originally printed in Philadelphia, 1882]. Comments: Over 925 marked graves, records from 1922 at church.

DARNESTOWN BAPTIST CHURCH CEMETERY
Directions: Route. 28 West to Darnestown. [A.D.C. Map: Montgomery, page 21, grid coordinates J-10.] Condition of cemetery: No longer extant. Inactive cemetery. Earliest known death: 1848. Most recent death: 1881. Famous person interred: Samuel T. Magruder. Location of transcribed records: Montgomery County Historical Society Library, 42 West Middle Lane, Rockville, Maryland 20850. Author: J. Thomas Scharf, A.M. Title: *History of Western Maryland*, page 762, Vol. I. Publisher: Regional Publishing Company [reprinted 1968], Baltimore, MD [originally printed in Philadelphia, 1882]. Comments: Church first built and used by Methodists, then used by the Baptists.

MONTGOMERY COUNTY CEMETERIES - CHURCH 165

DARNESTOWN PRESBYTERIAN CHURCH CEMETERY
Directions: Route 28 West, Darnestown Road, to Turkey Foot Road, cemetery and old church on left. [A.D.C. Map: Montgomery, page 21, grid coordinates K-10.] Condition of cemetery: Well kept. Active cemetery. Earliest known death: 1836. Most recent death: Present. Famous person interred: Edwin Warfield Broome. Veterans interred: WWI, WWII and other wars vets. Location of burial records: Church office. Date transcribed: 1985. Location of transcribed records: Montgomery County Historical Society Library, 42 West Middle Lane, Rockville, Maryland 20850. Author: J. Thomas Scharf, A.M. Title: *History of Western Maryland*, page 761, Vol. I. Publisher: Regional Publishing Company [reprinted 1968], Baltimore, MD [originally printed in Philadelphia, 1882]. Comments: Church records 1913-1923 and 1933 to present, years 1924-1932 missing.

EBENEZER CHURCH CEMETERY AT ASHTON (ASHTON CEMETERY, BOWEN FAMILY CEMETERY, AFRICAN METHODIST EPISCOPAL CHURCH)
Directions: Route 650 North, New Hampshire Avenue, to Ashton, right on 108, cemetery on right. [A.D.C. Map: Montgomery, page 25, grid coordinates K-1.] Condition of cemetery: Well kept. Active cemetery. Earliest known death: 1893. Most recent death: Present. In 1936, 3 record volumes, 1887-1937, at the M.E. Parsonage at Burtonsville. Date transcribed: 1980. Location of transcribed records: Montgomery County Historical Society Library, 42 West Middle Lane, Rockville, Maryland 20850. Comments: At least 15 marked graves, African-American congregation.

ELIJAH UNITED METHODIST CHURCH CEMETERY AT POOLESVILLE (ELIJAH REST METHODIST EPISCOPAL CHURCH)
Directions: Route 28 West, left on 109, church and cemetery on right. [A.D.C. Map: Montgomery, page 19, grid coordinates K-1.] Condition of cemetery: Well kept. Active cemetery. Earliest known death: 1881. Most recent death: Present. Veterans interred: WWII and other wars vets. In 1936, 1 volume records, 1909-?. Date transcribed: 1982. Location of transcribed records: Montgomery County Historical Society Library, 42 West Middle Lane, Rockville, Maryland 20850. Comments: Over 150 marked graves, African-American congregation, first church built 1871, present church built after 1950.

EMORY GROVE CEMETERY (EMORY GROVE MEMORIAL METHODIST EPISCOPAL CHURCH)
Directions: Route 124 North to 18100 Gaithersburg-Laytonsville Road. [A.D.C. Map: Montgomery, page 23, grid coordinates G-1.] Condition of cemetery: Overgrown, located behind Emory Grove Park, entrance beside Longview Elementary School. Inactive cemetery. Earliest known death: 1912. Most recent death: Present. Veterans interred: WWII Vets. In 1936, 1 volume of records, 1926-1936, earlier records lost, church organized 1878. Date transcribed: 1982. Location of transcribed records: Montgomery County Historical Society Library, 42 West Middle Lane, Rockville, Maryland 20850. Comments: Over 80 readable marked graves and many unmarked ones, African-American cemetery.

EMORY GROVE UNITED METHODIST CHURCH BURIAL AREA (EMORY GROVE MEMORIAL CHURCH)
Directions: Route 124 North, Laytonsville Road, left on Emory Grove Road, church on left. [A.D.C. Map: Montgomery, page 23, grid coordinates G-2.] Condition of cemetery: Well kept. Inactive cemetery. Earliest known death: 1906. Most recent death: 1923. Famous person interred: Rev. A.B. Dorsey. Date transcribed: 1990. Location of transcribed records: Montgomery County Historical Society Library, 42 West Middle Lane, Rockville, Maryland 20850. Comments: One grave marker for minister and wife in backyard, African-American congregation, church organized 1878.

FLOWER HILL CHURCH OF THE BRETHREN CEMETERY AT REDLAND
Directions: Route 124 North, right on Muncaster Mill Road, church and cemetery on right. [A.D.C. Map: Montgomery, page 23, grid coordinates J-1.] Condition of cemetery: Well kept. Active cemetery. Earliest known death: 1933. Most recent death: Present. Veterans interred: WWII Vets. In 1937, 1 record volume, 1935-1937, in possession of pastor, no earlier records. Location of burial records: Church office. Date transcribed: 1989. Location of transcribed records: Montgomery County Historical Society Library, 42 West Middle Lane, Rockville, Maryland 20850. Comments: Over 98 marked graves.

FRIENDS MEETING HOUSE CEMETERY AT SANDY SPRING (FRIENDS MEETING HOUSE CEMETERY)
Directions: Route 108 East, right on Meeting House Road, church and cemetery on left. [A.D.C. Map: Montgomery, page 25, grid coordinates H-2.] Condition of cemetery: Well kept. Active cemetery. Earliest known

MONTGOMERY COUNTY CEMETERIES - CHURCH 167

death: 1805. Most recent death: Present. Veterans interred: Civil War and WWI vets. Date transcribed: 1975. Location of transcribed records: Montgomery County Historical Society Library, 42 West Middle Lane, Rockville, Maryland 20850. Author: J. Thomas Scharf, A.M. Title: *History of Western Maryland*, page 776, Vol. I. Publisher: Regional Publishing Company [reprinted 1968], Baltimore, MD (originally printed in Philadelphia, 1882]. Comments: Over 600 marked graves.

FRIENDSHIP UNITED METHODIST CHURCH CEMETERY AT DAMASCUS
Directions: Route 27 North, Ridge Road, beyond Damascus, church and cemetery on right. [A.D.C. Map: Montgomery, page 2, grid coordinates C-10.] Condition of cemetery: Well kept. Active cemetery. Earliest known death: 1885. Most recent death: Present. Veterans interred: WWI and WWII vets. Date transcribed: 1989. Location of transcribed records: Montgomery County Historical Society Library, 42 West Middle Lane, Rockville, Maryland 20850. Comments: Over 154 marked graves, African-American congregation.

GATE OF HEAVEN CEMETERY AT SILVER SPRING
Directions: Route 97 North, Georgia Avenue, cemetery on right. [A.D.C. Map: Montgomery, page 33, grid coordinates G-1.] Condition of cemetery: Well kept. Active cemetery. Earliest known death: 1957. Most recent death: Present. Location of burial records: Gate of Heaven Cemetery office. Over 2,000 interments, owned by the Catholic Cemeteries of the Archdiocese of Washington, Inc.

GERMANTOWN BAPTIST CHURCH CEMETERY, UNION CHAPEL CEMETERY
Directions: Route 28 North, right on Route 118, right on Riffle Ford Road, church on right. [A.D.C. Map: Montgomery, page 21, grid coordinates J-2.] Condition of cemetery: Well kept, on road from Pleasant Hills to Old Germantown. Active cemetery. Earliest known death: 1881. Most recent death: Present. Veterans interred: WWI, WWII and other wars vets. Lapsed from 1924 to 1932, originally old Union Chapel at Pleasant Hills (now Darnestown). Date transcribed: 1989. Location of transcribed records: Montgomery County Historical Society Library, 42 West Middle Lane, Rockville, Maryland 20850. Author: J. Thomas Scharf, A.M. Title: *History of Western Maryland*, page 762, Vol. I. Publisher: Regional Publishing Company [reprinted 1968], Baltimore, MD [originally printed in Philadelphia, 1882]. Comments: Over 115 marked graves, in 1936 1 volume records, 1932-1937, earlier records not located.

GERMANTOWN METHODIST EPISCOPAL CHURCH CEMETERY (TRINITY METHODIST EPISCOPAL CHURCH CEMETERY)
Directions: Route I-270 to Germantown exit, Route 118 South, church on right. [A.D.C. Map: Montgomery, page 13, grid coordinates A-10.] Condition of cemetery: Unknown, original church building sold March 1903, but adjacent cemetery was reserved. Earliest known death: 1876. Most recent death: 1896. In 1937, 1 record volume, 1888-1890, Laytonsville parsonage, 3 volumes, 1890-1937, Gaithersburg. Date transcribed: 1959. Location of transcribed records: Montgomery County Historical Society Library, 42 West Middle Lane, Rockville, Maryland 20850. Author: J. Thomas Scharf, A.M. Title: *History of Western Maryland*, page 785, Vol. I. Publisher: Regional Publishing Company [reprinted 1968], Baltimore, MD [originally printed in Philadelphia, 1882]. Comments: Four known marked graves, church organized 1867, has never lapsed.

GOOD HOPE UNION UNITED METHODIST CHURCH CEMETERY AT COLESVILLE (GOOD HOPE METHODIST EPISCOPAL CHURCH CEMETERY)
Directions: Route 650 North, right on Cape May Road which becomes Good Hope Road, church on right. [A.D.C. Map: Montgomery, page 26, grid coordinates D-11.] Condition of cemetery: Well kept. Active cemetery. Earliest known death: 1882. Most recent death: Present. Veterans interred: WWII Vet. Organized 1913, 2 record volumes 1918-1937, at parsonage, earlier records destroyed by fire. Date transcribed: 1981. Location of transcribed records: Montgomery County Historical Society Library, 42 West Middle Lane, Rockville, Maryland 20850. Comments: Over 100 marked graves, African-American congregation.

GOSHEN MEETING HOUSE METHODIST EPISCOPAL CHURCH SOUTH CEMETERY (GOSHEN METHODIST CHURCH CEMETERY, GOSHEN MEETING HOUSE)
Directions: Route 124 North, left on Brink Road, cemetery on left. [A.D.C. Map: Montgomery, page 14, grid coordinates F-4.] Condition of cemetery: Well kept, over 275 marked graves. Active cemetery. Earliest known death: 1817. Most recent death: Present. In 1936, 4 record volumes, 1856-1905, Rockville Circuit, 3 volumes, 1905-1937, Laytonsville parsonage. Date transcribed: 1975. Location of transcribed records: Montgomery County Historical Society Library, 42 West Middle Lane, Rockville, Maryland 20850. Author: J. Thomas Scharf, A.M. Title: *History of Western Maryland*, page 718, Vol. I. Publisher: Regional Publishing Company [reprinted 1968], Baltimore, MD [originally printed in Philadel-

phia, 1882]. Comments: Church sold to Mennonites, cemetery still owned by Methodist cemetery trustees, church organized 1790.

GRACE EPISCOPAL CHURCH CEMETERY AT SILVER SPRING
Directions: Route 97 North, Georgia Avenue, right on Grace Church Road, church on left. [A.D.C. Map: Montgomery, page 39, grid coordinates F-1.] Condition of cemetery: Well kept. Active cemetery. Earliest known death: 1846. Most recent death: Present. Veterans interred: Civil War, WWI and other wars vets. Location of transcribed records: Montgomery County Historical Society Library, 42 West Middle Lane, Rockville, Maryland 20850. Author: J. Thomas Scharf, A.M. Title: *History of Western Maryland*, page 760, Vol. I. Publisher: Regional Publishing Company [reprinted 1968], Baltimore, MD [originally printed in Philadelphia, 1882]. Comments: Over 282 marked graves plus 17 Civil War soldiers buried 1864.

HAWLINGS RIVER CHAPEL CHURCH CEMETERY NEAR LAYTONSVILLE (BELL CEMETERY, ST. BARTHOLOMEW'S PROTESTANT EPISCOPAL CHURCH)
Directions: Two miles east of Laytonsville, on hilltop off Sundown Road, located on Wilcox farm. [A.D.C. Map: Montgomery, page 15, grid coordinates F-2.] Condition of cemetery: Poor, overgrown. Inactive cemetery. Location of transcribed records: Montgomery County Historical Society Library, 42 West Middle Lane, Rockville, Maryland 20850. Comments: Four marked graves, church was predecessor of St. Bartholomew's Episcopal Church, Laytonsville.

HERMON PRESBYTERIAN CHURCH CEMETERY AT BETHESDA
Directions: Seven Locks Road South, right on Lilly Stone Drive, right on Persimmon Tree Lane. [A.D.C. Map: Montgomery, page 37, grid coordinates F-5.] Condition of cemetery: Well kept, near Congressional Country Club Golf Course. Active cemetery. Earliest known death: 1880. Most recent death: Present. Veterans interred: WWII vets. Date transcribed: 1977. Location of transcribed records: Montgomery County Historical Society Library, 42 West Middle Lane, Rockville, Maryland 20850. Comments: Over 45 marked graves, church founded in 1874.

HOWARD CHAPEL METHODIST EPISCOPAL CHURCH CEMETERY AT UNITY
Directions: Sundown Road East, left on Howard Chapel Road, cemetery on left. [A.D.C. Map: Montgomery, page 8, grid coordinates A-11.] Condition of cemetery: Poor, part of Patuxent River State Park, recently

cleaned up by a Girl Scout. Inactive cemetery. Earliest known death: 1901. Most recent death: 1950. Date transcribed: 1992. Location of transcribed records: Montgomery County Historical Society Library, 42 West Middle Lane, Rockville, Maryland 20850. Comments: At least 17 marked graves, African-American cemetery located at corner of Howard Chapel Road and Elton Farm Road.

HYATTSTOWN CHRISTIAN CHURCH CEMETERY
Directions: Route 355 North, cemetery on right at bottom of hill before entering Hyattstown. [A.D.C. Map: Montgomery, page 4, grid coordinates E-4.] Condition of cemetery: Well kept. Active cemetery. Earliest known death: 1813. Most recent death: Present. Veterans interred: WWI Vets. In 1936, 1 record volume, 1913-1936, earlier records lost. Date transcribed: 1989. Location of transcribed records: Montgomery County Historical Society Library, 41 West Middle Lane, Rockville, Maryland 20850. Author: Jacob Mehrling Holdcraft. Title: *Names In Stone, 75,000 Cemetery Inscriptions From Frederick County, Maryland*, Vol. I and II. Publisher: The Monocacy Book Company [second printing 1972], Redwood City, California [printed in Ann Arbor, Michigan, 1966]. Comments: Present church built 1870 up hill and on opposite side of Route 355, original church site in cemetery.

HYATTSTOWN UNITED METHODIST CHURCH CEMETERY (HYATTSTOWN METHODIST EPISCOPAL CHURCH)
Directions: Route 355 North, church and cemetery on right at north end of Hyattstown. [A.D.C. Map: Montgomery, page 4, grid coordinates E-3.] Condition of cemetery: Well kept, located at top of long hill. Active cemetery. Earliest known death: 1823. Most recent death: Present. Veterans interred: WWI, WWII and other wars vets. In 1936, 5 volumes, 1857-1937, at Clarksburg parsonage, earlier records lost, church organized 1804. Date transcribed: 1989. Location of transcribed records: Montgomery County Historical Society Library, 42 West Middle Lane, Rockville, Maryland 20850. Author: Jacob Mehrling Holdcraft. Title: *Names In Stone, 75,000 Cemetery Inscriptions From Frederick County, Maryland*, Vol. I and II. Publisher: The Monocacy Book Company [second printing 1972], Redwood City, California [printed in Ann Arbor, Michigan, 1966]. Comments: Over 500 marked graves.

JERUSALEM BAPTIST CHURCH CEMETERY (NEW) NEAR POOLESVILLE (JERUSALEM NEW SCHOOL BAPTIST CHURCH CEMETERY)

Directions: Route 28 North, Darnestown Road, left on Jerusalem Road, right on Jerusalem Church Road. [A.D.C. Map: Montgomery, page 11, grid coordinates B-13.] Condition of cemetery: Well kept. Active cemetery. Earliest known death: 1958. Most recent death: Present. Veterans interred: WWII vets. In 1936, 1 volume of minutes, 1922-1937, earlier records lost in fire that destroyed the church. Date transcribed: 1983. Location of transcribed records: Montgomery County Historical Society Library, 42 West Middle Lane, Rockville, Maryland 20850. Comments: At least 9 marked graves, African-American congregation, church organized 1882.

JERUSALEM BAPTIST CHURCH CEMETERY (OLD) NEAR POOLESVILLE

Directions: Route 28, left on Jerusalem Road, right on Jerusalem Church Road, right on Jerusalem Church Terrace. [A.D.C. Map: Montgomery, page 11, grid coordinates B-12.] Condition of cemetery: Unknown. Active cemetery. Earliest known death: 1934. Most recent death: Present. Veterans interred: Other wars vets. In 1936, 1 volume of minutes, 1920-1936, earlier records lost, church organized about 1869. Date transcribed: 1983. Location of transcribed records: Montgomery County Historical Society Library, 42 West Middle Lane, Rockville, Maryland 20850. Comments: Over 44 marked graves, 34 with initials only, African-American congregation.

JOHN WESLEY UNITED METHODIST CHURCH CEMETERY NEAR CLARKSBURG (PLEASANT VIEW METHODIST EPISCOPAL CHURCH CEMETERY, JOHN WESLEY METHODIST EPISCOPAL CHURCH CEMETERY)

Directions: Route 355 North at corner of Running Brooke Drive, on left, one mile South of Clarksburg. [A.D.C. Map: Montgomery, page 13, grid coordinates C-1.] Condition of cemetery: Well kept. Active cemetery. Earliest known death: 1886. Most recent death: Present. Veterans interred: WWI, WWII and other wars vets. In 1936, 1 volume records, 1890-1937, located at Clarksburg parsonage, church organized 1890. Date transcribed: 1987. Location of transcribed records: Montgomery County Historical Society Library, 42 West Middle Lane, Rockville, Maryland 20850. Comments: Over 219 marked graves, African-American congregation.

LAYTONSVILLE CEMETERY NEXT TO ST. PAUL UNITED METHODIST CHURCH (ST. PAUL METHODIST EPISCOPAL CHURCH CEMETERY)
Directions: Route 108 North, cemetery located on left at North end of Laytonsville. [A.D.C. Map: Montgomery, page 15, grid coordinates A-3.] Condition of cemetery: Well kept, located at 21720 Laytonsville Road, next to St. Paul United Methodist Church. Active cemetery. Earliest known death: 1822. Most recent death: Present. Famous person interred: Henry R. Griffith. Veterans interred: Revolutionary, WWI, WWII and other wars vets. In 1936, 2 volumes of records, 1893-1936, at Laytonsville, earlier ones destroyed in fire. Date transcribed: 1975. Location of transcribed records: Montgomery County Historical Society Library, 42 West Middle Lane, Rockville, Maryland 20850. Author: J. Thomas Scharf, A.M. Title: *History of Western Maryland*, page 718, Vol. I. Publisher: Regional Publishing Company [reprinted 1968], Baltimore, MD [originally printed in Philadelphia, 1882]. Comments: Over 800 marked graves, owned by St Paul's, but used by community, church organized in 1866.

MONTGOMERY CHAPEL CHURCH CEMETERY AT HYATTSTOWN (MONTGOMERY CHAPEL METHODIST EPISCOPAL CHURCH)
Directions: Route 355 North, Frederick Road, cemetery and church on right. [A.D.C. Map: Montgomery, page 4, grid coordinates F-6.] Condition of cemetery: Recently cleaned up, was neglected and badly overgrown, church in poor condition in 1937. Inactive cemetery. Earliest known death: 1895. Most recent death: 1947. In 1937, 1 record volume, 1871-1937, at Clarksburg parsonage [Rev. J.E. Lewis at time]. Date transcribed: 1978. Location of transcribed records: Montgomery County Historical Society Library, 42 West Middle Lane, Rockville, Maryland 20850. Comments: At least 14 inscribed markers, several other graves, African-American congregation, church organized in 1871.

MONTGOMERY UNITED METHODIST CHURCH CEMETERY AT CLAGETTSVILLE (BROWN'S CHAPEL)
Directions: Route 27 North, Ridge Road, to Clagettsville, left on Route 80, Kemptown Road, cemetery on right. [A.D.C. Map: Montgomery, page 2, grid coordinates B-10.] Condition of cemetery: Well kept, cemetery still belongs to and used by Montgomery United Methodist Church. Active cemetery. Earliest known death: 1864. Most recent death: Present. Veterans interred: Civil War, WWI, WWII and other wars vets. In 1936, 11 record volumes at Kemptown parsonage, earlier records at New Market parsonage. Date transcribed: 1987. Location of transcribed records: Montgomery County Historical Society Library, 42 West Middle

Lane, Rockville, Maryland 20850. Comments: Over 700 marked graves, church beside cemetery sold to Damascus Church of God.

MT. CALVARY A.U.M.P. CHURCH CEMETERY AT SPENCERVILLE (MT. CALVARY AFRICAN UNION METHODIST PROTESTANT)

Directions: Route 198 West, Spencerville Road, right on Batson Road, church and cemetery on left. [A.D.C. Map: Montgomery, page 26, grid coordinates G-6.] Condition of cemetery: Well kept, church in very dilapidated condition in 1936. Active cemetery. Earliest known death: 1928. Most recent death: Present. In 1936 1 record volume, 1920-1937, at parsonage, no earlier records found. Date transcribed: 1981. Location of transcribed records: Montgomery County Historical Society Library, 42 West Middle Lane, Rockville, Maryland 20850. Comments: At least 9 marked graves, African-American congregation, church built in 1873.

MT. CARMEL UNITED METHODIST CHURCH CEMETERY AT SUNSHINE (MT. CARMEL METHODIST PROTESTANT CHURCH CEMETERY)

Directions: Route 97 North, Georgia Avenue, left on Mt. Carmel Cemetery Road, cemetery on right. [A.D.C. Map: Montgomery, page 8, grid coordinates C-13.] Condition of cemetery: Well kept. Active cemetery. Earliest known death: 1848. Most recent death: Present. Veterans interred: WWI, WWII and other wars vets. In 1937, 4 record volumes, 1958-1937, at Clarksville parsonage. Date transcribed: 1980. Location of transcribed records: Montgomery County Historical Society Library, 42 West Middle Lane, Rockville, Maryland 20850. Comments: Over 600 marked graves, church built prior to 1844.

MT. GLORY BAPTIST CHURCH CEMETERY AT CROPLEY ON CONDUIT ROAD

Directions: MacArthur Boulevard West, across from west end of the David Taylor Naval Ship Research Center. [A.D.C. Map: Montgomery, page 37, grid coordinates B-6.] Condition of cemetery: Unknown, remains probably removed when Clara Barton Parkway interchange was constructed. In 1937, 4 record volumes, 1915-1937, kept by Miss Emily Garner at Cropley. Records not transcribed. Comments: Church organized in 1897, 2nd church dedicated in 1920, still active in 1937 inactive before 1995.

MT. LEBANON METHODIST PROTESTANT CHURCH CEMETERY NEAR DAMASCUS

Directions: Route 108 Southeast, Damascus Road, church and cemetery on left. [A.D.C. Map: Montgomery, page 6, grid coordinates G-4.]

Condition of cemetery: Well kept. Active cemetery. Earliest known death: 1876. Most recent death: Present. Veterans interred: WWII Vets. By 1936, church records had been lost, church became inactive in 1926. Date transcribed: 1980. Location of transcribed records: Montgomery County Historical Society Library, 42 West Middle Lane, Rockville, Maryland 20850. Comments: Over 70 marked graves.

MT. PLEASANT UNITED METHODIST CHURCH CEMETERY AT DICKERSON (MT. PLEASANT METHODIST EPISCOPAL CHURCH SOUTH CEMETERY, MT. EPHRAIM METHODIST EPISCOPAL CHURCH CEMETERY)
Directions: Route 28 North, Dickerson Road, right on Mt. Ephraim Road, cemetery on right. [A.D.C. Map: Montgomery, page 3, grid coordinates E-3.] Condition of cemetery: Was badly neglected, overgrown in 1957, was still in use in 1937, stones broken and missing. Inactive cemetery. Most recent death: 1887. Earliest known death: 1918. Veterans interred: Civil War. In 1937, 4 record volumes, 1885-1937, at M.E. South Clarksburg parsonage. Date transcribed: 1983. Location of transcribed records: Montgomery County Historical Society Library, 42 West Middle Lane, Rockville, Maryland 20850. Comments: Over 48 marked graves, many graves unmarked, congregation still using cemetery in 1973.

MT. PLEASANT UNITED METHODIST CHURCH CEMETERY AT NORBECK (MT. PLEASANT METHODIST EPISCOPAL CHURCH)
Directions: Route 28 East, left on Muncaster Mill Road, cemetery on right. [A.D.C. Map: Montgomery, page 24, grid coordinates K-9.] Condition of cemetery: Well kept. Active cemetery. Earliest known death: 1893. Most recent death: Present. In 1937, 2 record volumes, 1922-1937, at Rockville parsonage, church organized in 1885. Date transcribed: 1983. Location of transcribed records: Montgomery County Historical Society Library, 42 West Middle Lane, Rockville, Maryland 20850. Comments: Over 35 marked graves, African-American congregation, located next to Norbeck Recreation Center.

MT. TABOR UNITED METHODIST CHURCH CEMETERY AT ETCHISON (MT. TABOR METHODIST EPISCOPAL CHURCH CEMETERY)
Directions: Route 108 North, church and cemetery on right in Etchison. [A.D.C. Map: Montgomery, page 7, grid coordinates A-9.] Condition of cemetery: Well kept. Active cemetery. Earliest known death: 1884. Most recent death: Present. Veterans interred: WWII Vets. In 1936, 3 record volumes, 1888-1936, at Laytonsville parsonage. Date transcribed: 1980.

Location of transcribed records: Montgomery County Historical Society Library, 42 West Middle Lane, Rockville, Maryland 20850. Comments: Over 90 marked graves.

MT. VIEW UNITED METHODIST CHURCH CEMETERY AT PURDUM (MT. VIEW METHODIST PROTESTANT CHURCH CEMETERY)
Directions: Bethesda Church Road North, left on Johnson Drive, right on Mt. View Road, cemetery on right. [A.D.C. Map: Montgomery, page 5, grid coordinates G-3.] Condition of cemetery: Well kept. Active cemetery. Earliest known death: 1874. Most recent death: Present. Veterans interred: WWI and WWII vets. In 1937, 3 record volumes, 1893-1937, at Kemptown parsonage records, 1875-1893, at New Market. Date transcribed: 1989. Location of transcribed records: Montgomery County Historical Society Library, 42 West Middle Lane, Rockville, Maryland 20850. Comments: Over 180 marked graves, church built in 1875.

MT. ZION METHODIST EPISCOPAL CHURCH CEMETERY AT BIG WOODS (MT. ZION METHODIST EPISCOPAL CHURCH CEMETERY)
Directions: Route 109 South, church and cemetery on right. [A.D.C. Map: Montgomery, page 11, grid coordinates C-5.] Condition of cemetery: Well kept, markers not transcribed. In 1936, 1 record volume, 1932-1937, earlier records not found. Comments: African-American congregation, church organized in 1888.

MT. ZION UNITED METHODIST CHURCH CEMETERY AT MT. ZION
Directions: Route 108 North, Olney Laytonsville Road, right on Zion Road, cemetery on left. [A.D.C. Map: Montgomery, page 15, grid coordinates G-8.] Condition of cemetery: Well kept. Active cemetery. Earliest known death: 1899. Most recent death: Present. Veterans interred: WWI, WWII and other wars vets. Date transcribed: 1982. Location of transcribed records: Montgomery County Historical Society Library, 42 West Middle Lane, Rockville, Maryland 20850. Comments: Over 85 marked graves, African-American congregation.

NEELSVILLE PRESBYTERIAN CHURCH CEMETERY
Directions: Route 355 North, Frederick Road, church and cemetery on right, just past Martin Luther King J.H.S. [A.D.C. Map: Montgomery, page 13, grid coordinates F-6.] Condition of cemetery: Well kept. Active cemetery. Earliest known death: 1849. Most recent death: Present. Veterans interred: WWII and other wars vets. Date transcribed: 1976. Location of transcribed records: Montgomery County Historical Society Library, 42 West Middle Lane, Rockville, Maryland 20850. Author: J.

Thomas Scharf, A.M. Title: *History of Western Maryland*, page 726, Vol. I. Publisher: Regional Publishing Company, [reprinted 1968], Baltimore, MD [originally printed in Philadelphia, 1882]. Comments: Over 450 marked graves.

OAK CHAPEL UNITED METHODIST CHURCH CEMETERY AT MT. ZION (LAYHILL CEMETERY, OAK GROVE CEMETERY)
Directions: Route 97 North, right on Bel Pre Road, left on Layhill Road, church and cemetery on left. [A.D.C. Map: Montgomery, page 25, grid coordinates E-11.] Condition of cemetery: Well kept. Inactive cemetery. Earliest known death: 1877. Most recent death: 1952. Veterans interred: Civil War. Date transcribed: 1981. Location of transcribed records: Montgomery County Historical Society Library, 42 West Middle Lane, Rockville, Maryland 20850. Comments: At least 80 marked graves.

OAK GROVE AFRICAN METHODIST EPISCOPAL ZION CHURCH CEMETERY AT MT. ZION
Directions: Route 108 North, Olney-Laytonsville Road, right on Zion Road, church and cemetery on left. [A.D.C. Map: Montgomery, page 15, grid coordinates G-7.] Condition of cemetery: Part well kept, part in woods is densely overgrown. Active cemetery. Earliest known death: 1934. Most recent death: Present. Veterans interred: WWII vets. Date transcribed: 1990. Location of transcribed records: Montgomery County Historical Society Library, 42 West Middle Lane, Rockville, Maryland 20850. Comments: At least 14 marked graves and many unmarked interments.

OAKWOOD METHODIST EPISCOPAL CHURCH AT NORWOOD
Directions: No longer exists, was located at Norwood. [A.D.C. Map: Montgomery, page 25, grid coordinates G-6.] Condition of cemetery: In 1937, grave yard located on church grounds, was fast disappearing due to neglect. This cemetery is non-extant. Church lapsed in 1914, church built 1880, class organized 1867 or 1868. Markers not transcribed. Comments: Church was on Spencerville Circuit, 2 record volumes, 1880-1914, at Burtonsville parsonage.

PLEASANT GROVE COMMUNITY CHURCH CEMETERY AT PURDUM (PLEASANT GROVE METHODIST EPISCOPAL CHURCH CEMETERY)
Directions: Route 27 North, left on Bethesda Church Road, left on Johnson Drive, cemetery on right. [A.D.C. Map: Montgomery, page 5, grid coordinates G-3.] Condition of cemetery: Well kept. Active cemetery.

MONTGOMERY COUNTY CEMETERIES - CHURCH   177

Earliest known death: 1869. Most recent death: Present. Date transcribed: 1989. Location of transcribed records: Montgomery County Historical Society Library, 42 West Middle Lane, Rockville, Maryland 20850. Comments: Over 60 marked graves, African-American congregation, church built about 1868.

PLEASANT HILLS METHODIST EPISCOPAL CHURCH SOUTH CEMETERY AT DARNESTOWN, UNION METHODIST CHURCH CEMETERY, BAPTIST MEETING HOUSE CHURCH CEMETERY
Directions: Cemetery destroyed by Kelly family sometime after 1951, originally a church cemetery. [A.D.C. Map: Montgomery, page 21.] Location of cemetery: No longer exists, church built in 1844 by Methodists, later used by the Baptists. This cemetery is non-extant. Earliest known death: 1846. Most recent death: 1947. In 1936, 2 record volume, 1857-1880, Rockville circuit, 1880-1908, 2 volume M.E. South Clarksburg parsonage. Location of transcribed records: Montgomery County Historical Society Library, 42 West Middle Lane, Rockville, Maryland 20850. Author: J. Thomas Scharf, A.M. Title: *History of Western Maryland*, page 762, Vol. I. Publisher: Regional Publishing Company [reprinted 1968], Baltimore, MD [originally printed in Philadelphia, 1882]. Comments: 49 marked and 66 unmarked graves, active until 1947. 1 volume of records, 1908-1917, at Potomac parsonage.

PLEASANT VIEW UNITED METHODIST CHURCH CEMETERY AT QUINCE ORCHARD (PLEASANT VIEW METHODIST EPISCOPAL CHURCH, MOUNT OF OLIVES CHURCH)
Directions: Route 28 West, near Quince Orchard. [A.D.C. Map: Montgomery, page 22, grid coordinates H-10.] Condition of cemetery: Well kept. Active cemetery. Earliest known death: 1890. Most recent death: Present. Veterans interred: WWII Vets. In 1937, no vital record books located only a current list of members existed. Date transcribed: 1990. Location of transcribed records: Montgomery County Historical Society Library, 42 West Middle Lane, Rockville, Maryland 20850. Comments: Over 63 marked graves, church organized in 1888.

POOLESVILLE METHODIST EPISCOPAL CHURCH CEMETERY
Directions: Route 109 South, to Fisher Avenue, Town Hall on left. [A.D.C. Map: Montgomery, page 19, grid coordinates K-2.] Condition of cemetery: Cemetery next to church, in 1936, most markers removed or displaced, survivors unreadable. This cemetery is non-extant. Earliest known death: 1839. Church organized 1816, defunct after Civil War, building sold in 1892 to YMCA. Author: J. Thomas Scharf, A.M. Title: *History of Western*

Maryland, page 734, Vol. I. Publisher: Regional Publishing Company [reprinted 1968], Baltimore, MD [originally printed in Philadelphia, 1882]. Comments: In 1936, no surviving records located.

POPLAR GROVE BAPTIST CHURCH CEMETERY AT DARNESTOWN
Directions: Route 28 West, Darnestown Road, left on Jones Lane, church and cemetery on left. [A.D.C. Map: Montgomery, page 22, grid coordinates C-11.] Condition of cemetery: Well kept, church organized in 1892. Active cemetery. Earliest known death: 1910. Most recent death: Present. Veterans interred: WWII Vets. In 1936, 3 record volumes, 1917-1937, kept by Mrs. Klennard Davis, Black Rock Mill. Date transcribed: 1990. Location of transcribed records: Montgomery County Historical Society Library, 41 West Middle Lane, Rockville, Maryland 20850. Comments: Over 33 marked graves, African-American congregation.

POTOMAC UNITED METHODIST CHURCH CEMETERY (POTOMAC CHAPEL METHODIST EPISCOPAL CHURCH, CAPTAIN JOHN'S PRESBYTERIAN CHURCH)
Directions: Route 189 South, Falls Road, church and cemetery on right. [A.D.C. Map: Montgomery, page 31, grid coordinates B-11.] Condition of cemetery: Well kept. Active cemetery. Earliest known death: 1793. Most recent death: Present. Veterans interred: WWI and WWII vets. In 1936, 4 record volumes, 1858-1905, Rockville Circuit, 3 volumes, 1908-1937, Potomac Circuit. Location of burial records: Church office. Date transcribed: 1982. Location of transcribed records: Montgomery County Historical Society Library, 42 West Middle Lane, Rockville, Maryland 20850. Author: J. Thomas Scharf, A.M. Title: *History of Western Maryland*, pages 787 and 788, Vol. I. Publisher: Regional Publishing Company [reprinted 1968], Baltimore, MD [originally printed in Philadelphia, 1882]. Comments: Over 1050 marked graves, church organized 1844.

ROCKVILLE BAPTIST CHURCH CEMETERY
Directions: Located at intersection of Washington and West Jefferson Streets, Rockville. [A.D.C. Map: Montgomery, page 23, grid coordinates J-13.] Condition of cemetery: Well kept, but has been vandalized, markers broken or removed. Inactive cemetery. Earliest known death: 1839. Most recent death: 1897. In 1936, C.H. Robertson had 2 record volume, Mrs. Russell Bogley had volume 1933-1937, other records lost. Date transcribed: 1979. Location of transcribed records: Montgomery County Historical Society Library, 42 West Middle Lane, Rockville, Maryland 20850. Author: J. Thomas Scharf, A.M. Title: *History of Western Maryland*, page 752, Vol. I. Publisher: Regional Publishing Company

[reprinted 1968], Baltimore, MD [originally printed in Philadelphia, 1882].
Comments: Over 43 marked graves.

ROUND OAK BAPTIST CHURCH CEMETERY AT SPENCERVILLE
Directions: 15812 Good Hope Road, between Harding Lane and Upland
Dr. [A.D.C. Map: Montgomery, page 26, grid coordinates E-8.] Condition
of cemetery: Many broken, worn and unreadable stones and markers,
many funeral home markers. Active cemetery. Earliest known death:
1898. Most recent death: Present. Date transcribed: 1981. Location of
transcribed records: Montgomery County Historical Society Library, 42
West Middle Lane, Rockville, Maryland 20850. Comments: Over 72
marked graves, African-American cemetery.

SALEM UNITED METHODIST CHURCH CEMETERY AT
BROOKEVILLE (SALEM METHODIST PROTESTANT CHURCH
CEMETERY)
Directions: Route 97 North, Georgia Avenue, cemetery on right, church
on left. [A.D.C. Map: Montgomery, page 16, grid coordinates C-9.] Condition of cemetery: Well kept. Active cemetery. Earliest known death:
1843. Most recent death: Present. Veterans interred: WWI and WWII
vets. In 1937, 4 record volumes, 1849-1937, at parsonage in Clarkesville
Methodist Protestant Church. Date transcribed: 1980. Location of
transcribed records: Montgomery County Historical Society Library, 42
West Middle Lane, Rockville, Maryland 20850. Author: J. Thomas Scharf,
A.M. Title: *History of Western Maryland*, page 781, Vol. I. Publisher:
Regional Publishing Company [reprinted 1968], Baltimore, MD [originally
printed in Philadelphia, 1882]. Comments: Over 240 marked, and many
unmarked graves.

SALEM UNITED METHODIST CHURCH OF CEDAR GROVE
CEMETERY (SALEM METHODIST EPISCOPAL CHURCH
CEMETERY)
Directions: Route 27 North, Ridge Road, church and cemetery on right.
[A.D.C. Map: Montgomery, page 5, grid coordinates G-10.] Condition of
cemetery: Well kept, 2 record volumes 1922-1937 at Damascus Parsonage.
Active cemetery. Earliest known death: 1841. Most recent death: Present.
Veterans interred: WWII Vets. In 1936, 3 record volumes 1858-1910 at
Clarksburg Parsonage, 3 volumes 1910-1922 at Laytonsville Parsonage.
Date transcribed: 1976. Location of transcribed records: Montgomery
County Historical Society Library, 42 West Middle Lane, Rockville,
Maryland 20850. Comments: Over 333 marked graves, church originally
built in 1850.

SENECA C.M.E. CHURCH CEMETERY AT VIOLET'S LOCK
Directions: Route 190 West, River Road, left on Violet's Lock Road, behind 2-story white house near river. [A.D.C. Map: Montgomery, page 29, grid coordinates C-3.] Condition of cemetery: Unknown. Active cemetery. Earliest known death: 1935. Most recent death: Present. Date transcribed: 1982. Location of transcribed records: Montgomery County Historical Society Library, 42 West Middle Lane, Rockville, Maryland 20850. Comments: Over 32 marked graves.

SITKA BAPTIST CHURCH CEMETERY IN HILLANDALE AREA
Directions: Probably no longer exists. Church was located in area of Naval Surface Weapons Center. [A.D.C. Map: Montgomery, page 34, grid coordinates H-9.] Condition of cemetery: Unknown, church leased to Seventh Day Adventists about 1930. This cemetery is non-extant. In 1937, no records located, those kept 1883-1897 destroyed by fire when church burned in 1897. Records not transcribed. Comments: African-American congregation, church was rebuilt in 1908.

ST. GABRIEL'S CATHOLIC CHURCH CEMETERY AT GREAT FALLS
Directions: Route 189 South, Falls Road to Alloway Drive, Potomac. [A.D.C. Map: Montgomery, page 36, grid coordinates J-2.] Condition of cemetery: Well kept, fence enclosed. Earliest known death: 1889. Most recent death: 1966. Veterans interred: WWII and other wars vets. Church was dedicated 2 May 1890. Date transcribed: 1977. Location of transcribed records: Montgomery County Historical Society Library, 42 West Middle Lane, Rockville, Maryland 20850. Comments: Church abandoned in 1920s when C&O Canal workers left the area.

ST. JOHN'S CATHOLIC CHURCH CEMETERY AT FOREST GLEN (CARROLL'S CHAPEL, CARROLL'S FAMILY CEMETERY)
Directions: Route 97 North, Georgia Avenue, left on Forest Glen Road, Route 192 West, right on Rosensteel Avenue. [A.D.C. Map: Montgomery, page 33, grid coordinates D-13.] Condition of cemetery: Well kept. Active cemetery. Earliest known death: 1790. Most recent death: Present. In 1936, records, 1813-1899 at Rockville, 1899-1936 at St John's Parish house. Location of transcribed records: Montgomery County Historical Society Library, 42 West Middle Lane, Rockville, Maryland 20850. Author: J. Thomas Scharf, A.M. Title: *History of Western Maryland*, page 759, Vol. I. Publisher: Regional Publishing Company [reprinted 1968], Baltimore, MD [originally printed in Philadelphia, 1882]. Comments: Interments begin before 1774, there are over 1939 burials recorded.

MONTGOMERY COUNTY CEMETERIES - CHURCH 181

ST. JOHN'S EPISCOPAL CHURCH CEMETERY AT OLNEY (ST. JOHN'S PROTESTANT EPISCOPAL CHURCH CEMETERY)
Directions: Route 97 North, Georgia Avenue, left on Route 108, Olney-Laytonsville Road, cemetery on right. [A.D.C. Map: Montgomery, page 16, grid coordinates B-13.] Condition of cemetery: Well kept, no more grave sites to be sold. Active cemetery. Earliest known death: 1836. Most recent death: Present. Veterans interred: Civil War, WWI and WWII vets. Date transcribed: 1975. Location of transcribed records: Montgomery County Historical Society Library, 42 West Middle Lane, Rockville, Maryland 20850. Author: J. Thomas Scharf, A.M. Title: *History of Western Maryland*, page 780, Vol. I. Publisher: Regional Publishing Company [reprinted 1968], Baltimore, MD [originally printed in Philadelphia, 1882]. Comments: Over 465 marked graves, some Waters Family interments moved here from Belmont, oldest marker 1788.

ST. LUKE'S EPISCOPAL CHURCH CEMETERY AT BRIGHTON (ST. LUKE'S PROTESTANT EPISCOPAL CHURCH CEMETERY)
Directions: Route 650 North, New Hampshire Avenue, left on Brighton Dam Road, church and cemetery on right. [A.D.C. Map: Montgomery, page 16, grid coordinates H-6.] Condition of cemetery: Well kept. Earliest known death: 1878. Most recent death: 1932. Date transcribed: 1975. Location of transcribed records: Montgomery County Historical Society Library, 42 West Middle Lane, Rockville, Maryland 20850. Comments: Over 10 marked graves.

ST. LUKE'S LUTHERAN CHURCH CEMETERY AT REDLAND
Directions: Route 355 North, right on Redland Road, left on Briardale Road by first house on right, 2nd driveway, in Blueberry Hill development. [A.D.C. Map: Montgomery, page 23, grid coordinates K-5.] Condition of cemetery: Well kept. Active cemetery. Earliest known death: 1919. Most recent death: Present. Date transcribed: 1981. Location of transcribed records: Montgomery County Historical Society Library, 42 West Middle Lane, Rockville, Maryland 20850. Comments: Over 154 marked graves.

ST. MARK'S EPISCOPAL CHURCH CEMETERY AT FAIRLAND (ST. MARK'S PROTESTANT EPISCOPAL CHURCH CEMETERY)
Directions: Route 29 North to Old Columbia Pike North, past East Randolph Road, church and cemetery on right. [A.D.C. Map: Montgomery, page 34, grid coordinates G-4.] Condition of cemetery: Well kept. Active cemetery. Earliest known death: 1862. Most recent death: Present. Veterans interred: Civil War, WWI and WWII vets. Date transcribed:

Society Library, 42 West Middle Lane, Rockville, Maryland 20850. Comments: Over 213 marked graves.

ST. MARK'S UNITED METHODIST CHURCH CEMETERY AT BOYDS, WHITE OAK CHAPEL
Directions: Route 121 South, through Boyds, left on White Ground Road, church and cemetery on right. [A.D.C. Map: Montgomery, page 12, grid coordinates D-9.] Condition of cemetery: Well kept, original church blew down in 1892. Active cemetery. Earliest known death: 1890. Most recent death: Present. In 1936, Addison Duffin reported the church never kept records. Date transcribed: 1982. Location of transcribed records: Montgomery County Historical Society Library, 42 West Middle Lane, Rockville, Maryland 20850. Comments: Over 57 marked graves, African-American congregation, 1st building stood about 20 feet back of present one.

ST. MARY'S CATHOLIC CHURCH CEMETERY (NEW) AT ROCKVILLE
Directions: Route 28 East, right on Baltimore Road, St. Mary's cemetery on left. [A.D.C. Map: Montgomery, page 24, grid coordinates C-13.] Condition of cemetery: Well kept. Active cemetery. Earliest known death: 1888. Most recent death: Present. Veterans interred: WWI, WWII and other wars vets. In 1937, 2 record volumes, 1813-1868, St Johns rectory, Forest Glen, 7 record volumes, 1869-1937, St Mary's Rockville. Date transcribed: 1980. Location of transcribed records: Montgomery County Historical Society Library, 42 West Middle Lane, Rockville, Maryland 20850. Comments: Over 750 graves, both marked and unmarked.

ST. MARY'S CATHOLIC CHURCH CEMETERY (OLD) AT ROCKVILLE
[A.D.C. Map: Montgomery, page 32, grid coordinates A-1.] Condition of cemetery: Well kept, many markers missing. Inactive cemetery. Earliest known death: 1832. Most recent death: 1953. Famous person interred: F. Scott Fitzgerald. Veterans interred: WWI Vets. See under St. Mary's "new" cemetery. Date transcribed: 1985. Location of transcribed records: Montgomery County Historical Society Library, 42 West Middle Lane, Rockville, Maryland 20850. Author: J. Thomas Scharf, A.M. Title: *History of Western Maryland*, page 751, Vol. I. Publisher: Regional Publishing Company [reprinted 1968], Baltimore, MD [originally printed in Philadelphia, 1882]. Comments: Church built in 1817, contains 288 marked and 183 unmarked graves, see new cemetery, Baltimore Road.

ST. MARY'S CATHOLIC SHRINE CHURCH CEMETERY AT BARNESVILLE

Directions: Route 117 Northwest, Barnesville Road, church and cemetery on left. Condition of cemetery: Well kept. Active cemetery. Earliest known death: 1820. Most recent death: Present. Veterans interred: Civil War, WWI, WWII and other wars vets. In 1936, records 1814-1936 at St John's at Forest Glen except 1 volume, 1836-1868, at Barnesville. Date transcribed: 1989. Location of transcribed records: Montgomery County Historical Society Library, 42 West Middle Lane, Rockville, Maryland 20850. Author: J. Thomas Scharf, A.M. Title: *History of Western Maryland*, page 731, Vol. I. Publisher: Regional Publishing Company [reprinted 1968], Baltimore, MD [originally printed in Philadelphia, 1882]. Comments: Church was built in 1808, until 1869 was pastored by Priests resident at Rockville.

ST. PAUL COMMUNITY CHURCH CEMETERY AT SUGARLAND

Directions: Route 190 West, River Road, right on Partnership Road, left on Sugarland Lane, cemetery on right. [A.D.C. Map: Montgomery, page 20, grid coordinates E-11.] Condition of cemetery: Well kept. Active cemetery. Earliest known death: 1905. Most recent death: Present. Veterans interred: WWI and WWII vets. Date transcribed: 1982. Location of transcribed records: Montgomery County Historical Society Library, 42 West Middle Lane, Rockville, Maryland 20850. Comments: Over 91 marked graves, African-American congregation.

ST. ROSE OF LIMA CATHOLIC CHURCH CEMETERY AT CLOPPERS

Directions: Route 117 West, Clopper Road, church and cemetery on right. [A.D.C. Map: Montgomery, page 22, grid coordinates F-1.] Condition of cemetery: Well kept, records 1840-1872, 1895-1937 at St. Martin's in Gaithersburg. Active cemetery. Earliest known death: 1837. Most recent death: Present. Famous person interred: William Rich Hutton. Veterans interred: Civil War and WWI vets. In 1937, records 1814-1835, 1868-1872, 1872-1895, at Barnesville, 1835-1868 at Forest Glen, see above. Date transcribed: 1980. Location of transcribed records: Montgomery County Historical Society Library, 42 West Middle Lane, Rockville, Maryland 20850. Comments: Over 385 marked graves.

SUGAR LOAF MOUNTAIN METHODIST EPISCOPAL CHURCH CEMETERY NEAR COMUS (SUGARLOAF CHAPEL, MOUNTAIN CHAPEL, SUGAR LOAF MOUNTAIN COMMUNITY CHURCH)

Directions: Route 109 South, Old Hundred Road, past Thurston Road, church and cemetery on right. [A.D.C. Map: Montgomery, page 4, grid coordinates A-7.] Condition of cemetery: Neglected, original church an octagonal log structure which stood near present site. Inactive cemetery. Church organized before 1788, 5 record volumes located at Clarksburg Parsonage in 1936. Author: Jacob Mehrling Holdcraft. Title: *Names In Stone, 75,000 Cemetery Inscriptions From Frederick County, Maryland*, Vol. I and II. Publisher: The Monocacy Book Company [second printing 1972], Redwood City, California [printed Ann Arbor, Michigan, 1966]. Comments: Remained a Methodist Episcopal Church, incorporation trustees buried in cemetery.

TRINITY METHODIST CHURCH CEMETERY AT GERMANTOWN
[A.D.C. Map: Montgomery, page 13, grid coordinates A-10.] Condition of cemetery: Well kept, abandoned but maintained by Boy Scouts. Inactive cemetery. Earliest known death: 1876. Most recent death: 1896. Date transcribed: 1989. Location of transcribed records: Montgomery County Historical Society Library, 42 West Middle Lane, Rockville, Maryland 20850. Author: J. Thomas Scharf, A.M. Title: *History of Western Maryland*, page 785, Vol. I. Publisher: Regional Publishing Company [reprinted 1968], Baltimore, MD [originally printed in Philadelphia, 1882]. Comments: At least 4 marked graves.

UNION WESLEY METHODIST CHURCH CEMETERY ON PINEY MEETING HOUSE ROAD (PINEY MEETING HOUSE CEMETERY, WIDEAR CEMETERY)
Directions: Piney Meeting House Road near Piney Glen Lane. [A.D.C. Map: Montgomery, page 30, grid coordinates G-6.] Condition of cemetery: Neglected for many years, cleaned up in 1990, stones in poor condition. Inactive cemetery. Earliest known death: 1953. Location of transcribed records: Montgomery County Historical Society Library, 42 West Middle Lane, Rockville, Maryland 20850. Comments: Four marked graves, African-American cemetery.

UPPER SENECA BAPTIST CHURCH CEMETERY AT CEDAR GROVE (WHITE OAK CHAPEL)
Directions: Route 27 North, Ridge Road, right on Davis Mill Road, church and cemetery on left. [A.D.C. Map: Montgomery, page 5, grid coordinates G-11.] Condition of cemetery: Well kept. Active cemetery. Earliest known death: 1864. Most recent death: Present. Veterans interred: WWII vets. In 1936, 1 record volume 1805-1857 in possession of E.D. Hawkins, Woodfield, later records in possession of Guy Watkins, Cedar Grove. Date transcribed: 1976. Location of transcribed records: Montgomery County Historical Society Library, 42 West Middle Lane, Rockville, Maryland

20850. Comments: Over 300 marked graves, is a Southern Baptist Church.

WARREN UNITED METHODIST CHURCH CEMETERY AT MARTINSBURG (WARREN METHODIST EPISCOPAL CHURCH CEMETERY, WARREN'S CHAPEL [AFRICAN M.E. CHURCH])
Directions: Route 107 West, Whites Ferry Road, church on right. [A.D.C. Map: Montgomery, page 10, grid coordinates A-12.] Condition of cemetery: Unknown. Inactive cemetery. In 1936, 1 record volume, 1903-?, church organized in 1900. Date transcribed: 1983. Location of transcribed records: Montgomery County Historical Society Library, 42 West Middle Lane, Rockville, Maryland 20850. Comments: Historic site, at least 15 marked graves.

WESLEY GROVE UNITED METHODIST CHURCH CEMETERY AT WOODFIELD (WESLEY GROVE METHODIST EPISCOPAL CHURCH CEMETERY)
Directions: Route 124 South, Woodfield Road, church and cemetery on right in Woodfield. [A.D.C. Map: Montgomery, page 6, grid coordinates D-10.] Condition of cemetery: Well kept. Active cemetery. Earliest known death: 1880. Most recent death: Present. Veterans interred: WWII and other wars vets. In 1936, 3 record volumes, 1888-1936, at Laytonsville parsonage. Date transcribed: 1977. Location of transcribed records: Montgomery County Historical Society Library, 42 West Middle Lane, Rockville, Maryland 20850. Comments: Over 158 marked graves, church established 1888.

WHITE OAK CHAPEL BAPTIST CHURCH NEAR CEDAR GROVE (PURDUM FAMILY BURYING GROUND)
Directions: Route 27 North, right on Davis Mill Road, left on Watkins Road, on hill on left before Kings Valley Road. [A.D.C. Map: Montgomery, page 5, grid coordinates G-11.] Condition of cemetery: Poor, iron fence enclosure has fallen down, located between Davis Mill and Kings Valley Roads. Inactive cemetery. Earliest known death: 1832. Most recent death: 1897. Date transcribed: 1978. Location of transcribed records: Montgomery County Historical Society Library, 42 West Middle Lane, Rockville, Maryland 20850. Comments: More Riggs family members buried here than Purdums.

DIRECTORY OF MARYLAND'S BURIAL GROUNDS

WILDWOOD BAPTIST CHURCH CEMETERY AT BETHESDA, MT. ZION BAPTIST CHURCH
Directions: Route 187 South, Old Georgetown Road, church and cemetery on right. [A.D.C. Map: Montgomery, page 32, grid coordinates D-11.] Condition of cemetery: Well kept. Active cemetery. Earliest known death: 1850. Most recent death: Present. Date transcribed: 1981. Location of transcribed records: Montgomery County Historical Society Library, 42 West Middle Lane, Rockville, Maryland 20850. Comments: Over 510 marked graves.

Public Cemeteries

POTTER'S FIELD AT ROCKVILLE
Directions: South on Monroe Street, cross Cabin John Parkway, left at Summit Apartments, cemetery on left. [A.D.C. Map: Montgomery, page 31, grid coordinates H-3.] Condition of cemetery: City sold property and contracted with National Parks Service to locate unmarked graves. This cemetery is non-extant. Has been relocated. Burials planned by Department of Works. Comments: Almost no marked graves. Human slave remains on old Riggs farm relocated to Poor Farm to make room for Laytonsville landfill.

PRINCE GEORGE'S COUNTY

Private Cemeteries

ADDISON FAMILY CEMETERY
Location: Stones moved to *Salubria* from *Colbrooke* near Street Barnabus Church at Oxon Hill. [A.D.C. map location: page 24, grid coordinates A2.] Earliest known death: 1841. Most recent death: 1860. Date transcribed: 1956. These transcribed records are held by Toaping Chapter, DAR. Author: P.G.C.G.S., Inc. Title: *Stones and Bones*. Publisher: Prince George's County Genealogical Society, Inc., P.O. 819, Bowie, MD 20718-0819 (1984).

ADDISON FAMILY CEMETERY AND VAULT
Location: One-half mile west of Indian Head Highway and 0.25 mile south of the Capital Beltway. [A.D.C. map location: page 23, grid coordinates D6.] Earliest known death: 1808. Most recent death: 1871.

Prominent individual interred: John Hanson. No burial records were kept. Date transcribed: 1955. These transcribed records are held by Toaping Chapter, DAR. Author: P.G.C.G.S., Inc. Title: *Stones And Bones*. Publisher: Prince George's County Genealogical Society, Inc., P.O. 819, Bowie, MD 20718-0819 (1984).

AITCHESON FAMILY GRAVEYARD
Location: Formally located at *Ellerslie*, between Dorset Road and I95, north of Sandy Spring Road. [A.D.C. map location: page 4, grid coordinates C3.] Earliest known death: 1863. Most recent death: 1866. Date transcribed: 1955. These transcribed records are held by Toaping Chapter, DAR. Author: P.G.C.G.S., Inc. Title: *Stones And Bones*. Publisher: Prince George's County Genealogical Society, Inc., P.O. Box 819, Bowie, MD 20718-0819 (1984). Additional comments: Remains were relocated to Ivy Hill Cemetery in Laurel, MD.

BADEN FAMILY GRAVEYARD
Location: Near Brooks Church, Naylor, MD [A.D.C. map location: page 34, grid coordinates E12.] Earliest known death: 1848. Most recent death: 1864. Date transcribed: 1955. These transcribed records are held by Toaping Chapter, DAR. Author: P.G.C.G.S., Inc. Title: *Stones And Bones*. Publisher: Prince George's County Genealogical Society, Inc., P.O. Box 819, Bowie, MD 20718-0819 (1984).

BAMBER GRAVE
Location: Located on Riggs Road south of old Adelphi Mill. [A.D.C. map location: page 7, grid coordinates B3.] Earliest known death: 1825. Most recent death: 1825. Date transcribed: 1955. These transcribed records are held by Toaping Chapter, DAR. Author: P.G.C.G.S., Inc. Title: *Stones And Bones*. Publisher: Prince George's County Genealogical Society, Inc., P.O. Box 819, Bowie, MD 20718-0819 (1984). Additional comments: The grave stone has been moved to Rock Creek Cemetery.

BAYNE FAMILY CEMETERY AND MONUMENT
Location: 2604 Kingsway Road off Bock Road near the Apple Grove Elementary School [A.D.C. map location: page 24, grid coordinates A8.] Earliest known death: 1800. Most recent death: 1901. Revolutionary War veterans. Date transcribed: 1983. These transcribed records are held by Toaping Chapter, DAR. Author: P.G.C.G.S., Inc. Title: *Stones And Bones*. Publisher: Prince George's County Genealogical Society, Inc., P.O. Box 819, Bowie, MD 20718-0819 (1984).

188   DIRECTORY OF MARYLAND'S BURIAL GROUNDS

BEALL FAMILY GRAVE
Location: On the White House place, on White House Road near Ritchie. [A.D.C. map location: page 19, grid coordinates K7.] Earliest known death: 1853. Most recent death: 1853. Date transcribed: 1955. These transcribed records are held by Toaping Chapter, DAR. Author: P.G.C.G.S., Inc. Title: *Stones And Bones*. Publisher: Prince George's County Genealogical Society, Inc., P.O. 819, Bowie, MD 20718-0819 (1984).

BEALL/LOVE FAMILY GRAVES
Location: In the cemetery across from *Middleton* place on old Route 5 near Camp Springs. [A.D.C. map location: page 24, grid coordinates H4.] Earliest known death: 1797. Most recent death: 1828. Date transcribed: 1955. These transcribed records are held by Toaping Chapter, DAR. Author: P.G.C.G.S., Inc. Title: *Stones And Bones*. Publisher: Prince George's County Genealogical Society, Inc., P.O. 819, Bowie, MD 20718-0819 (1984).

BEANES FAMILY CEMETERY
Location: Next to the Board of Education Service Center on Elm Street in Upper Marlboro, MD. [A.D.C. map location: page 27, grid coordinates B3.] Earliest known death: 1822. Most recent death: 1918. Revolutionary War veterans. Date transcribed: 1955. These transcribed records are held by Toaping Chapter, DAR. Author: P.G.C.G.S., Inc. Title: *Stones And Bones*. Publisher: Prince George's County Genealogical Society, Inc., P.O. Box 819, Bowie, MD 20718-0819 (1984).

BERRY FAMILY CEMETERY
Location: On the James Berry farm *Concord*, 8000 Walker Mill Road, District Heights. [A.D.C. map location: page 19, grid coordinates E5.] Earliest known death: 1793. Most recent death: 1876. Revolutionary War veterans. Date transcribed: 1955. These transcribed records are held by Toaping Chapter, DAR. Author: P.G.C.G.S., Inc. Title: *Stones And Bones*. Publisher: Prince George's County Genealogical Society, Inc., P.O. Box 819, Bowie, MD 20718-0819 (1984).

BERRY FAMILY CEMETERY
Location: On the former *Graden* estate of the Berry family on Central Avenue west of Largo. [A.D.C. map location: page 19, grid coordinates K2.] Earliest known death: 1846. Most recent death: 1850. Date transcribed: 1955. These transcribed records are held by Toaping Chapter, DAR. Author: P.G.C.G.S., Inc. Title: *Stones And Bones*.

PRINCE GEORGE'S COUNTY CEMETERIES - PRIVATE

Publisher: Prince George's County Genealogical Society, Inc., P.O. Box 819, Bowie, MD 20718-0819 (1984).

BERRY FAMILY CEMETERY
Location: *Independence* on Central Avenue. Earliest known death: 1835. Most recent death: 1886. Date transcribed: 1955. These transcribed records are held by Toaping Chapter, DAR. Author: P.G.C.G.S., Inc. Title: *Stones And Bones*. Publisher: Prince George's County Genealogical Society, Inc., P.O. Box 819, Bowie, MD 20718-0819 (1984).

BOTELER GRAVE
Location: Near Beltsville. [A.D.C. map location: page 7.] Earliest known death: 1886. Most recent death: 1886. Date transcribed: 1955. These transcribed records are held by Toaping Chapter, DAR. Author: P.G.C.G.S., Inc. Title: *Stones And Bones*. Publisher: Prince George's County Genealogical Society, Inc., P.O. Box 819, Bowie, MD 20718-0819 (1984).

BOWIE FAMILY CEMETERY
Location: *Friendship* on Central Avenue at Kolbe's Corner. [A.D.C. map location: page 20, grid coordinates F1.] Earliest known death: 1821. Most recent death: 1860. Date transcribed: 1955. These transcribed records are held by Toaping Chapter, DAR. Author: P.G.C.G.S., Inc. Title: *Stones And Bones*. Publisher: Prince George's County Genealogical Society, Inc., P.O. Box 819, Bowie, MD 20718-0819 (1984). Additional comments: Graves moved to St. Barnabus, Leeland.

BOWIE FAMILY CEMETERY
Location: Moved to Holy Trinity Church on Route 450 near Hillmeade Road. [A.D.C. map location: page 9, grid coordinates H13.] Earliest known death: 1811. Most recent death: 1897. Revolutionary War and Civil War veterans. Date transcribed: 1955. These transcribed records are held by Toaping Chapter, DAR. Author: P.G.C.G.S., Inc. Title: *Stones And Bones*. Publisher: Prince George's County Genealogical Society, Inc., P.O. Box 819, Bowie, MD 20718-0819 (1984).

BOWIE FAMILY CEMETERY
Location: *Fairview* (Oden Bowie estate) west of Church Road between Routes 50 and 450. [A.D.C. map location: page 14.] Earliest known death: 1809. Most recent death: 1948. Prominent individuals interred:

Oden Bowie, Governor of MD. Date transcribed: 1955. These transcribed records are held by Toaping Chapter, DAR. Author: P.G.C.G.S., Inc. Title: *Stones And Bones*. Publisher: Prince George's County Genealogical Society, Inc., P.O. Box 819, Bowie, MD 20718-0819 (1984).

BOWIE FAMILY CEMETERY
Location: On Route 450 at *Cedar Hill* 1/2 mile west of Highbridge Road near Holy Trinity Church. [A.D.C. map location: page 9, grid coordinates H13.] Earliest known death: 1809. Most recent death: 1871. Author: P.G.C.G.S., Inc. Title: *Stones And Bones*. Publisher: Prince George's County Genealogical Society, Inc., P.O. Box 819, Bowie, MD 20718-0819 (1984).

BOWIE FAMILY CEMETERY
Location: *Mattaponi* off of Mattiponi Road near Saint Thomas Road near Croom. [A.D.C. map location: page 34, grid coordinates D3.] Earliest known death: 1831. Most recent death: 1860. Date transcribed: 1955. These transcribed records are held by Toaping Chapter, DAR. Author: P.G.C.G.S., Inc. Title: *Stones And Bones*. Publisher: Prince George's County Genealogical Society, Inc., P.O. Box 819, Bowie, MD 20718-0819 (1984).

BRASHIERS GRAVE
Location: Unknown. [A.D.C. map location: page 4, grid coordinates E2.] Earliest known death: 1885. Most recent death: 1885. Date transcribed: 1855. Location of transcribed records: Toaping Chapter, DAR. Author: P.G.C.G.S., Inc. Title: *Stones And Bones*. Publisher: Prince George's County Genealogical Society, Inc., P.O. Box 819, Bowie, MD 20718-0819 (1984). Additional comments: Remains now located in Ivy Hill Cemetery, Laurel, MD.

BROWN/MILLER FAMILY CEMETERY
Location: Behind Agricultural Library, near 10300 Rhode Island Avenue, Beltsville, MD. [A.D.C. map location: page 7, grid coordinates G5.] Condition of cemetery: Very poor in June 1995. Vandalized in the 1980s. Periodically cleaned by local Boy Scout Troop. Earliest known death: 1840. Most recent death: 1910. Date transcribed: 1983. Author: P.G.C.G.S., Inc. Title: *Stones And Bones*. Publisher: Prince George's County Genealogical Society, Inc., P.O. Box 819, Bowie, MD 20718-0819 (1984).

CALVERT FAMILY CEMETERY
Location: 4609 Rittenhouse Street, Riverdale, MD. [A.D.C. map location: page 12, grid coordinates F2.] Earliest known death: 1821. Most recent death: 1864. Date transcribed: 1854. These transcribed records are held by Toaping Chapter, DAR. Author: P.G.C.G.S., Inc. Title: *Stones And Bones*. Publisher: Prince George's County Genealogical Society, Inc., P.O. Box 819, Bowie, MD 20718-0819 (1984).

CARTER CEMETERY
Location: *Goodwood* on Clagett Landing Road. [A.D.C. map location: page 22/23, grid coordinates G5/B5.] Earliest known death: 1845. Most recent death: 1845. Date transcribed: 1955. These transcribed records are held by Toaping Chapter, DAR. Author: P.G.C.G.S., Inc. Title: *Stones And Bones*. Publisher: Prince George's County Genealogical Society, Inc., P.O. Box 819, Bowie, MD 20718-0819 (1984). Additional comments: Grave and stone moved to St. Barnabus, Leeland.

CHIEF TURKEY TAYAC'S GRAVE (PISCATAWAY INDIAN OSSUARY) MOCKLEY POINT BURIAL GROUND
Location: From Farmington Road west on Bryan Pt. Road to Piscataway National Park [A.D.C. map location: page 29, grid coordinates H12.] Condition of cemetery: Good, occasional care. Used as Indian ceremonial site. June 1995.

CHISELIN STONE
Location: Just above Naylor on Route 382. [A.D.C. map location: page 34, grid coordinates C9.] Earliest known death: 1839. Most recent death: 1839. Date transcribed: 1983. Author: P.G.C.G.S., Inc. Title: *Stones And Bones*. Publisher: Prince George's County Genealogical Society, Inc., P.O. Box 819, Bowie, MD 20718-0819 (1984).

CLAGETT FAMILY CEMETERY
Location: *Weston* just off of Route 301 near Upper Marlboro, MD. [A.D.C. map location: page 27.] Earliest known death: 1732. Most recent death: 1948. Date transcribed: 1954. These transcribed records are held by Toaping Chapter, DAR. Author: P.G.C.G.S., Inc. Title: *Stones And Bones*. Publisher: Prince George's County Genealogical Society, Inc., P.O. Box 819, Bowie, MD 20718-0819 (1984).

CLAGETT FAMILY CEMETERY
Location: Between the Church and the old Croom railroad station at Croom Station. [A.D.C. map location: page 26, grid coordinates K10.]

Earliest known death: 1810. Most recent death: 1864. Prominent individuals interred: Bishop John Thos. Clagett. Date transcribed: 1955. These transcribed records are held by Toaping Chapter, DAR. Author: P.G.C.G.S., Inc. Title: *Stones And Bones*. Publisher: Prince George's County Genealogical Society, Inc., P.O. Box 819, Bowie, MD 20718-0819 (1984).

CLAGETT FAMILY CEMETERY
Location: 15901 Livingston Road, Accokeek, MD near Farmington Road west of Route 210. [A.D.C. map location: page 37, grid coordinates B3.] Condition of cemetery: Overgrown as of June 1995. Earliest known death: 1853. Most recent death: 1864. No burial records were kept. Date transcribed: 1983. Author: P.G.C.G.S., Inc. Title: *Stones And Bones*. Publisher: Prince George's County Genealogical Society, Inc., P.O. Box 819, Bowie, MD 20718-0819 (1984).

CLAGETT FAMILY GRAVEYARD
Location: White's Landing at 17303 White's Landing Road off Route 382, Croom Road. [A.D.C. map location: page 41, grid coordinates K4.] Condition of cemetery: Not found in June 1995. Author: P.G.C.G.S., Inc. Title: *Stones And Bones*. Publisher: Prince George's County Genealogical Society, Inc., P.O. Box 819, Bowie, MD 20718-0819 (1984).

CLAGETT GRAVE
Location: *Mt. Lubentia*, I95, east on Route 202, 3.3 miles to Route 603, on right. [A.D.C. map location: Prince George's, page 20, grid coordinates K10.] Condition of cemetery: Tombstones not visible. Earliest known death: 1792. Most recent death: 1792. No burial records were kept. Markers transcribed: 1983. Cemetery address: 603 Largo Road, Upper Marlboro, MD 20772. Author: P.G.C.G.S., Inc. Title: *Stones And Bones*. Publisher: Prince George's County Genealogical Society, Inc., P.O. Box 819, Bowie, MD 20718-0819 (1984).

CLAGGETT/WARING FAMILY CEMETERY
Location: *Mt. Pleasant* one mile off old Route 301 near Upper Marlboro. [A.D.C. map location: page 21, grid coordinates G12.] Earliest known death: 1795. Most recent death: 1900. Date transcribed: 1955. Author: P.G.C.G.S., Inc. Title: *Stones And Bones*. Publisher: Prince George's County Genealogical Society, Inc., P.O. Box 819, Bowie, MD 20718-0819 (1984).

CLARKE FAMILY CEMETERY
Location: *Willow Brook* on Route 301 south of Leeland Road. [A.D.C. map location: page 21, grid coordinates F8.] Earliest known death: 1815. Most recent death: 1864. Date transcribed: 1955. Author: P.G.C.G.S., Inc. Title: *Stones And Bones*. Publisher: Prince George's County Genealogical Society, Inc., P.O. Box 819, Bowie, MD 20718-0819 (1984).

CLARKE FAMILY CEMETERY
Location: On Route 301 just north of Central Avenue. [A.D.C. map location: page 15, grid coordinates G13.] Earliest known death: 1867. Most recent death: 1879. Date transcribed: 1955. These transcribed records are held by Toaping Chapter, DAR. Author: P.G.C.G.S., Inc. Title: *Stones And Bones*. Publisher: Prince George's County Genealogical Society, Inc., P.O. Box 819, Bowie, MD 20718-0819 (1984).

CONNICK FAMILY CEMETERY
Location: On Route 381 at 18807 Aquasco Road *Connick's Folly*, near Schmidt Envir. Educ. Center [A.D.C. map location: page 41, grid coordinates B11.] Condition of cemetery: Good condition, enclosed in iron fence as of June 1995. Earliest known death: 1861. Most recent death: 1887. Date transcribed: 1955. These transcribed records are held by Toaping Castle Chapter, DAR. Author: P.G.C.G.S., Inc. Title: *Stones And Bones*. Publisher: Prince George's County Genealogical Society, Inc., P.O. Box 819, Bowie, MD 20718-0819 (1984).

CONTEE FAMILY CEMETERY
Location: *The Valley* (Brookfield), Route 301, south on Route 382, Croom Road, 7 miles to 12607 Croom Road, Naylor, MD 20772. Earliest known death: 1740. Most recent death: 1811. Author: P.G.C.G.S., Inc. Title: *Stones And Bones*. Publisher: Prince George's County Genealogical Society, Inc., P.O. Box 819, Bowie, MD 20718-0819 (1984).

CONTEE FAMILY GRAVE
Location: On Mrs. Wood's farm near Ritchie, about six miles from Upper Marlboro. [A.D.C. map location: page 19.] Earliest known death: 1787. Most recent death: 1793. Author: P.G.C.G.S., Inc. Title: *Stones And Bones*. Publisher: Prince George's County Genealogical Society, Inc., P.O. Box 819, Bowie, MD 20718-0819 (1984).

COVINGTON GRAVE

Location: On Adams Farm near Patuxent River. 10.4 miles south of Poplar Hill (Route 381) to Aquasco Farm Road, left to end. [A.D.C. map location: Prince George's, page 44, grid coordinates C1.] Condition of cemetery: Inaccessible. Earliest known death: 1742. Most recent death: 1742. Date transcribed: 1955. No burial records were kept. These transcribed records are held by Toaping Castle Chapter, DAR. Author: P.G.C.G.S., Inc. Title: *Stones And Bones*. Publisher: Prince George's County Genealogical Society, Inc., P.O. Box 819, Bowie, MD 20718-0819 (1984).

CRAUFURD FAMILY CEMETERY

Location: At *Sasscer Home* at Crain Highway overlooking Upper Marlboro. [A.D.C. map location: page 27, grid coordinates B3.] Earliest known death: 1796. Most recent death: 1864. Author: P.G.C.G.S., Inc. Title: *Stones And Bones*. Publisher: Prince George's County Genealogical Society, Inc., P.O. Box 819, Bowie, MD 20718-0819 (1984).

CROSS FAMILY CEMETERY

Location: On Weaver farm *Locust Grove* on Enterprise Road between Route 50 and Lottsford Road. [A.D.C. map location: page 14, grid coordinates E8.] Earliest known death: 1850. Most recent death: 1880. Date transcribed: 1955. These transcribed records are held by Toaping Castle Chapter, DAR. Author: P.G.C.G.S., Inc. Title: *Stones And Bones*. Publisher: Prince George's County Genealogical Society, Inc., P.O. Box 819, Bowie, MD 20718-0819 (1984).

DAINGERFIELD/SEWELL FAMILY CEMETERY

Location: 7606 Woodyard Road, *His Lordship's Kindness*, about 2.8 miles south of Route 4. [A.D.C. map location: Prince George's County, page 25, grid coordinates H10.] Condition of cemetery: Perpetual care by Catholic Archdiocese of Washington, DC Earliest known death: 1810. Date transcribed: 1955. These transcribed records are held by Toaping Castle Chapter, DAR. Author: P.G.C.G.S., Inc. Title: *Stones And Bones*. Publisher: Prince George's County Genealogical Society, Inc., P.O. Box 819, Bowie, MD 20718-0819 (1984).

DARCEY FAMILY CEMETERY

Location: On Andrews Air Force Base. Through main gate, left on Perimeter Drive, right on Belle Chance Road. [A.D.C. map location: page 25.] Condition of cemetery: Well maintained. May 1995 Earliest known death: 1807. Most recent death: 1842. Location of records:

Forest Memorial United Methodist Church. Date transcribed: 1955.
These transcribed records are held by Toaping Castle Chapter, DAR.
Author: P.G.C.G.S., Inc. Title: *Stones And Bones*. Publisher: Prince
George's County Genealogical Society, Inc., P.O. Box 819, Bowie, MD
20718-0819 (1984). Additional comments: Go to Andrews A F Base
Visitors Center for additional information.

DARNALL FAMILY GRAVE
Location: On Clagett Landing Road, next farm beyond Goodwood, off
Route 301. [A.D.C. map location: page 21.] Earliest known death: 1835.
Most recent death: 1835. Date transcribed: 1955. Author: P.G.C.G.S.,
Inc. Title: *Stones And Bones*. Publisher: Prince George's County
Genealogical Society, Inc., P.O. Box 819, Bowie, MD 20718-0819 (1984).

DAWSON FAMILY MONUMENT
Location: In front of Drug Fair, Rosecroft Shopping Center, 3233
Brinkley Road, Oxon Hill, MD. [A.D.C. map location: page 24, grid
coordinates B5.] Earliest known death: 1727. Most recent death: 1930.
Date transcribed: 1976. Author: P.G.C.G.S., Inc. Title: *Stones And
Bones*. Publisher: Prince George's County Genealogical Society, Inc.,
P.O. Box 819, Bowie, MD 20718-0819 (1984).

DEAKINS FAMILY CEMETERY
Location: At 41st Avenue and Tennyson Road on block off Queens
Chapel Road, University Park. [A.D.C. map location: page 12, grid
coordinates C1.] Earliest known death: 1824. Most recent death: 1929.
Revolutionary War veterans. Date transcribed: 1955. These transcribed
records are held by Toaping Castle Chapter, DAR. Author: P.G.C.G.S.,
Inc. Title: *Stones And Bones*. Publisher: Prince George's County
Genealogical Society, Inc., P.O. Box 819, Bowie, MD 20718-0819 (1984).

DOWNING FAMILY CEMETERY
Location: On Route 382, Croom Road, near the Dobson Instrument
Company. [A.D.C. map location: page 26.] Earliest known death: 1940.
Most recent death: 1940. Date transcribed: 1955. Author: P.G.C.G.S.,
Inc. Title: *Stones And Bones*. Publisher: Prince George's County
Genealogical Society, Inc., P.O. Box 819, Bowie, MD 20718-0819 (1984).

DUCKETT FAMILY CEMETERY
Location: Northeast of intersection of Routes 3 and 450. [A.D.C. map
location: page 10, grid coordinates J11.] Condition of cemetery: Not
found in heavy overgrowth at site in June 1995. Earliest known death:

1809. Most recent death: 1834. Date transcribed: 1983. Author: P.G.C.G.S., Inc. Title: *Stones And Bones*. Publisher: Prince George's County Genealogical Society, Inc., P.O. Box 819, Bowie, MD 20718-0819 (1984).

DUNCAN GRAVE
Location: At the Alms House. 8401 D'Arcy Road, Upper Marlboro, MD 20772. [A.D.C. map location: Prince George's County, page 19, grid coordinates F8.] Condition of cemetery: Good, maintained. Earliest known death: 1931. Most recent death: 1931. Date transcribed: 1983. No burial records kept. Author: P.G.C.G.S., Inc. Title: *Stones And Bones*. Publisher: Prince George's County Genealogical Society, Inc., P.O. Box 819, Bowie, MD 20718-0819 (1984).

DUVALL FAMILY CEMETERY
Location: Near Cafeteria on Agriculture Research Center, Beltsville (near Beaver Dam Road). [A.D.C. map location: page 8.] Earliest known death: 1826. Most recent death: 1858. Date transcribed: 1983. Author: P.G.C.G.S., Inc. Title: *Stones And Bones*. Publisher: Prince George's County Genealogical Society, Inc., P.O. Box 819, Bowie, MD 20718-0819 (1984).

DUVALL FAMILY CEMETERY
Location: On Agriculture Research Center grounds near Muirkirk Road. Now fenced by Howard University. [A.D.C. map location: page 4.] Earliest known death: 1857. Most recent death: 1917. Date transcribed: 1983. Author: P.G.C.G.S., Inc. Title: *Stones And Bones*. Publisher: Prince George's County Genealogical Society, Inc., P.O. Box 819, Bowie, MD 20718-0819 (1984).

DUVALL FAMILY CEMETERY
Location: 3900 Mitchellville Road west of Route 197 near Route 301. [A.D.C. map location: page 15, grid coordinates G6.] Earliest known death: 1817. Most recent death: 1915. Date transcribed: 1983. Author: P.G.C.G.S., Inc. Title: *Stones And Bones*. Publisher: Prince George's County Genealogical Society, Inc., P.O. Box 819, Bowie, MD 20718-0819 (1984).

DUVALL FAMILY CEMETERY
Location: On Osborne Road about one-half mile west of Route 301 at *Greenland*. [A.D.C. map location: page 26, grid coordinates E8.] Earliest known death: 1852. Most recent death: 1866. Date transcribed:

1983. Author: P.G.C.G.S., Inc. Title: *Stones And Bones*. Publisher: Prince George's County Genealogical Society, Inc., P.O. Box 819, Bowie, MD 20718-0819 (1984).

DUVALL/DUVAL FAMILY CEMETERY
Location: Beyond dead end of Bell Station Road (on SHA R/W), Glen Dale, MD. [A.D.C. map location: page 14, grid coordinates F2.] Earliest known death: 1810. Most recent death: 1844. Date transcribed: 1983. Author: P.G.C.G.S., Inc. Title: *Stones And Bones*. Publisher: Prince George's County Genealogical Society, Inc., P.O. Box 819, Bowie, MD 20718-0819 (1984).

EARLY FAMILY CEMETERY
Location: Off Route 381 0.3 mile north of Ashbox Road and just north of Wilmer's Park. [A.D.C. map location: page 40, grid coordinates E5.] Condition of cemetery: Not found - June 1995. Earliest known death: 1847. Most recent death: 1875. Date transcribed: 1983. Author: P.G.C.G.S., Inc. Title: *Stones And Bones*. Publisher: Prince George's County Genealogical Society, Inc., P.O. Box 819, Bowie, MD 20718-0819 (1984).

EDELIN GRAVE
Location: On Marbury Farm on Steed Road, Stony Harbor. [A.D.C. map location: page 24, grid coordinates D13.] Earliest known death: 1815. Most recent death: 1815. Date transcribed: 1983. Author: P.G.C.G.S., Inc. Title: *Stones And Bones*. Publisher: Prince George's County Genealogical Society, Inc., P.O. Box 819, Bowie, MD 20718-0819 (1984).

FENNO STONE
Location: On Candy Hill Road near Naylor. [A.D.C. map location: page 34, grid coordinates D9.] Earliest known death: 1918. Most recent death: 1918. Date transcribed: 1983. Author: P.G.C.G.S., Inc. Title: *Stones And Bones*. Publisher: Prince George's County Genealogical Society, Inc., P.O. Box 819, Bowie, MD 20718-0819 (1984).

GANTT CENOTAPH
Location: On former *Nihil* estate on the western outskirts of Upper Marlboro. [A.D.C. map location: page 27, grid coordinates A3.] Condition of cemetery: Not found in June 1995. Earliest known death: 1863. Most recent death: 1863. Date transcribed: 1983. Author: P.G.C.G.S., Inc. Title: *Stones And Bones*. Publisher: Prince George's

County Genealogical Society, Inc., P.O. Box 819, Bowie, MD 20718-0819 (1984).

GIBBONS FAMILY CEMETERY
Location: On Galilee Farm, Gibbons Church Road, at Glen Arven near Brandywine off Route 381. [A.D.C. map location: page 40, grid coordinates C13.] Condition of cemetery: Cemetery not found in June 1995. Earliest known death: 1860. Most recent death: 1914. Date transcribed: 1983. Author: P.G.C.G.S., Inc. Title: *Stones And Bones*. Publisher: Prince George's County Genealogical Society, Inc., P.O. Box 819, Bowie, MD 20718-0819 (1984).

GREENFIELD FAMILY CEMETERY
Location: From Baden-Naylor Road, 0.5 mi. southeast on Nelson Road. Right on lane at barn (30 feet south of barn). [A.D.C. map location: page 41, grid coordinates C2.] Condition of cemetery: Poor & overgrown, 5 flat stones-June 1995. Earliest known death: 1715. Most recent death: 1760. No burial records were kept. Date transcribed: 1983. Author: P.G.C.G.S., Inc. Title: *Stones And Bones*. Publisher: Prince George's County Genealogical Society, Inc., P.O. Box 819, Bowie, MD 20718-0819 (1984).

GWYNN FAMILY CEMETERY
Location: On Floral Park Road (6200) opposite South Hill Road. [A.D.C. map location: page 31, grid coordinates K12.] Condition of cemetery: Overgrown as of June 1995. Earliest known death: 1853. Most recent death: 1864. No burial records were kept. Date transcribed: 1983. Author: P.G.C.G.S., Inc. Title: *Stones And Bones*. Publisher: Prince George's County Genealogical Society, Inc., P.O. Box 819, Bowie, MD 20718-0819 (1984).

HALL FAMILY CEMETERY
Location: On Soil Conservation Road near Beaver Dam Road on Agriculture Research Center. [A.D.C. map location: page 8, grid coordinates G6.] Earliest known death: 1829. Most recent death: 1834. Date transcribed: 1983. Author: P.G.C.G.S., Inc. Title: *Stones And Bones*. Publisher: Prince George's County Genealogical Society, Inc., P.O. Box 819, Bowie, MD 20718-0819 (1984).

HALL FAMILY CEMETERY
Location: Behind Bell Atlantic building on Church Road near Central Avenue, Route 214. [A.D.C. map location: page 15, grid coordinates

PRINCE GEORGE'S COUNTY CEMETERIES - PRIVATE

A13.] Earliest known death: 1862. Most recent death: 1960. Date transcribed: 1983. Author: P.G.C.G.S., Inc. Title: *Stones And Bones*. Publisher: Prince George's County Genealogical Society, Inc., P.O. Box 819, Bowie, MD 20718-0819 (1984).

HALL TOMBSTONE
Location: *Partnership* on Central Avenue, Route 214, midway between Routes 202 and 301. [A.D.C. map location: page 20.] Condition of cemetery: Not found in June 1995. Earliest known death: 1702. Most recent death: 1702. Date transcribed: 1983. Author: P.G.C.G.S., Inc. Title: *Stones And Bones*. Publisher: Prince George's County Genealogical Society, Inc., P.O. Box 819, Bowie, MD 20718-0819 (1984).

HALL/REED FAMILY CEMETERY
Location: Off Brooklyn Bridge Road near Dorset Road. [A.D.C. map location: page 4, grid coordinates D1.] Earliest known death: Unknown. Most recent death: 1919. Date transcribed: 1983. Author: P.G.C.G.S., Inc. Title: *Stones And Bones*. Publisher: Prince George's County Genealogical Society, Inc., P.O. Box 819, Bowie, MD 20718-0819 (1984).

HAMILTON FAMILY CEMETERY
Location: Near Greenbelt. [A.D.C. map location: page 8, grid coordinates B9.] Condition of cemetery: Overgrown. Headstones removed by City of Greenbelt. Earliest known death: 1819. Most recent death: 1857. No burial records were kept. Date transcribed: 1983. These transcribed records are held at the Greenbelt Municipal Building. Author: P.G.C.G.S., Inc. Title: *Stones And Bones*. Publisher: Prince George's County Genealogical Society, Inc., P.O. Box 819, Bowie, MD 20718-0819 (1984).

HARDISTY FAMILY CEMETERY
Location: Between 3503 and 3505 Mase Lane in Bowie. [A.D.C. map location: page 10, grid coordinates B12.] Condition of cemetery: Good condition as of June 1995. Earliest known death: 1831. Most recent death: 1879. Date transcribed: 1983. Author: P.G.C.G.S., Inc. Title: *Stones And Bones*. Publisher: Prince George's County Genealogical Society, Inc., P.O. Box 819, Bowie, MD 20718-0819 (1984).

HATTON FAMILY CEMETERY
Location: In the 13000 block of Livingston Road between Chalfont and Taylor Avenues, Piscataway, MD. [A.D.C. map location: page 30, grid coordinates J9.] Earliest known death: 1798. Most recent death: 1965.

Date transcribed: 1983. Author: P.G.C.G.S., Inc. Title: *Stones And Bones*. Publisher: Prince George's County Genealogical Society, Inc., P.O. Box 819, Bowie, MD 20718-0819 (1984).

HATTON FAMILY CEMETERY
Location: About 4 miles southwest of T.B. on Route 373 at 3561 Accokeek Road. [A.D.C. map location: page 38, grid coordinates D2.] Condition of cemetery: Poor, unattended as of June 1995. Earliest known death: 1842. Most recent death: 1899. No burial records were kept. Date transcribed: 1983. Author: P.G.C.G.S., Inc. Title: *Stones And Bones*. Publisher: Prince George's County Genealogical Society, Inc., P.O. Box 819, Bowie, MD 20718-0819 (1984).

HEBB FAMILY CEMETERY
Location: On Moore Park at 5200 Temple Hill Road. [A.D.C. map location: page 24, grid coordinates D3.] Earliest known death: 1819. Most recent death: 1819. Date transcribed: 1983. Author: P.G.C.G.S., Inc. Title: *Stones And Bones*. Publisher: Prince George's County Genealogical Society, Inc., P.O. Box 819, Bowie, MD 20718-0819 (1984).

HILL FAMILY CEMETERY
Location: On Hill farm on Hill Road in Landover. [A.D.C. map location: page 19, grid coordinates C1.] Earliest known death: 1905. Most recent death: 1907. Date transcribed: 1983. Author: P.G.C.G.S., Inc. Title: *Stones And Bones*. Publisher: Prince George's County Genealogical Society, Inc., P.O. Box 819, Bowie, MD 20718-0819 (1984).

HILL FAMILY CEMETERY
Location: *Woodland*, home of Dr. Sasscer on Route 4 just west of the Patuxent River. [A.D.C. map location: page 27, grid coordinates H4.] Condition of cemetery: Not found in June 1995. Earliest known death: 1819. Most recent death: 1917. Date transcribed: 1983. Author: P.G.C.G.S., Inc. Title: *Stones And Bones*. Publisher: Prince George's County Genealogical Society, Inc., P.O. Box 819, Bowie, MD 20718-0819 (1984).

HILLEARY FAMILY CEMETERY
Location: *Beechwood* on Route 301 near Leeland Road. [A.D.C. map location: page 21, grid coordinates F8.] Condition of cemetery: Not found in June 1995. Earliest known death: 1854. Most recent death: 1863. Civil War veterans. Date transcribed: 1983. Author: P.G.C.G.S.,

Inc. Title: *Stones And Bones*. Publisher: Prince George's County Genealogical Society, Inc., P.O. Box 819, Bowie, MD 20718-0819 (1984).

HILLEARY FAMILY CEMETERY
Location: Catholic Rest Home near Buena Vista on Lottsford Vista Road. [A.D.C. map location: page 14.] Earliest known death: 1820. Most recent death: 1821. Date transcribed: 1983. Author: P.G.C.G.S., Inc. Title: *Stones And Bones*. Publisher: Prince George's County Genealogical Society, Inc., P.O. Box 819, Bowie, MD 20718-0819 (1984).

HOLLYDAY FAMILY CEMETERY
Location: *Brookfield* on Fenno Road off Nottingham Road about 1.7 miles east of Route 382. [A.D.C. map location: page 34, grid coordinates H8.] Condition of cemetery: Not found in June 1995. Earliest known death: 1676. Most recent death: 1811. Date transcribed: 1983. Author: P.G.C.G.S., Inc. Title: *Stones And Bones*. Publisher: Prince George's County Genealogical Society, Inc., P.O. Box 819, Bowie, MD 20718-0819 (1984).

HOWARD FAMILY CEMETERY
Location: On Clagett Landing Road, Linden Hill. [A.D.C. map location: page 21.] Condition of cemetery: Not found in June 1995. Earliest known death: 1846. Most recent death: 1893. Date transcribed: 1983. Author: P.G.C.G.S., Inc. Title: *Stones And Bones*. Publisher: Prince George's County Genealogical Society, Inc., P.O. Box 819, Bowie, MD 20718-0819 (1984).

HUMPHREYS/EDELEN FAMILY CEMETERY
Location: Back of Grace United Methodist Church on Old Fort Road south of Gallahan Road. [A.D.C. map location: page 30, grid coordinates H6.] Earliest known death: 1814. Most recent death: 1841. Date transcribed: 1983. Author: P.G.C.G.S., Inc. Title: *Stones And Bones*. Publisher: Prince George's County Genealogical Society, Inc., P.O. Box 819, Bowie, MD 20718-0819 (1984).

ISAAC CEMETERY
Location: On Lancaster Lane off Route 197 (same side as post office). [A.D.C. map location: page 10, grid coordinates A12.] Earliest known death: 1855. Most recent death: 1858. Date transcribed: 1983. Author: P.G.C.G.S., Inc. Title: *Stones And Bones*. Publisher: Prince George's County Genealogical Society, Inc., P.O. Box 819, Bowie, MD 20718-0819 (1984).

JONES CEMETERY
Location: On Owen Tippett Place, Queen Anne Road (Hardesty Road). Now leased by 4-H Center. [A.D.C. map location: Prince George's 1994, page 22.] Condition of cemetery: Head stones removed. 4-H personnel know locations of graves. (May 1995). Earliest known death: 1849. Most recent death: 1849. Date transcribed: 1983. Author: P.G.C.G.S., Inc. Title: *Stones And Bones*. Publisher: Prince George's County Genealogical Society, Inc., P.O. Box 819, Bowie, MD 20718-0819 (1984).

JONES MEMORIAL GARDENS
Location: On Mitchellville Road just off Route 301 opposite Carroll Chapel/Mt. Sinai Church. [A.D.C. map location: Prince George's County, page 15, grid coordinates G11.] Condition of cemetery: Maintained and well marked. Earliest known death: 1912. Date transcribed: 1983. Author: P.G.C.G.S., Inc. Title: *Stones And Bones*. Publisher: Prince George's County Genealogical Society, Inc., P.O. Box 819, Bowie, MD 20718-0819 (1984).

LANSDALE GRAVE
Location: On Route 197 near Belair. [A.D.C. map location: page 15.] Condition of cemetery: Not found in June 1995. Earliest known death: 1805. Most recent death: 1805. Revolutionary War veterans. Date transcribed: 1983. Author: P.G.C.G.S., Inc. Title: *Stones And Bones*. Publisher: Prince George's County Genealogical Society, Inc., P.O. Box 819, Bowie, MD 20718-0819 (1984).

LLOYD FAMILY CEMETERY
Location: On Route 50 west of Glen Dale Road. [A.D.C. map location: page 14.] Condition of cemetery: Graves reinterred to Holy Trinity, Collington, November 21, 1966. Earliest known death: 1907. Most recent death: 1935. Date transcribed: 1983. Author: P.G.C.G.S., Inc. Title: *Stones And Bones*. Publisher: Prince George's County Genealogical Society, Inc., P.O. Box 819, Bowie, MD 20718-0819 (1984).

LYLES FAMILY CEMETERY
Location: On Riverview Road near Fort Washington. [A.D.C. map location: page 30, grid coordinates A3-A6.] Earliest known death: 1826. Most recent death: 1828. Date transcribed: 1983. Author: P.G.C.G.S., Inc. Title: *Stones And Bones*. Publisher: Prince George's County Genealogical Society, Inc., P.O. Box 819, Bowie, MD 20718-0819 (1984).

PRINCE GEORGE'S COUNTY CEMETERIES - PRIVATE 203

MACKALL FAMILY CEMETERY
Location: Off Route 381, 2.4 miles north on Keys Road, left on Plantation Drive, first right to cemetery. [A.D.C. map location: page 33, grid coordinates A12.] Condition of cemetery: Fair, inside 15' by 20' iron fence-June 1995. Earliest known death: 1822. Most recent death: 1862. There are veterans interred here. No burial records were kept. Date transcribed: 1983. Author: P.G.C.G.S., Inc. Title: *Stones And Bones*. Publisher: Prince George's County Genealogical Society, Inc., P.O. Box 819, Bowie, MD 20718-0819 (1984).

MAGRUDER FAMILY CEMETERY
Location: On Route 202 between Largo and Upper Marlboro, near Leeland. [A.D.C. map location: page 20.] Condition of cemetery: Not found in June 1995. Earliest known death: 1777. Most recent death: 1827. Date transcribed: 1983. Author: P.G.C.G.S., Inc. Title: *Stones And Bones*. Publisher: Prince George's County Genealogical Society, Inc., P.O. Box 819, Bowie, MD 20718-0819 (1984).

MAGRUDER FAMILY CEMETERY
Location: On Interprise Road, Route 193, at US 50. [A.D.C. map location: page 14, grid coordinates E6.] Earliest known death: 1843. Most recent death: 1923. Date transcribed: 1983. Author: P.G.C.G.S., Inc. Title: *Stones And Bones*. Publisher: Prince George's County Genealogical Society, Inc., P.O. Box 819, Bowie, MD 20718-0819 (1984).

MAGRUDER FAMILY CEMETERY
Location: Between the warehouses and the old Prince George's County Country Club near Country Club Road. [A.D.C. map location: page 13, grid coordinates A11.] Earliest known death: 1840. Most recent death: 1917. Date transcribed: 1983. Author: P.G.C.G.S., Inc. Title: *Stones And Bones*. Publisher: Prince George's County Genealogical Society, Inc., P.O. Box 819, Bowie, MD 20718-0819 (1984). Additional comments: All graves were moved to Fort Lincoln Cemetery in the early 1960s.

MAGRUDER/MCGREGOR FAMILY CEMETERY
Location: In a field at 10009 Westphalia Road, near Forestville off Route 4. [A.D.C. map location: page 19, grid coordinates K10.] Condition of cemetery: Not found in June 1995. Earliest known death: 1785. Most recent death: 1857. Date transcribed: 1983. Author: P.G.C.G.S., Inc. Title: *Stones And Bones*. Publisher: Prince George's

County Genealogical Society, Inc., P.O. Box 819, Bowie, MD 20718-0819 (1984).

MARBURY/FENDALL FAMILY CEMETERY
Location: At the corner of Tippett Road and Thrift Road off Route 223 near Hyde Field. [A.D.C. map location: Prince George's 1994, page 31, grid coordinates G6.] Condition of cemetery: Fair, occasional care. Earliest known death: 1848. Most recent death: 1866. Revolutionary War veterans. No burial records were kept. Date transcribed: 1955. These transcribed records are held by Toaping Castle Chapter DAR. Author: P.G.C.G.S., Inc. Title: *Stones And Bones*. Publisher: Prince George's County Genealogical Society, Inc., P.O. Box 819, Bowie, MD 20718-0819 (1984).

MARSHALL/SUMMERS FAMILY CEMETERY
Location: Formerly located near Andrews Air Force Base on Route 4 just east of Westphalia Road. [A.D.C. map location: page 19, grid coordinates F12.] Condition of cemetery: Graves moved to Epiphany Episcopal Church Cemetery on April 22, 1959. Earliest known death: 1843. Most recent death: 1863. Date transcribed: 1983. Author: P.G.C.G.S., Inc. Title: *Stones And Bones*. Publisher: Prince George's County Genealogical Society, Inc., P.O. Box 819, Bowie, MD 20718-0819 (1984).

MITCHELL FAMILY CEMETERY
Location: Behind 2411 Panther Lane between Peachwalker Drive and Porsche Court, Bowie, MD. [A.D.C. map location: page 15.] Earliest known death: 1859. Most recent death: 1862. Date transcribed: 1983. Author: P.G.C.G.S., Inc. Title: *Stones And Bones*. Publisher: Prince George's County Genealogical Society, Inc., P.O. Box 819, Bowie, MD 20718-0819 (1984).

MORSELL FAMILY GRAVE
Location: Grave was located on Wicomico Street near Caroline Avenue. [A.D.C. map location: page 7, grid coordinates H1.] Earliest known death: 1815. Most recent death: 1815. Date transcribed: 1983. Author: P.G.C.G.S., Inc. Title: *Stones And Bones*. Publisher: Prince George's County Genealogical Society, Inc., P.O. Box 819, Bowie, MD 20718-0819 (1984).

MULLIKEN GRAVES

Location: *Bellefields* on Duley Station Road off Old Indian Head Road near Route 301. [A.D.C. map location: page 33, grid coordinates D2.] Earliest known death: 1847. Most recent death: 1851. Date transcribed: 1983. Author: P.G.C.G.S., Inc. Title: *Stones And Bones*. Publisher: Prince George's County Genealogical Society, Inc., P.O. Box 819, Bowie, MD 20718-0819 (1984).

MULLIKIN FAMILY CEMETERY

Location: On Church Road about 1½ miles north of Route 214, opposite Tall Oaks School. [A.D.C. map location: page 15, grid coordinates A10.] Earliest known death: 1816. Most recent death: 1864. Date transcribed: 1983. Author: P.G.C.G.S., Inc. Title: *Stones And Bones*. Publisher: Prince George's County Genealogical Society, Inc., P.O. Box 819, Bowie, MD 20718-0819 (1984).

NAYLOR FAMILY CEMETERY

Location: Off Baden-Westwood Road between MD 381 and MD 382, 1 mile north of Westwood Road on Bald Eagle Road. [A.D.C. map location: page 41, grid coordinates E4.] Condition of cemetery: Good, 8-10 graves, June 1995. Earliest known death: 1878. Most recent death: 1953. Burial records were kept. Type of records kept: Interment and Tombstone. Location of records: See address above. Date transcribed: 1983. Author: P.G.C.G.S., Inc. Title: *Stones And Bones*. Publisher: Prince George's County Genealogical Society, Inc., P.O. Box 819, Bowie, MD 20718-0819 (1984).

OGLE FAMILY CEMETERY

Location: On grounds of Belair Mansion on Tulip Grove Drive. [A.D.C. map location: page 15, grid coordinates C2.] Condition of cemetery: Maintained. Earliest known death: 1838. Most recent death: 1859. Date transcribed: 1983. Author: P.G.C.G.S., Inc. Title: *Stones And Bones*. Publisher: Prince George's County Genealogical Society, Inc., P.O. Box 819, Bowie, MD 20718-0819 (1984).

ONION CEMETERY

Location: On Auburn Avenue near Riverdale Road. [A.D.C. map location: page 13, grid coordinates A2.] Condition of cemetery: Not found in June 1995. Earliest known death: 1865. Most recent death: 1865. Date transcribed: 1983. Author: P.G.C.G.S., Inc. Title: *Stones And Bones*. Publisher: Prince George's County Genealogical Society, Inc., P.O. Box 819, Bowie, MD 20718-0819 (1984).

206 *DIRECTORY OF MARYLAND'S BURIAL GROUNDS*

ORME/DALE CEMETERY
Location: Behind house 0.1 mile from Route 381 on Horsehead Road. [A.D.C. map location: Prince George's 1994, page 40, grid coordinates J8.] Earliest known death: 1850. Most recent death: 1907. No veterans interred here. Date transcribed: 1983. Author: P.G.C.G.S., Inc. Title: *Stones And Bones*. Publisher: Prince George's County Genealogical Society, Inc., P.O. Box 819, Bowie, MD 20718-0819 (1984).

OSBORN/TALBURTT FAMILY CEMETERY
Location: 10907 Westphalia Road near Ritchie Road. [A.D.C. map location: page 20, grid coordinates C10.] Earliest known death: 1834. Most recent death: 1894. Date transcribed: 1983. Author: P.G.C.G.S., Inc. Title: *Stones And Bones*. Publisher: Prince George's County Genealogical Society, Inc., P.O. Box 819, Bowie, MD 20718-0819 (1984).

OWENS FAMILY CEMETERY
Location: Located off Brooklyn Bridge Road behind Supplee Park on WSSC property. [A.D.C. map location: page 2, grid coordinates B13.] Condition of cemetery: Fence enclosed. Maintained by WSSC. Earliest known death: 1903. Most recent death: 1924. Date transcribed: 1983. Author: P.G.C.G.S., Inc. Title: *Stones And Bones*. Publisher: Prince George's County Genealogical Society, Inc., P.O. Box 819, Bowie, MD 20718-0819 (1984).

PEACH/WALKER FAMILY CEMETERY
Location: On Route 301 midway between Central Avenue and Route 50. [A.D.C. map location: page 15.] Earliest known death: 1841. Most recent death: 1918. Date transcribed: 1983. Author: P.G.C.G.S., Inc. Title: *Stones And Bones*. Publisher: Prince George's County Genealogical Society, Inc., P.O. Box 819, Bowie, MD 20718-0819 (1984).

PILES/PYLES GRAVEYARDS
Location: Unknown. It may have been at the intersection of Allentown Road and Lanham Lane. [A.D.C. map location: page 24, grid coordinates E8.] Earliest known death: 1865. Most recent death: 1865. Date transcribed: 1983. Author: P.G.C.G.S., Inc. Title: *Stones And Bones*. Publisher: Prince George's County Genealogical Society, Inc., P.O. Box 819, Bowie, MD 20718-0819 (1984).

PRATHER FAMILY CEMETERY
Location: Near railroad tracks, ½ mile south of Sunnyside Avenue, Beltsville. [A.D.C. map location: page 7, grid coordinates J5.] Earliest

known death: 1848. Most recent death: 1884. Date transcribed: 1983. Author: P.G.C.G.S., Inc. Title: *Stones And Bones*. Publisher: Prince George's County Genealogical Society, Inc., P.O. Box 819, Bowie, MD 20718-0819 (1984).

PUMPHREY/FRASER/WALKER CEMETERY
Location: Charles' Hill 3 miles northwest of Upper Marlboro on Route 4. [A.D.C. map location: page 26.] Earliest known death: 1841. Most recent death: 1849. Date transcribed: 1983. Author: P.G.C.G.S., Inc. Title: *Stones And Bones*. Publisher: Prince George's County Genealogical Society, Inc., P.O. Box 819, Bowie, MD 20718-0819 (1984).

RANDALL FAMILY CEMETERY
Location: On Tanyard Road near Route 382 south of Naylor. [A.D.C. map location: page 34, grid coordinates F11.] Earliest known death: 1803. Most recent death: 1803. Date transcribed: 1983. Author: P.G.C.G.S., Inc. Title: *Stones And Bones*. Publisher: Prince George's County Genealogical Society, Inc., P.O. Box 819, Bowie, MD 20718-0819 (1984).

RIVES FAMILY GRAVEYARD
Location: On Bladensburg Road near Eastern Avenue across from Fort Lincoln Cemetery. [A.D.C. map location: page 12, grid coordinates B8.] Earliest known death: 1853. Most recent death: 1869. Date transcribed: 1983. Author: P.G.C.G.S., Inc. Title: *Stones And Bones*. Publisher: Prince George's County Genealogical Society, Inc., P.O. Box 819, Bowie, MD 20718-0819 (1984).

ROBEY GRAVE
Location: 7619 Allendale Drive in Palmer Park. [A.D.C. map location: page 13, grid coordinates D11.] Earliest known death: 1909. Most recent death: 1909. Date transcribed: 1983. Author: P.G.C.G.S., Inc. Title: *Stones And Bones*. Publisher: Prince George's County Genealogical Society, Inc., P.O. Box 819, Bowie, MD 20718-0819 (1984).

SADIGSTONE GRAVE
Location: On Duley Station Road off Old Indian Head Road near Route 301 and Rosaryville Road. [A.D.C. map location: page 33, grid coordinates D2.] Earliest known death: 1830. Most recent death: 1830. Date transcribed: 1983. Author: P.G.C.G.S., Inc. Title: *Stones And Bones*. Publisher: Prince George's County Genealogical Society, Inc., P.O. Box 819, Bowie, MD 20718-0819 (1984).

SASSCER GRAVEYARD
Location: Zadok Sasscer farm near Upper Marlboro. [A.D.C. map location: page 27.] Earliest known death: 1847. Most recent death: 1865. Date transcribed: 1983. Author: P.G.C.G.S., Inc. Title: *Stones And Bones*. Publisher: Prince George's County Genealogical Society, Inc., P.O. Box 819, Bowie, MD 20718-0819 (1984).

SCOTT FAMILY GRAVEYARD
Location: Near Aquasco, 11 miles from Route 301 on St. Philip's Road, 0.1 mile off Route 381. [A.D.C. map location: page 43, grid coordinates F7.] Condition of cemetery: Maintained by Hoffman family, 1601 St. Philip's Road, May 1995. Earliest known death: 1848. Most recent death: 1891. Location of records: See Hoffman family at 16201 St. Philip's Road. Date transcribed: 1983. Author: P.G.C.G.S., Inc. Title: *Stones And Bones*. Publisher: Prince George's County Genealogical Society, Inc., P.O. Box 819, Bowie, MD 20718-0819 (1984).

SHERRIFF FAMILY CEMETERY
Location: On Sheriff Road near Route 202. [A.D.C. map location: page 13, grid coordinates E11.] Earliest known death: 1812. Most recent death: 1812. Date transcribed: 1983. Author: P.G.C.G.S., Inc. Title: *Stones And Bones*. Publisher: Prince George's County Genealogical Society, Inc., P.O. Box 819, Bowie, MD 20718-0819 (1984).

SHIPLEY FAMILY CEMETERY
Location: On hill north of Route 197 near Evergreen Parkway, 0.5 mile off Route 301 in Bowie. [A.D.C. map location: page Prince George's, grid coordinates 15.] Condition of cemetery: F5. Earliest known death: Overgrown. May 1995. Earliest known death: 1849. Most recent death: 1852. Date transcribed: 1983. Author: P.G.C.G.S., Inc. Title: *Stones And Bones*. Publisher: Prince George's County Genealogical Society, Inc., P.O. Box 819, Bowie, MD 20718-0819 (1984).

SIM FAMILY CEMETERY
Location: On Duley Station Road off Old Indian Head Road near Route 301 and Rosaryville Road. [A.D.C. map location: page 33, grid coordinates D2.] Earliest known death: 1771. Most recent death: 1771. Date transcribed: 1983. Author: P.G.C.G.S., Inc. Title: *Stones And Bones*. Publisher: Prince George's County Genealogical Society, Inc., P.O. Box 819, Bowie, MD 20718-0819 (1984).

SKINNER FAMILY CEMETERY
Location: On Route 382 just below Naylor on estate called *Mansfield*. [A.D.C. map location: page 34, grid coordinates E11.] Earliest known death: 1845. Most recent death: 1905. Date transcribed: 1983. Author: P.G.C.G.S., Inc. Title: *Stones And Bones*. Publisher: Prince George's County Genealogical Society, Inc., P.O. Box 819, Bowie, MD 20718-0819 (1984).

SMITH FAMILY CEMETERY
Location: On Leeland Road near Route 301. [A.D.C. map location: page 21, grid coordinates F8.] Earliest known death: 1828. Most recent death: 1854. Date transcribed: 1983. Author: P.G.C.G.S., Inc. Title: *Stones And Bones*. Publisher: Prince George's County Genealogical Society, Inc., P.O. Box 819, Bowie, MD 20718-0819 (1984).

SMITH FAMILY CEMETERY
Location: On Queen Anne Road near Route 301 on Poplar Ridge farm. [A.D.C. map location: Prince George's County, page 21, grid coordinates H3.] Earliest known death: 1794. Most recent death: 1815. Date transcribed: 1983. Author: P.G.C.G.S., Inc. Title: *Stones And Bones*. Publisher: Prince George's County Genealogical Society, Inc., P.O. Box 819, Bowie, MD 20718-0819 (1984).

SNOWDEN FAMILY CEMETERY, MONTPELIER
Location: On *Montpelier* estate on Route 197, south Laurel. [A.D.C. map location: page 4, grid coordinates J9.] Earliest known death: 1770. Most recent death: 1831. Date transcribed: 1983. Author: P.G.C.G.S., Inc. Title: *Stones And Bones*. Publisher: Prince George's County Genealogical Society, Inc., P.O. Box 819, Bowie, MD 20718-0819 (1984). Additional comments: Site was covered over because of vandalism. Location no longer known.

SNOWDEN FAMILY CEMETERY, OAKLANDS
Location: On Contee Road east of R.R Tracks near US 1, road leads to cemetery. [A.D.C. map location: Prince George's County, page 4, grid coordinates E8.] Condition of cemetery: No stones exist. Earliest known death: Unknown. Most recent death: Unknown. Date transcribed: 1977. Author: P.G.C.G.S., Inc. Title: *Stones And Bones*. Publisher: Prince George's County Genealogical Society, Inc., P.O. Box 819, Bowie, MD 20718-0819 (1984).

SOPER FAMILY CEMETERY
Location: On Auth Road on property owned and mined by the Buffalo Sand and Gravel Company. [A.D.C. map location: page 24, grid coordinates H2.] Earliest known death: 1881. Most recent death: 1882. Date transcribed: 1983. Author: P.G.C.G.S., Inc. Title: *Stones And Bones*. Publisher: Prince George's County Genealogical Society, Inc., P.O. Box 819, Bowie, MD 20718-0819 (1984).

STEED/EDELIN FAMILY CEMETERY
Location: On Steed Road near Allentown Road. [A.D.C. map location: page 24, grid coordinates B13.] Earliest known death: 1883. Most recent death: 1937. Date transcribed: 1983. Author: P.G.C.G.S., Inc. Title: *Stones And Bones*. Publisher: Prince George's County Genealogical Society, Inc., P.O. Box 819, Bowie, MD 20718-0819 (1984).

STEPHEN GRAVE
Location: The northeast corner of 59th Avenue and Sheridan Street, East Riverdale. [A.D.C. map location: page 12, grid coordinates H2.] Earliest known death: 1886. Most recent death: 1886. Date transcribed: 1983. Author: P.G.C.G.S., Inc. Title: *Stones And Bones*. Publisher: Prince George's County Genealogical Society, Inc., P.O. Box 819, Bowie, MD 20718-0819 (1984).

SUIT GRAVES
Location: Unknown. [A.D.C. map location: page 19, grid coordinates E11.] Earliest known death: 1862. Most recent death: 1863. Date transcribed: 1983. Author: P.G.C.G.S., Inc. Title: *Stones And Bones*. Publisher: Prince George's County Genealogical Society, Inc., P.O. Box 819, Bowie, MD 20718-0819 (1984).

TALBERT/HALL FAMILY CEMETERY
Location: On Cherry Tree Crossing Road, about 0.3 mile east of Route 301, Cheltenham. [A.D.C. map location: page 33, grid coordinates A6.] Earliest known death: 1852. Most recent death: 1946. Date transcribed: 1983. Author: P.G.C.G.S., Inc. Title: *Stones And Bones*. Publisher: Prince George's County Genealogical Society, Inc., P.O. Box 819, Bowie, MD 20718-0819 (1984).

TALBERT/TOLBERTT FAMILY CEMETERY (PERKINS FAMILY CEMETERY)
Location: At the corner of Springfield Road and Telegraph Road, south of Perkins Chapel. [A.D.C. map location: page 9, grid coordinates D7.]

PRINCE GEORGE'S COUNTY CEMETERIES - PRIVATE 211

Condition of cemetery: In heavy woods. Earliest known death: 1855. Most recent death: 1932. No burial records were kept. Date transcribed: 1983. Author: P.G.C.G.S., Inc. Title: *Stones And Bones*. Publisher: Prince George's County Genealogical Society, Inc., P.O. Box 819, Bowie, MD 20718-0819 (1984).

TAYMAN FAMILY CEMETERY

Location: On the Spicer Farm Cheltenham Road between Cheltenham and Rosaryville. [A.D.C. map location: page 33, grid coordinates D3.] Earliest known death: 1876. Most recent death: 1966. Date transcribed: 1983. Author: P.G.C.G.S., Inc. Title: *Stones And Bones*. Publisher: Prince George's County Genealogical Society, Inc., P.O. Box 819, Bowie, MD 20718-0819 (1984).

TOWNSHEND FAMILY CEMETERY

Location: 0.3 miles east of 12700 Brandywine Road on Washington Gas Company Property off Route 5 near T.B. [A.D.C. map location: Prince George's County 25th Edition 1994, page 32, grid coordinates B8.] Condition of cemetery: Poor, overgrown. Three graves with stones. June 1995. Earliest known death: 1801. Most recent death: 1864. Date transcribed: 1983. Author: P.G.C.G.S., Inc. Title: *Stones And Bones*. Publisher: Prince George's County Genealogical Society, Inc., P.O. Box 819, Bowie, MD 20718-0819 (1984).

TOWNSHEND (JOHN) GRAVE

Location: From Dyson Road, 0.5 mi. north on Missouri Avenue to grave site at intersection on left. [A.D.C. map location: page 32, grid coordinates G7.] Condition of cemetery: Overgrown, the gravestone is leaning against a tree as of June 1995. Earliest known death: 1846. Most recent death: 1846. Date transcribed: 1983. Author: P.G.C.G.S., Inc. Title: *Stones And Bones*. Publisher: Prince George's County Genealogical Society, Inc., P.O. Box 819, Bowie, MD 20718-0819 (1984).

TOWNSHEND/EARLY FAMILY CEMETERY

Location: In the woods in Cheltenham. [A.D.C. map location: page 32.] Condition of cemetery: Site is now under landfill. Earliest known death: 1815. Most recent death: 1816. Date transcribed: 1983. Author: P.G.C.G.S., Inc. Title: *Stones And Bones*. Publisher: Prince George's County Genealogical Society, Inc., P.O. Box 819, Bowie, MD 20718-0819 (1984).

212 DIRECTORY OF MARYLAND'S BURIAL GROUNDS

TRUEMAN FAMILY CEMETERY
Location: 11 miles east of Route 301 on Route 381 near the Aquasco Hardware Store. [A.D.C. map location: page 43, grid coordinates G7.] Condition of cemetery: Fair condition. May 1995. Earliest known death: 1917. No burial records were kept. Date transcribed: 1983. Author: P.G.C.G.S., Inc. Title: *Stones And Bones*. Publisher: Prince George's County Genealogical Society, Inc., P.O. Box 819, Bowie, MD 20718-0819 (1984).

TURNER FAMILY CEMETERY
Location: Formally located on Bond Hill farm on Gunpowder Road. Exact location unknown. [A.D.C. map location: page 3.] Condition of cemetery: Unknown. Earliest known death: 1866. Most recent death: 1950. Date transcribed: 1983. Author: P.G.C.G.S., Inc. Title: *Stones And Bones*. Publisher: Prince George's County Genealogical Society, Inc., P.O. Box 819, Bowie, MD 20718-0819 (1984).

TURNER FAMILY CEMETERY
Location: *Anchovy Hill* on Croom Road, Route 382, in Naylor. [A.D.C. map location: page 34, grid coordinates C9.] Earliest known death: 1852. Most recent death: 1949. Date transcribed: 1983. Author: P.G.C.G.S., Inc. Title: *Stones And Bones*. Publisher: Prince George's County Genealogical Society, Inc., P.O. Box 819, Bowie, MD 20718-0819 (1984).

TURNER FAMILY GRAVEYARD
Location: In the trees 50 yards east of Bond Mill Road behind second house from Brooklyn Bridge Road. [A.D.C. map location: page 4, grid coordinates B1.] Condition of cemetery: Not maintained. Site covered with trees and other growth. Earliest known death: Unknown. Most recent death: Unknown. Date transcribed: 1983. Author: P.G.C.G.S., Inc. Title: *Stones And Bones*. Publisher: Prince George's County Genealogical Society, Inc., P.O. Box 819, Bowie, MD 20718-0819 (1984).

TYLER FAMILY CEMETERY
Location: At the water tower in Upper Marlboro. [A.D.C. map location: page 27, grid coordinates A3.] Earliest known death: 1833. Most recent death: 1851. Date transcribed: 1983. Author: P.G.C.G.S., Inc. Title: *Stones And Bones*. Publisher: Prince George's County Genealogical Society, Inc., P.O. Box 819, Bowie, MD 20718-0819 (1984).

PRINCE GEORGE'S COUNTY CEMETERIES - PRIVATE

TYSON GRAVEYARD
Location: Formally located at *Alnwick* off US 1 in south Laurel. [A.D.C. map location: page 4, grid coordinates E6.] Condition of cemetery: It is believed that graves were moved to Ivy Hill Cemetery in Laurel. Earliest known death: 1883. Most recent death: 1883. Date transcribed: 1983. Author: P.G.C.G.S., Inc. Title: *Stones And Bones*. Publisher: Prince George's County Genealogical Society, Inc., P.O. Box 819, Bowie, MD 20718-0819 (1984).

WALKER FAMILY CEMETERY
Location: From Greenbelt Road, left on Walker Drive behind multilevel garage. [A.D.C. map location: Prince George's 1994, page 8, grid coordinates B11.] Condition of cemetery: Fair, enclosed by fence. DAR & Federal marker. May 1995. Earliest known death: 1807. Most recent death: 1842. Revolutionary War and veterans of other wars interred here. Burial records were kept. Location of records: Greenbelt Municipal Building. Date transcribed: 1983. Author: P.G.C.G.S., Inc. Title: *Stones And Bones*. Publisher: Prince George's County Genealogical Society, Inc., P.O. Box 819, Bowie, MD 20718-0819 (1984). Additional comments: At entrance on Walker Drive there is an Historic marker erected by City of Greenbelt.

WALL FAMILY CEMETERY
Location: 0.8 mile from Route 381 south of Dyson Road on lane. [A.D.C. map location: Prince George's, page 32, grid coordinates F8/F9.] Condition of cemetery: Poor, overgrown in June 1995. Earliest known death: 1801. Most recent death: 1814. No burial records were kept. Date transcribed: 1983. Author: P.G.C.G.S., Inc. Title: *Stones And Bones*. Publisher: Prince George's County Genealogical Society, Inc., P.O. Box 819, Bowie, MD 20718-0819 (1984).

WALL FAMILY CEMETERY
Location: Near Eagle Harbor. [A.D.C. map location: page 44, grid coordinates B9.] Condition of cemetery: Poor, not being maintained - May 1995. Earliest known death: 1819. Most recent death: 1850. Date transcribed: 1983. Author: P.G.C.G.S., Inc. Title: *Stones And Bones*. Publisher: Prince George's County Genealogical Society, Inc., P.O. Box 819, Bowie, MD 20718-0819 (1984).

WARING FAMILY CEMETERY
Location: On Enterprise Road (Route 193) on Capt. White's Enterprise Farm between Routes 214 and 50. [A.D.C. map location: page 14, grid coordinates E11.] Earliest known death: 1860. Most recent death: 1935. Date transcribed: 1983. Author: P.G.C.G.S., Inc. Title: *Stones And Bones*. Publisher: Prince George's County Genealogical Society, Inc., P.O. Box 819, Bowie, MD 20718-0819 (1984).

WARING GRAVES
Location: *Mt. Pleasant* near Old Route 4 and near the Patuxent River. [A.D.C. map location: page 27.] Earliest known death: 1795. Most recent death: 1795. Date transcribed: 1983. Author: P.G.C.G.S., Inc. Title: *Stones And Bones*. Publisher: Prince George's County Genealogical Society, Inc., P.O. Box 819, Bowie, MD 20718-0819 (1984).

WARING/HOLLYDAY CEMETERY
Location: From Baden, Naylor Road, 1/4 mile south of Molly Berry Road, 1/4 mile west on Harris Street. [A.D.C. map location: page 34, grid coordinates B13.] Condition of cemetery: Poor, overgrown, stones not visible as of June 1995. Earliest known death: 1806. Most recent death: 1883. No burial records were kept. Date transcribed: 1983. Author: P.G.C.G.S., Inc. Title: *Stones And Bones*. Publisher: Prince George's County Genealogical Society, Inc., P.O. Box 819, Bowie, MD 20718-0819 (1984).

WATSON FAMILY CEMETERY
Location: On Route 382 0.5 mile north of intersection with Route 381. [A.D.C. map location: page 41, grid coordinates C12.] Condition of cemetery: Poor, overgrown, 16 sunken graves with no markers as of June 1995. Earliest known death: Unknown. Most recent death: Unknown. No burial records were kept. Author: P.G.C.G.S., Inc. Title: *Stones And Bones*. Publisher: Prince George's County Genealogical Society, Inc., P.O. Box 819, Bowie, MD 20718-0819 (1984).

WHITESIDE AND WARFIELDS CEMETERY
Location: In Laurel, and may now be part of Ivy Hill Cemetery. [A.D.C. map location: page 4, grid coordinates E2.] Earliest known death: 1888. Most recent death: 1888. Date transcribed: 1983. Author: P.G.C.G.S., Inc. Title: *Stones And Bones*. Publisher: Prince George's County Genealogical Society, Inc., P.O. Box 819, Bowie, MD 20718-0819 (1984).

WILLIAMS/BERRY FAMILY CEMETERY
Location: *Seat Pleasant* on Central Avenue (Route 214) near Addison Road. [A.D.C. map location: page 18, grid coordinates K3.] Earliest known death: 1811. Most recent death: 1857. Date transcribed: 1983. Author: P.G.C.G.S., Inc. Title: *Stones And Bones*. Publisher: Prince George's County Genealogical Society, Inc., P.O. Box 819, Bowie, MD 20718-0819 (1984).

WILSON GRAVE
Location: 17310 Milltown Landing Road 0.8 mi. off Route 382, Croom Road. [A.D.C. map location: page 41, grid coordinates J10.] Condition of cemetery: Fair, ground cover over site. One stone. Earliest known death: 1857. Most recent death: 1872. Burial records kept: Tombstone and maps. Location of records: See address of cemetery. Date transcribed: 1983. Author: P.G.C.G.S., Inc. Title: *Stones And Bones*. Publisher: Prince George's County Genealogical Society, Inc., P.O. Box 819, Bowie, MD 20718-0819 (1984).

WORTHINGTON/CONTEE/BOWIE FAMILY CEMETERY
Location: *The Valley* on North Keys Road at Naylor. [A.D.C. map location: page 34, grid coordinates C9.] Earliest known death: 1734. Most recent death: 1951. Revolutionary War veterans interred here. Are gravemarkers transcribed: Yes. Date transcribed: 1983. Author: P.G.C.G.S., Inc. Title: *Stones And Bones*. Publisher: Prince George's County Genealogical Society, Inc., P.O. Box 819, Bowie, MD 20718-0819 (1984).

YOUNG FAMILY CEMETERY
Location: Oakland on Route 4. Earliest known death: 1836. Most recent death: 1915. Date transcribed: 1983. Author: P.G.C.G.S., Inc. Title: *Stones And Bones*. Publisher: Prince George's County Genealogical Society, Inc., P.O. Box 819, Bowie, MD 20718-0819 (1984).

Church Cemeteries

ADDISON CHAPEL OF ST. MATHEW'S EPISCOPAL CHURCH, ADDISON PARISH CEMETERY
Location: From MD 704, Martin Luther King Highway, northwest on Addison Road to 62nd Place. [A.D.C. map location: page 18, grid coordinates J1.] Earliest known death: 1809. Date transcribed: 1983. Author: P.G.C.G.S., Inc. Title: *Stones And Bones*. Publisher: Prince

George's County Genealogical Society, Inc., P.O. Box 819, Bowie, MD 20718-0819 (1984).

APOSTOLIC FAITH CHURCH CEMETERY
Location: At 4900 Accokeek Road (MD 373) 0.2 mile west of Danville Road. 3 miles west of Route 5. [A.D.C. map location: page 38, grid coordinates F1.] Condition of cemetery: Good condition as of June 1995.

ASBURY UNITED METHODIST CHURCH CEMETERY
Location: On Accokeek Road (MD 373) at Gardener Road. 3.3 miles west of Route 5. [A.D.C. map location: page 38, grid coordinates D2.] Condition of cemetery: Perpetual care. Burial records kept: Deed, plat, interment and maps. Location of records: See address above.

ASCENSION ROMAN CATHOLIC CHURCH CEMETERY
Location: 12700 Lanham-Severn Road, MD Route 564 in Bowie (Old Bowie). [A.D.C. map location: page 9, grid coordinates G7.] Condition of cemetery: Maintained. May 1995. Earliest known death: 1908. Revolutionary War, Civil War, WWI and WWII veterans. No burial records were kept. Date transcribed: 1983. Author: P.G.C. Genealogical Society. Title: *Stones And Bones*. Publisher: Prince George's County Genealogical Society, Inc., P.O. Box 819, Bowie, MD 20718-0819 (1984).

B'NAI ISRAEL CONGREGATION CEMETERY
Location: On St. Barnabus Road near Wheller Road in Oxon Hill, MD. [A.D.C. map location: Prince George's County 1994, page 24, grid coordinates A3.] Condition of cemetery: Perpetual care. Earliest known death: 1937.

BELLS UNITED METHODIST CHURCH
Location: 6016 Allentown Road, Camp Springs, MD about 0.1 mile east of Route 5, Branch Avenue. [A.D.C. map location: page 24, grid coordinates K5.] Earliest known death: 1856. Civil War, WWI and WWII veterans, in addition to veterans of other wars. Date transcribed: 1983. Author: P.G.C.G.S., Inc. Title: *Stones And Bones*. Publisher: Prince George's County Genealogical Society, Inc., P.O. Box 819, Bowie, MD 20718-0819 (1984).

BOONE'S CATHOLIC CHAPEL CEMETERY
Location: On Van Brady Road near Rosaryville. [A.D.C. map location: page 33, grid coordinates D4.] Earliest known death: 1833. Most recent

death: 1881. Date transcribed: 1983. Author: P.G.C.G.S., Inc. Title: *Stones And Bones*. Publisher: Prince George's County Genealogical Society, Inc., P.O. Box 819, Bowie, MD 20718-0819 (1984).

BROOKFIELD UNITED METHODIST CHURCH CEMETERY
Location: From Route 301, east on Croom Road (Route 382) about 7.5 miles to Candy Hill Road. [A.D.C. map location: page 34, grid coordinates C9.] Condition of cemetery: Perpetual care. Earliest known death: 1890. WWI and WWII veterans, in addition to veterans of other wars. Burial records kept: Interment. Location of records: See address above. Date transcribed: 1983. Author: P.G.C.G.S., Inc. Title: *Stones And Bones*. Publisher: Prince George's County Genealogical Society, Inc., P.O. Box 819, Bowie, MD 20718-0819 (1984).

BROOKS-MYERS UNITED METHODIST CHURCH CEMETERY
Location: On Brooks Church Road about 0.3 mile west of Croom Road (Route 382) Naylor, MD. [A.D.C. map location: page 34, grid coordinates E11.] Earliest known death: 1902. Date transcribed: 1983. Author: P.G.C.G.S., Inc. Title: *Stones And Bones*. Publisher: Prince George's County Genealogical Society, Inc., P.O. Box 819, Bowie, MD 20718-0819 (1984).

CARROLL CHAPEL (METHODIST) CEMETERY, (BETHEL APOSTOLIC CHURCH OF JESUS CHRIST)
Location: 1811 Mitchellville Road just off Route 301 2.6 miles south of US 50. [A.D.C. map location: page 15, grid coordinates G11.] Condition of cemetery: Minimal maintenance. Earliest known death: 1886. WWII veterans. Date transcribed: 1983. Author: P.G.C.G.S., Inc. Title: *Stones And Bones*. Publisher: Prince George's County Genealogical Society, Inc., P.O. Box 819, Bowie, MD 20718-0819 (1984).

CEDARVILLE ASSEMBLY OF GOD CHURCH CEMETERY (GRACE METHODIST EPISCOPAL CHURCH NORTH CEMETERY)
Location: On Cedarville Road about 0.8 mile West of Route 381, 4.5 mile East of US 301. [A.D.C. map location: page 40, grid coordinates D5.] Condition of cemetery: Perpetual care. Earliest known death: 1883. WWII veterans. Burial records kept: Deed, plat, interment and maps. Records kept at church. Date transcribed: 1983. Author: P.G.C.G.S., Inc. Title: *Stones And Bones*. Publisher: Prince George's County Genealogical Society, Inc., P.O. Box 819, Bowie, MD 20718-0819 (1984).

CHELTENHAM UNITED METHODIST CHURCH CEMETERY, (WESTWOOD METHODIST EPISCOPAL CHURCH)
Location: On west side of Route 301. 1/4 mile north of Veterans Memorial Cemetery, Cheltenham. [A.D.C. map location: page 33, grid coordinates A4.] Condition of cemetery: Well maintained. May 1995. Earliest known death: 1882. Location of records: Cheltenham United Methodist Church. Date transcribed: 1983. Author: P.G.C.G.S., Inc. Title: *Stones And Bones*. Publisher: Prince George's County Genealogical Society, Inc., P.O. Box 819, Bowie, MD 20718-0819 (1984).

CHRIST EPISCOPAL CHURCH CEMETERY
Location: 8710 Old Branch Avenue, Clinton, MD. [A.D.C. map location: page 24, grid coordinates K11.] Condition of cemetery: Perpetual care. Earliest known death: 1885. Burial records kept: Deed, plat, interment, tombstone and maps. Location of records: Church office. Date transcribed: 1983. Author: P.G.C.G.S., Inc. Title: *Stones And Bones*. Publisher: Prince George's County Genealogical Society, Inc., P.O. Box 819, Bowie, MD 20718-0819 (1984).

CHRIST EPISCOPAL CHURCH CEMETERY, ST. JOHN'S PARISH
Location: From Route 210, west on Livingston Road to Farmington Road, north to Bryan Point Road, right 0.3 mile. [A.D.C. map location: page 37, grid coordinates B3.] Condition of cemetery: Perpetual care. Earliest known death: 1775. Date transcribed: 1983. Author: P.G.C.G.S., Inc. Title: *Stones And Bones*. Publisher: Prince George's County Genealogical Society, Inc., P.O. Box 819, Bowie, MD 20718-0819 (1984).

CHRIST UNITED METHODIST CHURCH
John Wesley Methodist Episcopal Church Cemetery, merged with St Thomas United Methodist Church 1973.
Location: In Aquasco, MD 12 miles off Route 30 on Christ Church Road 0.3 mile off Route 381. [A.D.C. map location: page 43, grid coordinates F8.] Condition of cemetery: Well kept. Perpetual care. May 1995. Earliest known death: 1915. WWI and WWII veterans. Burial records kept: Deed, plat, interment, tombstone and maps. Location of records: Christ United Methodist Church. Date transcribed: 1983. Author: P.G.C.G.S., Inc. Title: *Stones And Bones*. Publisher: Prince George's County Genealogical Society, Inc., P.O. Box 819, Bowie, MD 20718-0819 (1984).

PRINCE GEORGE'S COUNTY CEMETERIES - CHURCH 219

CHURCH OF THE ATONEMENT (EPISCOPAL) CEMETERY
Location: Cheltenham Railroad near the extension of Frank Tippett Road, Cheltenham, MD. [A.D.C. map location: page 26, grid coordinates AB5.] Condition of cemetery: Fair condition. May 1995. Earliest known death: 1864. Most recent death: 1976. Date transcribed: 1983. Author: P.G.C.G.S., Inc. Title: *Stones And Bones*. Publisher: Prince George's County Genealogical Society, Inc., P.O. Box 819, Bowie, MD 20718-0819 (1984).

CHURCH OF THE HOLY ROSARY CEMETERY (CATHOLIC)
Location: At the junction of Route 301 and Rosaryville Road. [A.D.C. map location: page 33, grid coordinates C1.] Earliest known death: 1898. WWII veterans interred here. Date transcribed: 1983. Author: P.G.C.G.S., Inc. Title: *Stones And Bones*. Publisher: Prince George's County Genealogical Society, Inc., P.O. Box 819, Bowie, MD 20718-0819 (1984).

EPIPHANY EPISCOPAL CHURCH CEMETERY
Location: 3111 Ritchie Road near its intersection with Marlboro Pike in Forestville, MD. [A.D.C. map location: page 19, grid coordinates D10.] Earliest known death: 1875. Civil War, WWI and WWII veterans, in addition to veterans of other wars. Date transcribed: 1983. Author: P.G.C.G.S., Inc. Title: *Stones And Bones*. Publisher: Prince George's County Genealogical Society, Inc., P.O. Box 819, Bowie, MD 20718-0819 (1984).

EVERGREEN CEMETERY, THE OLD PRESBYTERIAN CEMETERY
Location: On 52nd Avenue near Newton Street in Bladensburg, MD. [A.D.C. map location: page 12, grid coordinates E7.] Earliest known death: 1749. WWI and WWII veterans, in addition to veterans of other wars. Date transcribed: 1983. Author: P.G.C.G.S., Inc. Title: *Stones And Bones*. Publisher: Prince George's County Genealogical Society, Inc., P.O. Box 819, Bowie, MD 20718-0819 (1984).

FIRST LUTHERAN CHURCH OF BOWIE
Location: 12710 Duckettown Road in Bowie, MD about one block from Old Laurel-Bowie Road. [A.D.C. map location: page 9, grid coordinates H7.] Earliest known death: 1919. WWII veterans interred here. Date transcribed: 1983. Author: P.G.C.G.S., Inc. Title: *Stones And Bones*. Publisher: Prince George's County Genealogical Society, Inc., P.O. Box 819, Bowie, MD 20718-0819 (1984).

FOREST GROVE METHODIST CHURCH CEMETERY

Location: On Andrews Air Force Base. From main gate, left on Perimeter, right on Patrick Avenue, left on Fetchet Avenue. [A.D.C. map location: page 25, grid coordinates G3.] Condition of cemetery: Well kept. May 1995. Earliest known death: 1874. Most recent death: 1938 Location of records: Forest Memorial United Methodist Church. Date transcribed: 1982. Author: P.G.C.G.S., Inc. Title: *Stones And Bones*. Publisher: Prince George's County Genealogical Society, Inc., P.O. Box 819, Bowie, MD 20718-0819 (1984). Additional comments: Go to Andrews Air Force Base Visitors Center for additional information.

FOREST MEMORIAL UNITED METHODIST CHURCH CEMETERY

Location: 3111 Forestville Road, Forestville, about 0.4 mile north of Route 4. [A.D.C. map location: page 19, grid coordinates D10.] Earliest known death: 1840. Date transcribed: 1982. Author: P.G.C.G.S., Inc. Title: *Stones And Bones*. Publisher: Prince George's County Genealogical Society, Inc., P.O. Box 819, Bowie, MD 20718-0819 (1984).

GIBBONS UNITED METHODIST CHURCH

Location: From Route 381 east on Keys Road to Gibbons Church Road, south to Cemetery at 14107. [A.D.C. map location: page 33, grid coordinates D12.] Condition of cemetery: Perpetual care. Earliest known death: 1907. WWII veterans. Burial records kept: Interment, tombstone and maps. Location of records: U M Church 14107 Gibbons Road, Brandywine, MD 20613. Date transcribed: 1983. Author: P.G.C.G.S., Inc. Title: *Stones And Bones*. Publisher: Prince George's County Genealogical Society, Inc., P.O. Box 819, Bowie, MD 20718-0819 (1984).

HADDAWAY CHAPEL METHODIST EPISCOPAL CHURCH CEMETERY (BRANCHVILLE METHODIST EPISCOPAL CHURCH, SOUTH)

Location: Formerly located on 60th Avenue in Berwyn Heights behind 6001 Greenbelt Road. [A.D.C. map location: Prince George's, page 7, grid coordinates H9.] Condition of cemetery: Remains relocated to Fort Lincoln Cemetery and other local cemeteries. Earliest known death: 1895. Most recent death: 1932. Location of records: Records are at College Park United Methodist Church. Date transcribed: 1983. Author: P.G.C.G.S., Inc. Title: *Stones And Bones*. Publisher: Prince George's County Genealogical Society, Inc., P.O. Box 819, Bowie, MD 20718-0819 (1984).

PRINCE GEORGE'S COUNTY CEMETERIES - CHURCH 221

HOLY FAMILY CATHOLIC CHURCH CEMETERY
Location: 12010 Woodmore Road about 0.4 mile from Enterprise Road in Mitchellville, MD. [A.D.C. map location: page 14, grid coordinates E10.] Earliest known death: 1938. Date transcribed: 1983. Author: P.G.C.G.S., Inc. Title: *Stones And Bones*. Publisher: Prince George's County Genealogical Society, Inc., P.O. Box 819, Bowie, MD 20718-0819 (1984).

HOLY TRINITY CHURCH (EPISCOPAL) CEMETERY
Location: Located off Route 450 between Highbridge Road and Hillmeade Road in Collington (Bowie). [A.D.C. map location: page 9, grid coordinates H13.] Earliest known death: 1735. Burial records kept: Interment. Date transcribed: 1983. Author: P.G.C.G.S., Inc. Title: *Stones And Bones*.

IMMANUEL UNITED METHODIST CHURCH CEMETERY (IMMANUAL METHODIST EPISCOPAL CHURCH SOUTH)
Location: 17400 Aquasco Road (Route 301) at Horsehead Road in Brandywine, MD. [A.D.C. map location: page 40, grid coordinates J7.] Condition of cemetery: Perpetual care. Earliest known death: 1867. WWI and WWII veterans, in addition to veterans of other wars. Are burial records kept: Yes. Type of records: Interment, tombstone and maps. Location of records: At church. Date transcribed: 1976. These transcribed records are held by: The Church. Author: P.G.C.G.S., Inc. Title: *Stones And Bones*. Publisher: Prince George's County Genealogical Society, Inc., P.O. Box 819, Bowie, MD 20718-0819 (1984).

LANHAM UNITED METHODIST CHURCH CEMETERY (FORMERLY WHITEFIELD CHAPEL)
Location: 5512 Whitfield Road about 0.3 mile south of Route 450 in Lanham, MD. [A.D.C. map location: Prince George's County, page 13, grid coordinates F3.] Condition of cemetery: Good condition as of June 1995. Earliest known death: 1866. WWI and WWII veterans, in addition to veterans of other wars. Date transcribed: 1982. Author: P.G.C.G.S., Inc. Title: *Stones And Bones*. Publisher: Prince George's County Genealogical Society, Inc., P.O. Box 819, Bowie, MD 20718-0819 (1984).

MCKENDREE METHODIST CHURCH CEMETERY
Location: From Route 5 south on Route 337 2.1 miles to 0.3 mi. past McKendree Road (cemetery on right). [A.D.C. map location: page 38,

grid coordinates H1.] Condition of cemetery: Fair condition as of June 1995. Earliest known death: 1842. Date transcribed: 1983. Author: P.G.C.G.S., Inc. Title: *Stones And Bones*. Publisher: Prince George's County Genealogical Society, Inc., P.O. Box 819, Bowie, MD 20718-0819 (1984).

MOUNT LEBANON CEMETERY
Location: On Riggs Road about 0.5 miles south of the Capital Beltway, I 495. [A.D.C. map location: page 6, grid coordinates A6.] Condition of cemetery: Perpetual care. Earliest known death: 1941. Burial records kept: Interment. Location of records: See address above.

MOUNT OAK UNITED METHODIST CHURCH CEMETERY
Location: On Church Road at Woodmore Road about 1.5 mile North of Central Avenue. [A.D.C. map location: page 15, grid coordinates A9.] Earliest known death: 1910. Date transcribed: 1983. Author: P.G.C.G.S., Inc. Title: *Stones And Bones*. Publisher: Prince George's County Genealogical Society, Inc., P.O. Box 819, Bowie, MD 20718-0819 (1984).

MT. CALVARY CATHOLIC CHURCH CEMETERY
Location: 6700 Marlboro Pike, District Heights, MD. [A.D.C. map location: page 19, grid coordinates A9.] Earliest known death: 1915. Date transcribed: 1983. Author: P.G.C.G.S., Inc. Title: *Stones And Bones*. Publisher: Prince George's County Genealogical Society, Inc., P.O. Box 819, Bowie, MD 20718-0819 (1984).

MT. CARMEL CATHOLIC CEMETERY, ST. MARY'S PARISH
Location: On Old Marlboro Pike just west of Brown Station Road, Upper Marlboro, MD. [A.D.C. map location: page 26, grid coordinates K2.] Condition of cemetery: Perpetual care. Earliest known death: 1831. Prominent individuals interred: Thomas Sim Lee, Governor of MD. Date transcribed: 1983. Author: P.G.C.G.S., Inc. Title: *Stones And Bones*. Publisher: Prince George's County Genealogical Society, Inc., P.O. Box 819, Bowie, MD 20718-0819 (1984).

MT. HOPE METHODIST EPISCOPAL CHURCH CEMETERY
Location: Off Temple Hills Road 0.25 mile north of Allentown Road, east to Wickham Drive to cemetery. [A.D.C. map location: page 24, grid coordinates G7.] Condition of cemetery: Unknown in June 1995.

MT. NEBO METHODIST CHURCH CEMETERY

Location: From Route 301 one mile south of Central Avenue. East on Queen Anne Road about 1.1 miles. [A.D.C. map location: page 21, grid coordinates K2.] Condition of cemetery: Maintained in good condition as of June 1995. Earliest known death: 1859. Date transcribed: 1983. Author: P.G.C.G.S., Inc. Title: *Stones And Bones*. Publisher: Prince George's County Genealogical Society, Inc., P.O. Box 819, Bowie, MD 20718-0819 (1984).

NATIONAL CAPITAL HEBREW CEMETERY

Location: From Central Avenue in Capitol Heights, MD, south on Larchmont to Fable Street, north to #4708. [A.D.C. map location: page 18, grid coordinates F/G4.] Burial records kept: Interment.

OLD STONE METHODIST CHURCH (THE)

Location: Formally located on Ninth Street off Park Hill Road in Laurel, MD. [A.D.C. map location: page 4, grid coordinates F2.] Earliest known death: 1845. Most recent death: 1905. No burial records were kept. Date transcribed: 1983. Author: P.G.C.G.S., Inc. Title: *Stones And Bones*. Publisher: Prince George's County Genealogical Society, Inc., P.O. Box 819, Bowie, MD 20718-0819 (1984). Additional comments: Status of graves is unknown. Apartment building now occupies site.

OXON HILL METHODIST CHURCH CEMETERY

Location: On Oxon Hill Road behind the post office near Livingston Road. [A.D.C. map location: page 23, grid coordinates G5.] Earliest known death: 1878. Most recent death: 1953. Date transcribed: 1983. Author: P.G.C.G.S., Inc. Title: *Stones And Bones*. Publisher: Prince George's County Genealogical Society, Inc., P.O. Box 819, Bowie, MD 20718-0819 (1984).

PERKINS CHAPEL, GLENN DALE UNITED METHODIST CHURCH CEMETERY

Location: On Springfield Road at Goodluck Road about 0.9 mile Northwest of Lanham-Severn Road. [A.D.C. map location: page 9, grid coordinates C7.] Condition of cemetery: Good Condition. May 1995. Earliest known death: 1871. Civil War, WWI and WWII veterans. No burial records were kept. Date transcribed: 1983. Author: P.G.C.G.S., Inc. Title: *Stones And Bones*. Publisher: Prince George's County Genealogical Society, Inc., P.O. Box 819, Bowie, MD 20718-0819 (1984).

PLEASANT GROVE METHODIST EPISCOPAL MEETING HOUSE CEMETERY
Location: In a wooded area on Springfield Road opposite an antenna field belonging to NASA. [A.D.C. map location: page 9, grid coordinates A5.] Earliest known death: 1903. Most recent death: 1952. Date transcribed: 1983. Author: P.G.C.G.S., Inc. Title: *Stones And Bones*. Publisher: Prince George's County Genealogical Society, Inc., P.O. Box 819, Bowie, MD 20718-0819 (1984).

PROVIDENCE UNITED METHODIST CHURCH (CURRENT NAME IS PROVIDENCE METHODIST CHURCH)
Location: From Route 210, east on Old Fort Road about 1.5 miles to 10610 Old Fort Road. [A.D.C. map location: Prince George's, page 30, grid coordinates J3.] Earliest known death: 1905. Date transcribed: 1983. Author: P.G.C. Genealogical Society. Title: *Stones and Bones*. Publisher: Prince George's County Genealogical Society, Inc., P.O. Box 819, Bowie, MD 20718-0819 (1984).

PROVIDENCE UNITED METHODIST CHURCH (THE PROVIDENCE METHODIST EPISCOPAL CHURCH, SOUTH)
Location: Opposite 12008 Old Fort Road, from Route 210 Indian Head Highway, east on Old Fort Road 2.5 miles. [A.D.C. map location: page 30, grid coordinates H6.] Earliest known death: 1871. Most recent death: 1871. Date transcribed: 1983. Author: P.G.C.G.S., Inc. Title: *Stones And Bones*. Publisher: Prince George's County Genealogical Society, Inc., P.O. Box 819, Bowie, MD 20718-0819 (1984).

QUEENS CHAPEL UNITED METHODIST CHURCH CEMETERY
Location: From US 1 East on Muirkirk Road to Old Muirkirk Road, left to cemetery, 7410 Old Muirkirk Road, Beltsville, MD 20705. [A.D.C. map location: page 4, grid coordinates C11.] Earliest known death: 1882. WWI, WWII, in addition to veterans of other wars. Markers transcribed: 1983. Burial records were kept. Author: P.G.C.G.S., Inc. Title: *Stones And Bones*. Publisher: Prince George's County Genealogical Society, Inc., P.O. Box 819, Bowie, MD 20718-0819 (1984).

RESURRECTION CATHOLIC CEMETERY
Location: On Route 223 (8000 Woodyard Road) 1.8 miles east of Route 5, Branch Avenue. [A.D.C. map location: page 25, grid coordinates G10.] Condition of cemetery: Perpetual care. Earliest known death: 1967. WWI and WWII veterans, in addition to veterans of other wars.

PRINCE GEORGE'S COUNTY CEMETERIES - CHURCH

Burial records kept: Deed, plat, interment, tombstone and maps.
Location of records: At office at above address.

RIDGLEY-ZION UNITED METHODIST CHURCH CEMETERY
Location: 8900 Central Avenue (Route 214) near the Capital Beltway at Brightseat Road. [A.D.C. map location: page 19, grid coordinates G2.] Earliest known death: 1913. Most recent death: 1948. Date transcribed: 1983. Author: P.G.C.G.S., Inc. Title: *Stones And Bones*. Publisher: Prince George's County Genealogical Society, Inc., P.O. Box 819, Bowie, MD 20718-0819 (1984).

SACRED HEART AT WHITE MARSH CATHOLIC CHURCH CEMETERY
Location: On a hill about 1/14 west of MD Route 3 on MD Route 450. [A.D.C. map location: page 10, grid coordinates G12.] Condition of cemetery: Good condition as of June 1995. Earliest known death: 1830. Date transcribed: 1983. Author: P.G.C.G.S., Inc. Title: *Stones And Bones*. Publisher: Prince George's County Genealogical Society, Inc., P.O. Box 819, Bowie, MD 20718-0819 (1984).

SAINT SIMON'S EPISCOPAL CHURCH CEMETERY
Location: On St. Thomas Church Road east of Croom Road, MD Route 382. [A.D.C. map location: page 34, grid coordinates A2.] Earliest known death: 1902. Date transcribed: 1983. Author: P.G.C.G.S., Inc. Title: *Stones And Bones*. Publisher: Prince George's County Genealogical Society, Inc., P.O. Box 819, Bowie, MD 20718-0819 (1984).

ST. BARNABUS' EPISCOPAL CHURCH CEMETERY, QUEEN ANNE PARISH, LEELAND
Location: On Oak Grove Road (MD Route 556) at Church Road South, Leeland. [A.D.C. map location: page 21, grid coordinates A5.] Earliest known death: 1867. Date transcribed: 1983. Author: P.G.C.G.S., Inc. Title: *Stones And Bones*. Publisher: Prince George's County Genealogical Society, Inc., P.O. Box 819, Bowie, MD 20718-0819 (1984).

ST. BARNABUS' EPISCOPAL CHURCH CEMETERY, ST. BARNABUS PARISH, OXON HILL
Location: 5203 St. Barnabus Road, Temple Hills, MD. [A.D.C. map location: page 24, grid coordinates A2.] Earliest known death: 1854. Burial records were kept. Date transcribed: 1983. Author: P.G.C.G.S., Inc. Title: *Stones And Bones*. Publisher: Prince George's County Genealogical Society, Inc., P.O. Box 819, Bowie, MD 20718-0819 (1984).

ST. DOMINIC'S CATHOLIC CHURCH CEMETERY (BOONE FAMILY CEMETERY)
Location: In Aquasco, MD, 11 miles from Route 301 on MD Route 381 opposite St. Philip's Road. [A.D.C. map location: page 43, grid coordinates G7.] Condition of cemetery: Well kept. Perpetual care May 1995. Earliest known death: 1875. Most recent death: 1959. Are burial records kept: No Location of records: St. Michael's Catholic Church, Baden, MD. Date transcribed: 1983. Author: P.G.C.G.S., Inc. Title: *Stones And Bones*. Publisher: Prince George's County Genealogical Society, Inc., P.O. Box 819, Bowie, MD 20718-0819 (1984). Additional comments: Burial is restricted to members of the Bowling family.

ST. GEORGE'S CHAPEL (EPISCOPAL) CEMETERY
Location: On Old Glendale Road between MD Route 564 Lanham-Severn Road and railroad tracks. [A.D.C. map location: page 9, grid coordinates B11.] Condition of cemetery: Good as of June 1995. Earliest known death: 1879. Burial records were kept. Date transcribed: 1983. Author: P.G.C.G.S., Inc. Title: *Stones And Bones*. Publisher: Prince George's County Genealogical Society, Inc., P.O. Box 819, Bowie, MD 20718-0819 (1984).

ST. IGNATIUS ROMAN CATHOLIC CHURCH CEMETERY
Location: 2400 Brinkley Road about 0.4 miles east of St. Barnabus Road. Oxen Hill. [A.D.C. map location: page 23, grid coordinates K5.] Earliest known death: 1854. Date transcribed: 1983. Author: P.G.C.G.S., Inc. Title: *Stones And Bones*. Publisher: Prince George's County Genealogical Society, Inc., P.O. Box 819, Bowie, MD 20718-0819 (1984).

ST. JOHN THE EVANGELIST CHURCH CEMETERY
Location: 8908 Old Branch Avenue about three-quarters of a mile North of Route 223 in Clinton. [A.D.C. map location: Prince George's County, page 24, grid coordinates K12.] Condition of cemetery: Perpetual care. Earliest known death: 1897. Burial records kept: Deed, plat and interment. Location of records: At church. Date transcribed: 1983. Author: P.G.C.G.S., Inc. Title: *Stones And Bones*. Publisher: Prince George's County Genealogical Society, Inc., P.O. Box 819, Bowie, MD 20718-0819 (1984).

ST. JOHN'S, BROAD CREEK, EPISCOPAL CHURCH GRAVEYARD
Location: 9801 Livingston Road near Indian Head Highway, Route 210. [A.D.C. map location: page 30, grid coordinates E1.] Earliest known

PRINCE GEORGE'S COUNTY CEMETERIES - CHURCH

death: 1807. Burial records were kept. Date transcribed: 1983. Author: P.G.C.G.S., Inc. Title: *Stones And Bones*. Publisher: Prince George's County Genealogical Society, Inc., P.O. Box 819, Bowie, MD 20718-0819 (1984).

ST. JOHN'S EPISCOPAL CHURCH, ZION PARISH
Location: From Capital Beltway, north on US 1 about two miles to MD 212, Powder Mill Road. Left to entrance. [A.D.C. map location: Prince George's County, page 7, grid coordinates J2.] Condition of cemetery: Perpetual care. Earliest known death: 1836. Prominent individuals interred: Gen. Rezin Beall, Rev. War. Revolutionary War, Civil War, WWI and WWII veterans, in addition to veterans of other wars. Burial records kept: Interment and maps. Location of records: Church office, 11040 Baltimore Avenue, Beltsville, MD. Date transcribed: 1983. Author: P.G.C. Genealogical Society. Title: *Stones And Bones*. Publisher: Prince George's County Genealogical Society, Inc., P.O. Box 819, Bowie, MD 20718-0819 (1984).

ST. JOSEPH'S CHURCH AND CHRISTIAN BROTHERS INSTITUTE CEMETERY
Location: US 1, Baltimore Avenue, and Ammendale Road at Beltsville, MD. [A.D.C. map location: page 3, grid coordinates K12.] Earliest known death: 1883. WWII veterans. Date transcribed: 1983. Author: P.G.C.G.S., Inc. Title: *Stones And Bones*. Publisher: Prince George's County Genealogical Society, Inc., P.O. Box 819, Bowie, MD 20718-0819 (1984).

ST. MARY OF THE MILLS CATHOLIC CHURCH CEMETERY
Location: Between 7th and 8th Streets behind Rectory near Main Street. [A.D.C. map location: page 4, grid coordinates G2.] Condition of cemetery: Perpetual care. Earliest known death: 1845. Civil War, WWI and WWII veterans, in addition to veterans of other wars.
Are burial records kept: Yes Location of records: St. Mary of the Mills Church. Date transcribed: 1983. Author: P.G.C.G.S., Inc. Title: *Stones And Bones*. Publisher: Prince George's County Genealogical Society, Inc., P.O. Box 819, Bowie, MD 20718-0819 (1984).

ST. MARY'S CATHOLIC CHURCH, PISCATAWAY
Location: 13401 Piscataway Road (MD Route 223) near Floral Park Road. [A.D.C. map location: page 30, grid coordinates K10.] Condition of cemetery: Perpetual care. Earliest known death: 1841. WWII veterans. Burial records kept: Deed, plat, interment and maps.

Location of records: Church office. Date transcribed: 1983. Author: P.G.C.G.S., Inc. Title: *Stones And Bones*. Publisher: Prince George's County Genealogical Society, Inc., P.O. Box 819, Bowie, MD 20718-0819 (1984).

ST. MARY'S EPISCOPAL CHURCH CEMETERY (ST. PAUL'S PARISH)
Location: In Aquasco on MD Route 381 at St. Mary's Church Road and Dr. Bowen Road. [A.D.C. map location: page 43, grid coordinates G6.] Condition of cemetery: Perpetual care. Earliest known death: 1851. Civil War, WWI and WWII veterans. Burial records kept: Interment and maps. Location of records: St. Paul's Episcopal Church (above). Date transcribed: 1983. Author: P.G.C.G.S., Inc. Title: *Stones And Bones*. Publisher: Prince George's County Genealogical Society, Inc., P.O. Box 819, Bowie, MD 20718-0819 (1984).

ST. PAUL'S EPISCOPAL CHURCH CEMETERY
Location: From MD 381, east on Baden-Westwood Road 1/2 mile. [A.D.C. map location: page 40, grid coordinates J5.] Condition of cemetery: Perpetual care. Earliest known death: 1818. WWI and WWII veterans. Burial records kept: Interment and maps. Location of records: Church. Date transcribed: 1983. Author: P.G.C.G.S., Inc. Title: *Stones And Bones*. Publisher: Prince George's County Genealogical Society, Inc., P.O. Box 819, Bowie, MD 20718-0819 (1984). Additional comments: Church is 300 years old. Many gravestone without dates appear older than 1818.

ST. PAUL'S METHODIST CHURCH
Location: 6634 St. Barnabus Road at Tucker Road, Oxon Hill, MD about 0.9 mile from I95. [A.D.C. map location: page 23, grid coordinates H6.] Earliest known death: 1896. Date transcribed: 1983. Author: P.G.C.G.S., Inc. Title: *Stones And Bones*. Publisher: Prince George's County Genealogical Society, Inc., P.O. Box 819, Bowie, MD 20718-0819 (1984).

ST. PHILIP'S EPISCOPAL CHURCH CEMETERY
Location: In Laurel, MD at Sixth, Main and Prince George Streets. [A.D.C. map location: page 4, grid coordinates G2.] Condition of cemetery: Perpetual care. Earliest known death: 1851. Most recent death: 1972. Burial records kept: Deed, plat, interment and maps. Location of records: St. Philip's Episcopal Church. Date transcribed: 1983. Author: P.G.C.G.S., Inc. Title: *Stones And Bones*. Publisher:

Prince George's County Genealogical Society, Inc., P.O. Box 819, Bowie, MD 20718-0819 (1984).

ST. PHILIP'S EPISCOPAL CHURCH CEMETERY
Location: From MD Route 381 in Aquasco, go 0.1 mile west on St. Philip's Road. [A.D.C. map location: page 43, grid coordinates F7.] Condition of cemetery: Perpetual care. Earliest known death: 1892. WWI and WWII veterans. Burial records kept: Deed, plat, interment and maps. Location of records: St. Philip's Church. Date transcribed: 1983. Author: P.G.C.G.S., Inc. Title: *Stones And Bones*. Publisher: Prince George's County Genealogical Society, Inc., P.O. Box 819, Bowie, MD 20718-0819 (1984).

ST. THOMAS' CHURCH CEMETERY (EPISCOPAL)
Location: From US 301, go east on MD 382 to St. Thomas Church Road, turn left to church. [A.D.C. map location: page 34, grid coordinates A2.] Earliest known death: 1780. Date transcribed: 1983. Author: P.G.C.G.S., Inc. Title: *Stones And Bones*. Publisher: Prince George's County Genealogical Society, Inc., P.O. Box 819, Bowie, MD 20718-0819 (1984).

TRINITY EPISCOPAL CHURCH CEMETERIES
Location: 14515 Church Street in Upper Marlboro, MD. [A.D.C. map location: page 27, grid coordinates B3.] Earliest known death: 1786. Date transcribed: 1983. Author: P.G.C.G.S., Inc. Title: *Stones And Bones*. Publisher: Prince George's County Genealogical Society, Inc., P.O. Box 819, Bowie, MD 20718-0819 (1984).

UNION BETHEL AME CHURCH CEMETERY
Location: On Floral Park Road 0.2 mile west of Brandywine Road. [A.D.C. map location: page 32, grid coordinates B10.] Condition of cemetery: Perpetual care. Earliest known death: 1887. Burial records kept: Interment and maps. Location of records: At church.

WESTPHALIA UNITED METHODIST CHURCH CEMETERY (JACKSON MEMORIAL CEMETERY OR ST. LUKE'S CHURCH CEMETERY)
Location: From Dower House Road, west on Dower House Road. West to Leapley Road. Left to cemetery. [A.D.C. map location: Prince George's, page 25, grid coordinates G5.] Earliest known death: 1903. Most recent death: 1937. WWII veterans. Date transcribed: 1983. Author: P.G.C.G.S., Inc. Title: *Stones And Bones*. Publisher: Prince

George's County Genealogical Society, Inc., P.O. Box 819, Bowie, MD 20718-0819 (1984).

WOODVILLE METHODIST CHURCH CEMETERY (DEMARR FARM CEMETERY)
Location: On Aquasco Road. (Route 381) about 1/2 mile South of Dr. Bowen Road near Eagle Harbor Road. [A.D.C. map location: page 43, grid coordinates G7.] Condition of cemetery: Well kept as of May 1995. Earliest known death: 1870. WWI veterans. Location of records: Methodist Church in Baden, MD. Date transcribed: 1983. Author: P.G.C.G.S., Inc. Title: *Stones And Bones*. Publisher: Prince George's County Genealogical Society, Inc., P.O. Box 819, Bowie, MD 20718-0819 (1984).

Public Cemeteries

CEDAR HILL CEMETERY (FOREST LAKE CEMETERY PRIOR TO 1913)
Location: 4111 Pennsylvania Avenue, Suitland, MD. [A.D.C. map location: Prince George's County 1994, page 18, grid coordinates D8.] Condition of cemetery: Perpetual care. Earliest known death: 1871. Civil War, WWI and WWII veterans, in addition to veterans of other wars. Burial records were kept. Types of records: Interment records, tombstone and maps. Location of records: See address above.

FOREST HILLS MEMORIAL GARDENS
Location: Near 10000 Brandywine Road, Clinton, MD. [A.D.C. map location: Prince George's County 1994, page 32, grid coordinates A1.]

FORT LINCOLN CEMETERY
Location: 3401 Bladensburg Road, Brentwood. On Alternate US 1 (Bladensburg Road) immediately north of the Washington, DC line. [A.D.C. map location: page 12, grid coordinates B8.] Condition of cemetery: Perpetual care. Earliest known death: 1928. WWI and WWII veterans, in addition to veterans of other wars. Burial records kept: Interment and maps. Location of records: See address above.

GEORGE WASHINGTON CEMETERY AND MAUSOLEUM
Location: On Riggs Road 0.5 mile south of I495 (Capital Beltway). [A.D.C. map location: page 6, grid coordinates K7.] Condition of

PRINCE GEORGE'S COUNTY CEMETERIES - PUBLIC

cemetery: Perpetual care. Earliest known death: 1931. Burial records kept: Interment.

HARMONY MEMORIAL PARK, HARMONEON 1825-1859 (MOVED); HARMONY CEMETERY 1959-1960 (MOVED)

Location: From I95, west on Route 202 (Landover Road) 0.25 mile to left on Sherriff Road 1.5 mile. [A.D.C. map location: page 13, grid coordinates B11.] Condition of cemetery: Perpetual care. Earliest known death: 1829. Burial records kept: Interment. Location of records: See address above.

IVY HILL CEMETERY (GREENWOOD CEMETERY)

Location: In Laurel, MD on Sandy Spring Road near and opposite Nichols Drive. [A.D.C. map location: page 4, grid coordinates E2.] Condition of cemetery: Perpetual care. Earliest known death: 1815. Civil War, WWI and WWII veterans, in addition to veterans of other wars. Burial records kept: Deed, plat, interment and maps. Location of records: Ivy Hill Association, Inc. Date transcribed: 1983. Author: P.G.C.G.S., Inc. Title: *Stones And Bones*. Publisher: Prince George's County Genealogical Society, Inc., P.O. Box 819, Bowie, MD 20718-0819 (1984).

LINCOLN MEMORIAL CEMETERY

Location: 4001 Suitland Road near Washington, DC line. [A.D.C. map location: page 18, grid coordinates C8.] Condition of cemetery: Perpetual care. Earliest known death: 1928

MARYLAND NATIONAL MEMORIAL PARK, NATIONAL CAPITAL MEMORIAL PARK 1930s-1953; CARVER MEMORIAL PARK 1953-1969

Location: On US 1, Baltimore Avenue, 2.4 miles south of Route 198 in Laurel, MD. [A.D.C. map location: page 4, grid coordinates D9.] Condition of cemetery: Perpetual care.

MARYLAND VETERANS' CEMETERY

Location: On Route 301, Crain Highway about 3.8 miles north of Route 5. [A.D.C. map location: page 33, grid coordinates A5.] Condition of cemetery: Perpetual care. Earliest known death: 1978. WWI and WWII veterans, in addition to veterans of other wars. Burial records kept: Interment and maps. Location of records: See above address.

SURRETT GRAVESTONE
Location: The Surrett House on Brandywine Road in the center of Clinton. [A.D.C. map location: page 24, grid coordinates K12.] Condition of cemetery: Only gravestone is here, stored in a box. Earliest known death: 1865. Most recent death: 1865. Date transcribed: 1983. Author: P.G.C.G.S., Inc. Title: *Stones And Bones*. Publisher: Prince George's County Genealogical Society, Inc., P.O. Box 819, Bowie, MD 20718-0819 (1984).

TURNER FAMILY CEMETERY (GREENBELT CEMETERY)
Location: On Ivy Lane off Route 201, Edmonston Road. [A.D.C. map location: page 8, grid coordinates A7.] Condition of cemetery: Maintained by City of Greenbelt. Flat headstones used now. Earliest known death: 1855. WWI and WWII veterans, in addition to veterans of other wars. Burial records kept: Deed, plat, interment, tombstone and maps. Location of records: Greenbelt Municipal Building. Date transcribed: 1983. These transcribed records are held at the Greenbelt Municipal Building. Author: P.G.C.G.S., Inc. Title: *Stones And Bones*. Publisher: Prince George's County Genealogical Society, Inc., P.O. Box 819, Bowie, MD 20718-0819 (1984). Additional comments: Original stones have been moved from site by Greenbelt City works department.

WASHINGTON NATIONAL CEMETERY, INC.
Location: 4101 Suitland Road about 0.6 miles from Washington, DC line. [A.D.C. map location: page 18, grid coordinates D9.] Condition of cemetery: Perpetual care. Earliest known death: 1934. Burial records kept: Interment. Location of records: See address above.

INDEX OF CEMETERIES

205th Street Cemetery, 1

-A-

Adam Shipley Family Cemetery, 74
Adams United Methodist Church Cemetery, 53
Addison Chapel of St. Mathew's Episcopal Church, 215
Addison Family Cemetery, 186
Addison Family Cemetery and Vault, 186
Addison Parish Cemetery, 215
African Methodist Episcopal Church, 165
Aitcheson Family Graveyard, 187
Albert Corey Cemetery, 1
Alesia Free Methodist Cemetery, 103
All Hallows Episcopal Church Cemetery, 54
All Hallows Episcopal Chapel Cemetery, 53
Allen Chapel African Methodist Episcopal Church Cemetery at Wheaton, 159
Allgire Family Cemetery, 75
Allnutt-Ayton-Bowman Family Burying Ground at Claysville, 135
Almshouse Cemetery, 131
Anderson Family Cemetery, 1
Andover/Camp Meade Cemetery, 1
Andrew Chapel Methodist Episcopal Church South, 163
Andrew Myers Cemetery, 91
Annapolis Hebrew Cemetery, 54
Annapolis Hebrew Cemetery, 2
Annapolis Junior High School Cemetery, 74
Annapolis National Cemetery, 72

Annapolis Neck Cemetery, 1
Apostolic Faith Church Cemetery, 216
Armiger Cemetery, 37
Arnold Asbury Methodist Church Cemetery, 54
Asbury Methodist Episcopal Church Cemetery, 160
Asbury Town-Neck United Methodist Church Cemetery, 54
Asbury United Methodist Church Cemetery, 216
Asbury United Methodist Church Cemetery, 54, 55
Asbury United Methodist Church Cemetery at Germantown, 160
Ascension Episcopal Church Cemetery, 103
Ascension Roman Catholic Church Cemetery, 216
Ash Memorial Cemetery at Sandy Spring, 135
Ashton Cemetery, 165
Ashton Methodist Episcopal Church Cemetery near Ashton, 160
Aspin Hill Memorial Park and Companion Cemetery, 135
Aud Family Burying Ground near Poolesville, 135
Avery Family Cemetery, 2
Awkard Gamily Burying Ground at Big Woods, 136

-B-

Bachman's Church, 111
Baden Family Graveyard, 187
Baile Family Cemetery, 75
Baldwin Marker, 2
Baldwin Memorial Methodist Church Cemetery, 55

Bamber Grave, 187
Baptist Road Cemetery, 104
Baptist Church Cemetery at
  Derwood, 140
Barchet Cemetery, 2
Barnes Family Cemetery, 75
Barnesville Methodist Episcopal
  Church Cemetery, 160
Baseman Family Cemetery, 76
Baptist Meeting House Church
  Cemetery, 177
Batson Family Burying Ground
  near Triadelphia, 136
Battee Cemetery, 2
Bauer's Church, 111
Baust United Church of Christ
  Cemetery, 104
Bay Frong Road Cemetery, 2
Bay Hills Golf Club Cemetery, 37
Bayne Family Cemetery and
  Monument, 187
Bayside Beach Road Cemetery, 3
Beall Family Burying Ground
  near Layhill, 136
Beall Family Grave, 188
Beall/Love Family Graves, 188
Beanes Family Cemetery, 188
Beard Hall Memorial Cemetery,
  41
Beasman Family Cemetery, 76
Beaver Family Cemetery, 76
Beggs Chapel Cemetery, 76
Beggs Family Cemetery, 76
Bell Cemetery, 169
Bellefield Cemetery, 27
Bells United Methodist Church,
  216
Belvoir Cemetery, 3
Bennett Cemetery, 77
Bennett Family Cemetery, 77
Benton-Shipley Cemetery, 3
Berry Family Cemetery, 188, 189

Beth Jacob Congregation
  Cemetery, 104
Bethany Methodist Episcopal
  Church Cemetery, 104
Bethel Apostolic Church of Jesus
  Christ, 217
Bethel Cemetery, 3
Bethel Methodist Episcopal
  Church Cemetery at Mt. Zion,
  161
Bethel United Methodist Church
  Cemetery, 105
Bethel-Carrollton Church of God
  Cemetery, 105
Bethesda Meeting House
  Cemetery at Bethesda, 161
Bethesda Methodist Episcopal
  Church Cemetery, 161
Bethesda United Methodist
  Church Cemetery, 105
Bethesda United Methodist
  Church Cemetery at
  Browningsville, 161
Bevan Family Cemetery, 3
Biggs and Waters Cemetery, 4
Bird-Chaney-Chew Cemetery, 4
Birkhead's Meadow Cemetery, 55
Bixler's United Methodist
  Church Cemetery, 106
B'Nai Israel Congregation
  Cemetery, 216
Bodkin Point Cemetery, 4
Bohmen Cemetery, 4
Bond Family Cemetery, 77
Bonifant Family Burying Ground
  near Layhill, 137
Boone Family Cemetery, 78, 226
Boone-Linstid Family Cemetery,
  4
Boone-Merriken Cemetery, 5
Boone's Catholic Chapel
  Cemetery, 216

INDEX OF CEMETERIES 235

Boring's Meeting House, 113
Boteler Grave, 189
Bowen Cemetery, 160
Bowen Family Cemetery, 165
Bower's Church, 111
Bowie Family Cemetery, 189, 190
Boyds Presbyterian Church Cemetery, 162
Boyer Burial Ground, 5
Branchville Methodist Episcopal Church, South, 220
Brandenburg United Methodist Church Cemetery, 106
Brashiers Grave, 190
Bready Family Burying Ground near Layhill, 137
Brewer Cemetery, 5
Brewer Family Gravestone, 5
Brewer Hill Cemetery, 5
Brick Methodist Church Cemetery, 120
Brock Bridge Road Cemetery, 56
Brooke Grove United Methodist Church Cemetery near Laytonsville, 162
Brookeville Methodist Episcopal Church Cemetery, 162
Brookfield United Methodist Church Cemetery, 217
Brooklyn Cemetery, 56
Brooks-Myers United Methodist Church Cemetery, 217
Brooksly Point Cemetery, 6
Brothers Family Cemetery, 78
Brown Family Burying Ground near Etchison, 137
Brown Nicholas Watkins Family Burying Ground near Damascus, 137
Brown-Carson Family Cemetery, 6

Brown/Miller Family Cemetery, 190
Brown/Owings Families Cemetery, 78
Brown's Chapel, 172
Browns-Oxbournes, 6
Brow's Meeting House, 108
Browsley Hall Cemetery, 9
Bruns/Braen Cemetery, 6
Buckingham Family Cemetery, 78
Burgess Family Burying Ground at Cabin John, 137
Burgess Graves, 6
Burley Creek Cemetery, 6
Burrage's End Cemetery, 50
Burton Family Burying Ground near Patuxent River, 138
BWI Cemetery, 58
Byrd Family Burying Ground near Dawsonville, 138

-C-

Cabin John Presbyterian Church, 161
Calvary U.M. Church, 121
Calvert Family Cemetery, 191
Camp Barrett Cemetery, 49
Caple Family Cemetery, 79
Captain John Presbyterian Church, 161
Captain John's Presbyterian Church, 178
Carpenters Hill Cemetery, 7
Carr Family Burying Ground at Burtonsville, 138
Carr Family Cemetery, 156
Carr Family Cemetery, 7
Carroll Chapel Cemetery, 217
Carroll Chapel Methodist Cemetery, 217
Carroll Family Burial Grounds, 7
Carroll Gardens Cemetery, 56

Carroll House Cemetery, 56
Carroll Memorial Gardens, 131
Carroll's Chapel, 180
Carroll's Family Cemetery, 180
Carter Cemetery, 191
Carver Memorial Park, 231
Cashell Family Burying Ground near Layhill, 138
Cassell Family Cemetery, 79
Cecil Plantation, 140
Cedar Drive Cemetery, 7
Cedar Grove Cemetery, 7
Cedar Hill Cemetery, 72, 230
Cedar Park Cemetery, 29
Cedarville Assembly of God Church Cemetery, 217
Cedarwood Cove Cemetery, 7
Celle Grove Road Cemetery, 55
Cemetery at Wilderness, 18
Cemetery, 8
Centenary United Methodist Church Cemetery, 56
Church of God Cemetery, 57
Charity Meeting House Cemetery, 106
Chartwell Country Club Cemetery, 42
Chartwell Golf Cemetery, 8
Cheltenham United Methodist Church Cemetery, 218
Chews United Methodist Church Cemetery, 56
Chief Turkey Tayac's Grave, 191
Chiselin Stone, 191
Christ Episcopal Church Cemetery, 57
Christ Episcopal Church Cemetery, 218
Christ United Methodist Church, 218
Christian Geiman Cemetery, 84

Church of the Atonement Cemetery, 219
Church of the Atonement Episcopal Cemetery, 219
Church of the Holy Rosary Catholic Cemetery, 219
Church of the Holy Rosary Cemetery, 219
Cissell-Trundle Family Burying Ground near Poolesville, 139
Clagett Family Cemetery, 191, 192
Clagett Family Graveyard, 192
Clagett Grave, 192
Claggett/Waring Family Cemetery, 192
Clark Cemetery, 8
Clark Family Burying Ground at Clarksburg, 139
Clark Family Cemetery, 8
Clark Station Road Cemetery, 8, 9
Clarke Family Cemetery, 193
Clarksburg Methodist Episcopal Church Cemetery, 162
Clarksburg United Methodist Church Cemetery, 162
Claytor Family Cemetery, 9
Clem Moore Grave, 9
Cold Saturday Farm Cemetery, 79
Coles Methodist Episcopal Church South, 163
Colesville United Methodist Church Cemetery, 163
Collins Grave, 9
Colored Cemetery on Brick Church Road, 107
Columbia Primitive Baptist Church Cemetery at Burtonsville, 163
Comus Cemetery, 158

INDEX OF CEMETERIES

Concord Methodist Episcopal Church Cemetery at Bethesda, 164
Condon Family Cemetery, 79
Connick Family Cemetery, 193
Conoway Family Cemetery, 80
Contee Family Cemetery, 193
Contee Family Grave, 193
Cook Family Cemetery, 80
Cook Family Cemetery, 9
Cooke Family Burying Ground at Redland, 139
Cove of Cork Memorial, 9
Covington Grave, 194
Crabb Family Burying Ground at Derwood, 139
Crandell-Smith Cemetery, 9
Craufurd Family Cemetery, 194
Crawford/Gosnell Families Cemetery, 80
Cromwell Grave, 10
Cross Family Cemetery, 194
Cross Roads Church Cemetery, 55
Crownsville State Hospital Cemetery, 10

-D-

Daingerfield/Sewell Family Cemetery, 194
Daker Cemetery, 10
Damascus United Methodist Church Cemetery, 164
Daniel Richards Cemetery, 95
Darcey Family Cemetery, 194
Darnall Family Cemetery, 10
Darnall Family Grave, 195
Darnell Family Burying Ground at Dawsonville, 140
Darnestown Baptist Church Cemetery, 164

Darnestown Presbyterian Church Cemetery, 165
David Geiman Cemetery, 84
Davidsonville United Methodist Church Cemetery, 57
Davis Family Burying Ground at Brookeville, 140
Davis Family Burying Ground on Cecil Plantation, 140
Davis Family Cemetery #1, 80
Davis Family Cemetery #2, 81
Davis/Waters Families Cemetery, 81
Dawson Family Cemetery, 10
Dawson Family Monument, 195
Day Family Cemetery, 87
Deakins Family Cemetery, 195
Deale Beach Road Cemetery, 72
Deale Episcopal Church Cemetery, 57
Deer Park Memorial Gardens, 131
Deer Park United Methodist Church Cemetery, 107
Defense Highway Cemetery, 11
Deichgraeber Family Cemetery, 11
Demarr Farm Cemetery, 230
Dennis Family Cemetery, 11
Dent Road Cemetery, 33
Derwood Cemetery, 140
Desellum Family Burying Ground at Gaithersburg, 141
Detour Methodist Protestant Church Cemetery, 107
Devillbiss Family Cemetery, 81
Disney Family Cemetery, 11
Ditty Tombstone, 11
Dods/Brooke/Scott Families Cemetery, 81
Dorsett Cemetery, 11
Dorsett-Duvall Cemetery, 12

Dorsey Family Burying Ground near Etchison, 141
Dorsey Family Burying Ground near Goshen, 141
Dorsey Family Cemetery, 82
Dorsey Road Cemetery, 12
Douty Family Cemetery, 82
Downing Family Cemetery, 195
Downs Cemetery, 12
Downs-Wellham Cemetery, 12
Downs-Wilham Cemetery, 12
Dr. Robert Franklin Cemetery, 12
Drury Family Cemetery, 13
Drury-Lyles Family Cemetery, 13
Dubois Cemetery, 13
Duckett Family Cemetery, 195
Duncan Grave, 196
Durner Family Cemetery, 13
Duvall Cemetery, 13, 70
Duvall Family Cemetery, 13, 72, 196
Duvall Family Chapel, 74
Duvall Grave, 14
Duvall-Merriken Cemetery, 14
Duvall/Duval Family Cemetery, 197

-E-

Early Family Cemetery, 197
East Park Drive Cemetery, 14
Ebenezer A.M.E. St. Paul's Cemetery, 57
Ebenezer Church Cemetery at Ashton, 165
Ebenezer United Methodist Church Cemetery, 107
Edelin Grave, 197
Edgewater Cemetery, 14
Edward's Ferry Cemetery, 141
Edwards M.E. Chapel Cemetery, 61

Elijah Methodist Church Cemetery at Poolesville, 165
Elijah Rest Methodist Episcopal Church, 165
Elizabeth Horn Tombstone, 88
Elizabeth J. and Ida M. Phillips Family Cemetery, 94
Elizabeth's Fancy Cemetery, 42
Ellsworth Cemetery, 108
Emmanuel Baptist Church, 116
Emmanuel United Church of Christ Cemetery, 104
Emory Grove Cemetery, 166
Emory Grove Memorial Church, 166
Emory Grove Memorial Methodist Episcopal Church, 166
Emory Grove United Methodist Church Burial Area, 166
Emory United Methodist Church Cemetery, 108
Epiphany Episcopal Church Cemetery, 58
Epiphany Episcopal Church Cemetery, 219
Evangelical Presbyterian Church Cemetery, 61
Evans Family Cemetery, 14, 83
Evergreen Cemetery, 219
Evergreen Memorial Gardens Cemetery, 131
Ezekiel Gillis' Grave, 31

-F-

Fair View United Methodist Church Cemetery, 108
Faith Chapel Methodist Episcopal Church South, 140
Farquhar/Shepherd/Webb Families Cemetery, 83
Fawcuett Avenue Cemetery, 14

INDEX OF CEMETERIES

Federal Methodist Episcopal Church, 163
Feis Family Cemetery, 15
Fenno Stone, 197
Ferdinand Duvall Grave, 73
Finksburg Methodist Church Cemetery, 108
Finksburg Methodist Episcopal Church South Cemetery, 109
First Lutheran Church of Bowie, 219
Fleming/Gosnell Cemetery, 95
Fletchall Family Burying Ground at Mt. Nebo, Poolesville, 142
Flinn Garner Cemetery, 84
Flower Hill Church of the Brethren Cemetery at Redland, 166
Forest Chapel Methodist Episcopal Church, 142
Forest Grove Methodist Church Cemetery, 220
Forest Haven Training School Cemetery, 15
Forest Hills Memorial Gardens, 230
Forest Home Academy Cemetery, 20
Forest Lake Cemetery, 230
Forest Memorial United Methodist Church Cemetery, 220
Forest Oak Cemetery at Gaithersburg, 142
Fort Lincoln Cemetery, 230
Fowler United Methodist Church, 58
Franklin Church Cemetery, 58
Franklin Family #1 Cemetery, 83
Franklin Family #2 Cemetery, 84
Freedom Methodist Episcopal Church South, 129

Friedhofer and Gary Cemetery, 15
Friends Meeting House Cemetery, 166
Friends Meeting House Cemetery at Sandy Spring, 166
Friendship Cemetery, 58
Friendship School Cemetery, 15
Friendship United Methodist Church Cemetery, 58
Friendship United Methodist Church Cemetery at Damascus, 167
Frizzellburg Church of God Cemetery, 109
Ft. Meade Cemetery #1, 37
Ft. Meade Cemetery #2, 3
Ft. Meade Cemetery #5, 15
Ft. Meade Cemetery #7, 48
Ft. Meade Cemetery #8, 12
Ft. Meade Cemetery #9, 70
Ft. Meade Cemetery #10, 4
Ft. Meade Cemetery #11, 49
Ft. Meade Cemetery #12, 44
Ft. Meade Cemetery #13, 22
Ft. Meade Cemetery #14, 13
Ft. Meade Cemetery #15, 21
Ft. Meade Cemetery #16, 53
Ft. Meade Cemetery #17, 32
Ft. Meade Cemetery #18, 28
Ft. Meade Cemetery #19, 35

-G-

Gaither Family Burying Ground at Unity, 143
Gaither Family Burying Ground at Gaithersburg, 142
Galesville Methodist Church Cemetery, 59
Gantt Cenotaph, 197
Gardens of Eternal Hope Cemetery, 131

Gardner-Anderson Cemetery, 15
Garner Family Cemetery, 84
Garrett Family Burying Ground near Shady Grove, 143
Garrison Family Cemetery, 84
Gate of Heaven Cemetery at Silver Spring, 167
Geiman Family Cemetery, 84
George Fox Cemetery, 16
George Richards Cemetery, 95
George Schmidt Farm Cemetery, 15
George Washington Cemetery and Mausoleum, 230
German Baptist Cemetery, 119
Germantown Methodist Episcopal Church Cemetery, 168
Gibbons Family Cemetery, 198
Gibbons United Methodist Church, 220
Gist Family Cemetery, 85
Glen Haven Memorial Park, 73
Glenn Dale United Methodist Church Cemetery, 223
Good Hope Methodist Episcopal Church Cemetery, 168
Good Hope Union United Methodist Church Cemetery at Colesville, 168
Gorsuch Family Cemetery, 85
Goshen Meeting House, 168
Goshen Meeting House Methodist Episcopal Church South Cemetery, 168
Goshen Methodist Church Cemetery, 168
Govenor's Bridge Road Cemetery, 16
Grace Episcopal Church Cemetery at Silver Spring, 169
Grace Methodist Episcopal Church North Cemetery, 217
Grace United Church of Christ Cemetery, 127
Graff-Musser Family Burying Ground near Germantown, 143
Green/Gardson Families Cemetery, 85
Greenbelt Cemetery, 232
Greenberry Family Cemetery, 16
Greenfield Family Cemetery, 198
Greenmount United Brethren in Christ, 109
Greenmount United Methodist Church Cemetery, 109
Greenock Road Cemetery, 16
Greens Lane Cemetery, 16
Greenwood Cemetery, 231
Greenwood Church Cemetery, 109
Griffith Family Burying Ground at Edgehill, 143
Griffith Family Burying on Warfield Farm, 144
Griffith Family Cemetery, 16
Griffith-Day Cemetery, 16
Groad Creek Episcopal Church Graveyard, 226
Gue Family Cemetery, 155
Gwynn Family Cemetery, 198

-H-

Haddaway Chapel Methodist Episcopal Church Cemetery, 220
Haines Family Cemetery, 86
Haiti Cemetery at Rockville, 144
Hall Family Cemetery, 87, 198
Hall Tombstone, 17, 199
Hall United Methodist Church Cemetery, 59
Hall Vault, 17
Hall/Reed Family Cemetery, 199
Hamilton Family Cemetery, 199

INDEX OF CEMETERIES 241

Hammond Cemetery, 17
Hampstead Cemetery, 110
Hancock Family Cemetery, 17
Hancock-Whittemore Cemetery, 17
Hardesty Family Cemetery, 18
Hardin/Harden Family Cemetery, 87
Harding Family Burying Ground near Cloverly, 144
Hardisty Family Cemetery, 199
Harding Family Burying Ground at Cloverly, 144
Harman Cemetery, 18
Harman Family Cemetery, 18
Harman-Disney Cemetery, 18
Harman-Lucas Cemetery, 18
Harmans Park Cemetery, 19
Harmoneon, 231
Harmony Cemetery, 231
Harmony Grove Methodist Church Cemetery, 110
Harmony Memorial Park, 231
Harris Family Cemetery, 87
Harrison Family Cemetery, 19
Hartge Family Cemetery, 19
Harvey Family Cemetery, 19
Harwood Cemetery, 19
Harwood Tombstone, 20
Hatton Family Cemetery, 199, 200
Hawlings River Chapel Church Cemetery near Laytonsville, 169
Hayes Family Burying Ground at Barnesville, 145
Hebb Family Cemetery, 200
Henry Baskum Shipley Cemetery, 97
Heritage Baptist Church Cemetery, 110

Hermon Presbyterian Church Cemetery at Bethesda, 169
Hershey Family Burying Ground at Comus, 145
Hesselius Family Cemetery, 20
Hickman Family Burying Ground, 141
Higgins Family Burying Ground at Parklawn, 145
Highland View Cemetery, 111
Highlands Cemetery, 20
Hill Family Cemetery, 200
Hillcrest Cemetery, 56
Hillcrest Memorial Cemetery, 73
Hilleary Family Cemetery, 200
Hilleary Family Cemetery, 201
Hiltabidel Family Cemetery, 87
Hines Family Cemetery, 20
Hodges Family Cemetery, 20
Holland Family Burying Ground at Prospect Hill, 145
Hollins Family Cemetery, 21
Holly Beach Farm Road Cemetery, 21
Hollyday Family Cemetery, 201
Holy Cross Cemetery, 59
Holy Family Catholic Church Cemetery, 221
Holy Trinity Church Cemetery, 221
Holy Trinity Church Episcopal Cemetery, 221
Holy Trinity Episcopal Cemetery, 111
Hood-Higgs Cemetery, 21
Hope Methodist Church Cemetery, 59
Hopkins Cemetery, 21
Hopkins Family Burying Ground near White Oak, 146
Hopkins Family Cemetery, 21
Horn Tombstone, 88

Hoskinson Family Burying
   Ground at Poolesville, 146
Houck Family Cemetery, 75
Howard Cemetery, 67
Howard Family Cemetery, 21,
   201
Howes Family Burying Ground
   near Middlebrook, 146
Humphreys/Edelen Family
   Cemetery, 201
Hyattstown Christian Church
   Cemetery, 170
Hyattstown Methodist Episcopal
   Church, 170
Hyattstown United Methodist
   Church Cemetery, 170

-I-

Idlewilde Cemetery, 35
Immanual Methodist Episcopal
   Church South, 221
Immanuel Lutheran Church
   Cemetery, 113
Immanuel United Methodist
   Church Cemetery, 221
Indian Creek Lane Cemetery, 22
Inglehart Cemetery, 22
Isaac Cemetery, 201
Ivy Hill Cemetery, 231
Ivy Neck Farm Cemetery, 22

-J-

Jackson Memorial Cemetery, 229
Jacobs Cemetery, 22
Jacobs Family Cemetery, 88
James Brown Family Burying
   Ground near Etchison, 137
Java Tombstone, 28
Jeffrey Family Cemetery, 22
Jeffrey Road Cemetery, 22

Jerusalem Baptist Church
   Cemetery, New, near Pooles-
   ville, 171
Jerusalem Baptist Church
   Cemetery, Old, near Pooles-
   ville, 171
Jerusalem Lutheran Church
   Cemetery, 111
Jerusalem New School Baptist
   Church Cemetery, 171
John Allgire Cemetery, 75
John Arnold Grave, 23
John Luther Miller Memorial
   Cemetery, 112
John Shipley Cemetery, 97
John Warner Cemetery, 101
John Wesley Methodist Episcopal
   Church Cemetery, 171
John Wesley United Methodist
   Church, 60
John Wesley United Methodist
   Church Cemetery near
   Clarksburg, 171
John Wesley Waterbury M.E.
   Church, 60
John Williams Family Cemetery,
   88
John Worthington Grave, 23
Johns Cemetery, 23
Johnson Cemetery, 23, 24
Johnson Family Cemetery, 23
Johnson Grave, 24
Johnson-Foreman Cemetery, 24
Johnsville United Methodist
   Church Cemetery, 112
Jonathan Dorsey Cemetery, 82
Jones Acres, 24
Jones Cemetery, 202
Jones Family Burying Ground at
   Mt. Zion, 146

INDEX OF CEMETERIES

Jones Family Burying Ground on Blunt Road near Great Seneca Park, 146
Jones Family Cemetery, 88
Jones Memorial Gardens, 202
Jordan Family Cemetery, 88
Joy Circle Cemetery, 60
Jubes Family Cemetery, 17
Judean Memorial Gardens near Olney, 147
Jumpers Hole Road Cemetery, 24
June Drive/June Way Cemetery, 25

-K-

Kemp Family Burying Ground near Layhill, 147
Key Slave Cemetery, 89
Keysville Union Cemetery, 112
Kinder Bros. Cattle Farm Cemetery, 30
Kinder Brothers Cattle Farm Cemetery, 25
Kinder Family Cemetery, 25
Kinder Park Cemetery, 25, 30
Kinder Park Family Plot, 25
King Family Burying Ground near Damascus, 147
King Family Burying Ground near Purdum, 147
King Family Property, 19
Kirkridge Presbyterian Church Cemetery, 112
Kneseth Israel Congregational Cemetery, 54
Kneseth Israel Congregational Cemetery, 2
Knopp Family Cemetery, 25
Koch Road Cemetery, 60
Kriders Church Cemetery, 123
Kurtz Family Cemetery, 89

-L-

Labrot Family Cemetery, 25
Lakemont Memorial Gardens, 73
Lakeview Memorial Park Cemetery, 132
Landis Family Cemetery, 89
Landis Slave Cemetery, 89
Langley Cemetery, 26
Langville Family Cemetery, 26
Lanham United Methodist Church Cemetery, 221
Lankford Family Cemetery, 26
Lansdale Grave, 202
Laurel Cemetery on Belair Road in Baltimore, 133
Lawson Family Cemetery, 99
Layhill Cemetery, 176
Laytonsville Cemetery nest to St. Paul United Methodist Church, 172
Lazarus Lutheran Church Cemetery, 113
Lazarus United Church of Christ, 113
Lea Family Cemetery, 159
Leatherwood Family Cemetery, 89
Leatherwood/Gunn/Fleming Families Cemetery, 90
Lee Cemetery, 26
Leeland, 225
Leister Family Cemetery, 90
Leister's Church, 124
Lemmon Family Cemetery, 90
Lewis Family Burying Ground at Lewisdale, 147
Lewis Shipley Family Cemetery, 97
Lighthouse Keeper's Cemetery, 26
Lily of the Valley Tabernacle Cemetery, 60

Lincoln Memorial Cemetery, 231
Lincoln Park Cemetery at Rockville, 148
Lindsay Family Cemetery, 90
Lineboro Cemetery, 132
Linstead Family Cemetery, 17
Linstead/Linstid Family Cemetery, 7
Linstid Family Cemetery, 17
Linstid-Hanshaw Burial Ground, 26
Linthicum Family Cemetery, 27
Linthicum Walks Cemetery, 61
Linthicum-Lee Cemetery, 27
Lloyd Family Cemetery, 202
Loghouse Cemetery, 90
Looper Property Cemetery, 24
Luce Creek Cemetery, 61
Lusby Family Cemetery, 27
Luther A. Palmer Memorial Cemetery, 61
Lyles Family Cemetery, 202
Lynch-Williams Family Cemetery, 27
Lynn Family Cemetery, 91

-M-

M.E. Cemetery, 74
Macedonia United Methodist Church Cemetery, 61
McElfresh Family Burying Ground at Hyattstown, 148
Mackall Family Cemetery, 203
McKendree Methodist Church Cemetery, 221
McKendree Road Cemetery, 29
McKinsey Woods Cemetery, 29
Mackubin Cemetery, 27
Macruder Family Burying Ground at the Ridge, 148
Magothy United Methodist Church Cemetery, 61

Magruder Family Burying Ground near Laytonsville, 148
Magruder Family Cemetery, 203
Magruder/McGregor Family Cemetery, 203
Major Thomas Francis Tombstone, 28
Manchester Bethel Church Cemetery, 113
Manchester Cemetery, 113
Manro/Conner Families Cemetery, 91
Marbury/Fendall Family Cemetery, 204
Mariott Cemetery, 28
Market Place Cemetery, 62
Marley Neck Road Cemetery, 28
Marshall/Summers Family Cemetery, 204
Martin Spalding Cemetery, 28
Maryland National Memorial Park, 231
Maryland Veterans Cemetery, 73
Maryland Veterans' Cemetery, 231
Marywood Drive Grave, 28
Marzoff Road Cemetery, 28
Mathias Harman Cemetery, 29
Max Lowman's Place, 37
Maxcy Family Cemetery, 29
Mayberry Church of God Cemetery, 114
Mayo United Methodist Church Cemetery, 62
Meadow Branch Church of the Brethren Cemetery, 114
Meek Family Cemetery, 6
Mercer Cemetery, 29
Merritt Family Cemetery, 30
Merson Family Burying Ground near Burtonsville, 149
Messiah Lutheran Church, 111

INDEX OF CEMETERIES

Methodist Protestant Church at Pleasant Gap, 110
Mewshaw Family Cemetery, 30
Meyn Family Cemetery, 30
Michael Haines Cemetery, 86
Michelle Court Cemetery, 30
Middle Plantation Cemetery, 30
Middleburg United Methodist Church Cemetery, 114
Midshipmen Memorial, 73
Milbur Cemetery, 31
Mill Creek Cemetery, 31
Mill Swamp Road Cemetery, 31
Miller Family Burying Ground at Alloway, 149
Miller Family Cemetery, 91
Millers United Brethren Church, 114
Millers United Methodist Church Cemetery, 114
Mitchell Family Cemetery, 204
Mobley-Magers-Arnold Family Burying Ground at Germantown, 149
Mockley Point Burial Ground, 191
Monocacy Cemetery Company at Beallsville, 149
Monocacy Cemetery Society of Montgomery County, 149
Montgomery Chapel Church Cemetery at Hyattstown, 172
Montgomery Chapel Methodist Episcopal Church, 172
Montgomery United Methodist Church Cemetery at Clagetsville, 172
Mordica Haines Grave, 86
Morehead Memorial Cemetery, 132
Morgan Road Cemetery, 31

Morgan's Chapel United Methodist Church Cemetery, 115
Morsell Family Grave, 204
Moses Lodge Cemetery near Cabin John, 150
Moss Family Plot, 31
Mount Lebanon Cemetery, 222
Mount Lebanon Church, 164
Mount Nebo Cemetery, 142
Mount Oak United Methodist Church Cemetery, 222
Mount of Olives Church, 177
Mountain Chapel, 183
Mountain Road Cemetery, 31
Mountain View Cemetery, 132
Mountain View Lutheran Cemetery, 115
Mountain View Methodist Church, 127
Mrs. Hill's Burying Ground, 31
Mt Ephraim Methodist Episcopal Church Cemetery, 174
Mt Zion Methodist Episcopal Church Cemetery, 175
Mt. Zion Methodist Episcopal Church Cemetery at Big Woods, 175
Mt. Calvary A.U.M.P. Church Cemetery at Spencerville, 173
Mt. Calvary African Union Methodist Protestant, 173
Mt. Calvary Catholic Church Cemetery, 222
Mt. Calvary Cemetery, 62
Mt. Calvary Chapel Cemetery, 62
Mt. Calvary Methodist Church Cemetery, 62, 63
Mt. Calvary United Methodist Church Cemetery, 63
Mt. Carmel Catholic Cemetery, 222

Mt. Carmel Methodist Protestant Church Cemetery, 173
Mt. Carmel United Methodist Cemetery, 63
Mt. Carmel United Methodist Church Cemetery at Sunshine, 173
Mt. Glory Baptist Church Cemetery at Cropley on Conduit Road, 173
Mt. Hope Methodist Episcopal Church Cemetery, 222
Mt. Joy Methodist Church Cemetery, 115
Mt. Lebanon Methodist Protestant Church Cemetery near Damascus, 173
Mt. Nebo Methodist Church Cemetery, 223
Mt. Olive United Methodist Church Cemetery, 115
Mt. Pilgrim Baptist Church Cemetery, 62
Mt. Pleasant Cemetery, 133
Mt. Pleasant Methodist Church Cemetery, 116
Mt. Pleasant Methodist Episcopal Church, 174
Mt. Pleasant Methodist Episcopal Church South Cemetery, 174
Mt. Pleasant United Methodist Church Cemetery at Dickerson, 174
Mt. Pleasant United Methodist Church Cemetery at Norbeck, 174
Mt. Steuart Cemetery, 6
Mt. Tabor Methodist Episcopal Church Cemetery, 174
Mt. Tabor United Methodist Church Cemetery, 63
Mt. Tabor United Methodist Church Cemetery at Etchison, 174
Mt. Union Brethren Church Cemetery, 116
Mt. Union Lutheran Church Cemetery, 116
Mt. View Methodist Protestant Church Cemetery, 175
Mt. View United Methodist Church Cemetery at Purdum, 175
Mt. Zion Baptist Church, 186
Mt. Zion Church, 161
Mt. Zion Methodist Cemetery, 117
Mt. Zion Methodist Church Cemetery, 63
Mt. Zion U.M. Church, 108
Mt. Zion United Methodist Church Cemetery, 64
Mt. Zion United Methodist Church Cemetery at Mt. Zion, 175
Mullikan Cemetery, 32
Mulliken Graves, 205
Mullikin Family Cemetery, 205
Murray/Beverly Cemetery, 32
Mutual Memorial Cemetery at Sandy Spring, 150
Myers Cemetery, 32
Myers Family Cemetery, 32, 91

-N-

Nathan Jones, 70
Nathan Jones Cemetery, 13
National Capital Hebrew Cemetery, 223
National Capital Memorial park, 231
Naval Academy Dairy Farm Cemetery, 17

INDEX OF CEMETERIES

Naylor Family Cemetery, 205
Neelsville Presbyterian Church Cemetery, 175
New Laurel Cemetery, 133
New Oakland Methodist Church Cemetery, 117
New Oakland Methodist Episcopal Church South, 117
New Port Cemetery, 133
New Windsor Presbyterian Church Cemetery, 117
Nicholas Wilson Cemetery, 102
Nichols Road Cemetery, 64
Nicodemus Family Cemetery, 92
Norbeck Memorial Park near Olney, 150
Norman Cemetery, 33
Norman's Retreat Cemetery, 45
Norris Cemetery, 33
Nusbaum Cemetery, 92, 96
Nusbaum/Nicodemus Families Cemetery, 92
Nutwell Family Cemetery, 33
Nutwell Grave, 33

-O-

Oak Chapel United Methodist Church Cemetery at Mt. Zion, 176
Oak Grove African Methodist Episcopal Zion Church Cemetery at Mt. Zion, 176
Oak Grove Cemetery, 176
Oakwood Methodist Episcopal Church at Norwood, 176
Obligation Cemetery, 46
Offutt Family Burying Ground at Dawsonville, 150
Offutt Family Burying Ground at Woodbyrne, 151
Ogg Family Cemetery, 93
Ogle Family Cemetery, 205

Oklahoma Road Cemetery, 93
Old Bethel Methodist Church Cemetery, 64
Old Christ Church Cemetery, 57
Old Cromwell Cemetery, 33
Old German Cemetery, 117
Old Herring Creek Cemetery, 69
Old Marley Methodist Church Cemetery, 66
Old Myers Burial Ground, 32
Old Oakland Methodist Church Cemetery, 118
Old Presbyterian Cemetery, The, 219
Old Pumphrey Cemetery, 37
Old Pumphrey Family Cemetery, 34
Old Ridout Cemetery, 34
Old Salem Cemetery, 74
Old St. Mark's Church Cemetery, 62
Old Stone Methodist Church, The, 223
Onion Cemetery, 205
Orme/Dale Cemetery, 206
Osborn/Talburtt Family Cemetery, 206
Our Lady of Sorrows Roman Catholic Church Cemetery, 64
Our Lady of the Fields Church Cemetery, 65
Outing/205th Cemetery, 34
Owen Brown Family Burying Ground, 137
Owen Family Burying Ground at Brookeville, 151
Owen Family Burying Ground at Norbeck, 151
Owens Family Burying Ground at Triadelphia, 151
Owens Family Cemetery, 34, 206
Owings Cemetery, 35

Owings Family Cemetery, 93
Owings Slave Cemetery, 93
Oxon Hill, 225
Oxon Hill Methodist Church
  Cemetery, 223

-P-
Parish-Mace Cemetery, 35
Parklawn Memorial Park at
  Rockville, 152
Parkway/Dorsey Cemetery, 35
Patapsco Baptist Church
  Cemetery, 118
Patapsco United Methodist
  Church Cemetery, 118
Patterson Family Cemetery, 94
Patuxent River Road Cemetery,
  35
Peach-Galloway Cemetery, 35
Peach/Walker Family Cemetery,
  206
Pearre Family Burying Ground
  near Comus, 152
Pendennis Cemetery, 23
Perkins Chapel, 223
Perkins Family Cemetery, 210
Perry Bennett Cemetery, 77
Peter Family Cemetery on Montevideo, 152
Peter Shipley Cemetery, 96
Pettebone Cemetery, 35
Phelps Cemetery, 35
Phillips Family Cemetery, 94
Phipps Cemetery, 36
Pickett Family Cemetery #1, 94
Pickett Family Cemetery #2, 94
Piles/Pyles Graveyards, 206
Pindell Family Cemetery, 36
Pindell Property Cemetery, 37
Pine Grove Cemetery, 133
Pinehurst Cemetery, 4

Piney Creek Church of the
  Brethren Cemetery, 119
Piney Creek Presbyterian
  Cemetery, 119
Piney Grove Methodist Church
  Cemetery, 65
Piney Meeting House Cemetery,
  184
Pipe Creek Church of the Brethren Cemetery, 119
Pipe Creek Friends Meeting
  Cemetery, 119
Pipe Creek United Methodist
  Church Cemetery, 120
Piscataway Indian Ossuary, 191
Pleasant Grove Community
  Church Cemetery at Purdum,
  176
Pleasant Grove Methodist
  Church Cemetery, 120
Pleasant Grove Methodist Episcopal Church, 120
Pleasant Grove Methodist Episcopal Church Cemetery, 176
Pleasant Grove Methodist Episcopal Meeting House
  Cemetery, 224
Pleasant Hill Farm Cemetery, 37
Pleasant Hills Methodist Episcopal Church South Cemetery
  at Darnestown, 177
Pleasant Plains of Damascus
  Church, 164
Pleasant Ridge Cemetery, 120
Pleasant Ridge Church of God,
  120
Pleasant Valley Cemetery, 134
Pleasant View Methodist Episcopal Church, 177
Pleasant View Methodist Episcopal Church Cemetery, 171

INDEX OF CEMETERIES

Pleasant View United Methodist Church Cemetery at Quince Orchard, 177
Plowman Family Cemetery, 94
Point Pleasant Cemetery, 65
Pool/Fleming Families Cemetery, 95
Poolesville Methodist Episcopal Church Cemetery, 177
Pool's Church Cemetery, 121
Poplar Grove Baptist Church Cemetery at Darnestown, 178
Post Cemetery, 37
Potomac Chapel Methodist Episcopal Church, 178
Potomac United Methodist Church Cemetery, 178
Potters Field, 131
Potter's Field at Rockville, 186
Poulson Family Cemetery, 95
Prather Family Burying Ground at Redland, 152
Prather Family Cemetery, 206
Primrose Hill Cemetery, 20
Providence Methodist Church, 224
Providence Methodist Church Cemetery, 121
Providence Methodist Episcopal Church, South, 224
Providence United Methodist Church, 224
Public, 186
Pumphrey Cemetery, 37
Pumphrey Family Cemetery, 37, 38
Pumphrey Farm Cemetery, 38
Pumphrey/Fraser/Walker Cemetery, 207
Purdum Family Burying Ground, 185

-Q-

Quaker Burial Grounds, 65
Quaker Meeting Cemetery, 119
Queen Anne Parish, 225
Queens Chapel United Methodist Church Cemetery, 224
Query Family Burying Ground at Darnestown, 152

-R-

Race Road Cemetery, 66
Randall Family Cemetery, 207
Redgrave-Nolen Family Cemetery, 38
Redmond Tombstone, 39
Redmore Drive/Court Cemetery, 39
Reservoir Road Cemetery Site near Patuxent River, 153
Resurrection Catholic Cemetery, 224
Richard Wight Cemetery, 102
Richards Family Cemetery, 95
Richardson Family Burying Ground at Mt. Airy at Sandy Spring, 153
Richardson Family Cemetery, 39
Ricketts Family Burying Ground near Middlebrook, 153
Ridge Presbyterian Church, 133
Ridgely-Worthington Cemetery, 39
Ridgley-Zion United Methodist Church Cemetery, 225
Ridout Family Cemetery, 39
Riggs Burying Ground at Locust Grove, 153
Riggs Family Burying Ground, 154
Riggs Family Burying Ground at Pleasant Hill, Brookeville, 154
Ring Family Cemetery, 66

Riva Road Cemetery, 35
Rives Family Graveyard, 207
Riviera Beach Cemetery, 40
Robertson-Counselman Family Burying Ground at Goshen, 154
Robey Grave, 207
Robinson Family Cemetery, 20
Robinson Grave, 40
Robinson-Gardner Cemetery, 40
Rockview Beach Cemetery, 40
Rockville Baptist Church Cemetery, 178
Rockville Cemetery Association, 154
Rockville Protestant Episcopal Church Cemetery, 154
Rockville Union Cemetery, 154
Rogers Family Cemetery, 40
Rolling Knolls Cemetery, 41
Roman Catholic Church Cemetery, 65
Rose Hill Cemetery, 21
Round Oak Baptist Church Cemetery at Spencerville, 179
Route 3 Cemetery, 41
Royal Beach Cemetery, 24
Runnymeade Cemetery, 92, 96
Rutland Cemetery, 41

-S-

Sacred Heart at White Marsh Catholic Church Cemetery, 225
Sadigstone Grave, 207
St. Andrew the Fisherman Episcopal Cemetery, 69
St. Anne's Cemetery, 69
St. Barnabus' Episcopal Church Cemetery, 225
St. Barnabus Parish, 225
St. Bartholomew's Protestant Episcopal Church, 169

St. Bartholomew's Roman Catholic Church Cemetery, 123
St. Benjamin's Church Cemetery, 123
St. Benjamin's Lutheran Church/Benjamin's U.C. of C., 123
St. Demetrios Greek Orthodox Cemetery, 44, 68
St. Dominic's Catholic Church Cemetery, 226
St. Gabriel's Catholic Church Cemetery at Great Falls, 180
St. George Barber Cemetery, 21, 67
St. George's Chapel Cemetery, 226
St. George's Chapel Episcopal Cemetery, 226
St. Ignatius Roman Catholic Church Cemetery, 226
St. Jacob's Lodge at Mt. Zion Church, 70
St. James Episcopal Parish Church Cemetery, 69
St. James the Less Cemetery, 57
St. James United Methodist Church Cemetery, 123
St. Jerome's Farm Cemetery, 10
St. John A.M.E. Zion Church Cemetery, 69
St. John the Evangelist Church Cemetery, 226
St. John's Catholic Church Cemetery at Forest Glen, 180
St. Johns Episcopal Church Cemetery, 70
St. John's Episcopal Church, 227
St. John's Episcopal Church Cemetery at Olney, 181
St. John's Episcopal Church Graveyard, 226

INDEX OF CEMETERIES 251

St. John's Evangelical Lutheran Cemetery, 124
St. John's Parish, 218
St. John's Protestant Episcopal Church Cemetery, 181
St. John's Roman Catholic Church Cemetery, 124
St. John's U.M. Church Cemetery, 110
St. Joseph's Church and Christian Brothers Institute Cemetery, 227
St. Joseph's Roman Catholic Church Cemetery, 124
St. Lawrence Roman Catholic Cemetery, 68
St. Luke's Church Cemetery, 229
St. Luke's Chapel Cemetery, 68
St. Luke's Episcopal Church Cemetery at Brighton, 181
St. Luke's Lutheran Church Cemetery, 125
St. Luke's Lutheran Church Cemetery at Redland, 181
St. Luke's Protestant Episcopal Church Cemetery, 181
St. Margaret's Episcopal Church Cemetery, 67
St. Mark Orthodox Church, 164
St. Mark's Episcopal Church Cemetery at Fairland, 181
St. Mark's Episcopal Chapel of St. James Parish, 50
St. Mark's Lutheran and Reformed Church Cemetery, 125
St. Mark's Protestant Episcopal Church Cemetery, 181
St. Mark's United Methodist Church Cemetery at Boyds, 182

St. Mary of the Mills Catholic Church Cemetery, 227
St. Mary's Cemetery, 70
St. Mary's Catholic Church Cemetery, New, at Rockville, 182
St. Mary's Catholic Church Cemetery, Old, at Rockville, 182
St. Mary's Catholic Church, Piscataway, 227
St. Mary's Catholic Shrine Church Cemetery at Barnesville, 183
St. Mary's Episcopal Church Cemetery, 228
St. mary's Evangelical Lutheran Church, 125
St. Mary's Lutheran and Reformed Church Cemetery, 125
St. Mary's Parish, 222
St. Mary's United Church of Christ, 125
St. Matthews Methodist Church Cemetery, 67
St. Matthews United Methodist Church Cemetery, 68
St. Paul Community Church Cemetery at Sugarland, 183
St. Paul Methodist Episcopal Church Cemetery, 172
St. Paul's Episcopal Church Cemetery, 68
St. Paul's Episcopal Church Cemetery, 228
St. Paul's Lutheran Cemetery, 115
St. Paul's Lutheran Church Cemetery, 125
St. Paul's Methodist Church, 228
St. Paul's Parish, 228

St. Peters P.E. Church Cemetery, 70
St. Peter's Parish Cemetery, 58
St. Philip's Episcopal Church Cemetery, 228, 229
St. Rose of Lima Catholic Church Cemetery at Cloppers, 183
Saint Simon's Episcopal Church Cemetery, 225
St. Stephens Church Road Cemetery, 45
St. Stephens Episcopal Church Cemetery, 67
St. Thomas' Church Cemetery, 229
St. Thomas' Episcopal Church Cemetery, 229
St. Thomas Roman Catholic Church Cemetery, 126
Salem Methodist Episcopal Church Cemetery, 179
Salem Methodist Protestant Church Cemetery, 179
Salem United Methodist Church Cemetery, 121
Salem United Methodist Church Cemetery at Brookeville, 179
Salem United Methodist Church of Cedar Grove Cemetery, 179
Sam and Tevis Cemetery, 77
Sam's Creek Church of the Brethren Cemetery, 121
Samuel Leatherwood Cemetery, 89
Sandymount United Methodist Church Cemetery, 122
Sasscer Graveyard, 208
Sater Family Cemetery, 96
Scenic Overlook Memorial, 73
Scheminart Family Cemetery, 41
Scott Family Cemetery, 41
Scott Family Graveyard, 208

Seal's Farm Family Burying Ground, 155
Selby Grove Cemetery, 41
Sellman Cemetery, 42
Seneca C.M.E. Church Cemetery at Violet's Lock, 180
Senseney Family Cemetery, 96
Severn Road Cemetery, 42
Sevier-Stewart Cemetery, 42
Shady Side Methodist Church Cemetery, 56
Shaw Family Burying Ground at Clarksburg, 155
Shaw Family Burying Ground near Laytonsville, 155
Sherberts Cemetery, 42
Sherriff Family Cemetery, 208
Shesley Road Cemetery, 42
Shiloh Baptist Cemetery, 122
Shiloh Park M.E. Church, 122
Shiloh United Methodist Church Cemetery, 122
Shipley Cemetery, 43, 96
Shipley Family Cemetery, 97, 208
Shoemaker Family Burying Ground near Westmoreland Hills, 155
Shriver Family Cemetery, 97
Shue Family Cemetery, 97
Silas First Baptist Church Cemetery, 66
Sim Family Cemetery, 208
Simmons Family Cemetery, 43
Sitka Baptist Church Cemetery in Hillandale Area, 180
Sixes Bridge Area Cemetery, 98
Skinner Family Cemetery, 209
Slave Cemetery, 98
Smith Cemetery, 43
Smith Family Burying Grounds, 43, 44
Smith Family Cemetery, 44, 209

INDEX OF CEMETERIES

Smith Farm Road Cemetery, 26
Snowden Cemetery, 44
Snowden Family Cemetery, 98
Snowden Family Cemetery, Montpelier, 209
Snowden Family Cemetery, Oaklands, 209
Sollers United Methodist Church Cemetery, 66
Solley Cemetery, 44, 66
Solley Road Cemetery, 67
Soper Family Cemetery, 210
Southern High School Cemetery, 2
Spca Area Cemetery, 44
Spencer Family Burying Ground at Dickerson, 156
Spencer Family Cemetery, 98
Spit Point Cemetery, 1
Springbrook Forest Citizens Association, 156
Springfield Cemetery, 122
Springfield State Hospital Cemetery, 134
Spurrier Family Cemetery, 99
Stallings Lane Cemetery, 45
Stansbury Family Cemetery, 99
Steed/Edelin Family Cemetery, 210
Stephen Grave, 210
Steuart Family Cemetery, 45
Stevenson Family Cemetery, 99
Steward-Norman Cemetery, 45
Stewart Family Cemetery, 45
Stewart/Stewert Hill Cemetery, 70
Stinchcomb Family Cemetery, 45, 46
Stinchcomb Grave, 46
Stinchcomb-Tydings Family Cemetery, 46
Stockett Family Cemetery, 46
Stocksdale Family Cemetery, 99
Stone Chapel United Methodist Church Cemetery, 126
Storms Family Cemetery, 99
Strawbridge United Methodist Church Cemetery, 126
Strevig Family Cemetery, 100
Stuart Hill Cemetery, 70
Sudley Cemetery, 23
Sugar Loaf Mountain Community Church, 183
Sugar Loaf Mountain Methodist Episcopal Church Cemetery near Comus, 183
SugarLoad Chapel, 183
Suit Graves, 210
Sulphur Springs Cemetery, 46
Summer Hill Estate Cemetery, 53
Summers Family Burying Ground at Rockville, 156
Sunderland-Prout Cemetery, 47
Sunnyside Cemetery, 94, 134
Sunrise Cemetery, 126
Surrett Gravestone, 232
Sweetser Cemetery, 47
Sycamore/Circle Roads Cemetery, 70

-T-

Talbert/Hall Family Cemetery, 210
Talbert/Tolbertt Family Cemetery, 210
Taneytown Reformed Cemetery, 127
Taylor/Ulrich Families Cemetery, 100
Taylorsville United Methodist Church Cemetery, 127
Taylorsville Churchyard Cemetery, 35

Tayman Family Cemetery, 211
Tener/Hooper Family Cemetery, 100
Tevis/Robosson and Shipley Families Cemetery, 101
Thomas Beasman Cemetery, 76
Thomas Solley Farm Cemetery, 47
Thomas-Wheeler Cemetery, 40
Thornton Family Burying Grounds, 10
Toop's Cemetery, 101
Townshend Family Cemetery, 211
Townshend Grave, 211
Townshend/Early Family Cemetery, 211
Trinity Episcopal Church Cemeteries, 229
Trinity Evangelical Lutheran Church Cemetery, 127
Trinity Lutheran Church Cemetery, 127, 128
Trinity Methodist Church Cemetery at Germantown, 184
Trinity Methodist Episcopal Church Cemetery, 168
Trinity U.C.C. Cemetery, 113
Trueman Family Cemetery, 212
Tucker Family Cemetery, 47
Tulip Hill Cemetery, 29
Tulip Oak/Golden Oak Cemetery, 71
Turner Family Cemetery, 212, 232
Tydings-Robosson Cemetery, 47
Tyler Family Cemetery, 212
Tyson Graveyard, 213

-U-

U.S. Naval Academy Cemetery, 74

Union Bethel A.M.E. Church Cemetery, 229
Union Bethel Church, 105
Union Cemetery, 113
Union Cemetery Association at Burtonsville, 156
Union Memorial Church Cemetery, 71
Union Methodist Church Cemetery, 177
Union Mills Cemetery, 132
Union Wesley Methodist Church Cemetery on Piney Meeting House Road, 184
Uniontown Church of God Cemetery, 128
Uniontown Methodist Church Cemetery, 128
United Brethren in Christ Cemetery, 128
Unnamed Cemetery, 48, 71
Unnamed Road Cemetery, 48
Upper Seneca Baptist Church Cemetery at Cedar Grove, 184

-V-

Ventnor/Pinehurst Cemetery, 48
Vineyard Vault, 17

-W-

W. Pasadena Road Cemetery, 48
Walker Family Cemetery, 213
Wall Family Cemetery, 213
Ward Family Burying Ground at Hunting Hills, 157
Ward of Faith Center Church Cemetery, 71
Ward Tombstone, 48
Warehime Family Cemetery, 101
Warfield Cemetery, 49
Warfield Family Cemetery, 48

INDEX OF CEMETERIES

Warfieldsburg Church of God, 110
Waring Family Cemetery, 214
Waring Graves, 214
Waring/Hollyday Cemetery, 214
Warner Family Cemetery, 101
Warren Methodist Episcopal Church Cemetery, 185
Warren United Methodist Church Cemetery at Martinsburg, 185
Warren's Chapel, 185
Warren's Chapel African M.E. Church, 185
Washington National Cemetery, Inc., 232
Waters Cemetery, 49
Waters Family Burying Ground at Belmont, 157
Waters Family Burying Ground at Germantown, 158
Waters Family Burying Ground near Goshen, 157
Waters Family Burying Ground near Laytonsville, 157
Waters Family Cemetery, 49
Waters Grave, 49
Watersville M.E. Church Cemetery, 129
Watson Family Cemetery, 214
Watts Cemetery, 49
Waugh Chapel Cemetery, 71
Ways Family Cemetery, 101
Wayson Property Cemetery, 50
Weedon Family Cemetery, 50
Weems Family Cemetery, 50
Weems-Sellman Family Cemetery, 50
Welch Family Cemetery, 50
Welling Family Burying Ground at Comus, 158
Wells Family Cemetery, 102
Welsh/Penn/Barnes Families Cemetery, 102
Wesley Chapel Cemetery, 129
Wesley Family Cemetery, 51
Wesley Freedom Methodist Church Cemetery, 129
Wesley Grove Methodist Episcopal Church Cemetery, 185
Wesley Grove United Methodist Church Cemetery, 71
Wesley Grove United Methodist Church Cemetery at Woodfield, 185
Wesley United Methodist Church Cemetery, 129
West River Quaker Burying Grounds, 65
West River Road Cemetery, 51
Western Chapel Cemetery, 130
Westminster Cemetery, 134
Westphalia United Methodist Church Cemetery, 229
Westwood Methodist Episcopal Church, 218
Wharf Creek Cemetery, 51
White Avenue Cemetery, 66
White Oak Chapel, 182, 184
White Oak Chapel Baptist Church near Cedar Grove, 185
White Rock Methodist Church Cemetery, 130
White-Barber Cemetery, 51
Whitefield Chapel, 221
Whitehall Cemetery, 39
Whitehall Creek Cemetery, 51
Whiteside and Warfields Cemetery, 214
Widear Cemetery, 184
Wight Family Cemetery, 102
Wildwood Baptist Church Cemetery at Bethesda, 186
Williams Cemetery, 52

Williams Family Cemetery, 51
Williams/Berry Family Cemetery, 215
Willow Tree Graveyard, 156
Wilson Family Cemetery, 102
Wilson Family Burying Ground at Ednor, 158
Wilson Grave, 215
Wilson Memorial United Methodist Church Cemetery, 72
Winfield Bible Church Cemetery, 120
Winters Church Cemetery, 125
Wisner Family Cemetery, 103
Wolf Cemetery, 134
Wolfe Cemetery, 134
Wood Family Burying Ground near Poolesville, 158
Wood Family Cemetery, 52
Woodfield Cemetery, 74
Woodfield-Ridgely Cemetery, 52
Woodside Cemetery at Brinklow, 159
Woodstock Tombstone, 28
Woodville Methodist Church Cemetery, 230
Woodward Cemetery, 53
Worthington Family Cemetery, 53
Worthington/Contee/Bowie Family Cemetery, 215
Wright Road Cemetery, 53

-Y-

Yieldhall Family Cemetery, 72
Yohn Family Cemetery, 103
Young Family Burying Ground at Poolesville, 159
Young Family Burying Ground near Damascus, 159
Young Family Cemetery, 215

-Z-

Zimmerman's Mennonite Cemetery, 130
Zion Methodist Protestant Church, 108
Zion Parish, 227
Zion United Methodist Church Cemetery, 131

www.ingramcontent.com/pod-product-compliance
Lightning Source LLC
Chambersburg PA
CBHW050135170426
43197CB00011B/1844